Eating Disorders in Contemporary French Women's Writing

Contemporary French and Francophone Cultures, 90

Contemporary French and Francophone Cultures

This series aims to provide a forum for new research on modern and contemporary French and francophone cultures and writing. The books published in *Contemporary French and Francophone Cultures* reflect a wide variety of critical practices and theoretical approaches, in harmony with the intellectual, cultural and social developments which have taken place over the past few decades. All manifestations of contemporary French and francophone culture and expression are considered, including literature, cinema, popular culture, theory. The volumes in the series will participate in the wider debate on key aspects of contemporary culture.

Recent titles in the series:

76 Anna Kemp, *Life as Creative Constraint: Autobiography and the Oulipo*

77 Maria Kathryn Tomlinson, *From Menstruation to the Menopause: The Female Fertility Cycle in Contemporary Women's Writing in French*

78 Kaoutar Harchi and Alexis Pernsteiner, *I Have Only One Language, and It Is Not Mine: A Struggle for Recognition*

79 Alison Rice, *Transpositions: Migration, Translation, Music*

80 Antonia Wimbush, *Autofiction: A Female Francophone Aesthetic of Exile*

81 Jacqueline Couti, *Sex, Sea, and Self: Sexuality and Nationalism in French Caribbean Discourses, 1924–1948*

82 Debra Kelly, *Fishes with Funny French Names: The French Restaurant in London from the Nineteenth to the Twenty-First Century*

83 Nikolaj Lübecker, *Twenty-First-Century Symbolism: Verlaine, Baudelaire, Mallarmé*

84 Ari J. Blatt, *The Topographic Imaginary: Attending to Place in Contemporary French Photography*

85 Martin Munro and Eliana Văgălău, *Jean-Claude Charles: A Reader's Guide*

86 Jiewon Baek, *Fictional Labor: Ethics and Cultural Production in the Digital Economy*

87 Oana Panaïté, *Necrofiction and The Politics of Literary Memory*

88 Sonja Stojanovic, *Mind the Ghost: Thinking Memory and the Untimely through Contemporary Fiction in French*

89 Lucy Swanson, *The Zombie in Contemporary French Caribbean Fiction*

LUCILLE CAIRNS

Eating Disorders in Contemporary French Women's Writing

LIVERPOOL UNIVERSITY PRESS

First published 2023 by
Liverpool University Press
4 Cambridge Street
Liverpool
L69 7ZU

British Library Cataloguing-in-Publication data
A British Library CIP record is available

ISBN 978-1-80207-795-7

Typeset by Carnegie Book Production, Lancaster

I dedicate this book to my mother, Dorothy Scott Cairns,

and to Keith Reader.

Contents

Acknowledgements

Thanks to Charles Forsdick and Chloe Johnson at Liverpool University Press; to Sam Bailey for all translations that are not otherwise attributed, and to Kathryn Banks, Maddy Chalmers, David Cowling, Catherine Dousteyssier-Khoze, Jonathan Long, and the School of Modern Languages and Cultures at Durham University; to Sian Reynolds, Gill Rye, and the late Keith Reader; and especially to Kathryn Robson.

Publisher's Note

Lucille Cairns completed the first draft of this manuscript before sadly passing away in 2017. The manuscript has been completed posthumously and the publisher would like to thank all of the above for their work and support.

Preface

As Emilie Durand writes: 'Il est difficile de comprendre l'anorexie' [It is difficult to understand anorexia], because, although the symptoms are clearly identifiable, 'pour ce qui se passe dans la tête, c'est loin d'être évident' [as for what is going on in the mind, it's far from being clear].[1] This is echoed in other French autobiographical accounts of eating disorders: Justine, for example, writing in collaboration with Marie-Thérèse Cuny, observes that 'les gens ne comprennent pas l'anorexie' [people don't understand anorexia].[2] *Eating Disorders in Contemporary French Women's Writing* explores experiences of eating disorders – including anorexia nervosa, bulimia nervosa and bulimarexia, and binge eating disorder – narrated in the first person, focusing on 'the phenomenological, lived, embodied and affective experience of EDs [eating disorders] from the point of view of ex-sufferers, rather than from the point of view of clinicians, medical researchers, and theorists'. This book very strikingly foregrounds lived experiences and perspectives that have often been neglected in studies of eating disorders and offers ground-breaking insights into what it means to live with eating disorders, as well as the impact of different treatments and the possibility, in particular, of scriptotherapy or a 'writing cure'. I am writing this preface after Lucille's untimely death, before her book could be finalised for publication, and I am acutely aware of the importance of allowing her study to speak for itself. While offering some brief contextualisation of some of the issues raised by her analysis of the French case studies that form the main part of this

1 Durand, Emilie, *Ma folie ordinaire: allers et retours à l'hôpital Sainte-Anne* (Paris: Les Empêcheurs de tourner en rond, 2006), pp. 23–24.

2 Justine (avec la collaboration de Marie-Thérèse Cuny), *Ce matin j'ai décidé d'arrêter de manger* (Paris: Oh! Editions, 2007), p. 133.

book, I seek here to follow Lucille's principle of privileging the voices of those who have suffered from eating disorders and of foregrounding their experiences of illness, treatment, and recovery.

Eating disorders are clearly far from uncommon: approximately 2,500 new cases of anorexia nervosa, for example, are diagnosed annually in France, of which approximately 95 per cent are female.[3] Given that the mortality rate, as Lucille points out, is considerably higher than for most other psychiatric disorders, the question of treatment of eating disorders remains highly urgent. Some of the representations of treatment of eating disorders, particularly of the hospital environment, discussed in the case studies in this book are particularly shocking. In the chapter on anorexia nervosa, for example, Valérie Valère's *Le Pavillon des enfants fous* [The House of Mad Children] offers a forceful indictment of the psychiatric hospital in which the teenage Valérie was interned for anorexia, which is echoed, to some extent, in Marta Aleksandra Balinska's *Retour à la vie: quinze ans d'anorexie* [Return to Life: Fifteen Years of Anorexia], which recounts the controlling, punitive aspects of treatment given for Balinska's eating disorder over a very prolonged period of illness. Valère's treatment was in the 1970s, Balinska's in the 1980s and 1990s (and the latter also describes a brief episode in an English psychiatric hospital, which Lucille suggests is likely to be the Maudsley Hospital, and which Balinska depicts as degrading and invasive). This of course raises questions, first as to whether these two texts are representative of experiences of treatment of EDs in France over that period of the twentieth century, and second how the treatment in France may be compared with typical practice elsewhere. Finally, Lucille's extended primary corpus here covers an extensive time frame – including a couple of texts published since 2010 – but the six main case studies mostly recount treatment in the twentieth century. It is also, then, worth considering if and how approaches to treatment in France and beyond have changed in the twenty-first century. These questions are not easy to answer. Certainly, this book calls for further research into experiences and treatment of EDs since the millennium in France and elsewhere, not only focusing on medical or clinical reports, but also, following Lucille's approach here, exploring more recent first-person narratives of EDs rather than – or at least as well as – such reports. Nonetheless, these are important questions that I would like to address briefly here.

3 Senninger, Franck, *L'Anorexie: le miroir intérieur brisé* (Paris: Jouvence, 2004), p. 8.

In a study of clinical representations of treatment of anorexia nervosa in Britain published in 1999, Julie Hepworth describes the typical interventionist treatment for severe (life-threatening) anorexia through enteral feeding or other techniques permitted to keep the patient alive almost against his or her will to avoid mortality, which evidently simultaneously risks aggravating the condition further: 'clinical treatment is defined by the antagonism between the nurse and patient in which there is a struggle over weight gain, eating and "keeping food down"'.[4] This antagonism is compounded by negative perceptions of ED sufferers on the part of caregivers: Hepworth observes that they are typically seen as 'resistant',[5] while a 1991 US study of the ethics of forced feeding in severe cases of anorexia nervosa makes troubling references to the personalities of patients suffering EDs: 'many anorexic patients are unpleasant and demanding', 'black holes' that 'endlessly suck up emotional energy from caregivers'.[6] Hepworth also describes a system of punishments (isolation, restricted movement, surveillance)[7] and privileges (leaving the ward, using the telephone, for example)[8] that the clinical nursing staff interviewed by Hepworth take for granted as foundational to treating eating disorders but that reinforce the sufferer's feelings of alienation and separation from others. The structures depicted by Hepworth are not dissimilar to those recounted by, for example, Valère and Balinska, and chapter 1 of this book gives the sufferer's perspective on medical assumptions about personality types of anorectic patients (seen as liars) and on the hostility and even brutality underpinning their treatment regimes. Hepworth's study was published in 1999, and therefore documents twentieth-century practice in Britain, which appears not entirely dissimilar to that in France recounted in *Le Pavillon des enfants fous* and *Retour à la vie*, although the London hospital referred to by Balinska seems arguably even worse given the appalling conditions and the apparent disregard for human rights (which Lucille surmises result from over-stretched NHS budgets).

4 Hepworth, Julie, *The Social Construction of Anorexia Nervosa* (London: Sage, 1999), p. 92.

5 Hepworth, *The Social Construction of Anorexia Nervosa*, p. 94.

6 Hébert, Philip C. and Weingarten, Michael A., 'The ethics of forced feeding in anorexia nervosa', *Canadian Medical Association Journal*, 144, 2 (15 January 1991), 141–44 (143).

7 Hepworth, *The Social Construction of Anorexia Nervosa*, p. 91.

8 Hepworth, *The Social Construction of Anorexia Nervosa*, p. 93.

It would be unwise to suggest that there are no differences in approaches to EDs across different countries even within Europe: one study in 2002 looking at treatment of EDs in twelve sample EU countries found 'considerable variations', 'particularly in the use of inpatient provision', 'the average length of stay', and the 'treatment style' (ranging from 'a strict behavioural approach to individually designed client-centred therapy').[9] The variations in treatment make it difficult to generalise about treatment of EDs in different countries, a difficulty compounded due to the co-existence of various different modes of treatment within individual countries. It is clear, however, that late twentieth-century hospital-based treatment of eating disorders at least does seem to correspond in many ways to the French accounts included in this book.

Turning to the twenty-first century, in 2003, the French psychiatrist Marie-France Le Heuzey claimed that 'aujourd'hui, la prise en charge de l'anorexie mentale change : le « pavillon des enfants fous » appartient au passé' [today, the treatment of anorexia is changing: the 'house of mad children' belongs in the past], underscoring a shift in attitude from the stigmatisation and isolation implied by the term 'mad children' (and indeed from the treatment recounted by Valère, whose memoir she deliberately evokes) and a move towards a focus on listening to and understanding sufferers of EDs.[10] This is echoed in the 2010 recommendation from the Haute Autorité de Santé that in cases of children or adolescents, 'les équipes soignantes doivent accompagner les familles en se montrant empathiques et déculpabilisantes' [care teams must accompany families with empathy and without imputing guilt].[11] Both in the UK and in France, notions of best practice have moved towards setting up intensive family-based therapy (characterised in the UK by the leading 'Maudsley Method'), predicated on listening to the sufferer and his or her family. *The Clinician's Guide to Collaborative Caring in Eating Disorders: The New Maudsley Method* details the mantra LESS – 'listen', 'empathise', 'share', and 'support';[12] the importance of listening

9 Gowers, S.G. et al., 'Treatment aims and philosophy in the treatment of adolescent anorexia nervosa in Europe', *European Eating Disorders Review*, 10 (2002), 271–80 (279–80).

10 Le Heuzey, Marie-France, *L'Enfant anorexique: Comprendre et agir* (Paris: Odile Jacob, 2003), p. 12.

11 Haute Autorité de Santé, 'Anorexie mentale: prise en charge. Recommandations', https://www.has-sante.fr/portail/jcms/c_985715/fr/anorexie-mentale-prise-en-charge (30 September 2010), p. 22.

12 *The Clinician's Guide to Collaborative Caring in Eating Disorders: The New*

is also emphasised in other recent studies.[13] The 2016 'Maudsley Service Manual for Child and Adolescent Eating Disorders', meanwhile, notably repeats the word 'listening' twelve times. In theory, then, contemporary treatment of eating disorders may be seen to respond, in part, to the imperative to listen to ED sufferers that Lucille articulates here – but this does not, of course, mean that ED sufferers feel that they are being listened to, nor indeed that the practice reflects the theory. This seems particularly striking in the most severe cases of EDs (like those in the case studies in this book) that entail hospitalisation. The 'Maudsley Service Manual for Child and Adolescent Eating Disorders' warns against hospitalisation except in the most severe cases ('One hospital admission reduces the chance of a positive outcome; two admissions makes the future look even bleaker'[14]) and there is a noticeable absence of the language of punishment and privilege noted above in the accounts of hospital treatment. Nonetheless, where patients are required to be hospitalised, the manual still recommends supervision (which could be taken to be synonymous with surveillance), time limits for meals, and prohibition of toilet access for at least thirty minutes after eating.[15] These modes of treatment must inevitably be perceived by those compelled to conform to these restrictions as punitive and invasive, even though they are evidently intended for support.

To return to lived experiences of eating disorders, two texts alluded to in this book present contrasting perspectives of treatment that span the twentieth and twenty-first centuries. The first, Alice Bairoch's *Voyage en anorexie* (which is not named in Lucille's extended corpus because it is Swiss, not French and that, despite its title, recounts bulimic episodes as well as anorexia nervosa), may be seen to contradict Le Heuzey's claim in 2003 that treatment has radically altered since Valère's account of it from the 1970s. Bairoch recounts how when hospitalised for anorexia

Maudsley Method, edited by Janet Treasure, Ulrike Schmidt, and Pam Macdonald (London/New York: Routledge, 2009), p. 101.

13 Goodheart, Kristin, Clopton, James R. and Robert-McComb, Jacalyn J. (eds), *Eating Disorders in Women and Children: Prevention, Stress Management* (Boca Raton, FL: CRC Press/Taylor & Francis, 2000), p. 291.

14 Eisler, Ivan, Simic, Mima, Blessitt, Esther, Dodge, Liz et al., 'Maudsley Service Manual for Child and Adolescent Eating Disorders', https://www.national.slam.nhs.uk/wp-content/uploads/2011/11/Maudsley-Service-Manual-for-Child-and-Adolescent-Eating-Disorders-July-2016.pdf (2016), p. 35.

15 'Maudsley Service Manual for Child and Adolescent Eating Disorders', 100. There is also reference to enteral feeding where required (118).

nervosa in that same year (2003), she was forced to spend her first week in isolation (allowed no text messages, phone calls, or visits)[16] in a prison-like environment:

> Ils ont mis ma porte sous alarme, fermé la fenêtre et le lavabo à clef. Même pour m'habiller, je dois leur demander d'ouvrir mon armoire, elle aussi verrouillée. Ils disent qu'ils font tout cela pour mon bien. C'est impossible, ils veulent me punir, m'enfermer. Ma chambre ressemble à une prison. [They put an alarm on my door, locked the window and the bathroom. Even to get dressed, I have to ask them to open my wardrobe, which is also locked. They say they are doing it all for my benefit. It's impossible, they want to punish me, lock me up. My bedroom looks like a prison.][17]

Although Bairoch was subsequently allowed visits, phone calls, and text messages, the locked, alarmed doors and windows remained, while she was also accused of hiding food and forced to endure an invasive room search; she admits that she was terrified of one of her doctors.[18] Her descriptions of hospital treatment – while admittedly recounting experience in Switzerland rather than in France – find striking echoes in Valère's and Balinska's and, for example, in Emilie Durand's *Ma folie ordinaire: allers et retours à l'hôpital Sainte-Anne*, wherein Durand describes being watched both during mealtimes and even when alone in her room (through a viewing panel in the door) and having her study time for the *bac* removed as a punishment for particular forms of behaviour.[19] By contrast, Delphine de Vigan's 2001 autofictional text *Jours sans faim* (which recounts experience of anorexia nervosa more than a decade earlier, before the so-called change in treatment claimed by Le Heuzey) portrays treatment very differently: as Nathalie Morello writes, 'Unlike the prison-like environment described in Valère's text, the hospital and its ward dedicated to treating nutritional disorders are represented as an open space, illustrating the different therapeutic approaches in psychiatric and public hospitals.'[20] The protagonist,

16 Bairoch, Alice, *Voyage en anorexie* (Paris: Presses du Belvédère, 2007), p. 117.

17 Bairoch, *Voyage en anorexie*, p. 111.

18 Bairoch, *Voyage en anorexie*, pp. 128–30.

19 Durand, *Ma folie ordinaire*, p. 34.

20 Morello, Nathalie, 'Anorexia, anger, agency: Investigating quests for self in three contemporary narratives in French', in Francesca Calamita, Petra Bagley, and Kathryn Robson (eds), *Starvation, Food Obsession and Identity: Eating Disorders in Contemporary Women's Writing* (Oxford: Peter Lang, 2017), pp. 121–41 (p. 127).

Laure, recounts visits from friends and family and visits outside the ward and describes a doctor who prioritises narrative (story-telling) over power-play and thereby enables her to heal. She highlights that he asked her to let him help her recover, that he never weighed her without warning, and that his trust in her instilled in her a confidence that inspired her to gain weight and to heal.[21] Yet even within what Laure registers as a highly supportive environment, the relentless descriptions of enforced meals, monitored weight gain, and particularly the insertion of the feeding tube (a 'serpent' [snake]) highlight the extent to which even humane treatment can be registered as violent and invasive by the individual who feels she has little choice other than to endure it.[22] Part of the feeling of entrapment is an effect of the illness itself, which imprisons sufferers within their own bodies: she describes herself as 'piégée dans un corps qui la domine' [trapped in a body that dominates her], which finds resonance in Lucille's analysis of spatiality, to which I will return later.[23] For now, though, it is worth emphasising the impact of severe anorexia nervosa, for example, on mental health (the importance of this is reiterated in Lucille's conclusion), and the extent to which sufferers are likely to find extensive surveillance and removal of privacy in hospital particularly difficult due to the nature of their illness. Bairoch's narrative emphasises how difficult it is for an individual severely affected by an ED to be rational about treatment in its early stages and, as she begins to recover, she recounts changing her perspective towards the medics responsible for her care: 'Quelque chose en moi a changé' [something inside me has changed]; 'tout en moi était faussé par cette horrible maladie' [everything in me was distorted by this horrible illness]; 'Je commence à comprendre que le but des infirmières n'est pas de me détruire' [I am starting to understand that the aim of the nurses is not to destroy me]; 'on ne peut pas être gentil avec une maladie comme l'anorexie' [you can't be kind with an illness like anorexia] (142). This is not, of course, to suggest that the structures that deny her the right to open or close doors and windows without permission are not oppressive. If there are no 'kinder' options, to borrow her terminology, her text, like those discussed in this book, urgently calls for less punitive and damaging measures to be found. Bairoch's text does, however, highlight

21 de Vigan, Delphine, *Jours sans faim* (Paris: J'ai lu, 2009), first published 2001 under the pseudonym Lou Delvig, p. 124.

22 Vigan, *Jours sans faim*, p. 18.

23 Vigan, *Jours sans faim*, p. 81.

that sufferers may experience heightened anxiety or even paranoia while severely ill, that the gap between their experience and the point of view of the medical staff is difficult to bridge, and finally that the attempt on the part of medical professionals to understand better the perspectives of patients with EDs is particularly fraught.[24] Lucille's study aims precisely to further our understanding of what it means to suffer from and be treated for different eating disorders, but also to propose alternative modes of recovery (she advocates scriptotherapy, a 'writing cure', in her conclusion, for example), through close readings of her chosen corpus of French autobiographical and autofictional texts.

As Lucille herself observes elsewhere, there has been a 'relatively slow appearance of anorexia on the scene of French women's writing'[25] in comparison with English-language texts. Listing French accounts of anorexia in an article published in 2015, she writes:

> With the exception of those of Atlan and Valère, none of these texts appeared before the 1990s, and roughly half of them have appeared in the 2000s. This contrasts with anglophone, female-authored texts about anorexia, which started proliferating from the early 1980s. The relatively slow appearance of anorexia on the scene of French women's writing perhaps reflects what appears to be a lower incidence of anorexia among young females (the demographic most affected) in France compared to global incidences: as is detailed more thoroughly below, around 2 per cent for France compared with up to 10 per cent worldwide.[26]

In the extended primary corpus that forms the basis for this book, one (*Le Pavillon des enfants fous*) was published in the 1970s, four in the 1980s, twelve in the 1990s, and 28 since 2000, of which 26 were published between 2000 and 2010. As Nathalie Morello puts it, 'it was at the turn of the millennium that narratives of anorexia flourished' in France.[27] There is no clear evidence that this striking rise in autobiographical/autofictional writing about EDs post-2000 in France mirrors a parallel rise in cases of EDs – it is more likely that EDs became more culturally

24 Senninger observes, 'L'anorexie est une vengeance, une rebellion qui se retourne contre soi' (20), as 'plutôt que d'exprimer contre l'autre sa colère', the anorexic turns his or her aggression into a battle 'contre la nourriture' (23); this struggle with food is also a thinly veiled combat with others.

25 Cairns, Lucille, 'Bodily dis-ease in contemporary French women's writing: Two case studies', *French Studies*, 69, 4 (October 2015), 494–508 (495).

26 Cairns, 'Bodily dis-ease in contemporary French women's writing', 495.

27 Morello, 'Anorexia, anger, agency', p. 122.

visible and thus narratable in this period. The increase in published accounts of EDs corresponds first to a rise in autobiography more widely (if we accept that 'memoir has become *the* genre in the skittish period around the turn of the millennium'[28]) and second to an increase in the narrative accounts of illness and disability in the early twenty-first century. ED memoirs also belong to what Hunsacker Hawkins calls 'pathography', (auto)biography or life-writing that recounts illness and treatment, as well as recovery or even (in the case of biographies) death.[29] The increase in published narratives of illness and disability, Couser suggests, reflects at once 'the destigmatisation of illness and disability' and 'the extension of identity politics to illness';[30] partly these texts mirror a cultural shift in attitudes towards disease, but also a change in conception of identity, wherein illness/disease become integral to – rather than interruptions in – a notion of self and in the construction of autobiography more widely.[31] This is highlighted in the French autobiographical writing that forms the extended primary corpus here, which both evokes and interrogates the relation between EDs, identity construction, and narrative.

The extended corpus ranges from memoirs (including those written in collaboration with professional writers)[32] to autofictional accounts by well-known prize-winning (auto)fictional writers like Amélie Nothomb or Delphine de Vigan. The six texts that form the case studies for this book – all clearly autobiographical bar Rodrigue's *La peau à l'envers. Le roman vrai d'une boulimique*, which 'blends fictional and autobiographical elements, but with a heavy weighting of the latter' – are representative of the extended corpus within which the vast majority of texts are self confessedly straightforwardly autobiographical, with a few (Geneviève Brisac's *Petite*, for example) classifiable as 'autofiction' and what Lucille describes as a single fictional novel: Fawzia Zourai's *Ce pays dont je meurs* (1999).[33] This is not, of course, the only text in the

28 Gilmore, Leigh, *The Limits of Autobiography: Trauma and Testimony* (London: Cornell University Press, 2001), p. 1.

29 Hawkins, Hunsacker, *Reconstructing Illness: Studies in Pathography* (West Lafayette, IN: Purdue University Press, 1999).

30 Couser, Thomas, *Recovering Bodies: Illness, Disability and Life Writing* (Madison, WI: University of Wisconsin Press, 1997), p. 8.

31 Couser, *Recovering Bodies*, p. 5.

32 Justine (avec la collaboration de Marie-Thérèse Cuny), *Ce matin j'ai décidé d'arrêter de manger*, cited above, is one such example.

33 Zourai, Fawzia, *Ce pays dont je meurs* (Paris: Ramsay, 1999).

primary corpus that could be described as fictional: Amélie Nothomb's *Robert des noms propres*, which has been aptly described as a traumatic 'fairytale',[34] is presumably not presented as an autobiography or even as autofiction, but Nothomb's own well-documented experience of eating disorders seems to be what differentiates this, in Lucille's framework, from Zourai's text. What draws all of the texts in the corpus together, then, is their status as 'testimonies' to the lived experience of EDs (*Ce pays dont je meurs*, while fictional, is included as it is 'importantly, based on a real, mediatized case of death by anorexia nervosa in France'). The point of this book is to focus on texts written out of lived experiences of EDs, which are explored in extraordinary and vital detail, and are linked repeatedly back to and compared with clinical accounts of EDs.

In a review essay of Megan Warin's book *Abject Relations: Everyday Worlds of Anorexia*,[35] Debra Ferreday observes the following:

> Such is the contemporary preoccupation with the relation between bodies and images, that the relation between bodies themselves is almost entirely under-theorized, nor is there any meaningful account of the lived experience of anorexia that does not conform to the overcoming/journey narrative of the misery memoir. The cultural tendency either to reduce anorexia to abject spectacle or to elevate it to heroic myth makes Warin's project, of paying attention to the 'everyday worlds of anorexia', all the more timely. Moving beyond cultural narratives that position the anorexic body as spectacle, that hold out the promise of an encounter with the disgusting body, Warin's book is concerned with what it might mean to allow anorexics to speak as subjects. By keeping her participants 'out of the grasping reach' of those who want only to gaze on the disgusting spectacle of 'the really skinny one', it might be possible for the anorexic subject to speak. Whether s/he will be heard remains to be seen.[36]

This book shifts away from the binary of 'abject spectacle' versus 'heroic myth' not only by allowing 'the anorexic subject to speak', but also by 'paying attention to' the 'everyday worlds of anorexia' (and, of course, other eating disorders) in impressive and acute detail. It is indeed

34 McIlvanney, Siobhán, '"Il était une fois...": Trauma and the fairytale in Amélie Nothomb's *Robert des noms propres*', *Dalhousie French Studies*, 81 (2007), 19–28.

35 Warin, Megan, *Abject Relations: Everyday Worlds of Anorexia* (Piscataway, NJ: Rutgers University Press, 2010).

36 Ferreday, Debra, 'Anorexia and abjection: A review essay', *Body & Society*, 18, 2 (2012), 139–55 (153).

partly Lucille's painstaking and meticulous analysis of detailed aspects of living with EDs that offers insights that could and should inform clinical responses to EDs. Some of the conclusions drawn – to give the examples that stand out to me, but there are others, too, that warrant further attention – are crucial to shifting attitudes to and treatment of EDs. First, I would like to point to Lucille's assertion that 'binge eating disorder is certainly as dangerous an ED as anorexia nervosa and bulimia nervosa', despite being generally perceived to be somehow less serious, and her convincing insistence that it therefore urgently needs further research. Second, the recognition that eating disorders provoke mental as well as, or even more than, physical suffering, also needs to be taken seriously. Finally, the last few pages on space and the potential benefits of scriptotherapy could fruitfully be developed further in various ways – through further academic research or clinical study, but equally through creative therapy, for example. I would like to end by suggesting that the notion of giving space, as well as voice, to sufferers of EDs seems to be a crucial step forward, in a context in which, as Lucille powerfully argues, experiences of EDs are bound up in a lack of personal space, both literal (the restricted space of the hospital room likened to a prison; the invasive intrusion of bodily boundaries via forced tube-feeding, for example) and figurative. In privileging the voices of sufferers of EDs (and the plural here is important: there is no singular and universal narrative perspective), this book creates space in which and from which the sufferers of EDs can both speak and be heard.

Kathryn Robson, Newcastle

Introduction

Timeshells

This book examines French literary, and largely testimonial, inscriptions of eating disorders (hereinafter abbreviated to EDs, and 'eating disorder' to ED). Its general overarching aim is to make a significant and singular contribution to two main and conjoined academic fields. These fields are literary studies on the one hand, and on the other hand the medical humanities, with the latter having long been interested in narratives of health and ill-health. As the reviewer for the proposal from which this book emerged observed, 'the cross-fertilisation of fields such as the humanities (literature) and sciences (medicine) [...] should [...] result in a better understanding of the pathology and push the boundaries in terms of writing cures [...]'. I address the concept of 'writing cures' briefly later on in this Introduction, and more fully in the Conclusion to this book. To return to the Introduction, it is to be hoped that my book will also contribute to improved understanding of EDs among scholars in cultural studies, feminism, gender studies, philosophy, psychiatry, psychoanalysis, and sociology – and to enhanced understanding of EDs among health-care practitioners treating, or with future prospects of treating, ED sufferers. Further comments made by the reviewer for the proposal from which this book originally emerged are worth citing:

> While research in science is illuminating to understand the phenomenon,[1] it has also been criticised for being too quantitative or over-reliant on the DSM IV (and now V). The proposed book offers an interesting complement, by focusing on more qualitative data (subjective, lived experiences).

1 That is, the phenomenon of EDs.

DSM stands for *Diagnostic and Statistical Manual of Mental Disorders*, the most recent version of which is *DSM-5*, published in 2013. The reviewer also remarked:

> [P]revious research [...] made it clear EDs (in particular anorexia) were at some point a social, cultural, and medical construction, for which doctors needed patients, hence the consequently high prevalence of cases. It is therefore essential [...] to take stock of a situation where EDs themselves must be thoroughly unpacked, as their very construction as a pathology cannot be ignored.

That 'EDs (in particular anorexia) were at some point a social, cultural, and medical construction' is certainly true, as I will go on to elaborate. It is worth noting that the feminist poststructuralist scholar Maree Burns goes considerably further than the reviewer in this contention – too far, in my view:

> [M]y starting point for this analysis insists that anorexia and bulimia do not exist independently of the discourses that describe them. There are therefore no truths to be uncovered about eating disorders or about the women who practise them. Anorexia and bulimia are, instead, understood to be constituted by the very knowledges that seek to depict and 'know' them.[2]

Burns's position neglects the irrefutable materialities of anorexia nervosa and bulimia nervosa. And while I concur with the reviewer's assertion, 'EDs (in particular anorexia) were at some point a social, cultural, and medical construction', this may, though, be no more true than of any other recognised illness. All recognised illnesses are nosologically 'constructed' by medical researchers and clinicians insofar as a recognised illness is, in one sense, the end result of the recording and grouping together of a given set of symptoms, and the subsequent conferring on them of a medical label, thus rendering them a pathologising 'construction'. Nonetheless, this does not diminish the validity of the assertion that 'EDs (in particular anorexia) were at some point a social, cultural, and medical construction'.

The 'at some point' could be nuanced: some scholars argue that anorexia nervosa at least has probably always existed. Others agree with the 'at some point', but that point is very far back in recorded human history. Three examples are from Mara Selvini Palazzoli, Angela

2 Burns, Maree, 'Eating like an ox: Femininity and dualistic constructions of bulimia and anorexia', *Feminism and Psychology*, 14, 2 (2004), 269–95 (272–73).

McCarthy and Margie Thomson, and Philippe Jeammet. Palazzoli observed the following in 1978:

> Two Italian authors, Accornero and Baraldi, have claimed that the earliest account of anorexia nervosa was given by Simone Porta, a sixteenth-century Genovese, but the more general view is that the first detailed description came from the pen of Richard Morton, a seventeenth-century English physician. In his *Phthisiologia, seu Exercitationes de Phthisis* (1689), Morton used the term 'nervous atrophy' to refer to a form of consumption that was not accompanied by fever or dyspnoea but went hand in hand with a loss of appetite and digestive difficulties. Morton not only gave two fairly detailed case histories but also described the chief characteristics of the disease – namely amenorrhea, lack of appetite, constipation, extreme emaciation ('like a skeleton only clad with skin') and overactivity.[3]

Angela McCarthy and Margie Thomson, in 1996, traced both anorexia nervosa and bulimia nervosa much further back in time: 'it is interesting to consider that there are mentions of anorexia- and bulimia-type symptoms throughout history, from as early as fourth-century Greece'.[4] And in 2004, Philippe Jeammet converged with them apropos anorexia nervosa:

> En effet, l'anorexie mentale est loin d'être une pathologie nouvelle ; on la reconnaît déjà dans certaines descriptions datant de l'Antiquité, greco-romaine et même égyptienne, et, au XIe siècle, le médecin et philosophe Avicenne rapportait l'histoire d'un jeune prince qui, refusant de se nourrir, se laissait dépérir.[5]
>
> Indeed, anorexia nervosa is far from a new illness; it is already recognisable in certain descriptions dating from Antiquity, Greco-Roman and even Egyptian, and, in the eleventh century, the doctor and philosopher Avicenna related the story of a young prince who, refusing to eat, was allowing himself to waste away.

Yet anorexia nervosa – and bulimia nervosa – as we now conceptualise (or 'construct') them have one vital component that does not

3 Palazzoli, Mara Selvini, *Self-Starvation: From Individual to Family Therapy in the Treatment of Anorexia Nervosa* (New York/London: Jason Aronson, 1978), p. 4.

4 McCarthy, Angela and Thomson, Margie, *Hungry Heart: Anorexia and Bulimia* (Auckland: Hodder Moa Beckett, 1996), p. 13.

5 Jeammet, Philippe, *Anorexie Boulimie. Les paradoxes de l'adolescence* (Paris: Hachette Littératures, 2004), p. 228.

appear to have figured in any of the putative cases cited in distant history: namely, fear of weight gain, and indeed relentless pursuit of weight loss. Having said that, I recognise other researchers/psychiatrists contend that in certain cultures what appears to be anorexia nervosa at least manifests itself without 'fat phobia'. One example is from two psychiatrists:

> [I]n a study of 70 anorexic patients in Hong Kong, Lee et al. (1993) reported that 58.6% displayed no conscious fear of becoming fat, and in large-scale surveys in Singapore, anorexic respondents usually related no fat phobia (Kok & Tian, 1994). Instead, these non-fat phobic patients used epigastric bloating, no hunger, or simply 'don't know' as legitimations of fat phobia.[6]

Yet much may be hidden behind the words 'no *conscious* fear' (my emphasis). The two psychiatrists proceed to refer to other studies, concluding thus on a historicising note:

> These findings parallel Western reports of anorexia nervosa at the turn of the century in which fat phobia was not stated as the precipitant for morbid food restriction. Prior to the medicalisation of anorexia nervosa in this century, the religious and political nature of food refusal was a starting point for understanding eating disturbance, not a caboose to a genetic-pharmacological train. Historical accounts of asceticism certainly suggest that both the onset and reduction of self starvation mirror changes in oppressed individuals' opportunities for overt recognition and advancement (Vandereycken & van Deth, 1993).[7]

Another example of the constructedness of EDs generally, not just anorexia nervosa, in the twentieth and twenty-first centuries is the fact that several changes have occurred for their diagnosis in the successive versions of the *Diagnostic and Statistical Manual of Mental Disorders*. These changes indicate that EDs are not immutable but rather, from a nosological perspective, constructions built on certain symptoms, whose presumed causes have shown some significant alterations over time (causative interpretations often reflecting shifting social and cultural values, one key instance being the increasing valorisation in the twentieth century of thinness and of food control). A further illustration

6 Katzman, M.A. and Lee, S., 'Beyond body image: The integration of feminist and transcultural theories in the understanding of self-starvation', *International Journal of Eating Disorders*, 22, 4 (1997), 385–94 (388).

7 Katzman and Lee, 'Beyond body image', 388.

of labile perceptions of, and in this case indeed *de*-construction of anorexia nervosa, is the fact that for two decades in the earlier part of the twentieth century many cases of anorexia nervosa were no longer recognised as such, but nosologically transformed into another illness consisting merely in physical dysfunction (with no psychological disturbance). As Palazzoli recalled:

> In 1914 Morris Simmonds, a Hamburg physician, described a fatal case of cachexia[8] which, at autopsy, showed atrophy of the anterior lobe of the pituitary. Two years later Simmonds gave an anatomical as well as a clinical description of two further cases.
>
> Simmonds' discovery misled physicians into attaching too much importance to the emaciation. As a result cases of anorexia nervosa were commonly mistaken for Simmonds' disease, and in about 1916 the term 'anorexia nervosa' was allowed to fall into disuse. Typical cases of adolescent anorexia nervosa were treated as cases of pituitary marasmus, and this confused state of affairs continued until the late 1930s.[9]

That this transduction of anorexia nervosa, and its consequences – drastically reduced estimations of its prevalence, and therefore lamentably inadequate treatment or no treatment at all – endured from 1914 to the late 1930s illustrates how stagnation in medical approaches to anorexia nervosa (the best known, but also by far the earliest recognised of the three EDs studied in this book) can occur. Helen Malson explains this particular transduction in terms of historically changing epistemological trends:

> During the early part of the twentieth century the problem of 'anorexia nervosa' was taken up by the psychoanalysts and was thereby reconstituted as an object of psychoanalytic discourse. [...]
>
> The early 1920s, however, saw the growing influence of the logical positivist approach to science, in which empirically verifiable 'objective fact' was posited as the only 'true' form of scientific knowledge (see Chapter 1). Clearly psychoanalytic accounts of anorexia did not meet these positivist criteria for Truth, and by the 1920s and 1930s explanations of anorexia as an endocrinal dysfunction came to predominate (Bruch, 1974).[10]

8 Cachexia means weakness and wasting of the body due to severe chronic illness.

9 Palazzoli, *Self-Starvation*, pp. 7–8.

10 Malson, Helen, *The Thin Woman: Feminism, Post-Structuralism and the Social Psychology of Anorexia Nervosa* (London/New York: Routledge, 1998), p. 77.

Another illustration furnished by Malson of such historically changing epistemological trends in 'professional' approaches to anorexia nervosa is the following:

> By the beginning of the 1940s there arose an international interest in 'psychosomatic disorders', and texts on 'anorexia' again became increasingly concerned with producing theories about psychological rather than physical aetiologies (see Tostrup, 1990) so that 'anorexia' was again discursively constituted as psychologically meaningful.[11]

So, already in this Introduction, I have taken 'stock of a situation' where EDs themselves must be thoroughly unpacked, as their very construction as a pathology 'cannot be ignored'. An example of how I further do so later on is in the section on Camille de Peretti in Chapter 2, which draws attention to the vehement assertion (or what psychoanalytically oriented clinicians would dismiss as a defence mechanism) of her protagonist Camille (based on de Peretti herself) that everyone is, in some sense, ill – and Camille's meaning here is clearly that everyone is, in some sense, mentally rather than physically 'ill'. This assertion is also made in another French testimony to eating-disordered illness, Emilie Durand's *Ma folie ordinaire: allers et retours à l'hôpital Sainte-Anne* (2006),[12] in which Durand contests normative concepts of sanity and insanity in the context of EDs.

The new grounds I hope to break in this book are, put briefly, to throw light upon the phenomenological, lived, embodied, and affective experience of EDs from the point of view of ex-sufferers, rather than from the point of view of clinicians, medical researchers, and theorists. Fulfilment of such a pedagogical aim is, I believe, urgent, given the grave public health challenge that EDs represent, the high mortality rates of ED sufferers, and the imperative of academic research having impact upon society at large. The significant, singular contribution this book aims to make will be achieved by fostering greater understanding of experiences of EDs, which constitute a grave public-health challenge in the Western world (although EDs have also recently increased outside of the West). One aspect of this challenge, on which I elaborate below, is that the best-known ED among the general public, anorexia nervosa, 'is now the third most common chronic

11 Malson, *The Thin Woman*, p. 77.

12 Durand, Emilie, *Ma folie ordinaire: allers et retours à l'hôpital Sainte-Anne* (Paris: Les Empêcheurs de tourner en rond, 2006).

disease among female adolescents'.[13] More specific objectives of this book supporting that aim are to examine the most common types of EDs as represented in contemporary French women's literature. These EDs are: anorexia nervosa, restrictor type – that is, not involving purgation of food through vomiting, laxative abuse, etc.; bulimia nervosa/bulimarexia (the two terms are not strictly speaking fungible, since bulimarexia involves bulimia nervosa with periods of anorexia nervosa, whereas some bulimics do not go through any such periods, controlling their weight instead by purging); and binge eating disorder. My overall primary corpus (see Bibliography for the complete list) comprises 45 largely autobiographical (occasionally autofictional, and in a tiny number among the 45, possibly fictional)[14] texts that represent EDs phenomenologically,[15] with such writing testifying subjectively to the embodied and affective impacts of these EDs on the sufferer. Presentation and analysis of such testimonies will be instructive to all the types of scholars mentioned in paragraph 1 above and to clinicians, but within literary studies it is likely to be of particular relevance to those working in *gendered* literary studies, since it analyses solely female-authored French writing. Males self-evidently suffer from EDs too, but *much* less commonly, and it is far beyond the possible scope of this book to address the specificities of male experiences of EDs.

One important aim of the book is thus to expand and deepen knowledge of women's EDs and of their lived experience. This is vital, because

13 Raveneau, G., Feinstein, R., Rosen, L.M., and Fisher, M., 'Attitudes and knowledge levels of nurses and residents caring for adolescents with an eating disorder', *International Journal of Adolescent Medicine and Health*, 26, 1 (2014), 131–36 ((131).

14 Fawzia Zourai's *Ce pays dont je meurs* (Paris: Ramsay, 1999) is an exception in the primary corpus, because it is definitely a fictional text – although, importantly, based on a real, mediatised case of death by anorexia nervosa in France. It has the merit of being an example of North African francophone women's writing about anorexia nervosa, unlike the other 44 primary texts I examine in this book.

15 On a phenomenological approach, see John Sours: 'Phenomenology, a presuppositionless inquiry in search of essences, not apparent by ordinary observation, is a technique for discovering what lies behind appearances by trying to experience them as the subject of the investigation.' Sours, John A., *Starving to Death in a Sea of Objects: The Anorexia Nervosa Syndrome* (New York/London: Jason Aronson, 1980), note 1, p. 269.

> [o]ver the last few decades, there has been a dramatic increase in the prevalence and incidence of eating disorders (EDs) among children and adolescents. The mortality rate for patients of all ages with anorexia nervosa (AN) is approximately 5.6% per decade, the highest among all psychiatric disorders.[16]

While these percentage rates may not appear high to some readers, it is surely of grave concern that more anorectics die from their illness than do sufferers of any other psychiatric illness. The secondary literature is replete with attestation to the anorectic's risk of death, such as, 'Anorexia nervosa is associated with a substantial risk of death and suicide'[17] and, 'The standardized mortality ratios in AN are between 5 to 10 times greater than in normal controls, and considerably higher than those reported for most other psychiatric disturbances, being the highest in bingeing-purging type AN.'[18] The elevated mortality rates for anorexia nervosa in particular are also registered in an English-language personal testimony by Emma Woolf that demonstrates wide knowledge beyond her own experience of the illness: 'Anorexia has a higher mortality rate than any other mental illness: up to 20 per cent of sufferers will die, either from medical complications or suicide.'[19] And the grave concern should not be restricted to anorectics, for there is also a raised mortality rate in other EDs: 'All-cause standardized mortality ratios were significantly elevated for bulimia nervosa and for eating disorders not otherwise specified.'[20] The formulation 'eating disorders not otherwise specified' is often acronymised as 'EDNOS', and an alternative term used for this diagnosis is 'atypical eating disorder'. It is relevant to note that '[i]n DSM-5, EDNOS is replaced by two residual ED diagnoses: OSFED, which among others contains

16 Raveneau et al., 'Attitudes and knowledge levels of nurses and residents', 131.

17 Herzog, D.B., Greenword, D.N., Dorer, D.J., Flores, A.T., Ekeblad, E.R., Richards, A., Blais, M.A., and Keller, M.B., 'Mortality in eating disorders: A descriptive study', *International Journal of Eating Disorders*, 28, 1 (2000), 20–26 (21).

18 Latzer, Yael, Merrick, Joay, and Stein, Daniel (eds), *Understanding Eating Disorders: Integrating Culture, Psychology and Biology* (New York: Nova Science Publishers, 2011), p. 3.

19 Woolf, Emma, *An Apple a Day: A Memoir of Love and Recovery from Anorexia* (London: Summersdale, 2012), p. 59.

20 Crow, S.J., Peterson, C.B., Swanson, S.A., Raymond, N.C., Specker, S., Eckert, E.D., and Mitchell, J.E., 'Increased mortality in bulimia nervosa and other eating disorders', *American Journal of Psychiatry*, 166, 12 (2009), 1342–46.

subthreshold BN and BED, and UFED, an aspecific ED diagnosis where insufficient information is available'.[21] (OSFED is an acronym for Other Specified Feeding or Eating Disorder, BN for Bulimia Nervosa, BED for Binge Eating Disorder, and UFED for Unspecified Feeding or Eating Disorder.)

Estimations of the rates of EDs vary in the voluminous secondary literature, presumably due at least in part to methodological differences in arriving at the estimations. Thus, for example, Hoek states, 'In Europe, anorexia nervosa is reported by 1–4%, bulimia nervosa by 1–2%, and binge eating disorder (BED) by 1–4% of women.'[22] Lewis and Nicholls 2016, on the other hand, affirm different rates:

> The prevalence of AN is around 0.3–0.5%, with a peak age of onset between 15 and 18, cases steadily increasing from age 10 and occurring in children as young as 7. High-risk populations (athletes, models, ballet dancers) have higher prevalence rates. BN tends to occur later. The prevalence is just under 1%, with a slightly later mean age of onset with cases reported from about 12 years. [...] Prevalence rates for BED range from around 2–3% [...]. BED is probably under-recognised, and in young people may look more like loss of control over eating than true bingeing.[23]

However, rather than referring to Europe alone as does Hoek, Lewis and Nicholls's figures appear to be global, or at least to refer to the Western world generally. French rates specifically may differ marginally from these global rates. In 2001 the French psychologist Christian Mormont and psychiatrist Marc Ansseau gave a figure of 0.5 to 1 per cent of the population for the incidence of anorexia nervosa.[24]

21 Dahlgren, Camilla Lindvall, 'Transitioning from DSM-IV to DSM-5: A systematic review of eating disorder prevalence assessment', *International Journal of Eating Disorders*, 49 (2016), 975–97 (976). Note that most clinicians have used and continue to use the criteria for diagnosis of EDs set out in the successive versions of the *DSM* (*Diagnostic and Statistical Manual of Mental Disorders*), or the *ICD* (*International Classification of Diseases*), which was developed in 1992. *ICD-11* was published in 2019.

22 Hoek, H.W., 'Review of the worldwide epidemiology of eating disorders', *Current Opinion in Psychiatry*, 29, 6 (November 2016), 336–39 (336).

23 Lewis., B. and Nicholls, D., 'Behavioural eating disorders', *Paediatrics and Child Health*, 26, 12 (December 2016), 519–26 (519).

24 See Christian Mormont and Marc Ansseau, 'Anorexie', in Marcel Crahay and Christine Goffinet (eds), *Regards croisés sur l'anorexie* (Liège: Les Editions de l'Université de Liège, 2001), pp. 11–13 (p. 11).

In 2008 Corcos et al. gave a generally higher rate for anorexia nervosa: '[l]a prévalence vie entière pour le sexe féminin de l'anorexie mentale varie entre 0,3 et 3%' [the lifetime prevalence of female anorexia nervosa varies between 0.3% and 3%], adding that the rate for bulimia nervosa was 'entre 2 et 5% selon les études' [between 2 and 5% according to studies].[25] More recent figures for France are provided in a previous publication of mine, although I was only able to obtain information on figures for adolescents or young adolescents, no information being supplied by INSERM for rates where the ED had a later onset age:

> In France, the INSERM (Institut national de la santé de la recherche médicale) reports that '[u]ne étude épidémiologique menée en France en 2008 auprès d'adolescents dans leur 18e année indique que l'anorexie mentale a concerné 0,5% de ces jeunes filles et 0,03% des garçons entre 12 et 17 ans' [an epidemiological study conducted in France in 2008 with 18-year-old adolescents indicates that anorexia nervosa affected 0.5% of the girls and 0.03% of the boys between the ages of 12 and 17].[26] A different source gives the slightly higher figure of 2 per cent for the incidence of anorexia in France [...]: '2% des adolescentes présentent des formes d'anorexie. L'anorexie concerne 9 filles pour un garçon. Elle se manifeste à l'adolescence, entre 15 et 18 ans notamment' [2% of adolescent girls have forms of anorexia. Anorexia affects 9 girls for every boy. It appears during adolescence, especially between the ages of 15 and 18]; and that '8 à 10% des adolescentes souffrent de boulimie. [...] C'est une maladie à 90% féminine. La boulimie se manifeste vers l'âge de 19 ans' [8 to 10% of adolescent girls suffer from bulimia. [...] It is a 90% female disease. Bulimia appears around the age of 19].[27]

However, the Lewis and Nicholls article, not specifically focused on France or Europe in general and the most recently published study of all those mentioned above, importantly provides figures that are not

25 Corcos, Maurice, Lamas, Claire, Pham-Scottez, Alexandra, and Doyen, Catherine, *L'anorexie mentale: déni et réalités* (Rueil-Malmaison: Doin, 2008), p. 44.

26 Institut national de la santé et de la recherche médicale (Inserm), 'Anorexie mentale', http://www.inserm.fr/thematiques/neurosciences-sciences-cognitives-neurologie-psychiatrie/dossiers-d-information/anorexie-mentale (accessed 27 April 2015).

27 Cairns, Lucille, 'Bodily dis-ease in contemporary French women's writing: Two case studies', *French Studies*, 69, 4 (October 2015), 494–508 (497–98).

limited to children and adolescents. Finally, it is worth noting that '[t]he combined prevalence of anorexia nervosa (AN), bulimia nervosa (BN), binge eating disorder (BED), and EDNOS is around 10% of girls and young women'.[28]

Given these data, it is worrying that no generally effective treatments as yet exist for EDs. It is equally worrying, if logically correlated to this dearth, that in a literature review examining the level of knowledge of EDs possessed by healthcare professionals, '[o]nly one study reported that clinicians have an adequate knowledge of EDs'.[29] Similarly perturbing are the often very negative attitudes and affect of healthcare professionals apropos the eating-disordered patients for whom they are meant to be caring. In an overall review of 21 articles, Seah et al. 2017 affirm the following:

> Twelve papers explored the attitudes of healthcare professionals toward working with patients with EDs. The majority of the studies reported negative feelings toward patients with EDs, while only two studies reported positive feelings.
>
> Four studies from the US reported negative emotions toward patients with EDs. Frustration was a commonly expressed emotion by 68.8% of the residents who worked in an inpatient adolescent medicine unit (n = 82) [...]. However, another study (n = 124) on psychologists and psychiatrists from various units reported low levels of frustration, with these professionals instead expressing higher levels of boredom and anger, and feelings of failure and incompetency towards patients with EDs [...]. Feelings of helplessness and emotional distress were recorded in a study of healthcare professionals working in ED treatment centers (n = 298) [...] and in general units (n = 183) [...].
>
> Two studies conducted in Australia also revealed negative emotions of healthcare professionals. Patients with EDs were viewed as 'manipulative' and 'non-compliant', causing annoyance in healthcare professionals [...].
>
> Three studies explored the attitudes of different healthcare professionals. 68.8% of the residents (n =34) in a study expressed feelings of frustration, compared to 45.2% of the nurses (n =14) [...]. Psychiatrists

28 Latzer, Merrick, and Stein (eds), *Understanding Eating Disorders*, pp. 237–49 (p. 238).

29 Seah, X.Y., Tham, X.C., Kamaruzaman, N.R., and Yobas, P., 'Knowledge, attitudes and challenges of healthcare professionals managing people with eating disorders: A literature review', *Archives of Psychiatric Nursing*, 31 (2017), 125–36 (126).

> were reported to have higher levels of anger and frustration, and feelings of aggression toward patients with EDs, than psychologists [...].[30]
>
> Patients with EDs face more stigmatizing attitudes than psychiatric patients suffering more general conditions, such as depression [...].[31]

An ancillary aim of this book is to mitigate as far as is realistically achievable such negative, stigmatising attitudes among healthcare practitioners treating ED sufferers, through highlighting the phenomenological, lived experience of EDs – an experience of intense misery emerging poignantly from the 45 primary texts. One particular aspect of clinicians' inadequate knowledge is of deep ethical concern. In Raveneau et al.'s 2014 study, nurses and physicians answered a questionnaire revealing that '[m]ore than half of all respondents (58.2%) thought that ED patients were responsible for their disease "always" or "in most cases"'.[32] The belief of these nurses and physicians is interrogated by the findings of my own research on the 45 primary texts written by women who in the majority of cases have themselves suffered from an ED. This belief reflects a popular cliché that EDs, particularly anorexia nervosa and bulimia nervosa/bulimarexia, are selfishly self-inflicted (selfishly because of the intense distress they cause the sufferer's family and the drain on public health-care budgets that ED treatment entails). Moreover, the belief betrays on the part of those who are meant to provide caring, non-judgemental treatment a moralising prejudice against patients with EDs. In contrast to controlled, voluntaristic self-infliction of their illness, the primary texts express, in some cases intermittently, a sense of the ED sufferer's total *lack* of control, both over food intake (be it too little or too much) and over her general syndromal behaviour. In fact, one prominent feature in these testimonies is the metaphor of the ED as an alien force, exterior to the suffering self, and not infrequently personified as a despotic mistress (the female gender of this force perhaps reflecting the massively greater preponderance of EDs in females as opposed to males).[33] This personification of the ED as an

30 Seah et al., 'Knowledge, attitudes and challenges of healthcare professionals', 132–33.

31 Seah et al., 'Knowledge, attitudes and challenges of healthcare professionals', 134.

32 Raveneau et al., 'Attitudes and knowledge levels of nurses and residents', 131.

33 One similar metaphor featuring anorexia as a despotic force exterior to the anorectic self is Lanor in Lou Delvig's *Jours sans faim* (Paris: Éd. France loisirs, 2001). Kathryn Robson describes Lanor as 'an imagined anorexic alter ego [...]

exterior force demonstrates the sufferer's sense of having no personal control over her disorder.

The research questions that drive this book are the following. 1. How are EDs represented phenomenologically in French autobiographical texts? 2. What are the literary, stylistic, and rhetorical devices deployed to represent these EDs? 3. How do these primary texts converge with, diverge from, and/or constitute challenges to accounts of EDs found in the clinical and medical research literature? 4. What can scholars in the medical humanities and health-care practitioners learn from these divergences and challenges? I address these questions through close readings of French narratives of EDs.[34]

With respect to research context, this book builds on two of my previous publications on EDs in French women's writing: '*Dissidences charnelles*: The female body in revolt', in James Baldwin, James Fowler, and Shane Weller (eds), *The Flesh in the Text* (Oxford: Peter Lang, 2007), pp. 205–25; and 'Bodily dis-ease in contemporary French women's writing: Two case studies', *French Studies*, 69, 4 (October 2015), 494–508. The book is further informed by the modest but growing number of journal articles or edited-volume chapters dealing with EDs in French women's writing (mainly, it has to be said, with anorexia nervosa rather

a skeletal figure whispering in her ear, tempting her to refuse to eat'. Robson, Kathryn, 'Voicing abjection: Narratives of anorexia in contemporary French women's (life-)writing', *L'Esprit Createur*, 56, 2 (Summer 2016), 108–20 (112).

34 France was a pioneer in recording instances of what would eventually come to be known in English as anorexia nervosa (as previously stated, the best known of all EDs). As early as 1789, Naudeau, a French physician, published a long account of a fatal case of what would now be termed anorexia nervosa (Naudeau, J., 'Observations sur une maladie nerveuse accompagnée d'un dégoût extraordinaire pour les aliments', *J. méd. Chir. Et pharmacol.*, 80, 197 (1789)). The first doctor (narrowly preceding the English clinical surgeon William Gull) to identify anorexia nervosa was French: Ernest Charles Lasègue, Professor of Clinical Medicine in the University of Paris. In April 1873 Lasègue published a paper named 'On hysterical anorexia' (Lasègue, E.C., 'On hysterical anorexia', *Med, Tms, Gaz.*, 2, 265 (1873)). Further indications of France's prominent role in the study of anorexia nervosa are made in the secondary literature: 'Gull's assertion that anorexia must be distinguished from hysteria was supported by French authorities (Deniau, Sollier, Regis, Girou, Ballet and Charcot) all of whom centred their attention on the nosological problem' (Palazzoli 1978: 6).

than either of the other two EDs with which I deal), details of which are supplied in the footnote to this observation.[35] However, some of these

35 Cairns, Lucille, '*Dissidences charnelles*: The female body in revolt', in James Baldwin, James Fowler, and Shane Weller (eds), *The Flesh in the Text* (Oxford: Peter Lang, 2007), pp. 205–25; Cairns, Lucille, 'Bodily dis-ease in contemporary French women's writing: Two case studies', *French Studies*, 69, 4 (October 2015), 494–508; Damlé, Amaleena, 'The becoming of anorexia and text in Amélie Nothomb's *Robert des noms propres* and Delphine de Vigan's *Jours sans faim*', in Amaleena Damlé and Gill Rye (eds), *Women's Writing in Twenty-First-Century France: Life as Literature* (Cardiff: University of Wales Press, 2013), pp. 113–26; Githire, Njeri, 'The semiotics of (not)-eating: Fasting, anorexia, and hunger strike in Ananda Devi's *Le Voile de Draupadi*', *Nottingham French Studies*, 48, 1 (2009), 82–93; Havercroft, Barbara, 'Paper thin: Agency and anorexia in Geneviève Brisac's *Petite*', in Valerie Raoul et (eds), *Unfitting Stories: Narrative Approaches to Disease, Disability, and Trauma* (Waterloo, ON: Wilfred Laurier University Press, 2007), pp. 61–69; Jackson, Laura, 'Purging the self: Transcribing the divided, anorexic subject in Geneviève Brisac's *Petite* and Camille de Peretti's *Thornytorinx*', in Adrienne Angelo and Erika Fülöp (eds), *Protean Selves: First-Person Voices in Twenty-First-Century French and Francophone Narratives* (Newcastle: Cambridge Scholars Publishing, 2014), pp. 166–79; Kemp, Anna, 'The child as artist in Amélie Nothomb's *Robert des noms propres*', *French Studies*, 66 (2012), 54–67; Kemp, Anna, '"Le passeport de la douleur ou rien": Fawzia Zouari's *Ce Pays dont je meurs* and the politics of pain', *Contemporary French Civilization*, 41 (2016), 49–67; Meuret, Isabelle, 'Entre secret et sacré: l'écriture "féminine" de Geneviève Brisac et Liliane Atlan', *Revue des Lettres et de Traduction* , 9 (2003), 307–18; Meuret, Isabelle, 'L'Anorexie: entre aliénation "mentale" et revendication d'altérité: le cas des écrivaines algériennes', *International Journal of Francophone Studies*, 12, 1 (2009), 19–35; Morello, Nathalie, 'Anorexia, anger, agency: Investigating quests for self in three contemporary narratives in French', in Francesca Calamita, Petra Bagley and Kathryn Robson (eds), *Starvation, Food Obsession and Identity: Eating Disorders in Post-1968 Women's Writing* (Oxford: Peter Lang, 2017), pp. 121–41; Robson, Kathryn, 'Voicing abjection: Narratives of anorexia in contemporary French women's (life-)writing', *L'Esprit Createur*, 56, 2 (Summer 2016), 108–20; Rodgers, Catherine, 'Nothomb's anorexic beauties', in Susan Bainbrigge and Jeanette den Toonder (eds), *Amélie Nothomb: Authorship, Identity, and Narrative Practice* (New York: Peter Lang, 2003), pp. 50–63; Rodgers, Julie, 'Body politics in *Truismes*: "The tyranny of slenderness"', in *Marie Darrieussecq*, in Helena Chadderton and Gill Rye (eds), *Dalhousie French Studies* [special issue], 98 (Spring 2012), 29–39; Rodgers, Julie, 'Double voices and splintered selves: The dialectic of anorexia in Ying Chen's *Querelle d'un squelette avec son double*', in Francesca Calamita, Petra Bagley, and Kathryn Robson (eds), *Starvation, Food Obsession and Identity: Eating Disorders in Post-1968 Women's Writing* (Oxford: Peter Lang, 2017), pp. 213–34; Vitiello, Joëlle, 'Le double meurtrier chez Sabrina Kherbiche',

articles and edited-volume chapters consider such EDs only fleetingly. And in terms of book-length studies on the topic, there is none that has the same focus and remit as my own. Only one other book bears any possible comparison with my own, insofar as it focuses solely on French literature: Patricia McEachern's *Deprivation and Power: The Emergence of Anorexia Nervosa in Nineteenth-Century France* (1998).[36] However, McEachern's book only discusses limited literary inscriptions of anorexia nervosa, whereas my own examines EDs more generally; she focuses on a non-contemporary period (1835–89), examining putatively anorexic female characters in seven novels written by four French male authors (Flaubert, Les Frères Goncourt, and Maupassant), in contrast with my own primary corpus of 45 late twentieth- and early twenty-first-century autobiographical (and occasionally autofictional) texts written by a wide range of French female authors. Likewise, my own book's scope is wider than that of Isabelle Meuret's two, viz. *L'anorexie créatrice* (2006)[37] and *Writing Size Zero: Figuring Anorexia in Contemporary World Literatures* (2007).[38] This is because, as with McEachern, Meuret's two books study only anorexia nervosa (and not infrequently the primary texts she studies inscribe anorexia, denoting simple absence of appetite, rather than anorexia nervosa); they are not devoted to French literature; and their approach is quasi-scienticist – for example, predicating a grammatology of 'anorexic signs' in her chosen primary texts – whereas my focus is on the phenomenology of the lived experience of EDs, which include but are not restricted to anorexia nervosa. Finally with respect to research context, my project draws on a high number of secondary texts, by which I mean: literary-critical texts; texts written by clinicians; medically research-based texts; and theoretical/philosophical texts – for example, Gilles Deleuze and Claire Parnet's *Dialogues* (1977);[39] Julia

in Frédérique Chevillot and Colette Trout (eds), *Rebelles et criminelles chez les écrivaines d'expression française* (Amsterdam: Rodopi, 2013), pp. 129–45. To this list of publications should be added the very fine, but as yet unpublished doctoral thesis of Karin Bernfeld, *Écriture du corps et discours clinique dans les autobiographies d'anorexie-boulimie* (Université Paris Diderot – Paris 7, 2013).

36 McEachern, Patricia, *Deprivation and Power: The Emergence of Anorexia Nervosa in Nineteenth-Century France* (Westport, CT/London: Greenwood Press, 1998).

37 Meuret, Isabelle, *L'anorexie créatrice* (Paris: Klincksieck, 2006).

38 Meuret, Isabelle, *Writing Size Zero: Figuring Anorexia in Contemporary World Literatures* (Brussels, Belgium/New York: Peter Lang, 2007).

39 Deleuze, Gilles and Parnet, Claire, *Dialogues* (Paris: Flammarion, 1977).

Kristeva's *Pouvoirs de l'horreur: essai sur l'abjection* (1980);[40] Jacques Lacan's *Les quatre concepts fondamentaux de la psychanalyse, Livre XI* (1973)[41] and *Le Séminaire, Livre IV: La Relation d'objet* (1994).[42]

My methodology will be multi- and inter-disciplinary, presenting approaches to/findings from writings on EDs in (presented in alphabetical, not hierarchical order) clinical practice, critical theory, feminism, gendered cultural studies, literary studies, philosophy, psychiatry, psychoanalysis, and sociology. Part of my methodology will be to acknowledge and indeed practise the cross-fertilisation of fields such as the humanities (that is, literary study) and sciences (medicine), but I will certainly not glibly reconcile or conflate the two fields. Study of the primary texts is complemented by ample but eclectic reference, and *sometimes challenge*, to clinical, medically research-based, or theoretical publications on EDs. Such challenge involves, inter alia, identifying scotoma in some of these publications. One example is Kestemberg et al.'s blindness to the fact that their entirely valid recognition of 'l'orgasme de la faim' [the orgasm of hunger] in anorexia nervosa (and, one might add, in its food-deprivational stages, of bulimia nervosa/bulimarexia) ignores the fact that an important element of the 'high' induced by hunger is its promise of weight loss.[43] Another example is my foregrounding the broad range of factors, some sociocultural, that in the primary texts predispose the sufferer to developing an ED but that, when sociocultural, are often ignored by mental health professionals treating (as opposed to researchers working on) EDs. This disregard is captured well in the following remarks from Katzman and Lee (1997), in the context of anorexia nervosa in particular: 'Mental health professionals working in the field of prevention may find that the scope of their theorizing (and thus impact) will remain limited, unless a more comprehensive definition of sociocultural influences is adopted.'[44]

40 Kristeva, Julia, *Pouvoirs de l'horreur: essai sur l'abjection* (Paris: Seuil, 1980).

41 Lacan, Jacques, *Les quatre concepts fondamentaux de la psychanalyse, Livre XI* (Paris: Seuil, 1973).

42 Lacan, Jacques, *Le Séminaire, Livre IV: la Relation d'objet* (Paris: Seuil, 1994).

43 Kestemberg, E., Kestemberg, J., and Decobert, S., *La Faim et le Corps. Une étude psychanalytique de l'anorexie mentale* (Paris: Presses Universitaires de France, 1972).

44 Katzman, M.A. and Lee, S., 'Beyond body image: The integration of feminist

While I will build upon the existing critical texts on the topic of EDs, my methodology aims to go beyond them, offering genuinely new insights.

Particular factors to be drawn out by this book include the following. One is the therapeutic role of writing about traumatic experiences, which EDs certainly do constitute. The conclusion to one set of empirical studies is eminently worth citing:

> Writing about stressful events has been studied in groups of varying education, in several languages, and multiple countries. Within the United States, writing about stressful events has produced similar benefits for senior professionals with advanced degrees and maximum security prisoners with little education. Differences among college students' ethnicity or native language have not been related to outcomes. Additionally, the writing paradigm has consistently produced positive results among French-speaking Belgians (16), Spanish-speaking residents of Mexico City (29), multiple samples of adults and students in The Netherlands (17), and medical students in New Zealand (20). [...] We are excited by the potential of sharing one's story through writing [...]. The power of a coherent narrative is just beginning to be understood; it may represent a fundamental link between the experience of stressful events and subsequent health.[45]

As indicated above, more detailed study of the therapeutic role of writing about traumatic experiences is made in the Conclusion to this book. Another feature that will become evident in this book is the predominant role of metaphor in the literary, stylistic, and rhetorical devices deployed in the primary texts to represent EDs (see research question 3 above). Metaphors are deployed abundantly in the 45 primary texts covered by this book, and they are generally ontological metaphors: 'ways of viewing events, activities, emotions, ideas, etc., as entities and substances'.[46] One reason for this special role of metaphor is the heavy freighting of embodiment – clearly of central significance in EDs – in Conceptual Metaphor Theory (CMT):

and transcultural theories in the understanding of self-starvation', *International Journal of Eating Disorders*, 22, 4 (1997), 385–94 (391).

45 Smyth, Joshua M. and Pennebaker, James W., 'Translating emotional experiences into words as a coping tool', in C.R. Snyder (ed.), *Coping: The Psychology of What Works* (New York NY/Oxford: Oxford University Press, 1999), pp. 70–89 [pp. 75 and 85].

46 Lakoff, George and Johnson, Mark, *Metaphors We Live By* (Chicago, IL/ London: University of Chicago Press, 1980), p. 25.

> 'Through metaphor, body and mind are inextricably intertwined', Geary (2012: 93) notes, echoing another core idea of CMT first introduced by Lakoff and Johnson (1999), emphasizing that many standardized conceptual metaphors have their experiential basis in the functioning of the human body (compare Frank et al., 2008). Because all human beings basically share a very similar body, CMT argues, metaphorical language that has bodily experiences as a frame of reference represents the perfect medium to share complicated emotional experiences interpersonally [...].[47]

Other reasons, closely related to the first, for paying special and critical attention to the role of metaphor are again twofold. One is the axiomatic difficulty of those with anorexia nervosa and bulimia nervosa/bulimarexia especially in accurately and objectively conceptualising their body size and body shape, as opposed to merely 'feeling' it, usually as objects of hatred – metaphors work by evoking images and sensations rather than by conscious, reasoned conceptualisation. Another is the mind–body split/mind–body dualism that is a pervasive trope in my corpus of 45 primary texts. As noted in the quotation directly above, James Geary, in *I Is an Other. The Secret Life of Metaphor and How it Shapes the Way We See the World*, states, 'Through metaphor, body and mind are inextricably linked.'[48] Ostensibly, this inextricability of body and mind is the complete antithesis of the mind–body split/dualism trope, but the use of conceptual metaphor may be a way of overcoming that split/dualism, at least by the autobiographical or autofictional narrator of testimonies to EDs. For a discrete but not dissimilar intellectual tack, namely the notion that conceptual/cognitive metaphor has helped at least one such (in this case anglophone) narrator, Marya Hornbacher[49] very powerfully to convey the phenomenological reality of anorexia and bulimia to a wide readership, see Senkbeil and Hoppe (2016).[50]

47 Senkbeil, Karsten and Hoppe, Nicola, '"The sickness stands at your shoulder…": Embodiment and cognitive metaphor in Hornbacher's *Wasted: A Memoir of Anorexia and Bulimia*', *Language and Literature*, 25, 1 (2016), 3–17 (6). The text in which Lakoff and Johnson first introduced this 'core idea' is Lakoff, George and Johnson, Mark, *Metaphors We Live By* (Chicago and London: University of Chicago Press, 1980).

48 Geary, James, *I is an Other: The Secret Life of Metaphor and How it Shapes the Way We See the World* (New York: HarperCollins, 2011), p. 93.

49 Hornbacher, Marya, *Wasted: A Memoir of Anorexia and Bulimia* (New York: HarperCollins, 1988).

50 Senkbeil and Hoppe, '"The sickness stands at your shoulder…"', 3–17.

The structure of the book is thus. A Bibliographical Appendix (see pp. 261–79) identifies (in alphabetical, not hierarchical order) commonalities – salient and recurring points, tropes, and motifs – emerging from the 45 primary texts testifying to three different types of ED. This appendix also provides numerous and full bibliographical references to such points, tropes, and motifs found in the secondary literature (clinical, medically research based, and critical theory). The Bibliographical Appendix is intended for readers to refer to as they approach the three main chapters that follow this Introduction and that deal with the six case studies. The commonalities covered here are (in alphabetical order), addiction (to hunger, food, over-exercising, among other possibilities), creativity or creation of a new self, distorted body image, hyperactivity or overachievement, language, metaphor, mind/body dualism, mother/daughter relationship, purity or transcendence of the body/flesh, (self-)surveillance, sexual abuse or self-abuse, the role of socio-cultural factors in the development of EDs, spatiality, the 'vide' (void), and writing as therapy. Chapters 1, 2, and 3 each examine two different literary 'case studies' per chapter, illustrating the three distinct types of ED delineated above. The six case studies, while arguably quite extreme in their accounts, have been chosen as being representative of the larger corpus and are all verifiably autobiographical texts (albeit with some name changes in certain cases): they thus, vitally, 'speak from experience', and it is for this reason that they have been selected as points of focus here. In each of these three chapters, the case studies are analysed in order of publication date, starting with the earlier, in order that the reader may discern any possible developments over time in the EDs under scrutiny. Chapter 1 focuses on anorexia nervosa (restrictor type: no purgation). The two representative case studies here are Valérie Valère's *Le Pavillon des enfants fous* (1978)[51] and Marta Aleksandra Balinska's *Retour à la vie: quinze ans d'anorexie* (2003).[52] Chapter 2 focuses on bulimia nervosa, or, in a nomenclatural variant, bulimarexia. The two representative case studies here are Valérie Rodrigue's *La peau à l'envers. Le roman vrai d'une boulimique* (1989)[53] and Camille de

51 Valère, Valérie, *Le Pavillon des enfants fous* (Paris: Stock, 1978).

52 Balinska, Marta Aleksandra, *Retour à la vie: quinze ans d'anorexie* (Paris: Odile Jacob, 2003).

53 Rodrigue, Valérie, *La peau à l'envers. Le roman vrai d'une boulimique* (Paris: Robert Laffont, 1989).

Peretti's *Thornytorinx* (2005).[54] Chapter 3 focuses on binge eating disorder. The two representative case studies here are Annick Loupias's *La Tortue sur le dos: ma lutte contre la boulimie* (2001)[55] and Anne Calife's *Meurs la faim* (2010; first published 1999).[56] The book ends on a Conclusion that briefly synthesises the findings of the previous chapters; engages critically with and challenges the pronouncements of major theorists, such as Gilles Deleuze, Julia Kristeva, and Jacques Lacan, on EDs; compares them with feminist theorists on the topic; offers a new supplement to the hypothesis articulated at the end of my 2015 *French Studies* article on EDs and spatiality; and assesses the concept of scriptotherapy with respect to EDs.

54 de Peretti, Camille, *Thornytorinx* (Paris: Belfond, 2005).

55 Loupias, Annick, with Louise Lambert-Lagacé and Annette Richard, *La Tortue sur le dos: ma lutte contre la boulimie* (Quebec: Éditions de l'homme, 2001).

56 Calife, Anne, *Meurs la faim* (The Menthol House, 2010); previously published under the name of Colmerauer, Anne, *Meurs la faim* (Paris: Gallimard, 1999).

CHAPTER ONE

Anorexia Nervosa (Restrictor Type)

Section 1.1

Valérie Valère's *Le Pavillon des enfants fous* (1978)[1] is one of the first published personal testimonies of anorexia nervosa in France, and to the best of my knowledge the first depicting such early onset of the illness: the author was only 12 when interned in hospital (where she spent her 13th birthday), and only 15 when she wrote her account of that internment.[2] There is only one other text in the primary corpus written at a similarly young age: Mathilde Monaque's *Trouble tête. Journal intime d'une dépression* (2006),[3] but in this case the hospitalisation occurred when the author was 14 and a half years old (Monaque 2006: 15). Valère's book's title is elucidated in evocation of the sign on the hospital building to which she is admitted against her will, 'HOPITAL. PAVILLON DES ENFANTS FOUS' ['HOSPITAL. MAD CHILDREN'S WING'] (p. 27). The veracity of this sign is highly dubious: it seems instead to project Valère's own disaffected view of the institution.

Born in 1961, Valérie Valère committed suicide at the age of 21 in 1982. Clerc 1987[4] indicates that Valère relapsed into anorexic behaviour

1 Valère, Valérie, *Le Pavillon des enfants fous* (Paris: Stock, 1978).

2 She weighed only 30 kilos (4 stones 10 lbs) at the time of hospitalisation (p. 45), but no indication is given of her height, so it is impossible to ascertain her Body Mass Index (BMI). However, comparing the target weight set for her with the heights (which are mentioned) and target weights set for other anorectic patients in the same hospital, the reader can infer that she is very short – probably under 5 feet tall. This inference is supported by Clerc, Isabelle, *Valérie Valère: un seul regard m'aurait suffi* (Paris: Perrin, 1987), pp. 99, 164.

3 Monaque, Mathilde, *Trouble tête. Journal intime d'une dépression* (Paris: Éditions des Arènes, 2006).

4 My general evaluation of Clerc's text is as follows. Clerc does seem to provide many perceptive, or at the very least credible, surmises about the object of her study,

after her discharge from hospital, even though she was never hospitalised again.[5] *Le Pavillon des enfants fous* was a huge literary and commercial success, and was subsequently translated into ten languages. During the remainder of her sadly short life, Valère also published other texts: novels that met with both critical acclaim and commercial success. Such success may be partly explained by the contention of Clerc that Valère's work caught the mood of a whole generation: 'Toute une génération s'est identifiée à Valérie…' [a whole generation identified with Valérie…].[6] Valère became the focus of intense media attention, appearing on television and radio in *Apostrophes* and *Radioscopie*.

The publisher's foreword ('Avertissement de l'éditeur', p. 5) states that Valère considered *Le Pavillon des enfants fous* to be a testimony ('témoignage'), and cites her own comments on this testimony:

Valérie Valère, based on attentive and empathetic reading of Valère's publications, notably *Le Pavillon des enfants fous*. However, Clerc's is not a scholarly work. It provides no bibliography, and when Clerc does very occasionally cite any secondary texts, her references are inadequate. Clerc purports to understand Valère, but the reader has no clue as to the bases of this understanding. There are direct quotations from Valère's own works, and these are stated in Clerc's prefatory material as being the following: *Le Pavillon des enfants fous* (Paris: Stock, 1979); *Malika ou un jour comme tous les autres* (Paris: Stock, 1979); *Obsession blanche* (Paris: Stock, 1981); and *Magnificia love* (inédit). Yet when Clerc does cite Valère, she rarely indicates from which of these texts she is citing. Some of Clerc's passages are mere paraphrases of what Valère wrote in *Le Pavillon des enfants fous*. Further, Clerc's passages in the first-person voice are often not citations from Valère's own works, and seem thus to be Clerc's own projections onto the object of her study, whom she never actually met (see p. 179). It appears that she bases her projections on information gleaned from those who *did* know Valère, whom she thanks in a note at the end of her book: 'Je remercie Gabriel Gonin, héritier spirituel de Valérie Valère, qui m'a fourni des éléments biographiques ; Christian de Bartillat qui a eu l'idée de ce livre ; tous ceux qui ont connu Valérie et m'ont parlé d'elle ; A.M. Métaillé, que je cite, pour son éclairage sur les années 60 ; Chantal Chawaf pour le soutien moral qu'elle m'a apporté' [I thank Gabriel Gonin, spiritual heir to Valérie Valère, who provided me with biographical elements; Christian de Bartillat who had the idea for this book; all those who knew Valérie and spoke to me about her; A.M. Métaillé, whom I quote, for his perspective on the 60s; Chantal Chawaf for the moral support she gave me].

5 Clerc indicates that Valère's will contained the following: '*Je souhaite que mes droits d'auteur soient utilisés pour la fondation d'une communauté thérapeutique pour anorexiques*' [*I wish for my royalties to be used for the foundation of a therapeutic community for anorectics*] (Clerc 1987: 170; her emphasis).

6 Clerc 1987: 12.

> Ce n'est pas une œuvre littéraire. Je ne me suis pas mise à écrire calmement dans la solitude de ma chambre, la pensée claire recherchant le mot juste. Il n'y a pas de mots raisonnables pour décrire le monde des fous. Je me refuse à transformer ce texte en une écriture soignée, polie. Il ne s'agit pas d'une chose abstraite, de fantasmes intellectuels, mais d'une souffrance endurée. Je ne traduis pas de jolis sentiments et je ne raconte pas une histoire avec des enchaînements bien logiques.

> This is not a literary work. I did not start writing quietly in the solitude of my room, with a clear mind looking for the right word. There are no reasonable words to describe the world of the mad. I refuse to turn this text into neat, polite writing. It is not about something abstract or intellectual fantasies, but endured suffering. I do not translate pretty feelings and I do not tell a story with logical sequences.

Valère's insistence on the unpolished style of her testimony strikes me as rather too modest if it implies that this was due to underdeveloped writerly skills. In substantiation of my reservation, it should be registered that the publisher follows the citation from Valère with the comment 'C'est *volontairement* que Valérie a laissé des répétitions de mots devenant obsessionnels comme "sale", ou des phrases leitmotive comme "ils ne m'auront pas"' [Valerie has *voluntarily* left in repetitions of words bordering on obsessive like "dirty", or leitmotifs like "they won't get me"] (p. 5; my emphasis). 'Ils ne m'auront pas' [They won't get me] is indeed a leitmotif, along with variants therefore, such as 'Vous ne m'aurez pas. Non, vous ne m'aurez pas !' [You won't get me. No, you won't get me!] (p. 28); 'Vous ne m'aurez pas' [You won't get me] (p. 29); 'je vais étouffer de sanglots, je le voudrais ! Comme ça, ils ne m'auraient pas !' [I'm going to choke with sobs, I'd like it! That way, they wouldn't get me!] (p. 30); 'S'ils croient m'avoir avec leur prison' [If they think they've got me with their prison] (p. 30); 'Toi non plus tu ne m'auras pas' [You won't get me either] (p. 37); 'On finira bien par t'avoir ! NON !' [We'll get you in the end! NO!] (p. 52); 'Celle-là, elle va m'avoir' [That one there, she's going to get me] (p. 70); 'tu ne m'auras pas' [you won't get me] (p. 90). These repeated defiant ejaculations express the young girl's deep mistrust of and defiant resistance to treatment, as well as a quasi-paranoia (which, given at least her initial, punitive treatment, is understandable).

Rather than as an unpolished piece of writing, I would qualify *Le Pavillon des enfants fous* as stylistically arresting. Notwithstanding narrative and genuinely dialogic passages, it contains a high proportion of enraged, violent internal monologue that periodically mutates into contumacious, provocative, sometimes insulting apostrophe, or into dialogue where it is unclear whether the dialogue is with real other people or an internal psychic process signalling self-division/self-splitting. The same uncertainty applies to certain monologic sections. For instance, on p. 71 some readers will be unsure whether the violent diatribe against Valère and her anorexia nervosa comes from the nurse to whom she has just referred, or whether – perhaps more probably – it is a projection onto that nurse of her own anticipation of the nurse's thoughts, her imagining of the nurse's contempt for her, and also an instance, perhaps partially ironic, of self-recrimination that both acknowledges and implicitly satirises medical models of the typical anorectic:

> Un énorme bol de café trop sucré, des tartines de bâtard… Tu vas les manger, espèce de sale môme. Ne dis pas qu'elles sont infectes, tu n'y as même pas goûté. Et puis, avec toi, tout est infect. Tu mens en plus. Tu n'as pas faim, ne me fais pas rire, tu n'as pas mangé depuis des mois ! […] Prends ta tartine ! Ne respire pas, sinon, tu vas trouver une excuse. Si tu ne sens pas l'odeur ça passera vite… Mon cœur se retourne, attention tout est fini. Je la repose et sirote le café. Tu es vraiment con ! essaie encore une fois, merde, ce n'est pas si compliqué ! Avoue que c'est risible, non ? Ne plus savoir manger ! Attention. Je ne respire pas. Je l'attrape fermement. Je ne la regarde pas. J'ouvre la bouche. Je fais entrer ce que je peux. Trop, ça m'érafle la gorge, ça se bat pour entrer dans le tuyau, ça m'étouffe. Merde, j'en veux pas !
>
> Et voilà ! ah ! je vous énerve ! Je vous comprends. (p. 71)

> A huge bowl of coffee that's too sweet, slices of bread… You'll eat them, you little brat. Don't say they're disgusting, you haven't even tasted them. And besides, with you everything is disgusting. You're also lying. You're not hungry, don't make me laugh, you've not eaten in months! […] Take your sandwich! Don't inhale, otherwise you'll find an excuse. If you don't smell the smell it will be over quickly… My heart squirms, look out, it's all over. I'm putting it back and drinking the coffee. You're really stupid! Try again, shit, it's not that complicated! You've got to admit it's ridiculous, right? To not know how to eat! Watch this. I don't inhale. I grip it firmly. I don't look at it. I open my mouth. I put in what I can. Too much, it catches my throat, it fights to get into the pipe, it chokes me. Shit, I don't want it!
>
> There you go! Ah! I annoy you! I get it.

The book's tone is exclamatory, interrogatory, accusatory, agitated, sometimes even manic. These tonal traits reflect the young girl's searing sense of injustice at being, as she experiences it, imprisoned. For example, she refers to 'leur prison' [their prison] (p. 30) to designate the hospital to which she has been committed against her will. And in effect, she is indeed imprisoned in this psychiatric hospital, her room being locked, with basic rights (such as being allowed to read and write) denied until she gains weight. Her resentment at this treatment is acerbically conveyed.

Her testimony laceratingly rejects prevailing clinical convictions, whether psychiatric or psychoanalytically based, about the aetiology and symptomatology of anorexia nervosa. That rejection is eloquent, although some readers may feel it arises primarily not so much from the actual falsity of such convictions as from her deep ire at being glibly categorised and homogenised by the psychiatric institution and by the hegemonic clinico-medical discourses on which that institution is founded. The following passage, particularly in the opening three rhetorical questions, artfully expresses that intense sense of injustice, and reflects the punitive nature of her initial hospital treatment:

> Mais quel crime ai-je donc commis ? Ai-je tué quelqu'un et perdu ensuite la mémoire ? Ai-je tué, volé ? Non, j'ai fait un choix. Il ne les concerne pas, ce n'est pas eux qui en souffrent, je suis « inoffensive ». Je les déteste ceux qui disent que je leur fais du mal en me laissant mourir. Ils ne peuvent pas savoir, je ne leur dirai pas, d'ailleurs ils ne m'aiment pas, ce n'est pas ainsi qu'on aime. « Il est interdit de disposer de votre personne à votre gré, mademoiselle, vous ne vous appartenez pas, votre corps est à nous. » (pp. 8–9)

> But what crime did I commit? Did I kill someone and then lose my memory? Did I kill, steal? No, I made a choice. It's nothing to do with them, it is not they who suffer, I am 'harmless'. I hate the ones who say that I hurt them by letting myself die. They can't know, I won't tell them, besides they don't love me, that's not how to love someone. 'It is forbidden to do what you want with your body, mademoiselle, you do not belong to yourself, your body is ours.'

This passage additionally conveys in 'Non, j'ai fait un choix' [No, I made a choice] Valère's voluntarism (though this is later weakened) in her anorexic conduct, with a defiance that will also be found in one of the other primary texts to be examined in depth (in Chapter 3), viz. Camille de Peretti's *Thornytorinx* (2005).[7] Valère's book ends, in its 'Épilogue', on reprised denunciation of the (patriarchal: 'messieurs les

7 de Peretti, Camille, *Thornytorinx* (Paris: Belfond, 2005).

psys' [Messrs shrinks]) psychiatric institution, and also on an ironic relativisation, even negation, of the construct of madness on which psychiatrists depend for their living.

> Mais faites attention, messieurs les psys, vous qui lisez ce mal de vivre avec un sourire au coin des lèvres, elle vous guette cette mendiante dont vous avez tellement peur qu'il vous a fallu créer des institutions pour la briser, l'enfermer... c'est contagieux, vous savez, la folie. (p. 158)

> But be careful, Messrs shrinks, you who read this pain of living with a smile on the corner of your lips, she's watching you this beggar you're so afraid of that you have to create institutions to break her, to lock her up... it's contagious, you know, madness.

That relativisation or even negation is also particularly prominent in one of the other primary texts, viz. Emilie Durand's *Ma folie ordinaire: allers et retours à l'hôpital Sainte-Anne* (2006).[8]

Contempt is voiced for psychoanalytic theories of anorexia nervosa as a refusal of femininity and mature female sexuality (p. 97). As Helen Malson points out, 'Psychoanalytic discourse thus constitutes "anorexia" as a symptomatic manifestation of unresolved Oedipal and pre-Oedipal conflicts associated in particular with inadequate ego development and with a failure to accept female psycho-sexual maturity.'[9] In response to questions from one of the male medical staff who appears to be either a psychoanalyst or a psychoanalytically informed psychiatrist, Valère poses the mocking rhetorical question, 'D'ailleurs, vous savez bien que je veux être un "mec" sans toutes ces conneries de seins, de futilités et de règles, ça fait partie de vos théories, n'est-ce pas ?' [Besides, you know that I want to be a 'guy' without all that crap of boobs, futilities and periods, that's all part of your theories, isn't it?] (p. 97). But in fact, at least in this respect, her own wishes do correspond in certain respects to such theories, for she does indeed not want to have breasts or ovaries: 'Moi, je veux être comme un garcon, sans poitrine, sans ovaires' [Me, I want to be like a boy, with no chest, no ovaries] (p. 98). However, she does not want to be male insofar as she does not want male genitalia: 'mais sans sexe non plus... ça fait

8 Durand, Emilie, *Ma folie ordinaire: allers et retours à l'hôpital Sainte-Anne* (Paris: Les Empêcheurs de tourner en rond, 2006).

9 Malson, Helen, *The Thin Woman: Feminism, Post-Structuralism and the Social Psychology of Anorexia Nervosa* (London/New York: Routledge, 1998), pp. 86–87.

mal quand on se cogne...' [but with no penis either... that hurts when it gets hit] (p. 98). And while angrily admitting (p. 98) that she does manifest many elements in clinical/psychoanalytic models of the typical anorectic, such as overinvestment in school work, an absent paternal figure, an (overly) protective mother figure, she also inwardly contests the validity of theories based on refusal of femininity: 'Pourtant ça ne peut pas coller, il y a aussi des garçons qui font des "anorexies"' [But that doesn't make sense, there are also boys who do 'anorexias'] (p. 98), and disdainfully issues a silent challenge: 'Alors, qu'est-ce que vous en faites de votre refus de féminité, hein ? Vous avez l'air malin !' [So, what are you going to do with your refusal of femininity, huh? You seem so smart!] (p. 98).

Later in the text there is a similarly cynical rejection of other elements of psychoanalytic theory, such as the Oedipal complex. In reference to her father, she states in silent apostrophe, 'Ne crains rien, je ne crois pas avoir le complexe d'Œdipe. D'ailleurs, je ne le trouve pas assez beau' [Don't worry, I don't think I have an Oedipal complex. Besides, I don't find him handsome enough] (p. 105). There is further contemptuous dismissal of clinical convictions about anorexia nervosa – here, the belief that it only occurs in highly intelligent girls: 'Encore une de leurs fausses et stupides théories' [Another of their false and stupid theories] (p. 118). Similarly, Valère later denies the dogma of psychiatrists that anorexia nervosa descends upon its victims suddenly and independently of their own volition:

> Car ce que disent les psychiatres est faux, ça n'arrive pas comme ça sans qu'on l'ait voulu et mûrement réfléchi. On ne peut pas du jour au lendemain ne plus connaître la faim, ne plus avoir besoin de rien, c'est faux ! (pp. 111–12)

> Because what psychiatrists say is wrong, it does not just happen like that without being wanted and carefully thought out. We can't change overnight so we no longer know hunger, no longer need anything, it's wrong!

Beyond those staff operating on psychoanalytic bases, Valère contemptuously refuses to communicate with the collective, enemy 'Other' of the medical establishment in general. This is illustrated, inter alia, in her comment apropos a doctor not identified as a psychiatrist who visits her in hospital. Her comment signifies a resolve to retain some kind of interiority for herself, even if her body has been expropriated for its own uses by the medical corps:

> Il peut rester des heures, des jours même, il n'entendra pas ma voix. Au moins, je garderai quelque chose à moi, pour moi. Ils ne m'auront pas tout entière, ils n'auront pas ma voix, ni mes pensées, rien... pourtant ils possèdent déjà mon corps, ma liberté, malgré tout ils accaparent une partie de mon esprit. (p. 19)
>
> He can stay hours, even days, he will not hear my voice. At least I'll keep something for myself. They won't get all of me, they won't get my voice, my thoughts, nothing... yet they already have my body, my freedom, despite everything they take up a part of my mind.

Valère's sense of the injustice of the involuntary hospital treatment she receives is rendered through details of the coercive and often punitive nature of the so-called 'rewards' regime. On 'involuntary', it should be noted proleptically that the detrimental effects on anorectics of enforced hospitalisation are conveyed in her post-discharge sense of despair about ever psychically being able to escape from its psychic scars – a form of ascotomisation:

> Ils m'ont gardée dans leurs griffes, j'ai conservé l'angoisse d'un emprisonnement, la colère refoulée d'une injustice, la rage de l'impuissance. [...] Je suis restée là-bas, dans la chambre vingt-sept, avec mes refus, avec ce mal de vivre. Et je crois bien que je n'arriverai jamais à en sortir. (pp. 55–56)
>
> They kept me in their clutches, I kept the anguish of imprisonment, the repressed anger of an injustice, the rage of impotence. [...] I stayed there, in room twenty-seven, with my refusal, with this pain of living. And I think I'll never get out of it.

Returning to the punitive aspects of the 'rewards' regime, these include the granting of certain basic rights only after coldly calibrated amounts of weight gain have been attained: 'Je ne peux pas lire parce que les livres sont la récompense de mille grammes, je ne peux pas écrire parce que le papier se paie ici au moins deux mille grammes, la clef qui ne tournera plus : trois mille, le bain chaud quatre mille...' [I cannot read because books are the reward of a thousand grams, I cannot write because the paper itself costs at least two thousand grams here, the key that won't turn anymore: three thousand, hot bath four thousand...] (p. 10). One of the coercive aspects is implicit in the following question posed to her: '« On t'a dit que tu aurais droit à une visite à trente-cinq kilos ? »' ['Were you told that you would have the right to a visit at thirty-five kilos?'] (p. 59). Later in the narrative, interdiction by the medical team on eating any more than the meals served (food brought by visitors) is decried as sadism, an attempt to prolong the anorectic's prison sentence (p. 125).

At this juncture, it is important to remember that *Le Pavillon des enfants fous* was based on Valère's experiences in the early 1970s. In more recent years, at least some researchers have stressed the importance of avoiding at least perceptions of punitive treatment, and the importance also of hospital staff's compassion. One example, albeit from the US rather than from France, is the following: 'It is also useful for staff to communicate that they are not seeking to engage in control battles and have no punitive intentions when using interventions that the patient may experience as aversive. [...] Refeeding programs should be implemented in nurturing emotional contexts.'[10] Yet despite this helpful advice from researchers, the so-called 'contract' regime – which will be discussed in greater depth in the section below on Balinska – remains to this day the most common type of inpatient treatment for anorexia nervosa in France and elsewhere.

Mendacity is another charge Valère levels at the clinicians treating her. A sense of having been lied to emerges in the disparity between on the one hand the psychoanalyst's initial statement that what mattered was not her weight but the causes of her refusal to eat, and on the other hand the discovery that she would not be released from hospital until she had gained nine kilograms.[11] This deceit is extended to all of the medical team:

> La première fois, elle m'a menti, *comme tous les autres.* Elle m'a dit que le poids n'avait pas d'importance, qu'il fallait seulement découvrir les causes de ce refus, le mécanisme qui m'y avait amenée. On me laisserait

10 Yager, Joel et al., 'Practice guideline for the treatment of patients with eating disorders, Third edition', *The American Journal of Psychiatry*, 163, 7 (July 2006), pp. 7 and 23. While this is a US reference, French medical responses to the treatment of eating disorders have also changed, in theory at least: see the preface.

11 Since the 1970s, researchers have implicitly recognised the error in such mendacity. One indication of this implicit recognition is the following: 'The initial interview is the first step in treatment, engaging both patient and family in the therapeutic endeavour, and it is extremely important that the format and style of the initial or early interviews be aimed at developing a sense of openness and *trust* between the patient and the assessing clinician.' Touyz, S.T., Garner, D.M., and Beumont, P.J.V., 'The inpatient management of the adolescent patient with anorexia nervosa', *Eating Disorders in Adolescence: Anorexia Nervosa and Bulimia Nervosa* (Berlin: Walter de Gruyter & Co., 1995), pp. 247–70 (249; my emphasis).

> sortir lorsque j'aurais trouvé, lorsque j'aurai pris un peu de poids. Elle ne m'avait pas dit que ce « peu de poids » c'étaient neuf kilos [...] (p. 59; my emphasis).
>
> The first time she lied to me, *like everyone else.* She told me that the weight did not matter, that it was only necessary to discover the causes of this refusal, the mechanism that had brought me there. I would be let out when I found some, when I gained a little weight. She did not tell me that this 'little weight' was nine kilos [...]

An additional source of Valère's sense of the injustice of the hospital treatment she receives is the perception that she is in fact treated not as a patient but as a criminal. The motif of wrongly imputed criminality features on several occasions, along with its pendants of imprisonment and punishment. At one very early point, she communicates the impression of having been framed due solely to her refusal of the world/other human beings: 'Quel crime ai-je donc commis ? Refuser le monde : crime puni de prison à perpétuité. Ils me manipulent comme un vulgaire ramassis d'os, dénué de toute pensée, de tout sentiment' [What crime have I committed? Denying the world: a crime punished with life imprisonment. They manipulate me like a crude bunch of bones, devoid of any thought, any feeling] (p. 12). Other examples occur on pages 8, 9, 12, and 75, reinforcing Valère's rancour. Although this rancour mainly targets the nursing staff, naturally enough given that she has the most contact with them, it does extend more generally to the whole clinical team in charge of her case. Given this, it is useful to recall the American Psychiatric Association's warning: 'Regardless of the clinical or theoretical approach used in treatment, some patients with EDs challenge clinicians' understanding and in some instances provoke countertransference reactions, particularly in response to patients' communications of aggression and defiance.'[12] And Valère certainly makes both such communications, with bitter vim.

Recurring to Valère's refusal of the world/other human beings, this seems to stem from misanthropy, indeed a deep disgust for humankind spawned by the deeply unedifying example of her parents' behaviour and from the lack of positive counter-examples in adults beyond her parents. Here Elspeth Probyn's observations are pertinent:

> [I]n terms of anorexia, instead of conceiving of the anorexic as a victim of social forces, it may be that she is also registering profound disgust

12 Yager et al. 2006: 27.

> at those around her. Rather than placing her as a hapless cipher, this reveals the strength of the anorexic's response to the world: 'it/you are disgusting, I will not take you in'.[13]

Homing in on Valère's parents as the prototype of her disgust for humankind, while I would not extrapolate, as Mara Selvini Palazzoli seems to do on the basis of her work with the families of anorectics, to all cases of anorectics' parents, the following remarks from Palazzoli certainly do apply to Valère's parents: 'All of the parents of the anorexics I have treated seemed to have intense neurotic conflicts [...]. At no time did I come across parents with a mature emotional relationship to each other, superficial appearances to the contrary.'[14]

Given such a profoundly negative view of life and of humankind, it is not surprising that Valère sees no point in living. Contrary to many assertions in the secondary literature (though not all),[15] her anorexia nervosa appears to be a hidden method of slow suicide, or desired suicide (cf. Othilie Bailly's *L'Enfant qui se laissait mourir* [1992]):[16] 'Je suis seule. Dehors, le monde est en train de rire, de s'amuser, de parler, je suis seule, seule avec mon corps, qui ne veut rien, qui ne demande rien, sauf de mourir' (p. 12) [I am alone. Outside, the world is laughing, having fun, and talking, I am alone, alone with my body, which wants nothing, which asks for nothing, except to die]. This suicidal disposition, inscribed very early on in the narrative, is soon reinscribed, along with the will to make her own choice between life or death, despite awareness that this choice has now been clinically confiscated: 'Je n'ai pas demandé la vie, je n'en veux plus. Maintenant j'ai le droit de choisir' [I didn't ask for life, I don't want it anymore. Now I have

13 Probyn, Elspeth, *Carnal Appetites: FoodSexIdentities* (London/New York: Routledge, 2000), p. 141.

14 Palazzoli, Mara Selvini, *Self-Starvation: From Individual to Family Therapy in the Treatment of Anorexia Nervosa* (New York/London: Jason Aronson, 1978), pp. 38–39.

15 One of the exceptions to this norm in the secondary literature is '[p]sychological explanatory models' that do indeed view anorectic patients as 'undertaking a passive form of suicide'. See Treasure, Janet, Todd, Gill, and Szmukler, George, 'The inpatient treatment of anorexia nervosa', in George Szmukler, Chris Dare, and Janet Treasure (eds), *Handbook of Eating Disorders: Theory, Treatment and Research* (Chichester/New York/Brisbane/Toronto/Singapore: John Wiley & Sons, 1995; reprinted 1996), pp. 275–91 (286).

16 Bailly, Othilie, *L'Enfant qui se laissait mourir* (Paris: le Grand livre du mois, 1992).

the right to choose] (p. 15). The alienation from and contempt for society and humankind become more narrowly focused on one of its microcosm, viz. her parents, whom she believes never wanted her to be born and do not genuinely care about her:

> Je n'y peux rien si ma mère n'a pas utilisé les contraceptifs. C'est normal que je détruise ce que mon « père » et ma « mère » ont créé. Ils disent l'avoir fait pour moi, alors, pourquoi ne me laissent-ils pas choisir maintenant ? Ils s'en foutent pas mal de ce que je pense, ils veulent garder leur « chose » et puis ils ne voudraient pas avoir à feindre un chagrin qu'ils n'éprouveraient pas. (p. 15)

> I can't help it if my mother didn't use contraceptives. It is natural for me to destroy what my 'father' and 'mother' have created. They say they did it for me, so why don't they let me choose now? They don't care about what I think, they want to keep their 'thing' and also they wouldn't like to have to feign a sorrow they wouldn't really feel.

That belief is validated on p. 106, when her mother tells her (with the 'Nous' [We] referring to the mother and the father), 'Nous ne voulions pas avoir d'enfant' [We didn't want to have a child]. Although the mother had continued by claiming, 'Mais quand tu étais là, nous étions bien contents' [But when you were there, we were happy], she had instantly negated this with respect to Valère's father, claiming, 'Sauf ton père qui ne voulait pas d'une fille' [Except your father, who didn't want a girl], and had added even more damagingly, 'Il disait que tu étais laide, toute rouge, sans un cheveu' [He said you were ugly, all red, and without any hair].

This suicidal predisposition includes nihilism (the 'ils' [they] in the following referring to members of society in general):

> ils disent que l'amour est la plus merveilleuse des choses, ils disent que c'est le but de la vie, mais ils disent tant de choses stupides… Je ne crois pas à leur optimisme ni à leur joie de vivre, mais *je ne crois à rien…* (p. 130; my emphasis)

> they say that love is the most wonderful thing, they say it's the purpose of life, but they say so many stupid things… I don't believe in their optimism or their *joie de vivre*, but *I don't believe in anything…*

This nihilism had been manifest much earlier on, in a comment on human society generally: 'ils l'aiment leur garce de vie, ils sont prêts à donner n'importe quoi pour continuer à vivre ! Et pour vivre quoi ? leur sale bouffe, leur sale baise' [they love their bitch of a life, they're ready to give anything to continue living! And to live what? Their filthy food, their filthy fuck] (p. 30). Contrary to Valère's will to make her own choice between life or death, one of the nurses, threatening her with tube-feeding if she refuses to eat, confirms the abrogation of her right to dispose of her own life: 'On ne peut pas te laisser mourir, le suicide est encore interdit' [We cannot let you die, suicide is still forbidden] (p. 17). The tone of Valère's response – 'C'est dommage' [That's a shame] (p. 17) – is characteristic of her tone throughout the testimony: caustically defiant.

The desire for, or at least fearlessness of, death is reiterated in 'je n'ai pas peur de cette mort que vous redoutez tellement !' [I'm not afraid of that death you fear so much!] (p. 16). Further reiteration of her suicidal ideation, and of the judgemental attitude of others towards her nihilism, is redolent in the following: 'Je n'ai plus la force de courir, plus la force de crier, non, je ne veux pas vivre, je n'ai donc pas appris qu'on les blâme ces gens qui ne « profitent » pas de la vie ?' [I no longer have the strength to run, nor the strength to shout, no, I do not want to live, so have I not learnt that we blame those people who do not 'enjoy' life?] (p. 20). Much later on, and for the first time, she consciously identifies her self-starvation as a deliberate attempt at suicide, and moreover plans another such attempt, once released from hospital, through despair at life:

> Comment peut-on vivre ? C'est impossible ! Qu'ils me laissent sortir et on verra ! Je recommencerai mon suicide raté, je repenserai aux mêmes choses que celles qui ont envahi mes pensées le jour où j'ai décidé de me tuer en cessant de manger. (p. 111)

> How can we live? It's impossible! If only they let me out and then we'd see! I'll restart my failed suicide attempt, I'll rethink the same things that invaded my thoughts the day I decided to kill myself by not eating.

Yet designation of self-starvation as a form of suicide is later qualified. She indicates that the suicidal project was not at first consciously planned: 'Mais je ne savais pas exactement que j'organisais mon suicide, inconsciemment je le devinais mais je n'aurais jamais voulu l'admettre…' [But I did not quite know that I was planning my suicide, unconsciously I guessed it but I would never have wanted to admit it…] (p. 118). Shortly afterwards she probes the precept of anorexia nervosa as a form of suicide, suggesting that it is a long drawn-out, painful form – but also proffering the counter-argument that it may in fact in some cases at least be more a cry for help than a genuine attempt at suicide: 'Une anorexie représentait un suicide long et douloureux, peut-être une sorte d'appel au secours […]' [Anorexia represents a long and painful suicide, perhaps a sort of cry for help] (p. 122).

Turning from the moot question of whether or not anorexia nervosa is a form of long, 'passive' suicide, let us now examine broader issues relating to Valère's case. In certain respects, hers is an atypical case of anorexia nervosa, for she does not appear to have a distorted body image that overestimates body size (a distorted body image being one of the diagnostic criteria for anorexia nervosa). For instance, at the start of her hospitalisation she mentions 'mes cuisses maigres et décharnées' [my skinny and scrawny thighs] (p. 7), and refers to herself as being 'plus rien que des os et un cadavre' [no more than bones and a corpse] (p. 26). A few researchers have remarked, 'Not all patients with anorexia nervosa have a distorted perception of themselves'.[17] However, this remark is preceded by the important point, 'A "distorted body image" was included as one of the five necessary criteria for the diagnosis of anorexia nervosa in DSM-III-R (APA, 1987).'[18] (As explained in the Introduction, *DSM* stands for *Diagnostic and Statistical Manual of Mental Disorders*, the most recent version of which is *DSM-5*, published in 2013.) Yet despite having initially recognised her emaciation, when informed that she needs to gain at least eight kilos Valère's response does reveal a distorted estimation of just how underweight she is: 'Huit ! Mais c'est énorme. Vous vous rendez compte, huit kilos ! Je serais grosse, laide et comme ça ils pourront continuer à se moquer de moi' [Eight! But that's enormous. Do you realise, eight kilos! I would be fat, ugly and that way they'll be able to continue to make fun of me] (p. 55).

Again there is subversion of much of the secondary literature on anorexia nervosa, particularly that of psychoanalytic inspiration, here in its theory of the anorectic girl's over-attachment to her mother. There is only one exception to that subversion, where the following resonates with psychoanalytically inspired models that assert the anorectic's unconscious wish to rebel against the mother's power and control: 'Elle ne supportait pas ce défi, c'était la preuve que je l'avais bien choisi' [She could not bear this challenge, that was the proof that I had chosen it well] (p. 24). Otherwise the portrait is of a mother–daughter relationship

17 Beumont, P.V.J., Russell, J.D. and Touyz, S.W., 'Psychological concerns in the maintenance of dieting disorders', in Szmukler et al. 1995, pp. 221–41 (232).

18 Beumont et al. 1995: 232.

where, far from over-enmeshment or fusion, there is cold distance, which in the daughter gradually turns into hatred, with Valère describing her mother as a horrible ugly woman whom she detests, who is insincere, who will put on a show of caring for her daughter in order to project a respectable maternal image, and whom she never wants to see again in her life. The profound contempt Valère feels for her mother is also expressed in her reaction when her mother emotionally blackmails her, by pleading that she cooperate fully with the hospital regime in order to be discharged as soon as possible and stop hurting her, the mother, who views her own distress as greater than her daughter's.

> « Tu seras raisonnable, me recommandait-elle. Hein, pour sortir vite et ne pas me faire trop de peine ? ça sera encore plus dur pour moi que pour toi… tu le sais bien. » Évidemment, c'est à elle qu'elle pensait, une vraie compétition à qui souffrirait le plus ! (p. 26)

> 'You will be reasonable,' she advised me. 'Eh? Come out quickly and don't bother me too much? It will be even harder for me than for you … you know that well.' Of course, she was thinking of herself, a real competition of who would suffer the most!

Valère's perception of her mother's self pity seems to be validated by a statement that, according to Clerc, Valère's mother made several years after her daughter's hospitalisation:

> à la suite de la parution du *Pavillon*, j'ai reçu des lettres de parents d'anorexiques. J'ai compris une chose : l'anorexique se nourrit de haine. Ma vie n'a pas été facile, mon mari m'a abandonnée quand elle était petite. J'ai élevé seule mes deux enfants. Maintenant, je vis avec un ami que Valérie n'accepte pas. C'est malheureux…[19]

> Soon after the publication of *Pavillon*, I received letters from parents of anorectics. I understood one thing: anorexia feeds on hatred. My life has not been easy, my husband abandoned me when she was little. I raised my two children by myself. Now, I live with a boyfriend who Valérie is not accepting of. It's sad…

But the fact that Valère's relationship with her mother subverts the common theoretical model of the anorectic girl's over-attachment to her mother does not mean that her relationship with her mother was not a crucial part in the aetiology and the prolongation of Valère's anorexia nervosa: quite the contrary, for that noxious relationship clearly played

19 Clerc 1987: 160.

a key role.[20] My point is that the dysfunction of this relationship lay not in over-attachment, but in its antithesis on the mother's side: what appears to have been a cold detachment from her child and a flagrant failure to meet that child's need for love and nurturing. One qualification should be made here: the mother's cold detachment from her child did not preclude a surveillance of her that could be viewed by some as invasiveness. In my opinion this would be not emotional invasiveness but control: refusal to grant her child any right to privacy and personal space (spatiality in EDs has been addressed in a 2015 article of mine;[21] see also the Conclusion to this book). Indeed, Valère recalls her mother having opened up her locked notebook without permission and having forced her to open up her treasure box (p. 115). Returning to the broader model of the anorexigenic mother found in the secondary literature, one of whose traits is over-protectiveness, there is proof of the opposite in Valère's case. Upon her discharge from hospital, her mother actually inflicts physical violence on her: when Valère refuses to attend the appointment with a psychoanalyst that her mother has arranged without consulting her, rolling up like a ball on the floor and weeping, her mother traps her by grabbing her by the hair (p. 149).

Further subversion of clinical and particularly psychoanalytic models of the anorectic that posit an unhealthily enmeshed, fusional relationship with the mother occurs in Valère's analepses. These reinscribe her alienation from (in the following, connoted by the scare quotes around the word 'mère' [mother]) and contempt for her mother: 'L'heure des repas était particulièrement insupportable. Cette femme au teint mat, ma « mère », pleurait quelquefois, criait toujours et me révoltait' [Mealtimes were particularly unbearable. This dull-faced woman, my 'mother', sometimes cried, always screamed and was revolting to me] (p. 24). More radical alienation from her mother is conveyed when Valère presents her mother's unexpected arrival in her hospital room as the arrival of a complete stranger: 'À onze heures, une femme toute drôle entre avec un grand sourire' [At eleven o'clock, an odd woman comes in with a big smile] (p. 71). Likewise, she later refers to her mother as 'une dame' [a lady] (p. 104) and as 'la femme qui va venir me chercher' [the woman who will come looking for me] (p. 136).

20 For evidence of this in Valère's extradiegetic life, see Clerc 1987: 26, 31, 34, 68.

21 Cairns, Lucille, 'Bodily dis-ease in contemporary French women's writing: Two case studies', *French Studies*, 69, 4 (October 2015), 494–508 (499–500).

On maternal visits, narrative confusion appears to arise in announcement of the prospect of a first visit from her mother, whereas in fact Valère has already narrated the occurrence of such a visit (p. 84; see also p. 71). Was this first visit a figment of her imagination? Some readers may judge her an unreliable narrator, but others may well consider that, if it *was* a figment of her imagination, this merely emphasises the phobic disgust about all contact with her mother she had developed. Indeed, this is closely followed by further evidence of her antipathy for her mother, from which she extrapolates to assert the hollow and insincere play-acting constituting maternal 'love' universally: 'Maintenant je me suis rendu compte de cette hypocrisie, de ce charlatanisme qu'on nomme "amour maternel"!' [Now I have realised this hypocrisy, this charlatanism that we call 'motherly love'] (p. 85). Shortly afterwards, there is expression of the deepest hatred possible for her mother as the latter appraises her body, which she feels is being infiltrated by a maternal gaze (isomorphic with the common trope of the anorectic's lack of personal space and privacy: see my article of 2015 and the Conclusion to this book): 'Je sens son regard s'infiltrer sous mes vêtements, se promener sur mon corps, pour constater l'amélioration de mon état. Je la déteste ! [...] Je crois que je n'ai jamais autant détesté quelqu'un de toute ma vie' [I feel her gaze slip under my clothes, walk around my body to assess the improvement of my condition. I hate her! [...] I don't think I've ever hated anyone so much in my life] (p. 95). Part of this hatred is the conviction that her mother regards her as a 'thing', an insentient object rather than a human being: 'Voilà, elle a rempli son devoir, elle est venue voir sa "chose", maintenant elle peut partir sans scrupules et même avec l'orgueil d'avoir mis sa fille entre de bonnes mains' [There, she has fulfilled her duty, she has come to see her 'thing', Now she can leave without scruples and with the pride of having left her daughter in good hands] (p. 97).

Recurring to Valère's resistance to psychoanalytically based components of her hospital treatment, this is forcefully rendered by her stubborn mutism faced with a psychoanalyst's questions, for example about whether she had not been affected when her father had left the family home. This question is typical of psychoanalytically based approaches to anorexia nervosa, which construct the father as an 'absent' figure, usually emotionally but also in some cases physically.[22]

22 To take just two examples, Palazzoli asserts 'the father is usually an emotional absentee, generally overshadowed, and secretly or openly belittled, by his wife' (Palazzoli 1978: 39), and Jeammet 2004: 207 also notes of the typical

The unilateral 'dialogue' in which she refuses to answer questions is prefaced by the bitter, categorical statements made in her own head but addressed silently to the psychoanalyst: 'Je ne veux pas parler. Je ne veux pas que vous sachiez quoi que ce soit de moi. Je refuse votre aide. Je ne suis pas malade et vous le savez, c'est pour ça que je n'ai pas besoin de vous parler' [I don't want to speak. I don't want you to know anything about me. I refuse your help. I am not ill and you know it, that's why I have no need to talk to you] (p. 29). While she has a right to desist from cooperating with the psychoanalyst, her insistence that she is not ill does obviously reveal one key element of anorexic psychopathology.

Valère's bitterness is not limited to the psychoanalysts who treat her in hospital. She sarcastically ventriloquises the discourse of clinicians on the anorectic (reflecting, incidentally, a wider public perception) that asserts that anorexia nervosa is a choice, and who thus condemn its sufferers in moralising terms: 'Allons, ne vous prenez-vous pas un peu trop au sérieux, mademoiselle ? Il y en a des milliers de gens enfermés dans des cachots depuis plus longtemps que vous ! D'ailleurs, on vous avait prévenue. *Il ne tenait qu'à vous d'éviter d'être ici*' [Come on, don't you take yourself a little too seriously, miss? There are thousands of people who have been locked up in cells for much longer than you! Besides, you had been warned. *It was up to you to avoid being here*] (p. 31; my emphasis). Her response to this imagined external rebuke – and the apprehension of the external voice may suggest slight schizophrenic tendencies – is vicious and deliberately vulgar: 'Non, ce n'est pas vrai ! Tais-toi sale voix ! Tu ne te montres même pas, tu es trop hypocrite, sale putain !' [No, that's not true! Shut your filthy mouth. You don't even show yourself, you are too much of a hypocrite, you piece of shit!' (p. 32), and could be interpreted by some readers as paranoia, or even psychosis. Nonetheless, that response reflects the empirical reality of many of those professionals involved in hospital treatment of anorexia nervosa. See my references in the Introduction to Seah et al. 2017, showing that clinicians generally have inadequate knowledge of EDs, and to Raveneau et al.'s 2014 study revealing that '[m]ore than half of all nurses and residents (58.2%) thought that ED patients were responsible for their disease "always" or "in most cases"'.

anorectic a 'relation décevante au père, marquée par l'effacement ou l'absence de ce dernier' [relationship of disappointment with her father, marked by his erasure or absence].

That attitude documented by Raveneau et al. 2014 – while it does not refer to treatment in France – correlates with the conduct of certain nurses treating Valère. Witness-bearing is made to the egregiously brutal conduct of (some of) the nursing staff: 'Regardez-les, ils s'énervent devant mon indifférence ; "Tu vas le manger, tu vas le manger, oui ? Mange-le ou je te donne une gifle... Tu la veux, tu la veux, réponds, sale môme, tu vas le manger ? "' [Look at them, they get angry at my indifference; 'You're going to eat it, you're going to eat it, yes? Eat it or I'll give you a slap... You want it, you want it, answer me, dirty brat, will you eat it?'] (p. 35). This brutality is even more egregious later on, when one of the nurses tries to force-feed her:

> elle m'attrape la main et m'écarte les dents avec la fourchette jusqu'à ce que ma bouche s'ouvre. Je bouge la tête dans tous les sens et à peu près les neuf dixièmes du plateau atterissent par terre et sur sa blouse. (p. 67)[23]

> she grabs my hand and parts my teeth with the fork until my mouth opens. I move my head in all directions and about nine-tenths of the tray lands on the floor and on her blouse.

The unethical, harsh conduct of (some of) the nursing staff is also flagrant on p. 41, although this time it takes the form of a more insidious, non-physical threat – more a psychic undermining: 'Mais cesse donc de dire : ces enfants fous, tu en fais partie, tu es folle toi aussi, sinon tu ne serais pas là. Tu entends, tu es folle, tu entends, folle, f,o,l,l,e' [But stop saying: these crazy children, you are part of it, you are crazy too, otherwise you wouldn't be here. You hear, you are crazy, you hear, crazy, c.r.a.z.y' (p. 41). Some of the nursing staff actually, and asininely, encourage competitiveness in weight loss among anorectics:

> « – Eh bien, alors fais un geste. Tu sais, c'est la première bouchée qui est difficile, après ça passe tout seul. Et puis tu verras ça ira vite si tu fais juste un petit effort au début. Tu sais, ici, j'ai vu des filles encore plus maigres que toi. Je me souviens d'une qui pesait vingt-cinq kilos pour un mètre soixante ! »

23 This egregiously unethical, indeed brutal, conduct of (some of) the nursing staff in the hospital where the 13-year-old Valérie is 'treated' for anorexia nervosa in 1973 in France runs entirely counter to the exhortations made 22 years later in Beumont, Russell, and Touyz 1995: 255: 'The nursing staff on the unit is responsible for the day-to-day management of the patients and must be well versed in the psychopathology of anorexia nervosa. The importance of the nursing staff in the successful management of these patients cannot be sufficiently emphasized.'

C'est la compétition, eh bien alors, j'ai encore cinq kilos à perdre !' (p. 45)

'Well, then make a gesture. You know, it's the first bite that's difficult, after it happens by itself. And then you'll see it go quickly if you make just a little effort at the beginning. You know, here I've seen girls even skinnier than you. I remember one who weighed twenty-five kilos for six feet!'

So it's a competition, well then, I still have five pounds to lose!

Despite her animosity towards and resistance to the entire hospital team treating her, at one point Valère lets slip her mental shield according to which there is nothing wrong with her by admitting that she does not understand, but would like to understand, her condition. This seems to imply a vague recognition of her psychopathology:

Je n'en sais rien, espèce de con ! en tout cas, je ne tenterai jamais de vous l'expliquer. Il n'y a qu'à moi que je peux essayer. Après tout, j'en ai rien à foutre, ça me plairait quand même de savoir, mais c'est moi qui trouverai ; vous ne l'inscrirez pas dans votre dossier, non, il n'y a que moi que ça regarde. (p. 34)

I don't know anything about it, you moron! In any case, I will never try to explain it to you. I can only try to explain it to myself. After all, I don't give a shit, still, I'd like to know, but it's me who will find it; you won't put it in your file, no, it concerns nobody but me.

Similarly, shortly afterwards her narrative expresses a wish to comprehend why she wants to starve herself to death:

Je ne suis qu'une imbécile, ce ne sont pas des solutions de se laisser mourir de faim. Oui, je sais, cela m'avance à quoi ? [...] J'aimerais bien le savoir, très exactement. L'ennuyeux, c'est que je ne pense pas que ce soit une chose précise, claire. C'est un ensemble : le déplorable résultat de treize ans de vie dans leur monde foutu. Qu'attendaient-ils d'autre ? La reconnaissance ? (p. 49)

I'm just an idiot, it's not a solution to starve yourself. Yes, I know, how does that help me? [...] I would like to know, exactly. The boring thing is that I don't think it's a precise, clear thing. It is a group of things: the deplorable result of thirteen years of life in their screwed up world. What else did they expect? Gratitude?

The last three sentences here ooze a pus-like rancour against the whole world, which has its roots in the deeply negative vision of humankind born of her parents' unedifying conduct. It has already been hinted on p. 41 that the discord between her parents, their failure to hide their ugly conjugal conflicts from her, had been deeply traumatic, and possibly a trigger to her anorexia nervosa, even if she herself does not posit this aetiology (cf. pp. 46, 47, 115, 116). Unconsciously murderous – and according to Valère in her use of the word 'lucidité' [lucidity], justifiably murderous – feelings towards her parents are expressed: 'J'ai dû tuer un de mes parents dans un moment de lucidité, ce qu'eux appellent moment de l'inconscient' [I had to kill one of my parents in a moment of lucidity, which they call moment of the unconscious] (p. 37).

Deep disgust for her parents is indeed cuttingly expressed, confirming in a very general sense the findings of clinical and psychoanalytic researchers that anorectics often emerge from dysfunctional families, but with the striking difference that unlike the typical anorectic presented in the secondary literature, she is acutely aware of this dysfunction, and freely admits her fear of it. Referring first to her mother and then to her father, she proclaims, 'Elle est hypocrite, aveugle, névrosée et sans énergie. Lui est traître, menteur, schizophrène, obsédé sexuel, frustré… je ne vous dirai pas tout, il y en a trop, ça me fait peur' [She is hypocritical, blind, neurotic and without energy. He is a traitor, liar, schizophrenic, obsessed with sex, frustrated… I won't tell you everything, there are too many, it scares me] (p. 39). The psychopathogenic relationship of Valère's mother to her own mother, noted by some of the secondary literature as characteristic of anorectic family constellations, is evidenced here: 'Ma mère […] a été traumatisée par sa maman qui lui répétait qu'elle était une bonne à rien, qu'elle était laide, paresseuse, et que jamais elle ne saurait séduire les hommes' [My mother […] was traumatised by her mom who repeated to her that she was a good-for-nothing, that she was ugly, lazy and that she'd never be attractive to men] (p. 39; cf. p. 117). Whether or not this indicates genetic or environmental causation in the transmission of EDs is a moot point, but what seems plain is the presence of possible intergenerational predisposing maternal factors in the onset of Valère's own ED. The following assertion by Sours certainly seems relevant to Valère's case: 'The mother of the anorectic is an emotionally immature woman who often continues to be dependent on her own mother, also a controlling woman who can only criticize her daughter and try to control her life.'[24]

24 Sours, John A., *Starving to Death in a Sea of Objects: The Anorexia Nervosa Syndrome* (New York/London: Jason Aronson, 1980), p. 6.

Triggered by her parents' lamentable behaviour, Valère's general misanthropy is psychologically legible, and causes her to choose solitude over having friends. However, there is another facet to this choice: she explicitly states a wish not to experience a permanent need for others (p. 42). The anorectic's fear of intimacy with and resulting dependency on other human beings is a classic feature of the secondary literature. From this optic, the anorexic wish not to need food correlates with a more general wish to transcend basic human needs, which include attachment to other human beings. This seems to correspond to Lacan's theory when he refers to 'la véritable fonction d'un symptôme comme celui de l'anorexie mentale' [the true function of a symptom like that of anorexia nervosa], claiming, 'Je vous ai déjà dit que l'anorexie mentale n'est pas un *ne pas manger*, mais un *ne rien manger*. J'insiste – cela veut dire *manger rien*. Rien, c'est justement quelque chose qui existe sur le plan symbolique' [I have already told you that anorexia nervosa is not about *not eating*, but about *eating nothing*. I insist – it means *eating nothing*. Nothing is in fact something that exists on the symbolic plan].[25] The inference to be drawn from Lacan's statement is that the anorectic wants to ingest nothing, which extends symbolically from food to the company of other human beings. (See the Conclusion for analysis of Lacan's words.)

Having made the choice of solitude, Valère extols the latter via metaphor, personifying it as a beautiful mistress (p. 42). On p. 61, she extends the personification of solitude by saying she is in love with it, but also engages with the concept of solitude more cognitively, wondering if it is perhaps a form of pride, of pretentiousness, or of cowardly conflict-avoidance. What is clear in this dual approach is her immense difficulty in interpersonal relationships. These difficulties also emerge on p. 82, and the causation here is clear: a deep lack of confidence in her ability genuinely to be liked and appreciated by others. Metaphor, again personification, is part of her psychic dealings with the concept of death: 'la mort. J'ai hâte de la connaître. [...] je sais qu'elle est belle, c'est la plus belle femme jamais vue' [death. I can't wait to meet her [...] I know that she's beautiful, the most beautiful woman ever seen] (p. 51). A different, but striking metaphor is that of a second skin bursting as she bursts into tears, as if her harsh carapace of angry resistance conceals intense inner distress, albeit interpreted as anger and contempt:

25 Lacan, Jacques, *Le Séminaire, Livre IV: La Relation d'objet* (Paris: Seuil, 1994) [Texte établi par Jacques-Alain Miller], pp. 184–85 (184).

> Il y a une nouvelle infirmière du matin, elle revient de vacances, une petite femme énergique et autoritaire. Le jour où elle arrive, ma seconde peau vient d'éclater, et je ne peux plus arrêter les larmes, coléreuses, rageuses, méprisantes, des sanglots qui m'étouffent presque. (p. 67)

> There is a new nurse in the morning, she's back from vacation, a small woman who is energetic and authoritarian. The day she arrives, my second skin has just burst, and I can't stop the tears, angry, rageful, contemptuous, sobs that almost choke me.

The ontological metaphor of multiple skins is extended as she evokes a third skin bursting (prompted, tellingly given what has been discussed above about the mother–daughter relationship, by a remark from a nurse who says she is going to ask the doctors if Valère's mother can visit), with the piercing detail of pus emerging from within her, as if she were a polluted entity: 'Elle avait réussi à faire éclater la troisième peau. Putride le pus n'en finissait plus de s'échapper, toujours plus virulent' [She had managed to burst her third skin. Putrid pus had not stopped escaping from it, still more virulent] (p. 69). Metaphor is again forcefully utilised to depict eating as a form of suicide and food as a poison: 'Je n'ai plus qu'à les bouffer leurs sales plateaux pour criminels endurcis ! Je n'ai plus qu'à accepter cette forme de suicide, avaler leur poison qui donne « la vie, la joie, la sortie » !' [I just have to eat their dirty trays meant for hardened criminals! I just have to accept this form of suicide, swallow their poison that gives 'life, joy, the way out'!] (p. 75). The metaphorisation of food as poison is reprised in the following reference to eating: 'j'ai péniblement essayé de mâcher, d'avaler... Chaque miette m'éraflait la gorge comme une lame de couteau affûtée, je devais m'y reprendre à plusieurs fois pour une malheureuse once de leur poison' [I tried painfully to chew, to swallow... Every crumb cut my throat like a sharp knife blade, I had to go back to it several times for an unfortunate ounce of their poison] (p. 75). (See the Conclusion, where I briefly discuss Julia Kristeva's views on food's status as a pollutant in certain cultural contexts.) As affirmed in my Introduction, metaphor is a pervasive stylistic trait in the primary corpus, and one form of metaphor is personification. Two other examples among many are found in Emilie Durand's *Ma folie ordinaire: allers et retours à l'hôpital Sainte-Anne* (2006) and Annick Loupias's *La Tortue sur le dos: ma lutte contre la boulimie* (2001),[26]

26 Loupias, Annick, with Louise Lambert-Lagacé and Annette Richard, *La Tortue sur le dos: ma lutte contre la boulimie* (Quebec: Éditions de l'homme, 2001).

one of the two case studies in Chapter 3, where anorexia nervosa and bulimia nervosa are figured as beautiful but evil mistresses. Ontological metaphors in these three texts all reveal morbid glorification of what is normatively considered deeply negative – solitude, death, life-threatening EDs – and, significantly, all three personify the ED as women, a not nugatory gendering, given that the vast majority of those with EDs are female.

Returning to the metaphor of her skins bursting, Valère's carapace of hostility and invulnerability is further punctured by a new sensation of guilt about refusing to eat, just after a nurse has shown her compassion and not treated her as mad (p. 70). But this sensation of guilt instantly transmutes into (arguably paranoid) hostility: 'C'était bien ce qu'ils cherchaient. Ce sont eux qui vous enferment et c'est vous qui avez tort' [That was what they were looking for. They are the ones who lock you up and it's you who are wrong] (p. 70). Nonetheless, she does begin to reflect on her hatred for the medical staff and on how the nurse's words had prompted a revival of self-hatred (p. 70). This process of reflection is augmented upon the arrival of another anorexic patient, which prompts a different perspective on her own self-starvation, for in another anorectic she condemns starving oneself to death as idiocy; moreover, this view serves as a salutary mirror to herself: 'En toi-même, tu la traitais bien d'idiote de s'être laisser mourir de faim, de s'être oubliée, de se montrer ainsi, presque invisible, inexistante... Tu es comme elle... Mange !' [In your mind you treated her like an idiot to have let herself starve to death, to be forgotten, to be seen like that, almost invisible, inexistent... You are like her... Eat!] (p. 78). Further cognitive progress appears to follow, when Valère silently decries as 'con' [stupid] the draconian alimentary restrictions previously imposed on herself by another anorectic patient (p. 89). A counter-argument would be that anorectics exhort other anorectics to eat in order to feel 'superior' to those who do 'capitulate' to eating, or eating more. Valère's narrative does not, however, appear to indicate such manipulation of other anorectics. On the topic of manipulation, Valère newly becomes aware that she is guilty of this, a process triggered by the presence of another anorectic with whom she is able to talk.

> Je commençais à entrevoir la vérité sur mes propres manipulations, celles de mes rêves. La chef de clinique ne repassa pas et permit aux infirmières de me donner des livres. Mais ce qui déclencha définitivement le mécanisme fut la présence de l'autre anorexique avec laquelle je pus parler un jour, en cachette, dans les lavabos. (pp. 78–79)

> I began to glimpse the truth about my own manipulations, those of my dreams. The head of the clinic did not come back and allowed the nurses to give me books. But what definitely triggered the mechanism was the presence of the other anorectic with whom I could speak one day, secretly, in the washbasins.

This new, more lucid perspective on herself increases as she comes to understand the frustration of the hospital staff at her anorexic self-destruction and defence mechanisms (p. 80).[27] Accompanying this conceptual breakthrough are the glimmerings of a nascent compassion for the other child patients in this psychiatric hospital, replacing her previous revulsion for them – even if her inveterate cynicism kicks in at realisation of her wish to help them (p. 81). In evocation of this new self-awareness and self-analysis, there is an interesting reprise of the skin metaphor deployed on pp. 67 and 69: 'j'aimerais les aider, et immédiatement je comprends la "stupidité" de cette impulsion, son inutilité. Je comprends aussi que mes peaux de fausse sensibilité sont loin d'être toutes tombées et que je suis profondément égoïste' [I would like to help them, and immediately I understand the 'stupidity' of this impulse, its uselessness. I also understand that my skins of false sensitivity are far from having all fallen away and that I am deeply selfish] (p. 81).

In tandem with her inveterate cynicism is her scathing condemnation of the psychiatric institution (cf. Emilie Durand) previously remarked on, for the suffering it has inflicted on those it has deemed insane, and for its actual ignorance. The condemnation is made with humorous sarcasm:

> Ces savants devraient posséder un équilibre neuropsychique tellement parfait qu'ils pourraient se permettre de devenir fous. Quand ils repasseraient de l'autre côté de la barrière ils se rendraient compte des souffrances qu'ils ont infligées et de l'incompréhension dont ils ont fait preuve. (p. 82)

> These scientists should have a neuropsychic balance so perfect that they could allow themselves to go crazy. When they went back to the other side of the fence they would realize the pain they had inflicted and the misunderstanding they had shown.

After she starts eating all hospital meals (plus, of her own volition, high-calorie snacks), with resultant weight gain, one form of suffering

27 See Brotman, A.W., Stern, T.A., and Herzog, D.B., 'Emotional reactions of house officers to patients with anorexia nervosa, diabetes and obesity', *International Journal of Eating Disorders*, 3 (1984), 71–77.

experienced is humiliation and self-disgust at having submitted to the psychiatric regime, and at having become, as she sees it, weakly compliant. The metaphor of the 'serpillière' [wet rag] is particularly resonant, expressing her sense of degradation in the regime's crushing of her revolt:

> La fille qui disait avec orgueil : "Ils ne m'auront pas", cette fille a disparu entre leurs murs de saleté, je suis perdue, ils en ont fabriqué une autre, larve, serpillière, une autre comme ils la voulaient... J'ai cédé à leur chantage, à leur désirs, à leur corruption. (p. 137)
>
> The girl who said with pride: 'They will not get me', this girl disappeared between their walls of dirt, I'm lost, they made another, larva, wet rag, another as they wanted... I have given in to their blackmail, their desires, their corruption.

There is also a sense of the psychiatric regime having dispossessed her of herself: 'Je ne suis rien. Je ne m'appartiens plus. Ils ont tout saccagé' [I am nothing. I no longer belong to myself. They have wrecked everything] (p. 140). The metaphorical use of the verb 'saccager' [to wreck] is potent, implying the violent criminality of that regime – ironically, given that she had felt it criminalised her: it has wrecked, devastated, even vandalised everything within her.

In fact, all three of the anorectics in this psychiatric hospital unit – Valère, Christine, and Dominique – denounce as disgraceful and traumatising, and revolt against, the methods deployed by the psychiatric institution to treat them (p. 88). These methods are revealed to be completely ineffective in the long term, as the resolve of these three anorectics is that they will comply with such methods in order to be liberated from the hospital and then achieve vengeance by starving themselves afresh, not being taken in again by the lies to which they had been victim prior to hospital admission (p. 89). Such compliance is augmented in Valère's case by an attempt to accelerate the point of discharge. Despite her professed antipathy for food, in addition to finally accepting the consumption of all hospital meals, she also starts to consume extra, calorifically rich foods in order to gain weight as quickly as possible and thus be released from the hospital she regards as a prison (pp. 10–19).

We have noted above that Valère rejects the dogma of psychiatrists according to which anorexia nervosa descends upon its victims suddenly and independently of their own volition:

> Car ce que disent les psychiatres est faux, ça n'arrive pas comme ça sans qu'on l'ait voulu et mûrement réfléchi. On ne peut pas du jour au lendemain ne plus connaître la faim, ne plus avoir besoin de rien, c'est faux ! C'est un entraînement, un but : ne plus être comme tous les autres, ne plus être esclave de cette exigence matérielle, ne plus jamais sentir ce plein au milieu du ventre, ni cette fausse joie qu'ils éprouvent lorsque le démon de la faim les tiraille. [...] (pp. 111–12)

> Because what psychiatrists say is wrong, it does not just happen like that without being wanted and carefully thought out. We can't change overnight so we no longer know hunger, no longer need anything, it's wrong! It is a training, a goal: to no longer be like all the others, no longer to be a slave to this material requirement, never to feel that full in the middle of your belly, nor this false joy that they experience when the demon of hunger pulls them. [...]

I referred above to Valère's '*professed* antipathy for food' (my emphasis), and indeed, her rendering above of the anorectic's descent into illness stresses a deliberate self-training. This self-training involves suppression of liking for food and tolerance of hunger, in order to free oneself from what she sees as enslavement to a base material demand and from a false pleasure. This 'false' pleasure is, in her view, experienced by a common humankind above which she wants to rise – and this wish is one of the salient motifs of the broader primary literature, viz, aspiration to a form of 'purity'.[28] The metaphor deployed of hunger as demonic ('le démon de la faim' [the demon of hunger]) also betrays her fear of hunger – revealingly, since for so long in her narrative hitherto she has expressed her hatred of food. This ambivalence towards food, eating, and hunger in the anorectic is abundantly recorded in the secondary literature.

A similar ambivalence prevails in her attitude towards body shape and weight in others. Morbid attraction to emaciation is betrayed in her description of another anorectic patient, Dominique: 'Grande fille d'os, j'aime ton corps, j'aime sa légèreté...' [Big girl of bone, I like your body, I like its lightness...] (p. 114). However, there appears to be a healthier counter-perspective in her trenchant remarks to another anorectic patient, Christine: 'Regarde tes jambes, les os de tes hanches malgré l'épaisseur du tissu ressortent comme des barres, ta silhouette affalée et laide, cette faiblesse maladive. Et ça te plaît !' [Look at your

28 See the section in the Bibliographical Appendix, 'Purity/Transcendence of the Flesh/Transcendence of the Need for Food that Sustains that Flesh'.

legs, the bones of your hips stand out like bars despite the thickness of the fabric, your slouched and ugly figure, this sickly weakness. And you like it!] (p. 118). Yet her ascription of ugliness in emaciation may, again, and as remarked above, be a form of manipulation, motivated by the competitive desire for another anorectic to gain weight. A proximate though not identical attitude emerges in Valère's mention of her and her fellow anorectics patients' attitude towards bulimia: 'La boulimie, c'était à la fois étonnant, incompréhensible pour nous... et un peu rassurant' [Bulimia was both amazing and incomprehensible to us... and a little reassuring] (p. 135). The admission that, while they cannot understand bulimia, they find it reassuring, and the suspension points that follow this admission, are cryptic. One interpretation is that others 'indulging' in over-eating may diminish their own sense of guilt about eating at all. Another, more cynical interpretation is that they are gratified to sense themselves superior to mere mortals enslaved to the temptations of food. Moreover, these anorectics' encouragement of a non-anorectic patient to eat all the cakes they have clandestinely accumulated vindicates abundant research findings of the anorectic's desire to cook, prepare food for others, or press food on others while she herself refrains from partaking of it.

Notwithstanding this desire, all three, as previously remarked, end up eating all that they are required to eat because otherwise they would never be released from hospital. When Valère reaches her target weight and is discharged from hospital, the flagrant lack of psychological help in the treatment regime she has followed is evident in her continuing depression and disenchantment with human society generally, which she frames as a basely commercial enterprise that will attempt to blackmail her just as the psychiatric regime had: 'Ainsi, c'est cela que j'ai voulu rejoindre, un univers de vente. Est-ce que je vais également me laisser prendre à ce chantage implicite ?' [So, that's what I wanted to join, a universe of sales. Will I also get caught up in this implicit blackmail?] (p. 147). That depression also subtends another statement made apropos abandoned children, the term she had earlier on used to qualify the paediatric patients in the psychiatric hospital: 'Je sais que je ne peux rien y faire sinon crier, un cri fou qui ne déchire que mon propre cœur, que ma propre vie, un cri pour les enfants abandonnés, un autre appel, une demande d'amour' [I know I can't do anything but scream, a mad cry that only tears my own heart, my own life, a cry for abandoned children, another call, a request for love] (p. 153). The last clause, 'une demande d'amour' [a request for love], seems to sum up the overall aetiology of her anorexia nervosa: a profoundly depressive revolt against a world in which the primary-care figures – the mother and father – had failed her, giving no demonstrable and consistent proof of love and esteem, and thus thwarting the development of any self-esteem and emotional health in their child.

That last clause occurs on the last page of the text proper. In the 'Épilogue', Valère reprises the motif of imprisonment, affirming its persistence since her release from hospital two years ago, but in a different form. For she now feels a prisoner of her own anxieties, of her own fears, of her own self, and, significantly, of her mother. Her decision to write the preceding narrative has, we learn, been motivated by an attempt to forget, to erase, to free herself from what she calls daily humiliations:

> Depuis plus de deux ans, ma vie, cette vie de prisonnière continue dans un décor quelque peu différent mais pour moi proche des cachots de l'hôpital. Prisonnière de mes angoisses, de mes craintes, prisonnière de moi-même et de « cette » femme, dans le vide sinistre de ma chambre, de cette chambre qui m'a été imposée, au risque de souffrir, j'ai choisi de parler pour oublier, pour rayer, pour me libérer de ces humiliations quotidiennes plus cruelles que les coups qui m'auraient permis de nourrir ma haine. (p. 155)

> For more than two years, my life, this life of a prisoner has continued in a somewhat different setting but for me close to the cells of the hospital. Prisoner of my anguish, of my fears, prisoner of myself and of 'that' woman, in the sinister void of my room, of this room which was imposed on me, at the risk of suffering, I chose to speak in order to forget, to cross out, to free myself from these daily humiliations more cruel than the blows that would have allowed me to feed my hatred.

This extract is infused by pathos. Yet the very last paragraph of the 'Épilogue', and thus the lasting impression for the reader, is a spiritedly arch denunciation of the (patriarchal: 'messieurs les psys' [Messrs shrinks]) psychiatric institution, and also a sourly ironic relativisation, even negation, of the construct of 'la folie' [madness] on which psychiatrists depend for their credibility and livelihood (p. 158; again, cf. Emilie Durand).

Section 1.2

Although both Valère's *Le Pavillon des enfants fous* and Marta Aleksandra Balinska's *Retour à la vie: quinze ans d'anorexie* (2003)[29] inscribe the experience of anorexia nervosa, restrictor type, the scope of the two texts is by no means homologous, and indeed they show many divergences as well as convergences, perhaps unsurprisingly given that the latter text recounts treatment in the 1980s and 1990s. One is that while Valère's testimony is very largely confined to rendering the experience of a short period of time, viz. that of her hospitalisation, Balinska's renders the phenomenology of anorexia nervosa over a long period of time (fifteen years), including two hospitalisations, and is concerned with day-to-day embodied and emotional experience of the condition. Another, and stark, contrast with Valère's text is tonal and stylistic. Balinska's tone is predominantly composed, meditative, often earnest; her register of language is elevated (illustrated, for instance, by use of the imperfect subjunctive); and her approach to anorexia nervosa is intellectually probing. These tonal, stylistic, and intellectual differences between Valère and Balinska are unsurprising given that Valère was only 15 when she wrote *Le Pavillon des enfants fous*, whereas Balinska was 38 at the time her *Retour à la vie: quinze ans d'anorexie* was published, and was, moreover, a researcher with a doctoral thesis to her name. On the question of intellectual differences, a conspicuous feature of Balinska's testimony is its challenge to various strands of medico-theoretico dogma pertaining to anorexia nervosa. Valère had certainly challenged these, but in a more emotive, less conceptually oriented fashion (although for her young age, her knowledge of psychoanalytic theory is impressive).

However, the more conceptually sophisticated tenor of Balinska's testimony does not preclude literary stylistic traits, including sometimes striking use of metaphor, and a certain poetry, in some cases literal poetry in the intercalation within framework prose of Balinska's own poems written during her 15 years of anorexia. Other intercalations which render *Retour à la vie: quinze ans d'anorexie* something of a hybrid text are extracts from her mother's written record of Balinska's incarceration in a French psychiatric hospital for treatment for anorexia, and a lengthy transcribed interview with Stanislaw Tomkiewicz, a

29 Balinska, Marta Aleksandra, *Retour à la vie: quinze ans d'anorexie* (Paris: Odile Jacob, 2003).

neuropsychiatric doctor upon whose interview with Balinska her book ends. While on the subject of Balinska's style, it is interesting that Tomkiewicz adds to the qualities I have enumerated above the following praise: 'Votre style est vivant, aiguisé comme une épée' [Your style is lively, sharpened like a sword] (p. 253).

Retour à la vie: quinze ans d'anorexie is explicitly designated a testimony (p. 254) by Balinska, who is part Jewish[30] (see p. 22 and p. 179). Discussion of the linking of Jewishness to anorexia nervosa is provided in a footnote.[31] For readers interested in this linkage, I would

30 Balinska is of dual heritage, being American on her mother's side and Polish-Jewish on her father's side (p. 22).

31 One fruitful line of enquiry that goes beyond the remit of my study but that I will examine briefly here is the extent to which autobiographical texts, or even autofictional texts, by French Jewish women such as Atlan, Balinska, Bernfeld, Brisac, Tohorah and Vasseur accurately reflect Jewish EDs in the extra-textual world. As early as 1986, Thomas Silber observed, 'One cannot help but notice, for instance, the fact that for many years anorexia nervosa has been encountered disproportionately among Jews.' See Silber, Thomas J., 'Anorexia nervosa in blacks and Hispanics', *International Journal of Eating Disorders*, 5, 1 (1986), 121–28 (127). Silber does not, however, support his claim with any empirical evidence, and there is no consensus among specialists as to whether anorexia nervosa is more common among Jews than non-Jews. Indeed, the exiguous body of research conducted on the subject contains some pronounced contradictions. Nonetheless, the conclusion drawn by one of the most thorough reviews of that body of research certainly merits consideration: 'although the clinical evidence is inconclusive regarding the exact rates of anorexia among the Jewish population and the Orthodox subset, the overwhelming anecdotal and scholarly evidence suggests that the rates are the same *if not higher* than in the general population'. See Peyser, Caroline, *Body and Soul: A Guide for Addressing Eating Disorders in a Jewish Education Setting* (Jerusalem: Academy for Torah Initiatives and Directions, 2005), p. 18; my emphasis. Even more exiguous is any body of serious scientific enquiry as to whether, as Betty E. Chesler put it in 2005, 'Holocaust survivors' exposure to deprivation and trauma, whether experienced at the onset of, or throughout WWII, contributed to the development of eating and weight problems among their offspring. To date, not a single study appears to address this issue.' See Chesler, Betty E., 'Implications of the Holocaust for eating and weight problems among survivors' offspring: An exploratory study', *European Eating Disorders Review*, 13, 1 (January 2005), 38–47 (38–39). Interestingly, Chesler affirms that 'almost all participants (Holocaust survivors' offspring) exhibit restrained or overeating syndromes, and under- or overweight' (45). It would seem that the majority of those empirical studies that do exist indeed suggest a higher risk of disordered eating in the first and second generation of Holocaust survivors.

But Zohar, Giladi, and Givati assert that '[w]hile there is research on the psychological sequelae of the Holocaust for survivors and for the second generation, there is nearly no controlled quantitative study of the implications for the third generation'. See Zohar, Ada H., Giladi, Lotem, and Givati, Timor, 'Holocaust exposure and disordered eating: A study of multi-generational transmission', *European Eating Disorders Review*, 15 (2007), 50–57 (51). It is as yet impossible to provide any satisfactory answer to the question as to why some first-, second- and third-generation Jews in fact over-eat, while others under-eat. Interestingly, Chesler concluded, 'Interviewees' restrained eating syndromes with low weight appear related to parental emigration from Europe by 1941; overeating syndromes with high weight appear related to parental incarceration in concentration camps' (38). More recently, see Weinberger-Litman, S.L., Latzer, Y., and Stein, D., 'A historical, cultural and empirical look at eating disorders and religiosity among Jewish women', in Yael Latzer, Joav Merrick, Daniel Stein (eds), *Understanding Eating Disorders: Integrating Culture, Psychology and Biology* (New York: Nova Science Publishers, 2011), pp. 109–22. Yet even they, basing their findings on the most up-to-date studies available, ascribe no definite, inexorable link between Jewishness and anorexia nervosa: 'This research is discussed and interpreted in light of cultural values and expectations placed upon young Jewish women. [...] Consistent with the general research examining religion and mental health, studies exploring the relationship between religion and EDs have shown that religiosity can have both a beneficial and a detrimental influence' (Weinberger-Litman et al., pp. 109 and 119). It would seem, then, that the secondary literature alone is inadequate to account for the anorexia inscribed in female Jewish-authored texts in French. One important missing element in such studies may well be consideration of gender, with a relative lack of attention having been paid to the crucial role in Jewish culture of the mother, and to the Jewish mother's famed tendency to press food upon her children. Readers may wish to consider the analysis in my monograph *Post-War Jewish Women's Writing in French* (Oxford: Legenda, 2011) of anorexia in the young Miriam Anissimov, a '1.5 generation' Jewish survivor of the Shoah; but here the anorexia does not qualify as anorexia *nervosa*, since Anissimov's various autofictional avatars do not fear weight gain; rather, they refuse or limit food due partly to resistance to their survivor mother's anxiety to feed her children often to excess, and due partly to identification with Shoah victims' involuntary starvation in the camps. In addition, I have studied cases of anorexia in Jewish girls/woman again in the writings of Anissimov but also in those of Sarah Kofman, another '1.5 generation' Jewish survivor of the Shoah, and in one case of genuine anorexia *nervosa* in a third-generation survivor, Karin Bernfeld, in a conference paper entitled 'Consuming guilt: Food and French Jewish women writers' for the Association for Jewish Studies Annual Conference, 12–14 July 2009. Zohar et al. 2007 observe revealingly that there is some evidence that Holocaust survivors formed more anxious and less secure attachment with their children, and especially women survivors with their daughters (Bar-On suggest consulting the primary texts by Liliane Atlan, Karin Bernfeld, Geneviève Brisac, Valérie Rodrigue (who forms one of my case studies in Chapter 2), and Nadine Vasseur (see the Bibliography of primary texts for bibliographical details). Further, I would encourage consideration of the oblique implication made by Balinska (p. 159) of transmission, be it vocal or silent (on silent transmission, see Abraham and Torok)[32] of second-/third-generation trauma from Jewish survivors of the Shoah, a transmission that, by extrapolation, could perhaps be interpreted as having contributed to the aetiology of Balinska's anorexia nervosa (a hermeneutics that Balinska herself seems to promote).

Balinsksa's testimony is not merely personal. First, it has a proclaimed ethical and sociotropic mission (cf. Durand's *Ma folie ordinaire: allers et retours à l'hôpital Sainte-Anne*):[33]

> C'est avant tout pour elles [les anorexiques] que j'écris, car j'ai l'espérance – peut-être folle – qu'elles verront dans mon récit un éclairage de leurs propres problèmes.
>
> Mais ce n'est pas uniquement pour elles. J'écris aussi pour leur entourage, pour ceux qui veulent les aider, les traiter. (Balinska: 12)
>
> It is above all for them [the anorectics] that I write, because I have hope – perhaps crazy – that they will see in my story an illumination of their own problems.
>
> But it's not just for them. I also write for those around them, for those who want to help them, to treat them.

et al. 1998; Brom, Kfir, and Dasberg 2001; Sagi-Schwartz et al. 2003). While enmeshed mother–daughter dyads with anxious attachment do not constitute psychopathology, many clinicians and theoreticians of EDs have described this family constellation as one that may increase the risk of EDs and particularly for anorexia nervosa (Bruch 1973, 1981; Minuchin, Roseman, and Baker 1988). See Zohar et al. 2007: 51. Finally, clinical psychologist Esther Altmann has observed the following: 'The Holocaust, with its haunting images of skeletal victims, hovers over the Jewish anorectic's self-induced starvation. One theory is that an unconscious, collective identification with grandparents who survived or relatives who perished may underlie eating disorders in the Jewish community.' See Esther Altmann, 'Anorexia and bulimia are amongst the most emotionally and physically devastating disorders affecting young Jewish women', http://www.myjewishlearning.com/article/eating-disorders-in-the-jewish-community/.

32 Abraham, Nicolas and Torok, Maria, *L'Ecorce et le noyau* (Paris: Flammarion, 1978).

33 Note that in Durand's case, the anorexia nervosa later mutates into binge-eating – a common mutation, whose occurrence is estimated at about 50 per cent in some of the secondary literature.

Second, it aims to widen debate about anorexia nervosa (p. 12); this involves vigorous challenge to certain strands of medico-clinical thinking that dictate and regulate clinical treatment of the anorexic body, and often degrade the anorexic individual. I will address this challenge later on in this section.

The longevity and severity of the author's illness are stressed in her opening paragraph (p. 11): she had anorexia nervosa for 15 years, from the ages of 15 to 30 (see pp. 35 and 47), from 1980 to 1995 (having been born in 1965: see p. 19). At the age of 23, she weighed 26kg/4 stones 2lbs, for a height of 1.65 metres/5 feet 4.75 inches. Given this longevity and severity, it is clinically atypical that she was only hospitalised twice (p. 249). Despite the prolonged suffering it has caused, Balinska does actually posit one – sole – salutary legacy of her anorexia nervosa: 'comme toute expérience qui nous amène aux portes de la mort, elle [l'anorexie] nous laisse un goût pour la vie et une jouissance de l'existence probablement bien plus prononcés que chez les autres' [as with every experience that brings us to the gates of death, it [anorexia] leaves us with a taste for life and an enjoyment of existence that is probably more pronounced than in other people] (p. 12). But this is only one salutary legacy, and the overwhelming impression conveyed by her testimony is of suffering.

Balinska questions the aetiology of her anorexia nervosa, with apt distinction between this condition and anorexia alone ('anorexia' meaning, literally, simple lack of appetite).

> Y avait-il eu, dès l'enfance, des signes précurseurs d'anorexie au sens propre ? Je ne me souviens d'aucun dégoût particulier pour la nourriture. Comme presque tous les enfants, il y avait deux, trois aliments que je n'aimais pas (les épinards et les champignons…), mais je ne souffrais pas de manque d'appétit. (p. 19)
>
> Had there been early signs of anorexia in the true sense in childhood? I do not remember any particular disgust for food. Like almost all children, there were two or three foods that I did not like (spinach and mushrooms …), but I did not suffer from lack of appetite.

A number of prodromal factors, however, are referred to. One is an experience at the age of 10, thus in a pre-anorexic period: 'Soudain, je fus prise d'un sentiment terrible d'angoisse : une sensation de vide et de déracinement total' [Suddenly, I was seized by a terrible feeling of anguish: a feeling of emptiness and total uprooting] (p. 20). The trope of 'le vide' [the void] is widespread in other primary texts covered in my book.[34] Another further predisposing/vulnerability factor was spatial displacement.[35]

> Quand j'ai eu 4 ans, nous avons commencé à voyager. Au cours des onze années qui suivirent nous avons changé de pays huit fois, vivant – en dehors de Princeton – à Paris, Lausanne, Grenoble et Vienne. Dans ma seizième année, nous nous sommes installés définitivement à Paris. (Balinska: pp. 23–24)

> When I was 4 we started traveling. Over the next eleven years, we changed country eight times, living – outside Princeton – in Paris, Lausanne, Grenoble and Vienna. In my sixteenth year, we settled permanently in Paris.

Parts of the secondary literature posit such moves, or migration, as possible pre-disposing/vulnerability factors to EDs.[36] Balinska recalls: 'Tout au long de ma période anorexique, il n'y avait que deux choses – impossibles – que je désirais : retrouver mon chien et retrouver la maison de Princeton' [Throughout my anorectic period, there were only two – impossible – things that I wanted: to find my dog and find the house in Princeton] (p. 3). This correlates with Sandra Tohorah's deep nostalgia, in her *La Mort patiente* (2005),[37] another of the personal testimonies on anorexia nervosa, for a now-lost originary home, in Tohorah's case Geneva, before deracination to France. It is reasonable to consider this spatial dislocation/migration as a possible predisposing/vulnerability factor to developing anorexia nervosa, given the following remark: 'In earlier works Katzman and Katzman and Lee have argued that EDs may be precipitated by problems with transition, dislocation, and oppression that produce solutions in manipulations of weight, diet and food.'[38] And at least two of the other 43 primary texts seem to bear this out: Fawzia

34 See the section '"Vide", Physical and Metaphysical', in the Bibliographical Appendix.

35 See the section 'Spatiality' in the Bibliographical Appendix. I also return to this in my Conclusion and spatiality in EDs has been addressed in a 2015 article of mine (Cairns 2015: 499–500).

36 One example is Katzman and Lee 1997: 387, 392.

37 Tohorah, Sandra, *La mort patiente* (Cestas: Élytis Editions, 2005).

38 Katzman, Melanie A., 'Eating disorders: Global marker of change', in Latzer et al. 2011: 84. Her references are Katzman, M.A., 'Feminist approaches to eating disorders: Placing the issues in context', in P. Bria, A. Ciocca, and S. De Risio (eds), *Psychotherapeutic Issues on Eating Disorders: Models, Methods and Results* (Rome: Società Editrice Universo, 1998), pp. 19–26; Katzman and Lee 1997.

Zourai, *Ce pays dont je meurs* (1999);[39] and Anne Calife's *Meurs la faim* (1999; republished 2010).[40] (Calife's text will form the last case study in my book.)

There is inflection and nuance to the common trope in the primary literature of the anorectic's lack of self-confidence/self-esteem, since Balinska states that despite her academic under-achievement, due to the frequent changes of school and education at those foreign schools in a number of languages she did not understand (all due to the frequent migrations of her family), she had *originally* believed herself to be intelligent. To this extent, she did not initially share the predisposing/vulnerability factor of lack of self-esteem that precedes the onset of anorexia nervosa in so many cases, but gradually acquires it (she refers to an inferiority complex on p. 25).

> À de rares exceptions près, j'avais été « mauvais élève » tout au long de ma scolarité. Pourtant, je ne rougis pas de l'avouer, je me *croyais* intelligente. Or, même si l'on est persuadé de ses propres mérites, il arrive un moment où, si tout le monde (ou en tout cas ceux qui occupent les places d'autorité dans la société) nous renvoie le message contraire, on finit par y souscrire. (p. 168)
>
> With rare exceptions, I had been a 'bad student' throughout my schooling. However, I do not blush to admit it, I *thought* myself intelligent. Now, even if one is convinced of one's own merits, there comes a moment when, if everyone (or at least those who occupy the places of authority in society) sends us the opposite message, we end up subscribing to it.

This displacement may have contributed to another possible predisposing/vulnerability factor in the development of Balinska's ED – her sense of alienation from the other girls at school: 'Les filles étaient gentilles, mais je n'avais rien en commun avec elles. Elles s'intéressaient déjà aux sorties, aux vêtements, alors que je passais mon temps à faire de la musique, à lire,

39 Zourai, Fawzia, *Ce pays dont je meurs* (Paris: Pocket, 2001). Note that the anorectic character in this novel, based on a real-life event of death by anorexia nervosa, was born in France to Algerian parents, so did not literally migrate. However, she was exposed to her family's traumas ensuing from the migration; went on frequent visits with this family back to Algeria, involving culture clashes between Algeria and her homeland France that could well have been destabilising; and wanted desperately, but failed, to be taken for a 'real' French person in France.

40 Calife, Anne, *Meurs la faim* (The Menthol House, 2010) (previously published under the name of Anne Colmerauer, *Meurs la faim* [Paris: Gallimard, 1999]).

à écrire des histoires' [The girls were kind, but I had nothing in common with them. They were already interested in going out and in clothes, while I passed my time making music, reading and writing stories] (p. 26). Her alterity becomes a psychological burden: 'ma solitude et le fait d'être « différente » à tant d'égards me pesaient' [my solitude and the fact of being 'different' weighed on me in so many ways] (p. 27)

Yet another predisposing/vulnerability factor was Balinska's prodromal revulsion for menstruation. In her commentary on this, the aspiration to purity that is a salient trait in a good number of the primary texts, and to which I will return, is implicit: 'L'autre aspect des règles qui me rebutait était un fort sentiment d' « impur » ; en somme, je trouvais cela dégoûtant' [The other aspect of periods that repelled me was a strong 'unclean' feeling; in short, I found it disgusting] (p. 36). Another avatar of this aspiration, or rather its abhorred negation, is her reaction to having enjoyed eating a piece of her birthday cake, for shortly afterwards she is engulfed by a sense of unbearable guilt and impurity: 'Un peu plus tard, en travaillant mon instrument de musique, je fus d'un seul coup prise d'un sentiment absolument insupportable de culpabilité et d'*impureté* à l'égard de l'aliment que je venais d'absorber' [A little later, while practising my musical instrument, I was suddenly struck by an absolutely unbearable feeling of guilt and *impurity* for the food I had just absorbed] (p. 41; my emphasis). Finally, the requirement from her gym teacher that pupils should for one week note down everything they ate, combined with her sister's counting of the morsels of bread she (Balinska the narrator) was consuming, destroyed her previously spontaneous relationship with eating (p. 36). Relevant in the secondary literature here is Muriel Darmon's sociological analysis of the role of *prescripteurs, incitateurs* and *prescripteurs*.[41] In Balinska's case, the gym teacher would qualify in Darmon's typology as a *prescripteur*: 'Les *prescripteurs* sont des professionnels. Ce peut être un médecin, un nutritionniste ou un entraîneur sportif, qui prescrit un régime spontanément ou à la demande de l'interviewée – cette dernière ayant pu auparavant être incitée à solliciter cette prescription' [*Prescripteurs* are professionals. It can be a doctor, a nutritionist or a sports trainer who prescribes a diet spontaneously or at the request of the interviewee – the latter having previously been encouraged to seek this prescription].[42]

41 Darmon, Muriel, *Devenir anorexique. Une approche sociologique* (Paris: La Découverte, 2003), pp. 112–13.

42 Darmon 2003: 112.

So much for the variety of possible predisposing/vulnerability factors in the genesis of Balinska's anorexia nervosa. Let us now examine her inscription of what happened once she had begun to fall prey to it. As remarked above, the chief emphasis of her testimony is on sheer suffering. There is a parallel with the infernal lexicon deployed by Durand and Loupias to evoke the intense anguish of EDs in general (on which I have previously commented in my 2015 article).[43] To evoke her descent into anorexia nervosa, Balinska uses the formulation 'descente aux enfers' [descent into hell] (p. 36), adding parenthetically 'le terme n'est pas trop fort' [the term is not too strong] (p. 36). As her anorexia becomes established, depression and anhedonia set in: 'Je me rendais compte de deux choses seulement : d'une part, j'étais déprimée, je pleurais beaucoup, je n'avais plus envie de rien' [I only realised two things: on the one hand, I was depressed, I cried a lot, I no longer wanted anything] (p. 41). And in a transcribed extract from Balinska's diary, dated 27 September 1981, she conveys the vividly painful memories of depression during her anorexic years: '*Je suis tellement déprimée que je ne sais plus quoi faire, ni penser*' [*I am so depressed that I don't know what to do anymore, nor what to think*] (p. 77; Balinska's emphasis).[44] Notation of such deep depression abuts onto another question: that of an unconscious wish for death. The theory that anorexia nervosa is a passive and/or unconscious form of suicide has already been discussed above in relation to Valère, for whom it was eminently relevant. In another transcribed extract from her diary, dated 29 July 1981, Balinska writes: '*Je ne veux pas mourir – la pensée même me terrifie. Mais vu comment les choses se passent, tu comprendras que cette pensée me visite dans mes rêves*' [*I do not want to die – the very thought terrifies me. But given what has happened, you will understand that this thought visits me in my dreams*] (p. 76; Balinska's emphasis). Again, this pull towards death, conscious or unconscious, has been noted by clinicians:

> During severe emaciation, it is hard to argue that death is far away, figuratively or realistically. The appearance of the patient attests to this fact and despite initial denial, many will recount death-related dream

43 Cairns 2015: passim.

44 Balinska uses italics when quoting from various sources such as her diary or letters or poems. Italics here and in other citations are Balinska's and reflect this practice.

imagery, concerns and preoccupations if enquiry is made in a suitably open-ended and impersonal manner (Jackson et al, 1993).[45]

See also p. 86, where her preoccupation with death, metaphorised as 'l'ombre de la mort' [the shadow of death], reappears.

> À ma sortie de la clinique commençait une longue période vécue dans l'ombre de la mort. J'étais tellement persuadée de ma mort prochaine que je trouvais inutile de m'acheter des vêtements : à quoi bon puisque je ne serais plus là pour les porter la saison suivante ? (p. 86)

> When I left the clinic, I began a long time living in the shadow of death. I was so convinced of my impending death that I found it useless to buy clothes: what good was it because I would not be there to wear them the following season?

The following cameo portrait of the anorexic syndrome is particularly powerful in its concise distillation of the condition's debilitating symptomatology and in its negative poeticisation of that condition as the valley of shadows of death (which concords with the metaphorical 'l'ombre de la mort' [shadow of death] of p. 86):

> Ces quelques phrases, que j'ai inscrites dans mon journal intime à 17 ans, résument à elles seules l'état anorexique : l'horreur du quotidien, la proximité de la mort, le désespoir, la lassitude totale, le froid glacial qui habite le corps et la peur du monde. L'expression biblique « la vallée de l'ombre de la mort » sied particulièrement bien à l'anorexie, car c'est la mort dans la vie, la vieillesse dans la jeunesse, la famine dans l'abondance et le froid en permanence. (p. 81)

> These few sentences, which I wrote in my diary at age 17, summarize alone the anorectic state: the horror of everyday life, the proximity of death, despair, total weariness, the freezing cold that inhabits the body and the fear of the world. The biblical expression 'the valley of the shadow of death' is particularly suited to anorexia, because it is death in life, old age in youth, famine in abundance and constant cold.

On a less dramatic note, but still of importance, are other aspects of her anorexic condition. One is exhausting over-investment in school

45 Beumont, P.V.J., Russell, J.D., and Touyz, S.W., 'Psychological concerns in the maintenance of dieting disorders', in Szmukler et al. 1995, pp. 221–41 (234). Their reference is to Jackson, C., Tabin, J., Russell, J., and Touyz, S.W., 'Themes of death: Helmut Thomas' anorexia nervosa (1987): A research note', *International Journal of Eating Disorders*, 14, 4 (1993), 433–37.

or university studies, identified in the secondary literature as standard among (young) anorectics (see: 'je me poussais de plus en plus pour réussir en classe, mettant un zèle extrême dans mon travail, passant les vacances de printemps à peaufiner un rapport d'histoire' [I pushed myself more and more to succeed in class, putting extreme zeal into my work, spending the spring holidays tweaking a history report] (p. 38). Isomorphic with this is the compulsion to be ever-, and over-, active, another common symptom of anorexia nervosa inscribed in much of the primary literature:[46]

> […] l'état anorexique détruit l'énergie propre aux âges jeunes et la remplace par une frénésie nerveuse. […]
>
> On entend souvent dire que les anorexiques sont des « hyperactives », douées d'une énergie peu commune. […] L'activité intense déployée par l'anorexique n'a pas comme moteur l'énergie naturelle d'un organisme en bonne santé, mais une force qui la pousse inexorablement à agir, alors qu'elle est épuisée. (p. 43)

> […] the anorectic state destroys the energy characteristic of young age and replaces it with a nervous frenzy. […]
>
> It is often said that anorectics are 'hyperactive', endowed with an unusual energy. […] The intense activity of the anorectic is not driven by the natural energy of a healthy body, but by a force that pushes it inexorably to act while it is exhausted.

Greatly exacerbating such fatigue in both cases (viz., quasi-demential studying, and hyper-activity more generally) is deeply inadequate sleep: 'Mon sommeil était léger, court, hanté par les cauchemars' [my sleep was light, short and haunted by nightmares] (p. 44). The punishing over-investment in study also reflects another trait commonly identified in the secondary literature as characterising anorectics: perfectionism. Bardone-Cone et al. 2007 report:

> Perfectionism has long been linked with eating disorders. Indeed, eating disorder pioneer Hilde Bruch characterised young anorexia nervosa (AN) patients as fulfilling 'every parent's and teacher's idea of perfection' and demonstrating 'pleasing superperfection' (Bruch, 1978, p. 59). While the link with AN is longstanding and broadly accepted, the relation of perfectionism to bulimia nervosa is less clear.[47]

46 See the section 'Hyperactivity/Hyperintellectuality/Over-investment in School or University Studies' in the Bibliographical Appendix.

47 Bardone-Cone, A.M., Wonderlich, S.A., Frost, R.O., Bulik, C.M., Mitchell, J.E., Uppala, S., and Simonich, H., 'Perfectionism and eating disorders: Current

> [...] the existing evidence supports premorbid perfectionism predicting eating disorders, especially AN.[48]

Such perfectionism is evinced in Balinska's (over-)reaction to receiving a bad mark in history, her favourite school subject, as she prepares for the *baccaulauréat*:

> [...] un jour, ayant reçu une mauvaise note en histoire alors que c'était ma matière préférée, je revins à la maison, me jetai sur mon lit et annonçai à mes parents que plus jamais je n'y retournerais. [...] Aucun des professeurs n'a essayé de m'aider à comprendre mes erreurs malgré mes demandes répétées. J'en conclus que je n'étais pas intellectuelle et je perdis toute confiance en moi-même. (pp. 87–88)

> [...] one day, having received a bad grade in history even though it was my favourite subject, I came home, threw myself on my bed and announced to my parents that never again would I return there. [...] None of the teachers tried to help me understand my mistakes despite my repeated requests. I concluded that I was not intellectual and I lost all confidence in myself.

The loss of any self-confidence simply aggravates her anorexic condition (moreover, the secondary literature identifies lack of self-confidence as already being a predisposing/vulnerability factor in the onset of anorexia).

Another facet of her anorexia nervosa is biological dysregulation: amenorrhea before significant weight loss, which Balinska presents as quasi-universal among pre-anorectics.

> J'avais perdu un peu de poids, mais de façon imperceptible – pas plus de un ou deux kilos, quoi qu'il en soit pas suffisamment pour provoquer une aménorhée, pourtant je n'avais plus mes règles. *Ce trait serait commun à presque toutes les anorexiques* : contrairement à *la « loi » biologique*, elles perdent leur règles *avant* que le processus d'amaigrissement ne se déclenche. (p. 39; first emphasis is mine)

> I had lost a little weight, but imperceptibly – no more than one or two kilos, whatever it was not enough to cause amenorrhea, yet I did not have my period anymore. *This trait would be common to almost all*

status and future directions', *Clinical Psychology Review*, 27 (2007), 384–405 (385). Their reference is to Bruch, Hilde, *The Golden Cage: The Enigma of Anorexia Nervosa* (Cambridge, MA: Harvard University Press, 1978).

48 Bardone-Cone et al. 2007: 392.

> *anorectics*: contrary to *the biological 'law'*, their periods stop *before* the severe weight loss begins.

This curious phenomenon is probably unfamiliar to most lay readers and is mentioned infrequently in the secondary literature. Exceptions to this paucity are provided in my endnote, but none of these substantiate Balinska's view of the phenomenon as quasi-universal.[49] On this specific point, Balinska's argument for the anorectic's quasi universal defiance

49 Examples of these exceptions include the following. In 1995, Arnold A. Andersen referred to '[t]he early loss of periods', but his hypothetical explanation for it, viz. that this early loss 'may reflect a non-specific endocrine response to weight loss in that group of individuals who only function normally at the upper part of a normally distributed weight range', does not apply to Balinska, who prior to becoming anorexic had functioned normally at a modest weight (she refers to herself as having been slim before onset of the illness). See Andersen, Arnold A., 'Sequencing treatment decisions: Cooperation or conflict between therapist and patient', in Szmukler et al. 1995, pp. 363–79 (373). In the same edited collection, Walter Vandereycken insisted '[b]ut an early onset of amenorrhea in anorexics, often occurring before any appreciable weight loss, as well as the persistence of menstrual dysfunction after recovery, remained to be explained. Russell began to speculate that some endocrine disturbances in anorexia nervosa were primary of [*sic*] nature, "not as a sequel of malnutrition but as a more fundamental feature of the illness" (Russell and Beardwood 1970: 361). Here, he hypothesised a failure of the anterior hypothalamic mechanisms concerned with the control of rhythmic gonadtrophin secretion.' See Vandereycken, Walter, 'Food for thought: Gerald Russell's writings on eating disorders', in Szmukler et al. 1995, pp. 401–6 (404). NB: the full reference for Russell and Beardwood, 1970: 361 is Russell, G.F.M. and Beardwood, C.J., 'Amenorrhoea in the feeding disorders: Anorexia nervosa and obesity', *Psychotherapy and Psychosomatics*, 18 (1970), 359–64 (361). In 2004, psychiatrist Philippe Jeammet observed, 'Il apparaît en effet clairement que le déficit pondéral ne peut, à lui seul, expliquer l'aménorrhée. Dans 20 % des cas, celle-ci précède l'amaigrissement' [It is clear to see that weight loss alone cannot explain amenorrhea. In 20% of cases, it precedes weight loss] (Jeammet 2004: 175). Two years later, in his *Eating and Weight Disorders* (Hove/New York: Psychology Press, 2006), p. 7, Carlos M. Grilo remarked: '[a]menorrhea, however, is sometimes seen in individuals before large weight losses, but is largely unknown by the lay public/non-medical specialists (and even by several such specialists)'. More recently, Winkler, Laura Al-Dakhiel, Frølich, Jacob Stampe, Schulpen, Maya and Støvling, René Klinkby, 'Body composition and menstrual status in adults with a history of anorexia nervosa – At what fat percentage is the menstrual cycle restored?', *International Journal of Eating Disorders*, 50, 4 (2017), 370–77 (371), stated, 'In many cases the menstrual bleeds will subside before a significant weight loss.'

of the 'laws' of biology (p. 39) – as encoded in the disciplines of medicine and clinical physiology – does not appear to be borne out by empirical evidence, but rather to be a questionable extrapolation and over-generalisation from her personal experience. But when she recounts her *own* experience of defying these biological 'laws', there is no such dubiety, and her points carry more weight. One instance is the statement that when she reached her lowest body weight ever, she had not in the preceding period been eating any less than usual.

A further facet of her illness signalled above, but worth expanding on here from a perspective other than that of the anorectic's aspiration to purity, is the crisis triggered by her eating a piece of the cake made for her 15th birthday:

> [...] j'étais parfaitement consciente que le dessert dans cette histoire était circonstanciel : il s'agissait en réalité d'un phénomène beaucoup plus grave : je perdais le contrôle de mes désirs – lesquels il s'agissait donc de nier. Dans mon for intérieur, j'étais affolée. À partir de ce jour-là, je ne me suis plus jamais sentie libre : j'étais mon propre esclave. Aujourd'hui, même si je suis « guérie », cette liberté ne m'est pas totalement revenue. (pp. 41–42)

> [...] I was perfectly aware that the dessert in this story was circumstantial: in reality it was a much more serious phenomenon: I lost control of my desires – those that I had to deny. Deep down in my heart, I was distraught. From that day on, I never felt free again: I was my own slave. Today, even though I am 'healed', this freedom has not completely returned to me.

The drive for control over one's desires and panic at its loss are common to the vast majority of anorectics. The metaphor of enslavement to oneself, or to the punitive anorectic self one has become, illustrates one of the sad paradoxes of anorexia nervosa: namely, the striving for self-control that becomes pathological in its drastic self-denial of food, and when successful leads to pride in such self-control, set against (intermittent) awareness of being enslaved to the condition, and thus of not being in control after all.

Another symptom – or perhaps put more accurately, underlying causal factor among others – of the anorexic condition is the quest for putative purity. This quest is prominent at several points in Balinska's text: see pp. 83, 84, 201, 247. On these pages, we witness mental transgression of the simple fact that all bodies need food to survive, along with figurative transformation of food into a bodily pollutant (as mentioned above, in my Conclusion I briefly discuss Julia Kristeva's views on food's status as a pollutant in certain cultural contexts). Crucially, this transgression, which is motivated by a quest for perceived inner purity, is linked to the wish, conscious or unconscious, to erect a boundary between the anorexic body and the exterior world (p. 83). (Interestingly, in 'la nourriture vient de l'extérieur souiller l'intérieur' [food comes from the exterior to contaminate the interior] (p. 83), Balinska uses exactly the same verb as Kristeva, 'souiller' [to contaminate], in Kristeva's statement 'toute nourriture est susceptible de souiller' [any food is likely to contaminate].[50]) Fear of the exterior, of everything that comes from the outside (reiterated on p. 247), indicates the anorectic's need to maintain a boundary between herself and everything that comes from outside oneself: at face value, primarily food, but also, and underlying the rejection of food, other human beings and relationships with them (p. 83). The secondary literature often finds that those who go on to develop anorexia nervosa have had difficulty in interpersonal relationships prior to the onset of their illness, and that the illness merely intensifies that difficulty. Finally on the motif of purity, the word 'pureté' [purity] on p. 84 is also used by Balinska to stress the need for any treatment to help the anorexic 'à comprendre ce que représente pour elle la notion de pureté afin de le traduire dans sa vie quotidienne autrement que par la logique de la privation' [to understand what the notion of purity represents for her in order to translate it into her daily life other than through the logic of deprivation]. Much later on in her testimony, Balinska makes her own efforts at such understanding, and in relation to her own case.

> Quelle est cette « pureté intérieure » ? La non-corruption, l'innocence, la virginité… la non-contamination par l'horreur du monde extérieur, et ainsi la non-participation à la souffrance des autres ? Oui, je crois rétrospectivement que la pureté signifiait pour moi, théoriquement, ne pas prendre part, d'aucune façon que ce soit, à ce qui engendre la souffrance. (p. 201)

> What is this 'inner purity'? Non-corruption, innocence, virginity… non-contamination by the horror of the outside world, and thus the non-participation in the suffering of others? Yes, I believe in hindsight that purity meant for me, theoretically, not to be involved, in any way whatsoever, in that which causes suffering.

50 Kristeva, Julia, *Pouvoirs de l'horreur: essai sur l'abjection* (Paris: Éditions du Seuil, 1980), p. 91.

(Cf. Marie Dupont's horror faced with the suffering of others in the world in her *Maman, pourquoi tu ne manges pas? Mon combat contre l'anorexie* [2007].)[51] The question that arises is: does the last sentence from the Balinska extract above have a genuinely sociotropic basis, or is it an unconscious attempt to exculpate herself from the rejection of other human beings who form a significant part of the feared exterior world – a rejection based on the difficulties in interpersonal relationships with other human beings remarked upon above?

Perhaps surprisingly, the greatest disabling feature of anorexia asserted by Balinska is the loss of one's youth (recall that a large proportion of anorectics develop the condition in adolescence).

> Quand je pense au handicap le plus lourd à porter dans l'anorexie, je pense à la perte de la jeunesse. Elle se situe à deux niveaux. D'une part, l'état anorexique détruit l'énergie propre aux âges jeunes et la remplace par une frénésie nerveuse. D'autre part, elle ôte à sa victime une partie fondamentale et irremplaçable de la vie : l'adolescence, voire, dans certains cas (comme le mien), la jeunesse toute entière. (p. 43)

> When I think of the most serious disability in anorexia, I think of the loss of youth. It is on two levels. On the one hand, the anorectic state destroys the energy characteristic of young age and replaces it with a nervous frenzy. On the other hand, it takes away from its victim a fundamental and irreplaceable part of life: adolescence, or, in some cases (like mine), the whole youth.

This is rarely reflected in the secondary literature on anorexic experience, but one exception is the following: 'the sufferer [...] is also in the process of losing years of her youth'.[52] Much later on, when the narrative is recounting recovery in her late twenties, Balinska gives a new conceptual twist to this observation about loss of one's youth when one suffers from anorexia nervosa before reaching adulthood. As well as destroying normal elements of youth, the illness also places the sufferer in a state of quasi-*childhood* vis-à-vis other human beings and relationships with them.

> Alors que mes contemporains avaient fait le cheminement de l'adolescence et de la première jeunesse, j'avais, moi, la double impression d'être

51 Dupont, Marie, *Maman, pourquoi tu ne manges pas ? Mon combat contre l'anorexie* (Paris: Philippe Rey, 2007), pp. 40–41 and 68.

52 Duker, Marilyn and Slade, Roger, *Anorexia Nervosa and Bulimia: How to Help* (Milton Keynes/Philadelphia, PA: Open University Press, 1988), p. 49.

> vieillie par l'épreuve [de 15 ans d'anorexie], mais presque enfant par ma connaissance du monde adulte. Intellectuellement, j'étais très développée, mais, pour de nombreux aspects de la vie courante, j'étais étonnamment naïve. (p. 214)

> While my peers had made the journey of adolescence and early youth, I had the dual impression of being aged by the experience [of 15 years of anorexia], but almost childlike in my knowledge of the adult world. Intellectually, I was very developed, but when it came to many aspects of everyday life, I was surprisingly naive.

Returning to the key aspect of anorexia nervosa stressed by Balinska over and over again, namely sheer suffering, insight into one avatar of the latter is given in the following extract. Its length is justified by the breadth of aperture it gives the reader onto the specific form of suffering inflicted on the anorectic by standard (French) hospital treatment of her condition in the 1980s:

> Tout d'abord, on m'a enfermée sans me stipuler les termes du « contrat », et j'ai mis six semaines avant de les comprendre. Dès lors, cela m'est apparu comme étant d'une hypocrisie totale : on n'allait même pas m'aider à comprendre la source de mon mal ; tout ce qu'on voulait, c'était de voir monter l'aiguille du pèse-personne. Se souciait-on vraiment de ce qui m'arriverait à la suite de mon hospitalisation ? Je n'arrivais pas à le croire et me sentais donc trahie par le monde des soignants qui était, forcément, le monde des adultes. Qui plus est, le milieu psychiatrique était dominé par les hommes, des hommes qui entraient dans ma chambre sans frapper, des hommes avec lesquels je devais converser, à 16 ans, en chemise de nuit, des hommes qui s'exprimaient par demi-phrases, traitaient mes propos d'absurdes et, souvent, qui partaient alors que j'étais en milieu de phrase. Qui m'écoutait, alors que l'anorexique meurt d'envie d'être entendue ? (p. 84)

> First of all, they locked me up without stipulating the terms of the 'contract', and it took me six weeks to understand them. From then on, it seemed to me to be utter hypocrisy: they weren't even going to help me understand the source of my pain; all they wanted was to see the scale needle go up. Were they really worried about what would happen to me as a result of my hospitalisation? I couldn't believe it and felt betrayed by the world of caregivers, which was, of course, the world of adults. What's more, the psychiatric environment was dominated by men, men who entered my room without knocking, men with whom I had to converse, aged 16, in nightgown, men who spoke in half-sentences, treated my remarks as absurd, and often left when I was in the middle of the sentence. Who listened to me when the anorexic was dying to be heard?

This quotation recalls an earlier (1970s) and broader critique of the noxious effects that can arise from psychiatrists' and psychoanalysts' (mis)treatment of their patients generally: Meares and Hobson (1977).[53] The quotation contains three striking elements. The first is the confluence with Valère's vehement sense of the medical corps' hypocrisy, in fact of its mendacity. The second is the confluence, in the last clause, with Durand's stress on the need for anorectics (and for Durand, those with mental health problems generally) to be listened to. On this defect, see the refreshingly honest admission by three specialists in the treatment of EDs: 'Therapeutic pitfalls which must be avoided include failing to listen to what the patient is saying.'[54] Another trio (including two of the same) of medical practitioners aver, precisely, that the clinician treating inpatient anorexic patients (though they are referring only to adolescent cases) should 'facilitate the expression of inner feelings' by such patients.[55] The third, but by no means least important element, is the patriarchally abusive nature of the male-dominated medical corps. Related to this, one 1988 critique in the secondary literature of that corps' conduct is of particular import.

> Feminists meanwhile are likely to see the problem of helping anorexics in the context of the whole historic struggle of women to regain control over their own bodies. For them it is an example to set alongside the issues of legitimacy, contraception and access to medical care for specifically female complaints. To accept that the effects of starvation play an important part in creating anorexia nervosa too easily seems to allow or condone coercive refeeding programmes, a course which, given the predominance of men in positions of power within the medical profession, tends to take the form of a classic male/female confrontation for control over a woman's body.[56]

This gendered approach tallies with a further recollection, namely that the only higher-status member of Balinska's 'care' team in the hospital who actually listened to her was a woman:

> À part une infirmière et quelques aides-soignantes qui avaient éprouvé pour moi de l'amitié, seul un soignant à proprement parler avait eu,

53 Meares, R. and Hobson, R., 'The persecutory therapist', *British Journal of Medical Psychology*, 50 (1977), 349–59 (passim).

54 Beumont, P.V.J., Russell, J.D. and Touyz, S.W., 'Psychological concerns in the maintenance of dieting disorders', in Szmukler et al. 1995, pp. 221–41 (237).

55 Touyz et al. 1995, pp. 247–70 (248).

56 Duker and Slade 1988: 35.

> au bout d'un certain temps, une attitude d'écoute envers moi. C'était la femme, médecin, que j'évoquais dans mon journal : Mme R. Elle avait été elle-même, disait-on, anorexique – les aides-soignantes me l'avaient rapporté – et souffrait à l'époque de tendances boulimiques : on l'avait vue à la cantine avaler des quantités insensées. À la regarder, elle n'était évidemment pas sortie de ses problèmes : très maigre, son trouble intérieur s'affichait sur son visage. Et cette circonstance me paraissait bizarre, injuste, absurde : Mme R., de l'autre côté en tant que médecin, était considérée comme « normale », elle était libre, elle était même censée me soigner, alors que moi, en tant que patiente, j'étais « anormale », emprisonnée, dépendante. Mme R. était la plus humaine et la plus intelligente dans son écoute. Les autres médecins, tous hommes, procédaient par la provocation. (p. 85)
>
> Apart from a nurse and some caregivers who had shown friendship to me, only one caregiver strictly speaking had displayed, after a while, a desire to listen to me. It was the woman, a doctor, whom I mentioned in my diary: Mrs. R. She had, apparently, been anorectic herself – the caregivers had told me – and was suffering at the time from bulimia: we had seen her in the canteen swallowing insane amounts of food. To look at her, she had obviously not overcome these problems: she was very thin and her inner trouble was displayed on her face. And this circumstance seemed strange, unjust and absurd to me: on the one hand, Mrs. R., as a doctor, was considered 'normal', she was free, she was even supposed to treat me, whereas me, as a patient, I was 'abnormal', imprisoned, dependent. Mrs. R. was the most humane and the most intelligent in way of listening. The other doctors, all men, proceeded by provocation.

Notable here are three elements: that the sole doctor who actually listens to Balinska is a woman; that this female doctor has personal experience of anorexia nervosa (and also of bulimia nervosa), and thus possesses insider insight; and that all the other doctors, all male, instead of trying to elicit verbal self-expression from her simply seek rather to provoke and thus, insidiously, to undermine their patient. Further types of destructive measures taken by the male doctors meant to be caring for Balinska are evidenced. One male doctor myopically reduces anorexia nervosa to a mere chemical disorder/disturbance, and so limits his treatment of Balinska to the sole administration of numerous anti-depressant and anxiolytic drugs. The side-effects of this incompetent doctor's 'treatment' include memory loss (p. 95), but also, more gravely, 'une inflammation de la paroi intestinale par surdosage médicamenteux' [an inflammation of the intestinal wall due to drug overdose] (p. 96).

Male doctors' abuse of power is less obvious in the valuable cross-cultural optic provided on inpatient treatment of anorexia nervosa in the 1980s (to be precise, in 1986, when Balinska was 21 years old). This optic is located in the diary account she subsequently composed of her second, and last, experience of hospitalisation for anorexia nervosa, this time in a large English psychiatric hospital situated in the London region (pp. 105–6). My surmise is that this English centre for EDs was the Maudsley Hospital, widely viewed as *the* leading British centre for treatment of such disorders. Balinska was unusually fortunate in being given the right to 'trial' the regime for one week, at the end of which she could decide to stay or leave (p. 106). Contrarily, she was unfortunate in finding the regime there intolerable, prompting her departure after eight days (p. 105).

There were several reasons for her departure. One was the coercive nature of the regime at this English hospital (cf. Valère's French hospital experience, and Balinska's own first experience of French hospital treatment for anorexia nervosa). One dimension to this coercion was emotional blackmail, exposed in the following: 'aucune des filles n'avait le droit de se lever de table tant que toutes n'avaient pas terminé de manger' [none of the girls were allowed to get up from the table until everyone had finished eating] (p. 113, footnote 3). Those patients who had themselves finished their meal, but were forbidden to leave the table because of another patient who had not, would almost inevitably feel resentment towards the slower eating patient, and could easily develop a hostile attitude towards her, leading them to exert emotional blackmail on the slower-eater (a practice with Foucauldian overtones). Other negative aspects of the treatment regime at this English hospital were not so much coercive or based on emotional blackmail, but rather denial of basic human rights to a modicum of privacy and to personal dignity. One example is '*Nous n'avions pas le droit de tirer les rideaux de peur que nous fissions de la gymnastique en cachette*' [*We were not allowed to draw the curtains because they were afraid we would do gymnastics in secret*] (p. 115; Balinska's emphasis). Further, although this is based on anecdote rather than proven evidence, the following comment from a fellow patient indicates the forensic sureveillance, presumably based at least partly on suspicion, to which anorexic patients are subjected: '*Chacun de tes gestes est rapporté, même si tu ne dis rien*' [*Every one of your gestures is reported, even if you say nothing*] (p. 122; Balinska's emphasis). Finally, although this may have been due to financial constraints imposed by an over-stretched NHS budget, the physical environment in which these patients are treated is degrading: 'Le service de psychiatrie général était sale, pour ne pas dire crasseux. La moquette de la salle de réunions était recouverte de taches et de mégots' [The general psychiatry ward was dirty, even filthy. The carpet in the meeting room was covered with stains and cigarette butts] (p. 123).

Although the following is obviously not confined to the English psychiatric hospital Balinska chose to leave after only eight days, we should heed her warning of the perniciously contaminatory effects of treating anorectics together, effects rarely if ever acknowledged by medical professions specialising in EDs:

> L'hospitalisation dans la région de Londres avait donc été un échec : si j'étais restée, j'en suis persuadée, je serais devenue encore plus marquée par le comportement anorexique, qui peut être contagieux entre filles atteintes du même mal. Je me souviens justement que les filles à Londres avaient attiré mon attention sur des sujets relatifs au corps et à la nourriture auxquels je n'avais pas jusque-là pensé, mais qui se sont rapidement ajouté à ma longue liste de « phobies ». (p. 126)
>
> Hospitalization in the London area had therefore been a failure: if I had remained, I am sure, I would have become even more marked by anorectic behavior, which can be contagious between girls with the same illness. I remember that the girls in London had drawn my attention to body and food topics that I had not previously thought of, but which quickly added to my long list of 'phobias'.

The main deleterious effect of treating inpatient anorectics together, Balinska suggests, is the morbid competitiveness about weight loss/food avoidance it provokes.

The fact that the doctors 'les photographiaient nues, de face et de profil, pour leurs recherches' [photographed them naked, front-on and in profile, for their research] (p. 127) reveals a degradation, or at least an affront to the anorexic patient's dignity, which has also been noted above, albeit flowing from different factors of this English hospital's treatment regime for anorexia nervosa. Moreover, the taking of photographs of anorectics naked, from the front and from the side, recalls the sinister practices of Nazi concentration camps. Not as chilling as the recall of such Nazi practices, but still implying the treatment of anorectics as prisoners (cf. Valère) is Balinska's designation of her fellow patients as 'copénitentiaires' [cellmates] (p. 127). The trope of anorectics as prisoners recurs later on; however, this time it denotes not the experience of hospitalisation, but rather the anorectic's entrapment in her own disturbed mind: '*Parfois, j'ai tellement faim que je rêve de certaines nourritures, tels des prisonniers de guerre*' [*Sometimes, I was so hungry that I dreamt of certain foods, just like prisoners of war did*] (p. 146; Balinska's emphasis).

Finally, Balinska's observations bring to light the disabling institutionalisation of anorectics who have undergone multiple hospitalisations, and their resulting inability to adapt to life outside hospital:

> En observant ces filles, dont la plupart en étaient à leur énième hospitalisation, et à écouter leurs récits d'autres filles anorexiques qu'elles avaient connues, j'ai compris que l' « institutionnalisation » façonnait des créatures qui n'avaient plus rien dans leur vie à part l'anorexie. Leur peur de l' « impur » extérieur n'étant pas allégée, mais au contraire aggravée, par l'attitude qu'elles rencontraient à l'hôpital – qui n'était autre que celle du bâton et de la carotte pour les « guérir » -, elles se protégeaient derrière le seul bouclier à leur disposition : leur maladie. C'était un cercle vicieux : plus elles subissaient d'hospitalisations, plus elles devenaient anorexiques car, interrompant études, travail, relations sociales, elles n'avaient plus rien pour meubler leurs vies et sentaient douloureusement, mais inconsciemment, qu'elles risquaient de perdre complètement leur identité. (p. 126)

> By observing these girls, most of whom were on their umpteenth hospitalization, and listening to their stories of other anorectic girls they had known, I realized that 'institutionalization' was shaping creatures that had nothing left in their lives apart from anorexia. Their fear of the 'impure' outside is not alleviated but, on the contrary, aggravated by the attitude they were met with at the hospital – which was none other than that of the stick and carrot to 'heal' them – they protected themselves behind the only shield at their disposal: their illness. It was a vicious circle: the more they were hospitalised, the more they became anorectic because, with their education, work and social relations interrupted, they had nothing left to fill their lives and felt painfully, but unconsciously, that they risked a complete loss of identity.

Turning to other significant aspects of Balinska's text, one such is the mind–body dualism/split featuring in much of my primary corpus.[57] This is initially found in a variant form in the following comment:

> Lorsqu'on est en pleine crise anorexique, il y a de brefs moments où l'on est persuadé de pouvoir s'aider soi-même. Par une espèce de jeu perfide,

57 See the section 'Mind–Body Split/Mind–Body Dualism' in the Bibliographical Appendix.

> l'esprit anorexique fait croire à sa victime qu'il peut la subjuguer par un simple acte de volonté. (p. 105)
>
> When one is in the midst of an anorectic crisis, there are brief moments when one is persuaded to be able to help oneself. By way of a deceitful game, the anorectic mind makes the victim believe that it can subjugate her by a simple act of volition.

The variant is that this is not so much a mind–body dualism/split as a dualism/split between an incorporeal 'anorexic mind' and a human subject who, it is implied, sometimes does not have such a mind. Later on, the mind–body dualism/split is less equivocal, but most unusually within the collective primary corpus it is presented positively:

> [...] la même capacité démesurée que j'avais de me séparer de moi-même, de sortir de mon corps, de le voir comme une entité étrangère à mon véritable être – cette capacité qui me faisait tant souffrir – me permettait aussi de me distancier des problèmes qu'elle engendrait : certes, je ne pouvais pas changer de raisonnement, mais j'en percevais l'absurdité. Et le fait de distinguer le sens du non-sens m'a empêchée de sombrer complètement dans la folie. (p. 147)
>
> [...] the same disproportionate ability I had to separate myself from myself, to exit my body, to see it as an entity foreign to my real being – this capacity that made me suffer so much – also allowed me to distance myself from problems that it engendered: certainly, I could not change the reasoning, but I perceived the absurdity in it. And distinguishing the meaning of nonsense prevented me from sinking completely into madness. (p.147)

Equally unequivocally, but decidedly negatively this time, the mind–body dualism/split is also poetically conveyed in Balinska's intertextual allusion to Lewis Carroll's *Alice's Adventures in Wonderland* (1865),[58] in which she posits several striking isomorphisms between Alice's experiences and those of anorectics.[59] One such isomorphism is the reaction to bodily transformation – in Alice's case, induced by a magic potion rather than the anorexic's conscious 'work' on modifying her body, but both being marked by the mind's sense of alienation from

58 Carroll, Lewis, *Alice's Adventures in Wonderland* (London: Macmillan, 1865).

59 See Senkbeil, Karsten and Hoppe, Nicola, '"The sickness stands at your shoulder...": Embodiment and cognitive metaphor in Hornbacher's *Wasted: A Memoir of Anorexia and Bulimia*', *Language and Literature*, 25, 1 (2016), 3–17 (12).

body, by loss of control of one's body, and by perception of one's body as an enemy:

> Mais, cette fois-ci, elle devint affreusement grande – si grande que ses jambes s'étaient allongées et éloignées d'elle et qu'elle dut envoyer des mots à ses pieds pour leur demander de se déplacer. D'un seul coup, elle s'était vue comme extérieure à son corps, un corps qu'elle ne reconnaissait plus, dont elle ne voulait plus. Cette image est extraordinaire dans sa proximité avec la vision anorexique. Car, quand on devient anorexique, on a l'impression d'un corps qui nous échappe, qu'on ne contrôle plus (tout en croyant tout faire pour le contrôler), qui est notre ennemi, qui nous empêche d'avancer, de même que la pauvre Alice était – du fait de sa taille trop grande ou trop petite – exclue du Pays des merveilles. (pp. 130–31)

> But this time she became frightfully tall – so great that her legs were stretched out and far away from her, and she had to send written directions to her feet to ask them to move. Suddenly, she saw herself as external to her body, a body she no longer recognised, which she no longer wanted. This image is extraordinary in its proximity to the anorectic vision. Because when we become anorectic, we have the impression of a body that escapes us, that we no longer control (while believing that we are doing everything to control it), which is our enemy, which prevents us from moving forward, in the same way that poor Alice was – because her size was either size too big or too small – excluded from Wonderland.

A second isomorphism between Alice's experiences and those of anorectics is the dark tunnel in which Alice is trapped and that Balinska deems a perfect metaphor for 'la traversée de l'anorexie' [the crossing of anorexia]:

> [...] on avance, mais on n'a pas l'impression d'aboutir, on se sent pris au piège, emprisonné dans des murs d'autant plus difficiles à abattre qu'ils sont invisibles et, tout comme Alice avait eu un aperçu du délicieux jardin, on souffre d'autant plus qu'on sait que, quelque part, il y a une porte de sortie, une autre vie, mais – pas plus qu'elle – on n'arrive à en trouver le chemin. (p. 131)

> [...] we move forward, but we do not have the impression of succeeding, we feel trapped, imprisoned between walls that are all the more difficult to defeat because they are invisible and, just like Alice had a glimpse of the delicious garden, we suffer all the more because we know that somewhere there is a way out, another life, but – no more than her – we cannot find the way.

A third such isomorphism is that of an oneiric existence detached from reality shared by Alice and, if not by all anorectics, then certainly by Balinska:

> Alice rêve ; elle n'est pas dans la réalité, et en fait elle attend de se réveiller. Tout au long de mon anorexie, je me suis sentie comme dans un rêve, ou plutôt dans un cauchemar, dont je n'arrivais pas à me libérer : c'était un brouillard épais, la nuit sourde. Combien de fois je me suis dit : « Si seulement je pouvais me réveiller ! Me réveiller ! » (p. 131)

> Alice dreams; she's not in reality, and in fact she's waiting to wake up. Throughout my anorexia, I felt like I was in a dream, or rather a nightmare, from which I could not free myself: it was a thick fog, the dull night. How many times have I said to myself, 'If only I could wake up! Wake up!'

A fourth isomorphism is the unjust 'justice' (judicial) system whose judgements are capriciously arbitrary yet menacingly sovereign. Just as Alice is arraigned in front of a jury, silenced, threatened by the Queen with decapitation, and stripped of any basic human rights, so Balinska felt she – and the anorectic patient generally – is treated similarly by the medical institution: 'De même qu'Alice, je me sentais jugée et punie de façon arbitraire et, de même qu'Alice, je savais que je n'avais pas le "droit" de parler avant d'avoir retrouvé ma "taille normale" – *car l'anorexique, elle, n'a aucun* droit' [Like Alice, I felt judged and punished arbitrarily and, also like Alice, I knew that I did not have the 'right' to speak until I had returned to my 'normal size' – *because she, the anorectic, has no rights*] (p. 132; Balinska's emphasis).

Finally, the mind–body dualism/split is also discernible in Balinska's ruminations on desire and the deep-rooted belief that anorectics deny themselves desire:

> On dit des anorexiques qu'elles s'interdisent le désir. Mais quel désir ? Le désir serait-il limité aux besoins physiologiques ou, plus précisément, les besoins du corps humain peuvent-ils être entièrement dissociés d'un désir d'ordre spirituel ? Si je m'interdisais de manger, je sentais en moi un désir dévorant de quelque chose que je n'arrivais pas à définir, mais dont l'absence ne me permettait pas de vivre. (p. 133)

> Anorexics are said to forbid desire. But what desire? Would desire be limited to physiological needs or, more precisely, can the needs of the human body be entirely dissociated from a desire for a spiritual order? If I forbade myself to eat, I felt in myself a consuming desire for something that I could not define, but whose absence did not allow me to live.

Other pathognomonic traits of anorexia nervosa are registered in Balinska's testimony. One is social isolation, caused by increasing absorption in the food–weight obsession, along with a desire to avoid any social situation involving eating or even drinking – as very many, if not all, social situations do. A potent simile is used to express Balinska's sense of immense – indeed, planetary – alienation from other human beings: 'Je me sentais piégée dans l'anorexie et je regardais les autres comme s'ils vivaient sur une autre planète dont j'étais séparée par un gouffre infranchissable' [I felt trapped within anorexia and I saw others as if they were living on another planet from which I was separated by an uncrossable chasm] (p. 137). Another pathognomonic trait of anorexia nervosa registered is the typical anorectic's self-denial not just of adequate food intake but also of adequate rest, and even of expenditure on items for oneself. All of these instances of excessive self-discipline (or, to put it in Foucauldian terms, self-surveillance, where the subject becomes her or his own persecutory slave to societal 'laws' or even simply societal expectations), I posit, spring from intense self-loathing and guilt feelings:

> *Je sais que ce n'est pas bien, mais mon antipathie envers moi-même est si intense que je ne peux plus me supporter. C'est comme si j'étais une masse tout entière de culpabilité. Je me sens* toujours *coupable – principalement en ce qui concerne la nourriture, bien sûr, mais pour presque tout le reste aussi : si je me repose, si je ne travaille pas assez, si je m'achète n'importe quoi. Le simple fait d'« etre » me rend coupable.* (p. 145; Balinska's emphasis)
>
> *I know it's not good, but my dislike of myself is so intense that I can't stand myself anymore. It's like I'm a whole mass of guilt. I always feel guilty – mostly about food, of course, but about almost everything else too: if I rest, if I do not work enough, if I buy anything. The mere fact of 'being' makes me guilty.*

Regarding the anorectic's excessive propensity to guilt feelings, Balinska's reflections on pp. 160–61 underscore both the anteriority of these feelings to her illness, and their aggravation at the onset of her illness, to the point where she thinks she has no right to exist, if existence includes pleasure in the face of other human beings' pain (pp. 160–61). As Duker and Slade comment, this heightened sensitivity to suffering in the whole world is characteristic of the anorectic, and their last sentence in the extract below is particularly pertinent to Balinska (cf. Balinska p. 201):

> However, because she cannot allow herself to be aware of another person's need, to acknowledge it, and then not at least try to make an

> effort to respond in a caring way, the sufferer is defenceless against another's wishes and obligations, whether clearly stated, or covert but sensed by her. She does not feel she has the right to refuse. If she does refuse or withdraw to avoid the situation, she feels unutterably guilty. So she is vulnerable not only in relation to her family and friends, but potentially to anyone she meets, including the would-be helper. Responding is the sufferer's responsibility. Characteristically she feels responsible for the whole world.[60]

Tellingly, they add at a later point:

> Being assertive over righteous causes is more acceptable. This kind of assertion is justified because it is on behalf of other people or things. But the whole idea of taking a stand for her own sake she will believe to be morally wrong.[61]

A further pathognomonic trait of anorexia nervosa – indeed one included in the criteria for diagnosis of the condition in the *Diagnostic and Statistical Manual of Mental Disorders*, 4th edition (1994) – and also an extremely common motif in the primary literature is the anorectic's distorted body image.[62] This surfaces in Balinska's reflections, but in inflected, more ambivalent terms than in most other cases in the primary corpus, showing intermittent signs of lucidity: '*Je me sens trop grosse, même si parfois je suis capable de voir combien mon cou est ridicule de maigreur, combien mon visage est enlaidi ; le simple fait de m'asseoir me fait mal au derrière*' [*I feel like I'm too fat, even though sometimes I can see how ridiculously thin my neck is, my face has become so ugly; the simple act of sitting down hurts my bottom*] (p. 146; Balinska's emphasis). And yet another pathognomonic trait of anorexia nervosa – arguably, the most vital predisposing/vulnerability factor, viz., lack of self-esteem/self-confidence – is implicit in Balinska's lack of self-confidence following many years of academic under-achievement, due, as explained above, to under-achievement at school due to highly frequent changes of school and schooling in different languages because of her parents' frequent moves from one country to another. Although she is accepted for postgraduate study in France, this success does nothing to restore her lost self-esteem/self-confidence, leading to overwork while

60 Duker and Slade 1988: 96–97.

61 Duker and Slade 1988: 207.

62 See the section 'Distorted Body-image/Over-estimation of Body Size' in the Bibliographical Appendix.

severely under-nourished (p. 170); over-investment in studies is, as mentioned before, a recurring motif in the primary corpus.

Bifurcating now from what Balinska's phenomenological account of her anorexia nervosa shares with the anorectic's standard pathognomonic traits, I observe that one entirely unique trait in Balinska's account is her narrative of being given hormonal treatment for her illness. This treatment's singularity is no doubt an unsurprising corollary of the medical corps' general dismissal of it as an ineffective treatment for the illness. The American Psychiatric Association classes it as one of the forms of treatment that have no proven value in the case of anorexia nervosa: 'Other somatic treatments, ranging from vitamin and hormone treatments to ECT, have been tried in uncontrolled studies. None has been shown to have specific value in the treatment of anorexia nervosa symptoms.'[63] Yet the hormonal treatment given to Balinska, which artificially induced menstruation, did in fact appear to have been highly beneficial to her (see pp. 180–81). It led to a gradual weight gain without her eating any more, a gain that is not reversed (pp. 181–82). This is a process that most anorexics would find terrifying. While Balinska, atypically, does not express any fear about weight gain, she certainly expresses fear, before the hormonal treatment begins, about the return of menstruation.

> J'allais donc avoir mes règles. L'idée m'était répugnante car avant tout j'avais *peur* de les avoir. Ce n'était pas seulement une hantise devant l' « impur », mais devant l'idée de saigner de façon incontrôlée, c'est-à-dire de ne plus pouvoir me maîtriser. Car, lorsqu'on est dans un état anorexique, on est dans la complète maîtrise de soi-même : *l'identité vient de la maîtrise qu'on a sur soi*, et seulement de là. (pp. 180–81; Balinska's emphasis)

> I was going to have my period. The idea was disgusting to me because above all I was *afraid* of having it. It was not only an obsession with the 'impure', but with the idea of bleeding uncontrollably, that is to say

63 Yager et al. 2006: 50. This statement is followed by a reference to Garfinkel, P.E. and Garner, D.M., *Anorexia Nervosa: A Multidimensional Perspective* (New York: Brunner/Mazel, 1982). See also a much earlier statement about general medical dismissal of hormone treatment for anorexia nervosa: 'Leading medical experts agree on only one point, namely on the uselessness and dangers of hormone therapy (oestrogens and anterior pituitary extracts) and above all of the pituitary transplants advocated by Bergmann, Kylin and Sauerbruch and many of their continental successors' (Palazzoli 1978: 100).

> not being able to control myself anymore. Because when you're in an anorectic state, you are in complete control of yourself: *identity comes from the control one has over oneself*, and only from there.

Of particular note here are the recurrent motif of (putative) purity as primordial for the anorectic and the primordial value placed by her on what she perceives as self-mastery (a delusion that is part of the psychopathology of her illness). The recurrent motif of (putative) purity is pursued in Balinska's following comments:

> Les premiers mois où j'ai subi ces règles artificiellement imposées, je les ai mal vécues. Mais, ensuite, je m'y suis habituée remarquablement vite et n'y prêtais plus beaucoup d'attention puisqu'elles n'étaient pas, pour ainsi dire, de ma « responsabilité » ; ainsi, quelque part je maintenais ma « pureté ». (p. 181)

> The first few months I underwent these artificially induced periods, I dealt with them badly. But then I got used to them remarkably quickly and did not pay much attention to them since they were not, so to speak, my 'responsibility'; so in a way I maintained my 'purity'.

It is interesting that she is able to overcome her dread of impurity with respect to menstruation, and rapidly to ignore it when it returns, by the ratiocination according to which this so-called impurity is not her responsibility, having been induced by medical intervention, and that she is thus retaining her inner purity.

However, it is important to note that Balinska does not ascribe her weight gain solely to this hormonal treatment – and to this extent she is inadvertently, if only partially, concurring with the statement above cited from the American Psychiatric Association. Other, vital reasons, immanent in the extract below, include her gradually opening up to a feared outside world. Fear of the exterior appears to be a highly common component of anorexic psychopathology. It is certainly one previously foregrounded by Balinska (see p. 83).

> Je ne crois pas que ma prise de poids vers les 30 ans fut le seul fait du traitement hormonal. Un autre élément vital a joué. En élargissant mon monde, en m'ouvrant petit à petit à cet extérieur qui m'avait fait si peur, je prenais (très lentement) confiance : confiance en moi, confiance en l'autre. De ce fait, je commençais à mieux accepter mon apparence, mon extérieur – en un mot, mon corps, cet « objet » honni jusque-là. Sans m'en rendre compte – car je ne saurais trop souligner que ce que je suis en train de décrire m'était parfaitement inconscient au moment où je le vivais -, je prenais des petits « risques », j'apprenais à « oser ».

> I don't think that my weight gain at around the age of 30 was solely the result of hormonal treatment. Another vital element played a part. By widening my world, opening myself little by little to that outside that had once made me so afraid, I (very slowly) gained confidence: confidence in myself, confidence in others. As a result, I began to better accept my appearance, my outside – in a word, my body, this 'object' that I had hated up until now. Without realizing it – because I cannot emphasize enough that what I am describing was totally unconscious at the moment when I was living it – I took small risks, I learned to 'dare'.

One of the risks she takes is to go swimming, which her doctors had advised against at the start of her anorexia nervosa (pp. 183–84). At the swimming pool, she becomes part of a community of regular swimmers, talking to them over coffee, which contributes to her re-socialisation and thus further erodes her fear of the outside world (p. 184). This re-socialisation gradually leads to a renewed desire for relationships with other human beings (pp. 184–85) – and as previously stated, both a classic predisposing/vulnerability trait, and also a feature aggravated by the illness, is difficulty in interpersonal relationships, which in itself meshes with fear of the 'outside world'.

A further sign of gradual recovery is an insight she has about her perfectionism: 'la réalisation que je ne pouvais rien entreprendre sans vouloir le faire à la perfection, car seule la perfection justifiait l'activité, et seule l'activité justifiait l'existence' [the realisation that I was never able to take anything on without wanting to do it to perfection, because perfection alone justified activity, and activity alone justified existence] (p. 200). Part of her recovery is taking the risk of failure, such as when she submits and defends a doctoral thesis (two months before her 28th birthday). This time her success does promote greater self-confidence, which in its turn contributes to her steady recovery (p. 210). Indeed, the greater self-confidence, even pride, blossoming from her success dramatically accelerates her weight gain, as is evident in the following passage where 'ce jour-là' [that day] refers to the day she successfully defends her thesis and is awarded her doctorate:

> Sur les photos prises ce jour-là, ma silhouette témoigne encore d'une maigreur anormale, facilement reconnaissable comme une maigreur anorexique, même si elle n'était déjà plus aussi aiguë que les années précédentes. À peine quelques mois plus tard, cette maigreur s'était largement estompée. Certes, on aurait dit que j'étais « trop mince », que j'avais « une petite nature », que j'étais « pâlotte », mais l'empreinte anorexique (qui n'est pas seulement due au petit poids mais aussi à un

regard effacé, distant) s'était estompée pour ne pas laisser de traces. (p. 211)

In the pictures taken that day, my figure is still abnormally thin, easily recognisable as anorectic thinness, even if it was already less acute than in previous years. Only a few months later, this thinness had largely faded. Admittedly, some would say that I was 'too thin', that I had 'a petite appearance', that I was 'pale', but the anorectic imprint (which is not only due to the low weight but also to an effaced, distant gaze) had faded without a trace.

Her continuing recovery is also implicit in the fact that after this success she starts a job, albeit a modest one, linked to the academic world, which she enjoys (pp. 211–12). Another index to her continuing recovery is her appetite for an existentially richer life: 'Je me mis à rêver de bien plus qu'une existence sans anorexie. D'un seul coup, je me découvris affamée par la vie. L'été inoubliable de mes 28 ans !' [I began to dream of more than an existence without anorexia. Suddenly, I found myself hungry for life. The unforgettable summer of my 28 years!] (p. 212). Note the word play within the lexical field of anorexia nervosa: while she has denied her physiological, bodily hunger, she now begins to experience a new 'hunger' for life. Appetitiveness, albeit existential rather than alimentary, is now supplanting her anorexic psychopathology.

Certain affective and cognitive aspects of her recovery that are less positive, such as the following, may surprise the reader, especially when juxtaposed with her renewed appetite for life: 'alors que je n'avais jamais pensé au suicide étant anorexique, j'y pensais (sans jamais l'approcher) périodiquement au cours des années de « guérison »' [although I had never thought of suicide while I was anorectic, I thought about it (without ever approaching it) occasionally during my years of 'recovery'] (p. 213). (The notation 'je n'avais jamais pensé au suicide étant anorexique' [I had never thought of suicide while I was anorectic] correlates with statements in the secondary literature arguing that, while appearing to be killing themselves, albeit slowly, anorectics do not actually want literally to die; cf. discussion of this matter in the section above on Valère.) This apparent paradox is explicated thus:

Comment l'expliquer ? Tout simplement parce que, ayant goûté à nouveau à la joie de vivre, les moments de peine me semblaient encore plus lourds à supporter. C'est comme le lendemain du départ d'un être cher : on se sent encore plus seul qu'avant son arrivée. (pp. 213–14)

> How to explain it? Simply because, having tasted anew the joy of living, the moments of pain seemed even harder for me to bear. It is like the day after the departure of a loved one: you feel even more alone than you did before their arrival.

Note the complete contrast with Valère, who did identify her own anorexia nervosa as a form of suicide, however slow.

I will now return to a feature of Balinska's testimony signposted in my introductory paragraphs: its conspicuous challenges to various strands of medico-theoretical dogma pertaining to anorexia nervosa. One such challenge is to the doxa, widespread particularly in psychoanalytic theorisations of causation, that the condition stems from fear and rejection of womanhood and female sexuality: 'Je n'ai jamais rejeté la féminité en tant que telle. Mais ma féminité, comme tout mon être, était infectée par l'anorexie, et je craignais de l'exposer, comme tout le reste, au monde extérieur' [I never rejected femininity as such. But my femininity, like my whole being, was infected by anorexia, and I feared exposing it, as with the rest, to the outside world] (p. 217). Salient here is a motif discussed above, viz. fear of the outside world, or, more specifically in this instance, of what is exterior to the body. Balinska expresses apprehension of the exterior, but this time the apprehension is of responses produced by her own 'exterior' – that is, her external appearance – on other human beings – in this case, on men: 'Avant de devenir anorexique, je me souviens d'un vague malaise à l'idée que les hommes puissent préférer mon apparence extérieure à mon moi intérieur' [Before becoming anorectic, I remember a vague unease caused by the idea that men might prefer my external appearance to my internal self] (p. 217). This discomfiture is expanded upon, and develops into an implicitly feminist denunciation of male doctors, particularly those working in psychiatric environments, in their objectification of the female body.

> De ce fait, j'ai développé une certaine appréhension des hommes dans leur rapport avec la féminité. Cette inquiétude m'a semblé être confirmée par l'attitude que j'ai rencontrée chez tant de médecins, hommes, que j'avais connus notamment en milieu psychiatrique : des hommes qui ne cessaient de me parler de ma féminité en termes qui me dégoûtaient, car j'avais l'impression de n'être qu'un objet, qu'un tuyau qu'on pourrait réparer en me gavant, en forçant mon organisme à avoir des règles. Leur emprise sur mon corps suscitait en moi un sentiment de révolte, mais jamais de rejet de la féminité, essence que je voulais au contraire cultiver par sa douceur, sa non-violence, sa pureté potentielle.

> As a result, I have developed a certain apprehension of men in their relationship with femininity. This concern seemed to me to be confirmed by the attitude I encountered in so many doctors, men, whom I had met particularly in a psychiatric environment: men who kept talking to me about my femininity in terms that disgusted me, because I had the impression of being only an object, a pipe that could be repaired by gorging myself, forcing my body to have periods. Their grip on my body aroused in me a feeling of revolt, but never a rejection of femininity, an essence that I wanted to cultivate due to its gentleness, its non-violence, its potential purity.

Two points stand out here: the often abusively patriarchal nature of the medical body noted above (the earlier mention had also been more specifically about male psychiatrists); and second, the recurring valorisation of purity. A different challenge to medico-clinical thinking that dictates and regulates clinical treatment of the anorexic body pertains to hospitalisation of the anorectic, and here an absurdity emerges:

> Je me souviens d'avoir fait référence à ma « maladie » au médecin qui, la première, m'avait diagnostiquée. Elle m'avait sèchement reprise, faisant valoir que l'anorexie n'était pas une maladie. De même, l'infirmière du service psychiatrique où j'étais hospitalisée me répétait sans cesse quand je pleurais : « Ce n'est pas une maladie que vous avez, il faut simplement que vous mangiez ». (pp. 234–35)

> I remember referring to my 'illness' to the doctor who first diagnosed me. She had replied curtly, arguing that anorexia was not an illness. Similarly, the nurse in the psychiatric ward where I was hospitalized kept repeating to me when I cried: 'This isn't a disease that you have, you just have to eat'.

If the medical establishment does not consider anorexia nervosa to be an illness, why should that establishment attempt to 'treat' it at all?

Balinska's challenge is achieved through questioning and denunciation of various axes of standard medical approaches to anorexia nervosa. Prominent among these is the power of psychiatrists to literally lock patients up in hospitals: 'le pouvoir qu'avait le monde psychiatrique à m'enfermer, à me priver de ma liberté' [the power that the psychiatric world had to lock me up, to deprive me of my liberty] (p. 55). Balinska's observation of the punitive power of the psychiatric institution over the anorectic and its legally sanctioned ability to divest her of any freedom is poignant, and resonates both with Valère's and Durand's texts. The power of psychiatrists over anorectics is also implicitly denounced in the words of the neuropsychiatric doctor Stanislaw Tomkiewicz transcribed at the end of Balinska's book:

> Je partage aussi entièrement votre conviction concernant le fameux « contrat ». Le mot « contrat », utilisé dans le contexte de l'hôpital psychiatrique, ne peut l'être que de manière manifestement frauduleuse car il n'y a de contrat qu'entre des personnes de force égale. Or le « contrat » lié avec les anorexiques n'est autre chose que « léonin », c'est-à-dire celui qu'un lion lie avec sa victime : « Si tu sautes trois fois, je te mange. Si tu sautes six fois, je te dévore. » Dans le cadre de l'institution, le psychiatre a effectivement tout le pouvoir. (p. 257)

> I also fully share your belief about the so-called 'contract'. The word 'contract', used in the context of the psychiatric hospital, can only be manifestly fraudulent because there can only be a contract between persons of equal strength. But the 'contract' made with the anorectic is nothing else than 'leonine', that is to say the one a lion makes with its victim: 'If you skip three times, I eat you. If you jump six times, I devour you.' In the framework of the institution, the psychiatrist does have all the power.

Another strategy is to intercalate her mother's notes, which are equally damning:

> *Il y avait une infirmière qui nous a souri et a été assez agréable, mais elle me dit de prendre rapidement congé, ce que j'ai fait sans soupçonner l'enfer qui attendait Marta.*
>
> *Comme nous l'avons appris bien plus tard, elle a été immédiatement assommée de médicaments et n'a aucun souvenir des premiers jours. [...] Même une fois qu'elle avait commencé à reprendre connaissance, personne ne venait la voir sauf pour lui apporter ses repas et ses médicaments. Elle demandait, elle implorait même, à voir les médecins, mais en vain. (C'étaient les vacances !) Son désespoir n'a fait que croître et durant plus de sept semaines elle s'est rebellée et a perdu encore plus de poids. Les médecins passaient la voir pendant quelques minutes (sans jamais frapper à la porte, évidemment), mais il n'y eut aucune espèce de thérapie. La bataille des volontés était engagée : ou bien Marta mangeait la nourriture qu'on lui apportait et prenait du poids, ou bien elle resterait emprisonnée et complètement coupée du monde extérieur. La porte de sa salle de bains était fermée à clé. En fait, il s'agissait d'une salle d'eau avec toilette et lavabo, seulement. Elle n'a pas pu se doucher ou se baigner une seule fois pendant tout son séjour et elle est revenue à la maison toute recouverte d'une infection cutanée. Parce qu'on suspectait qu'elle pût vomir ou jeter sa nourriture dans*

> *les toilettes, on l'obligeait à faire ses « besoins » dans un pot dans la chambre. [...] Pendant la canicule du mois d'août, on ne lui a pas permis d'ouvrir la fenêtre parce qu'on la soupçonnait de donner à manger aux pigeons. Ce ne fut qu'après une crise émotionnelle intense à la mi-août, lorsqu'elle fut à nouveau soumise à un lourd régime sédatif, qu'elle prit la décision de manger afin de reconquérir sa liberté mais, comme elle nous le dit souvent, elle résolut qu'une fois libre elle s'arrêterait de manger complètement.*' (pp. 61–63)
>
> *There was a nurse who smiled at us and was nice enough, but she told me to quickly take my leave, which I did without suspecting what hell was waiting for Marta.*
>
> *As we learned much later, she was immediately stunned with medication and has no memory of the early days. [...] Even once she had started to regain consciousness, no one came to see her except to bring her meals and medicine. She asked, she even begged to see the doctors, but to no avail. (It was the holidays!) Her despair only grew, and for more than seven weeks she rebelled and lost even more weight. The doctors went to see her for a few minutes (never knocking on the door, of course), but there was no kind of therapy. The battle of wills had begun: either Marta ate the food brought to her and gained weight, or else she would remain imprisoned and completely cut off from the outside world. The door to her bathroom was locked. In fact, it was a bathroom with only a toilet and a sink. She was not allowed to shower or bathe once during her entire stay, and she returned home with a skin infection. Because it was suspected that she could throw up or throw her food in the toilet, she was forced to do her 'business' in a pot in the room. [...] During the heat wave in August, she was not allowed to open her window because she was suspected of feeding the pigeons. It was only after an intense emotional crisis in mid-August, when she was again subjected to a heavy sedative regime, that she made the decision to eat to regain her freedom but, as she often tells us, she resolved to stop eating altogether as soon as she was free.*

The harmful nature of this treatment regime is particularly egregious in '*Elle n'a pas pu se doucher ou se baigner une seule fois pendant tout son séjour et elle est revenue à la maison toute recouverte d'une infection cutanée*' [*She was not allowed to shower or bathe once during her entire stay, and she returned home with a skin infection*]. Balinska's commentary on this extract penned by her mother includes one vital point, namely that her putative revolt, if it occurred at all, had been prompted by the complete lack of psychotherapeutic help (as opposed to mere physical treatment) offered by this hospital regime: 'je ne me suis pas consciemment « rebellée », mais *j'attendais* qu'on m'aide, *j'attendais* une assistance qui pût me permettre de m'aider moi-même' [I did not consciously 'rebel', but *I waited* for help, *I waited* for help that could allow me to help myself] (p. 63).

Further evidence of the inhumane nature of this hospital treatment for anorexia nervosa resides in the following recollection:

> [...] j'étais complètement seule sans rien, sans aucune visite. Je ne sortais jamais de ma chambre. Seuls les plateaux de nourriture quatre fois par jour m'apportaient un contact avec l'extérieur. [...] À mes demandes de téléphoner ou d'écrire à mes parents, je me vis opposer un refus total. [...] Il n'y avait, évidemment, aucune espèce de décoration dans la chambre, à part une croix gammée en face de mon lit qu'un malade avait probablement tracée et que personne ne s'était donné la peine d'effacer. (p. 64)

> [...] I was completely alone without anything, without a single visit. I never left my room. My only contact with the outside were the trays of food four times a day. [...] My requests to call or write to my parents were met with total refusal. [...] There was, obviously, no kind of decoration in the room, except for a swastika in front of my bed that a patient had probably drawn and that no one had bothered to erase.

Is this leaving of the swastika image on the wall of her hospital room a sinister metaphor for the concentrationary universe of the (then, but not completely extinct in the present day) standard psychiatric regime for anorexics? It certainly has connotations of Nazi/fascistic inhumanity (as had the photographing of anorectics naked, from the front and from the side, in the English hospital described above). That inhumanity also emerges poignantly in the following statement, especially in the lexical choices of 'insupportable' and 'torturait':

> Le « traitement » que je suivais était de conception simple : on rendait la vie de l'anorexique tellement insupportable qu'elle finissait par faire tout et n'importe quoi pour retrouver la liberté – y compris le pire de tout : manger. D'un seul coup, je compris qu'il n'y avait aucune thérapie dans cette histoire, que personne n'allait m'aider, que personne ne voulait me comprendre, que la clinique fixait ses taux de « réussite » uniquement sur la base d'un nombre de kilos pris par des filles au départ émaciées et qu'on torturait psychologiquement pour qu'elles finissent par manger. (p. 67)

> The 'treatment' I was following was simple: the life of the anorectic was made so unbearable that she ended up doing anything and everything

> to regain freedom – including the worst of all: eating. All of a sudden, I realized that there was no therapy in this story, no-one was going to help me, no-one wanted to understand me, and that the clinic was basing its 'success rate' solely on the number of kilos gained by initially emaciated girls who were psychologically tortured to make them eat.

In contrast with her depiction of the regime constructed and imposed by physicians and psychiatrists, Balinska's purview on the nursing staff who implement most of it rather than design it is more ambivalent. Early on, she asserts 'avouons-le, trop souvent il y a beaucoup d'agressivité et de mépris dans l'attitude des soignants envers les anorexiques' [Let's admit it, too often there is lots of aggression and contempt in the attitude held by carers towards anorectics] (p. 13). Admittedly, the noun 'soignants' [carers] is ambiguous, and could englobe all of those involved in her putative 'care': doctors, nurses, psychiatrists, etc.; but it does appear to refer to nurses here. In this initial stance, there is concurrence with Valère. However, later on, Balinska figuratively represents many of the less empowered staff encountered at the hospital, such as 'femmes de ménage' [cleaning ladies], 'aides-soignantes' [assistant nurses] – in addition to only one 'infirmière' [nurse] – as having been 'petits rayons de soleil' [little rays of sunshine] (p. 68). Significantly, given the risk to their job, they avow their complete indignation about the mandatory treatment of anorexic patients (p. 69). One psychiatric nurse shows particular lucidity apropos not just the brutality but also the ineffectuality of this treatment:

> Annabelle, une infirmière psychiatrique, [...] me raconta, de par ses expériences dans cette clinique et dans d'autres, que la majorité des filles soumises à ce traitement rechutaient rapidement par la suite puisqu'elles n'avaient eu aucune thérapie à part la punition et la récompense en fonction de la perte ou de la prise de kilos. Elles n'avaient donc pas « assimilé leur poids mentalement », comme elle disait. (p. 69)

> Annabelle, a psychiatric nurse, [...] told me that from her experiences in this and other clinics, the majority of girls undergoing this treatment soon relapsed afterwards because they had no other therapy apart from punishment or reward depending on whether they had lost or gained kilos. They had not 'mentally assimilated their weight', as she put it.

(On the point of 'punition' [punishment], at least some clinicians have stressed the importance of avoiding perceptions of punitive treatment. One example is the following: 'It is also useful for staff to communicate that they are not seeking to engage in control battles and have no punitive intentions when using interventions that the patient may experience as aversive.'[64]) An exception to this general enlightenment among the less-empowered hospital staff is another nurse, Léonora, who insists that anorexia is not an illness, and that Balinska simply needs to eat and gain weight (see p. 76). Léonora's more – to put it charitably – limited outlook may be to do with the fact that she is elderly ('La vieille infirmière' [The old nurse]) and thus probably not trained in the more diverse approaches to anorexia elaborated (although often not deployed) over the latter part of the twentieth century.

One prime target of Balinska's trenchant critique is the commonest approach to hospital treatment of anorexia. This is the so-called 'contract', mandatory and in fact entirely one-sided, whose humanity and ethical justification she implicitly refutes via rhetorical questions (cf. Valère):

> [...] je m'oppose formellement au traitement le plus accepté de l'anorexie : le fameux "contrat" selon lequel l'anorexique accepterait d'être punie jusqu'à ce qu'elle atteigne un certain poids. Le plus souvent, ce système donne des résultats dans l'immédiat, mais qu'en est-il du moyen et du long terme ? A-t-on aussi réfléchi au fait que ce traitement est dépourvu d'humanité et détruit les règles de base de l'éthique médicale ? (p. 13)

> [...] I absolutely oppose the most accepted treatment of anorexia: the so-called 'contract' according to which the anorectic agrees to be punished until she reaches a certain weight. Most often, this system produces immediate results, but what about the medium and long term? Has anyone thought about how this treatment is devoid of humanity and destroys the basic rules of medical ethics?

As we have seen, this is confluent with the critique of the 'contract' made by Tomkiewicz, a neuropsychiatric doctor (p. 257). It also concurs with the critique made by André J. Scheen, a doctor specialising in nutrition and metabolic illnesses:

> La technique du « contrat de poids » est souvent utilisée, mais pas toujours efficace. Elle consiste à fixer à la patiente des objectifs de reprise pondérale dans un délai donné ; si l'objectif est atteint, la patiente obtient un bénéfice secondaire défini de commun accord au départ du contrat, soit sous la forme d'une récompense (cadeau,...), soit sous la forme de l'évitement d'une punition (report d'une éventuelle hospitalisation, par exemple). Cette stratégie résout rarement le fond du problème [...].[65]

64 Yager et al. 2006: 7.

65 Scheen, André J., 'L'anorexie mentale: aspects medicaux', in Marcel Crahay et Christine Goffinet (eds), *Regards croisés sur l'anorexie* (Liège: Les Editions de l'Université de Liège , 2001), pp. 89–96 (p. 93).

> The 'weight contract' technique is often used, but is not always effective. It consists of setting the patient a series of weight recovery objectives within a given time; if the objective is reached, the patient obtains a secondary benefit defined by mutual agreement at the beginning of the contract, either in the form of a reward (gift,...) or in the form of the avoidance of a punishment (postponement of a possible hospitalisation, for example). This strategy rarely solves the root of the problem [...].

As we have seen above, Balinska states 'trop souvent il y a beaucoup d'agressivité et de mépris dans l'attitude des soignantes envers l'anorexique' [too often there is lots of aggression and contempt in the attitude held by carers towards anorectics] (p. 13). Aggression and disdain are perturbing in the context of what is meant to be therapeutic treatment for a patient. But even greater negativity is conferred upon hospital treatment of anorexia via the use of what Conceptual or Cognitive Metaphor Theory would call an ontological metaphor,[66] 'enfer' [hell] (p. 61), to qualify that treatment. In an intercalated text penned by Balinska's mother, the word 'enfer' is reprised in order to convey the horror of the psychiatric hospital regime to which her daughter is subjected. Hell has often been used as a metaphor (again, an ontological metaphor) to describe the experience of those interned in the concentration and death camps of World War Two. One particular notation already noted above that Balinska makes about her hospital room evokes precisely that experience: 'Il n'y avait, évidemment, aucune espèce de décoration dans la chambre, à part une croix gammée en face de mon lit qu'un malade avait probablement tracée et que personne ne s'était donné la peine d'effacer' (p. 64).

Balinska also questions and denounces medical preconceptions of the anorectic through her exposure of their reductive and myopic stereotyping. This stereotyping is the source of the suspicion mentioned above leading to degrading and inhumane treatment:

> [...] il était détestable d'être prise systématiquement pour une menteuse. C'était le « portrait-robot » de l'anorexique [...] qui le voulait, et il ne servait à rien que je dise que je ne vomissais jamais ma nourriture, que je ne la donnais pas au pigeons... (p. 70)

66 In Conceptual Metaphor Theory, ontological metaphors are defined by the pioneers of that theory, George Lakoff and Mark Johnson, as 'ways of viewing events, activities, emotions, ideas, etc., as entities and substances'. See Lakoff, George and Johnson, Mark, *Metaphors We Live By* (Chicago, IL/London: University of Chicago Press, 1980), p. 25.

> [...] it was horrible to be so systematically taken for a liar. It was the 'robot portrait' of the anorectic [...] that required it, and it was useless for me to say that I never vomited my food, that I did not give it to the pigeons...

Mention is made by three clinicians (Janet Treasure, Gill Todd, and George Szmukler) of 'the extreme view that patients are overpriviledged [*sic*] manipulators, liars and cheats who abuse medical attention (Naish, 1979)'.[67] Balinska later returns to this reductive stereotyping of the anorexic in her motif of reductive identikitting:

> Pire, même auprès du personnel soignant, l'anorexique répond à un schéma prédéterminé. Par conséquent, on a tendance à faire des amalgames entre toutes les anorexiques, qui répondraient, *grosso modo*, au même schéma : c'est ce que j'appelle le portrait-robot de l'anorexique. (p. 233)

> Worse, even in the eyes of the nursing staff, the anorectic responds to a predetermined pattern. Therefore, people tend to amalgamate all anorexics, thinking that they all follow, roughly speaking, the same pattern: this is what I call the robot portrait of the anorexic.

The cogency of her attack on reductive and schematic profiling of the anorectic is augmented by a canny strategy. This consists in first listing all the traits clinically ascribed, then specifying how only some of those traits were present in her own case, and how her own case also contained the opposite of several such traits.

> Quel est donc ce « portrait-robot » ? Une anorexique serait au départ une jeune fille un peu forte, perfectionniste, appartenant à une famille de classe aisée, avec une mère dominatrice ; afin de perdre du poids, elle pratiquerait le sport comme une forcenée, elle vomirait le peu de nourriture qu'elle absorbe, elle mentirait systématiquement à toutes et à tous, elle nierait absolument l'existence de son problème, elle ne verrait pas sa maigreur, elle se trouverait très bien comme elle est, elle ne serait pas du tout triste de son état, mais au contraire assez satisfaite. (p. 234)

> What is this 'robot portrait', then? An anorexic would initially be a girl who is a little thickset, perfectionist and from a well-off family with a domineering mother. In order to lose weight, she would play sport like

67 Treasure, Janet, Todd, Gill, and Szmukler, George, 'The inpatient treatment of anorexia nervosa', in Szmukler et al. 1995, pp. 275–91 (pp. 285–86). Their reference is to Naish, J.M., 'Problems of deception in medical practice', *Lancet*, ii (1979), 139–42.

> crazy, throwing up what little food she does eat, systematically lying to everyone and denying outright the existence of her problem. She would not see her thinness, believing herself to be fine as she is and her state would not make her sad in the slightest, but on the contrary quite satisfied.

Balinska's challenge is to the flattening homogenisation of these ascriptions, which ignore deviations such as her own:

> [...] j'étais une jeune fille mince, n'ayant jamais eu de problème de poids [...] je n'ai jamais pratiqué de sport, me sentant toujours fatiguée et fragile ; je n'ai pas vomi une seule fois ; je reconnaissais à tous (famille, médecins, amis) l'existence d'un problème qui me gâchait la vie ; je voyais ma maigreur qui me faisait honte (surtout sur les photos) [...] (p. 234)

> [...] I was a slender girl, having never had a weight problem [...] I never played sport, always feeling tired and fragile; I did not vomit once; I admitted to everyone (family, doctors, friends) the existence of a problem that was wasting my life; I saw my thinness and it made me ashamed (especially on the photos) [...]

Another target of Balinska's questioning and denunciation is the suffering caused – however non-intentionally in the better of cases – by normative hospital treatment regimes for anorexia. This suffering takes various forms, of which I will highlight the most prominent: the crass stereotyping evoked above, which in Balinska induced a sense of self-loss, coercion shading into emotional blackmail, deprivation of any privacy, and even what is construed as sadism. The sense of self-loss is figured by the ontological metaphor of 'une profonde blessure inguérissable, enfouie en moi' [a deep, incurable wound buried within me] (p. 79). It appears to ensue from the reductive identikitting of the anorexic mentioned earlier. It leads to a depression that at the time Balinska conceptualises, via the trope 'blessure inguérissable' [incurable wound], as permanent damage to her psychic integrity. As we have seen above, the experience of coercion shading into emotional blackmail also occurred in the English psychiatric hospital of national pre-eminence for its treatment of EDs in which Balinska stayed for a trial eight-day period. Coercion in standard hospital treatment regimes for anorexia is also mentioned by psychiatrist Philippe Jeammet, who partly explains it by the irritation and sense of impotence that anorectics induce in clinical staff, but also admits that it can lead to violent 'clinical' measures:

> C'est la dimension de défi propre à ces troubles du comportement alimentaire qui fait que ces patientes suscitent deux réactions[68] opposées, elles aussi : beaucoup d'intérêt, voire de fascination, mais également de l'irritation, un sentiment d'impuissance et des mesures thérapeutiques coercitives, voir violentes.[69]

> It is the challenging aspect specific to these eating disorders that causes these patients to elicit two opposite reactions [from clinical staff]: a lot of interest, even fascination, but also irritation, a feeling of helplessness, and coercive, even violent, therapeutic measures.

Finally, we come to the imputation of sadism – which again had also been made in Valère's 1978 account of hospital treatment of anorexia.[70] Balinska reproves this sadism via different discursive strategies. One is sarcastic reporting of the perverse rationale for it given by the medico-clinical establishment: 'l'anorexique étant avant tout sadique envers elle-même, elle réagira peut-être si l'agression vient de l'extérieur' [the anorexic, being above all sadistic towards herself, may react if the aggression comes from outside] (p. 236). See pp. 258 and 259, where highly unusually, that sadism is acknowledged, and denounced, by a clinical practitioner himself, Stanislaw Tomkiewicz. The gravity of her charge is reinforced by the pathos of the mismatch between the anorectic's wish for help and the hostility with which she is instead routinely rejected:

> [...] même si j'ai vite appris à me méfier des médecins et même si j'y allais avant tout pour rassurer mes parents, il y avait toujours en moi un espoir que je trouverais quelqu'un vraiment à mon écoute, avec du cœur, qui essaierait de m'aider. Ce que je trouvais presque systématiquement à la place, c'était un regard froid et souvent hostile, l'absence de dialogue, des mots agressifs, humiliants, provocateurs et gênants. (p. 246)

> [...] even though I quickly learned to be wary of doctors and even if I went first to reassure my parents, there was always a hope that I would find someone who would really listen to me, with their heart, someone who would try to help me. What I almost always found instead was a cold

68 Jeammet appears to be talking about the reactions of clinical staff treating anorectics and bulimics in hospital.

69 Jeammet 2004: 193.

70 While Valère does not use exactly the same adjective 'sadique' [sadistic] or its noun cognate 'sadisme' [sadism], this is certainly what she represents in her depiction of the medical staff treating anorexics in hospital. See also in Balinska's testimony other uses of this adjective/noun, for example on p. 236 and p. 258.

> and often hostile look, the absence of dialogue, aggressive, humiliating, provocative and embarrassing words.

This is a potent censure of the medical establishment's treatment of anorexic inpatients. As a remarkable exception to the rule, this imputation of sadism in clinical treatment of anorexia is reproved by a clinical practitioner – and a male one at that – Tomkiewicz, the neuropsychiatric doctor, on whose dialogue with Balinska her book ends.

> D'ailleurs, on se demande si le but du « contrat », en tant que méthode, est vraiment la guérison psychique de l'anorexique ou si on ne cherche pas plutôt à briser définitivement son caractère, à casser son légendaire orgueil (voir les écrits qui comparent les anorexiques à Antigone)[71] et à en faire une jeune femme effacée, obéissante et soumise au corps médical. Il n'est pas étonnant qu'une telle atmosphère attire parfois dans le service travaillant avec les anorexiques un personnel plus ou moins *sadique* qui transforme non sans jouissance la cure en lutte pour le pouvoir. Et, à partir de votre témoignage, je note qu'en termes de sadisme les Anglais n'ont rien à nous envier. (p. 258; my emphasis)

> Moreover, one wonders if the purpose of the 'contract', as a method, is really the psychic cure of the anorectic or if one does not try rather to definitively break her character, to break her legendary pride (see writings that compare anorectics to Antigone) and to make a young woman subdued, obedient and subject to the medical profession. It is not surprising that such an atmosphere sometimes attracts a more or less *sadistic* staff in the team working with the anorectic who, not without enjoyment, transform the cure into a struggle for power. And, from your account, I note that in terms of sadism the English have no reason to envy us.

Another singular exception to that rule is made by one of the psychiatrists/psychotherapists/doctors who had formerly treated Balinska: 'Puis, d'un seul coup, il avoua comme malgré lui : "Oui, si les médecins sont brutaux [*sic*] avec l'anorexique, c'est qu'ils se retrouvent face à leur ignorance"' [Then, all at once, he confessed in spite of himself: 'Yes, if the doctors are brutal [*sic*] with the anorectic, it is because they are confronted with their ignorance'] (p. 242).

71 Regarding Stanislaw Tomkiewicz's mention of 'les écrits qui comparent les anorexiques à Antigone' [writings that compare anorectics to Antigone], see, for example, Raimbault, Ginette and Eliacheff, Caroline, *Les indomptables. Figures de l'anorexie* (Paris: Odile Jacob, 2001 [first edition: 1989]).

As was one of her aims in writing her testimony (p. 12), Balinska encourages wider debate about anorexia nervosa, at one point through rhetorical questions, as seen in the second part of the extract below:

> Ainsi, il arrive souvent qu'on enferme les anorexiques dans des hôpitaux psychiatriques comme si elles étaient des « folles ». On les prive de leur liberté, de leur affaires personnelles, voire de leur intimité la plus primaire. Certes, on trouvera des explications raisonnées à ce traitement, mais a-t-on le droit d'incarcérer des personnes qui ne sont pas dangereuses pour les autres ? Un traitement sadique (tel que le reconnaissent certains soignants eux-mêmes) est-il jamais justifiable ? (pp. 226–27)

> Thus, it often happens that anorectics are locked up in psychiatric hospitals as if they were 'crazy'. They are deprived of their freedom, their personal belongings, even their most primary intimacy. Of course, we will find reasoned explanations for this treatment, but is it right to incarcerate people who are not dangerous to others? Is sadistic treatment (as recognised by some caregivers themselves) ever justifiable?

It is worth noting that the topos of anorexic inpatients as prisoners ('incarcérer' [incarcerate]), also present in Balinska's designation of her fellow patients as 'copénitentiaires' [cellmates] (p. 127), had, as we have seen, also featured in Valère's 1978 account. Comparing these two texts, it appears that a quarter of a century had seen no improvement in the phenomenological experience of anorexics' hospital treatment. To this we should add the fact that the negative homeostasis is common to both French and English inpatient regimes, showing undesirable transnational isomorphism. Talking of transnational isomorphism, and more specifically of parallels between France and England, the injustice felt by Balinska in what is apprehended as penitentiary treatment is conveyed creatively in the intertextual allusions to the English Lewis Carroll's *Alice in Wonderland*,[72] on which I have remarked above.

In sum, it is patent that Balinska regards the medical corps' treatment of anorectics as largely inhumane. Her evidence contradicts the entirely laudable recommendations for treatment of eating-disordered patients made by the American Psychiatric Association in 2006:

72 Note the same allusion in Senkbeil, Karsten and Hoppe, Nicola, '"The sickness stands at your shoulder...": Embodiment and cognitive metaphor in Hornbacher's *Wasted: A Memoir of Anorexia and Bulimia*', *Language and Literature*, 25, 1 (2016), 3–17 (12).

> At the very outset and through ongoing interaction with the patient, it is important for clinicians to attempt to build trust, establish mutual respect, and develop a therapeutic relationship that will serve as the basis for ongoing exploration and treatment of the problems associated with the eating disorder.[73] [...]
>
> Refeeding programs should be implemented in nurturing emotional contexts.[74]

It should now be obvious that such recommendations were certainly not followed in Balinska's (or Valère's) case. The vast majority of clinicians would probably react to Balinska's critiques in one of the following modes: simply not recognise her conceptuo-phenomenological account; counter her accusations, whether directly or by implication in their writings; or take these accusations on board, but proffer reasons why anorectics in their opinion (mis)conceive such treatment as inhumane. Consider the asseveration made in 2005 by Carlos M. Grilo of the Yale University School of Medicine:

> The experience of treating and/or caregiving for patients with anorexia nervosa are among the most challenging of any health problem yet have received relatively little attention. Venables (1930), in a remarkably astute and compassionate early account of the treatment of nine cases of AN, indicated the need for clinicians to exercise patience and emphasized the importance of not losing one's temper when working with such patients. The frustrations and negative reactions evoked by these patients are well known to clinicians (Strober, 2004) and well documented (Morgan, 1977).[75]

Angelyn Spignesi refers to the views that clinicians hold of anorectics as 'antagonistic, intolerant, authoritarian'.[76] Such views are also

73 Yager et al. 2006: 12.

74 Yager et al. 2006: 23.

75 Grilo 2006: 88. His references are to Strober, M., 'Managing the chronic, treatment-resistant patient with anorexia nervosa', *International Journal of Eating Disorders*, 36 (2004), 245–55; and Morgan, H.G., 'Fasting girls and our attitudes to them', *British Medical Journal*, 2, 6103 (1977), 1652–55.

76 Spignesi, Angelyn, *Starving Women: A Psychology of Anorexia* (Dallas, TX: Spring Publications, 1983), p. 8. Her references are to Thoma, H., *Anorexia Nervosa* (New York: International Universities Press, 1967); Palazzoli 1978; Dally, P. and Gomez, J., *Anorexia Nervosa* (London: William Heinemann Medical Books, Ltd., 1979); Ushakov, G.K., 'Anorexia nervosa', in J.G. Howells (ed.), *Modern Perspectives in Adolescent Psychiatry* (Edinburgh: Oliver & Boyd, 1971);

documented by Brotman et al. (1984).[77] Here, and as noted with respect to Valère's testimony, it is useful to recall the American Psychiatric Association's warning against the possibility of the clinician's countertransference (a term normally associated with psychoanalysis, but used more loosely by the American Psychiatric Association with respect to general clinical treatment of the eating-disordered patient): 'Regardless of the clinical or theoretical approach used in treatment, some patients with EDs challenge clinicians' understanding and in some instances provoke countertransference reactions, particularly in response to patients' communications of aggression and defiance.'[78] Unlike Valère, Balinska did not communicate either aggression or defiance towards the clinicians treating her, but the American Psychiatric Association only adds such communications as particularly compelling reasons for countertransference, rather than necessary ones.

A critique of the medical corps' treatment of anorexia that is similar to that of Balinska, but much more overtly politicised, and, crucially, written from the optic of a practicing psychotherapist with long experience of treating eating-disordered patients, is made in Susie Orbach's *Hunger Strike: The Anorectic's Struggle as a Metaphor for our Age* (first published in 1986).[79] Of particular pertinence in this work are pp. xxv–xxvi, which cogently criticise standard clinical attitudes towards anorectics, particularly the following extract.

> Assumptions about the anorexic have shifted little in the last few years and they include a sense of the manipulativeness, wilfulness, destructiveness and negativity of the patient to the exclusion of other thoughts and feelings. These kinds of attitudes that underlie treatment programmes bode badly for a cooperative patient-doctor relationship. (pp. xxv–xxvi)

Further, Orbach states, 'In my capacity as a therapist training others to work with anorectics, I frequently come across a fear of, a disdain for and a dismissive attitude towards the anorectic' (p. 113). However, Orbach's is not a wholesale condemnation of the medical corps' attitude towards anorectics, for she offers insightful analysis of the affect prompted in these clinicians by such patients:

Bruch, Hilde, *Eating Disorders* (London: Routledge and Kegan Paul, 1973); and Bruch 1978.

77 Brotman et al. 1984: 71–77.

78 Yager et al. 2006: 27.

79 Orbach, Susie, *Hunger Strike: The Anorectic's Struggle as a Metaphor for our Age* (London: Penguin, 1993 [first published by Faber and Faber, 1986]).

> [...] the nature of the syndrome stirs up strong feelings in others, feelings which include envy, frustration, rage. Such feelings can and do lead practitioners to mislay their compassion and replace it with a treatment that at its best is ineffectual, and at its worst coercive. (109)

Nonetheless, the overall tenor of Orbach's analysis is condemnatory of standard inpatient treatment of anorectics: 'the "treatment" proffered in many inpatient units is coercive, infantilizing and punitive' (p. 165).

Some other clinicians and researchers in the field of EDs do admit both negative clinical stereotyping of the anorectic and the deleterious treatment of her that are rooted in such stereotyping, again due to the negative affect produced in the medical corps by the condition. Thus, Ulrike Schmidt, a psychiatrist and academic, Jane Tiller, a senior registrar, and H. Gethin Morgan, a professor of psychiatry, observe the following:

> Personality traits may manifest as the anorexic patient's notorious denial of her illness, her obstinacy, and her deviousness. These create mistrust, hostility, frustration and outrage in those close to the sufferer, including those people working with her therapeutically (Morgan, 1977; Vandereycken, 1993). For example, young doctors were found to respond to anorexia nervosa patients with much more anger, stress and helplessness than to other physically ill patients (Brotman, Stern and Herzog, 1984).[80]

However, one at best moot, at worst dubious point in this observation is the attribution of the anorectic's 'denial of her illness, her obstinacy, and her deviousness' to '[p]ersonality traits'. Others would argue that such traits do not arise from the anorectic's basic personality, but from her illness, and that to conflate the two is a sign of ignorance. The ignorance – or to put it more charitably, the lack of understanding of anorexia nervosa – in doctors generally (as opposed to those specialising in EDs) is admitted in some of the secondary, medico-clinical literature. While not an overt admission of failure to understand anorexia nervosa, the following statement from two eminent medical authorities in the field of EDs, Janet Treasure and George Szmukler, who work at the

80 Schmidt, Ulrike, Tiller, Jane, and Morgan, H. Gethin, 'The social consequences of eating disorders', in Szmukler et al. 1995, pp. 259–70 (261–62). Their references are to Morgan, H.G., 'Fasting girls and our attitudes to them', *British Medical Journal*, 2, 6103 (1977), 1652–55; Vandereycken, W., 'Naughty girls and angry doctors: Eating disorder patients and their therapists', *International Review of Psychiatry*, 5 (1993), 13–18; and Brotman et al. 1984: 71–77.

Maudsley Hospital in London (along with a less prominent figure in that field, Gill Todd) is telling: 'The strides in our understanding of the treatment principles required for bulimia nervosa have overtaken those for anorexia nervosa.'[81] What comes closer to an eating-disorders researcher's admission of, if not ignorance, then inadequate understanding of EDs (which axiomatically include anorexia nervosa) generally in the medical profession is the following from Anita Jansen, a professor in the psychology of EDs: 'The lack of understanding mechanisms that cause, maintain and change eating disorders, currently is the biggest problem facing the science of eating disorders.'[82] On ignorance of the first factor mentioned by Jansen, viz. causation, P.G. Campbell, based at the time of his observation at the Royal Free Hospital in London, another prominent centre for treatment of EDs, proclaims the following.

> The eating disorders present a special kind of challenge to psychiatric approaches to theories of causality, particularly because they seem to implicate a strong degree of conscious choice, which may be actively hostile to medical or other therapeutic intervention. [...] Medical causes have not been identified despite a profusion of research, and medical treatments have had limited success and have probably caused much suffering and even avoidable deaths.[83]

Campbell mentions 'causes' of EDs. On the topic of causality, Balinska makes pertinent and convincing observations that, taken in their entirety, contend that many specific causal factors asserted by clinicians and theoreticians are at best questionable, at worst unfounded in reality. She instead implies that causation may well be multifactorial:

> Ainsi, il y a fixation sur le fait que basculer dans l'anorexie relève purement et simplement d'une réaction par rapport à une situation extérieure. C'est de cette façon qu'on peint le portrait type de l'anorexique, de ses parents (surtout de sa mère), de son environnement familial qui seraient autant de preuves de son mal.
>
> Soit. Je ne nie absolument pas que la composante psychologique dans l'anorexie est énorme. Simplement, je pense qu'elle ne peut pas à elle seule expliquer la survenue de cette maladie. [...]

81 Treasure, Janet, Todd, Gill, and Szmukler, George in Szmukler et al. 1995, pp. 275–91 (289).

82 Jansen, Anita, 'Eating disorders need more experimental psychopathology', *Behaviour Research and Therapy*, 86 (2016), 2–10 (2).

83 Campbell, P.G., 'What would a causal explanation of the eating disorders look like?', in Szmukler et al. 1995, pp. 49–64 (50).

Si l'on applique le même raisonnement à la genèse de l'anorexie dans son lien avec les facteurs psychologiques que l'on cite toujours – jeune fille perfectionniste, situation familiale difficile, etc. -, on trouvera la chose suivante : il y a beaucoup de jeunes filles perfectionnistes, grandissant dans des familles malheureuses *qui ne deviennent pas anorexiques*. Ainsi, vouloir imputer à ces seuls éléments la causalité d'une pathologie aussi grave et complexe que l'anorexie me paraît déraisonnable. [...]

Le contexte familial de la jeune fille anorexique joue très probablement un rôle dans l'enclenchement et l'évolution de sa maladie, bien que son importance soit difficile à déterminer et certainement variable, mais songeons à une chose. Quand bien même l'état anorexique d'une enfant aurait un lien causal avec son environnement, il ne sert à rien de culpabiliser les parents. (pp. 236–38)[84]

Thus, there is fixation on the fact that a turn to anorexia is purely and simply a reaction to an external situation. This is how we paint the typical portrait of the anorectic, her parents (especially her mother) and her family environment, all of which are used to provide many explanations for this illness.

So be it. I absolutely do not deny that the psychological component in anorexia is huge. Simply put, I do not think that it alone can explain the occurrence of this disease. [...]

If we apply the same reasoning to the genesis of anorexia in its link with the psychological factors that we always quote – perfectionist girl, difficult family situation, etc. – we will find the following: there are many

84 Clinicians increasingly recognise this point. See, for instance, Touyz et al. 1995: 247–70, who extend the point to families of anorectics in general rather than just their parents: 'It is important that families be approached in a non-blaming way' (p. 263). Similarly, the American Psychiatric Association warns: 'A clinician's articulation of theories that imply blame or permit family members to blame one another or themselves can alienate family members from involvement in the treatment and therefore be detrimental to the patient's care and recovery.' See Yager et al. 2006: 5. More recently, in a non-academic publication, Carrie Arnold also extends the point in the following report: 'In 2013, Hill, Knatz and Kaye applied for a grant from the US National Eating Disorders Association to fund a pilot study of what they called Neurobiologically Enhanced with Family/Friends Eating Disorder Trait Response (NEW FED-TR). Every aspect of the programme was based on what researchers understood about what happens in the brain of someone with anorexia, the goal being not just to improve treatment but also *to reduce blame and guilt among sufferers and families*.' Arnold, Carrie, 'Anorexia: You don't just grow out of it', *The Guardian*, 29 March 2016, http://www.theguardian.com/society/2016/mar/29/anorexia-you-dont-just-grow-out-of-it (my emphasis).

perfectionist girls, growing up in unhappy families *who do not become anorectic*. Thus, to want to attribute the causality of a pathology as serious and complex as anorexia to these elements alone seems to me unreasonable. [...]

The family situation of the anorectic girl most likely plays a role in the onset and progression of her illness, although its importance is difficult to determine and certainly variable, but let's think about one thing. Even if the anorectic state of a child has a causal link to her environment, there is no point in making parents feel guilty.

On the very last sentence in this lengthy extract, the compassionate exhortation not to make parents feel guilty about their child's anorexia could not stand in starker contrast to the stance taken by Valère, who misses no chance to point out the toxic effects on her of her own parents, from which any reasonable reader may infer at the very least their key contribution to the cause of her illness. In contrast, Balinska disculpates her parents, and makes a balanced judgement about the role of parents more generally among the various causal elements of anorexia nervosa:

> J'ai vu mes deux parents pleurer – pis, je les ai vus sangloter, implorer mon pardon pour une faute dont nous étions tous ignorants. [...]
>
> Faire prendre conscience aux parents des difficultés inexprimables de leur fille anorexique, des manifestations involontaires de sa maladie et de la réaction qu'il convient d'avoir ; les aider à surmonter des entraves éventuelles à la communication au sein de la famille ; leur suggérer des changements d'attitudes, voire de style de vie, dans le foyer familial qui pourraient aider leur enfant, me paraît hautement souhaitable. Mais culpabiliser les parents ne fait qu'empirer la situation : la tension augmente, l'atmosphère pourrit, et, inévitablement, la rancune s'installe : subir l'anorexie de son enfant est difficile, mais la porter est destructif. (pp. 238–39)

> I saw both my parents crying – worse, I saw them sobbing, begging my forgiveness for a failing we were all unaware of. [...]
>
> To make parents aware of the inexpressible difficulties of their anorectic daughter, the involuntary manifestations of her illness and the appropriate reaction; help them overcome potential barriers to communication within the family; to suggest changes of attitudes, or even of lifestyle in the family home that might help their child, seems to me highly desirable. But to make the parents feel guilty only makes the situation worse: the tension increases, the atmosphere sours, and, inevitably, the grudge sets in: enduring the anorexia of the child is difficult, but wearing it is destructive.

Reiteration of the multifactorial nature of causation is found in the following recollection, along with observation of the failure of any doctor (or psychotherapist) to explore one facet of her guilt complex (in passing, it is relevant to note that guilt complexes are extremely common in anorectics, and not just with respect to food intake):

> Un autre médecin, grand bourgeois, avait essayé de me convaincre que ma préoccupation pour la malnutrition dans les pays du Sud était déraisonnable puisque nous, Européens, avions « mérité » notre développement. Aucun médecin ou psychothérapeute n'a jamais essayé d'explorer avec moi le sentiment de culpabilité que j'avais envers les peuples qui souffraient. Certes, ce n'était peut-être pas la cause première de mon anorexie (si tant est qu'on puisse ordonner les causes…), mais puisque la culpabilité occupait une place si importante dans ma vision du monde, n'auraient-ils pas pu s'en servir comme porte d'entrée à un dialogue ? (pp. 242–43)

> Another doctor, a bourgeois, had tried to convince me that my concern for malnutrition in the Global South was unreasonable because we Europeans had 'deserved' our development. No doctor or psychotherapist has ever tried to explore with me the feeling of guilt I felt for the people who were suffering. Of course, this may not have been the root cause of my anorexia (if we could order the causes…), but since guilt was so important in my vision of the world, could they not have used it as a gateway to a dialogue?

Again, cf. Dupont's horror faced with the suffering of others in the world: Marie Dupont, *Maman, pourquoi tu ne manges pas? Mon combat contre l'anorexie*, pp. 40–41 and 68.

Returning to the question of personality-illness conflation, it should be acknowledged that just as one cannot help one's basic personality, one cannot help one's genetic make-up (and it could be argued that basic personality is also a product of genetic make-up, even if it obviously interacts with and is influenced by environmental factors). So it is of interest that Balinska implies there may have been a genetic component in her predisposition to depression – 'mon arrière-grand-mère avait toujours parlé de ces "genes Hirszfeld", de cette tendance dans la famille à la depression sévère' [my great-grandmother had always spoken of these 'Hirszfeld genes' and of this tendency in the family towards severe depression] (p. 222) Comorbidity in anorectics has long been recognised in clinical writings on anorexia nervosa: many individuals suffer from both anorexia nervosa and depression without the latter being in any way a verifiably causal factor in the former. More particularly relevant to my book is Balinska's specific reference to the possibility of genetic heredity[85] as at play in both anorexia nervosa and bulimia nervosa (a line of research that has recently become prominent, for instance in very recent hypotheses on the role of the insula): 'la recherche actuelle va dans le sens d'une forte prédisposition héréditaire, et plus précisément génétique, dans le développement de l'anorexie comme de la boulimie' [current research points towards the existence of a strong hereditary, or more accurately genetic, predisposition towards the development of anorexia and bulimia] (p. 228). Her implicit support for the postulate of genetic heredity of anorexia nervosa at least is bolstered by the fact that one of her ancestors had died of the illness in 1943: 'Marysia Hirszfeld est morte en 1943 d'anorexie mentale' [Marysia Hirszfeld died in 1943 from anorexia nervosa] (p. 223).

Sixty years separate the death of this ancestor from anorexia nervosa and Balinska's account of her own, far more recent experience of the illness. However, while seeming a long time, sixty years is a blink of the eye in terms of several centuries, and Balinska posits the historical continuity of anorexia nervosa over the centuries, despite the differences in perception of the phenomenon over those centuries (see the Introduction). The second half of the extract below is perspicacious.

> Plusieurs chercheurs ont montré, de façon convaincante, l'existence de l'anorexie (appelée par toutes sortes de noms et confondue avec d'autres maladies et états) à d'autres siècles et dans d'autres sociétés. L'anorexie mentale a probablement toujours existé, avec une incidence fluctuante (comme toutes les pathologies), sans être le produit pur de notre civilisation contemporaine. Songeons aussi que les maladies infectieuses autrefois si prévalentes devaient s'attaquer à l'organisme affaiblie d'une anorexique avant que son amaigrissement extrême ne soit identifié en tant que tel. Autrement dit, dans une société hautement « aseptisée » et vaccinée, une personne dénutrie survivra plus longtemps, suffisamment longtemps, en tout cas, pour que l'anorexie à la source de cette malnutrition soit repérée, identifiée et analysée. Cela peut-être explique que l'anorexie paraisse avant tout comme une maladie contemporaine. (p. 226)

> Several researchers have convincingly demonstrated the existence of anorexia (known by all kinds of names and confused with other diseases and conditions) in other centuries and other societies. Anorexia nervosa has probably always existed, with a fluctuating incidence (like all

85 See the section 'Biological/Genetic/Hereditary Factors' in the Bibliographical Appendix.

> pathologies), without being wholly the product of our contemporary civilization. We should also remember that once-prevalent infectious diseases must have attacked the weakened body of an anorectic before extreme weight loss became identifiable as such. In other words, in a highly 'sanitised' and vaccinated society, a malnourished person will survive longer, long enough, in any case, so that the anorexia at the source of this malnutrition may be located, identified and analyzed. This may explain why anorexia appears above all to be a contemporary disease.

Finally, it is worth briefly examining the dialogue between Balinska and the neuropsychiatric doctor Stanislaw Tomkiewicz that constitutes the postface of her book. Presumably with reference to her belief that '*pour l'anorexique le chemin vers la guérison est long, semé de rechutes, et une attitude « normale » envers la nourriture (c'est-à-dire sans arrière-pensées) n'est jamais rétablie*' [for the anorectic the path towards healing is long, fraught with relapses and a 'normal' attitude towards food (i.e., one without ulterior motives) is never restored] (p. 245; Balinska's emphasis), Tomkiewicz, after giving great praise to her book, makes a certain criticism.

> Je pense aussi que vous êtes trop pessimiste s'agissant d'une attitude « spéciale » envers la nourriture qui ne disparaîtrait jamais de la vie d'une ex-anorexique. Au contraire, j'ai observé des personnes ayant souffert d'une anorexie qui mangent et qui parlent de la nourriture comme n'importe qui : à moins que l'art de cacher leurs véritables sentiments ne soit insondable. (p. 254)

> I also think that you are too pessimistic about a 'special' attitude towards food that would never disappear from the life of an ex-anorectic. On the contrary, I have observed people who have suffered from anorexia who eat and who talk about food like anyone else: unless the art of hiding their true feelings is unfathomable.

From his clinical position, he continues with his more positive portrait:

> Au cours de cette psychothérapie, j'essaye d'amener *en douceur* les patientes à comprendre la liaison sexe-nourriture et d'éveiller en elles le désir de devenir femme, y compris en acceptant et en ayant leurs règles. Sur ce point, précis mais important, la quasi-totalité de mes patientes (sauf celles que j'ai accepté de soigner sans espoir de guérison lorsqu'elles en sont arrivées au stade d'anorexie chronique, âgées de plus de 30 ans) a fait ce pas décisif sur le chemin de la guérison. (p. 260)

> During this psychotherapy, I try to *gently* bring the patients to understand the sex-food connection and awaken in them the desire to become a

> woman, including accepting and having their period. On this point, precise but important, almost all of my patients (except those aged over 30 that I agreed to take care of without hope of cure when they arrived at the stage of chronic anorexia) take this decisive step on the path of healing.

Two opposing inferences may be made from these two criticisms. One is that Balinska's work is indeed overly pessimistic. The other is that Tomkiewicz is observing 'from the outside', never having suffered 'from the inside' the anorexia nervosa forming the object of her testimony. Additionally, his second criticism betrays in its first sentence the doxa prevalent among clinicians and theoreticians working in the field of anorexia nervosa that it is primarily a fear of feminine identity and of 'woman's' reproductive nature. This is merely a theory, one among many on causation, and one that Balinska has rejected in her own case. Perhaps the more reliable authority should be taken to be the individual with 'insider knowledge' – Balinska herself.

Conclusion

In sum, it is patent that both Valère and Balinska regard the medical corps' treatment of anorectics as largely barbaric. Predictably, antithetical perspectives are normatively found among clinicians – not just doctors, but also nurses who work directly with patients rather than in a laboratory or as a researcher[86] – and by theoreticians whose work informs those clinicians. The vast majority would probably react to Valère's and Balinska's critiques in one of the following ways. One: simply discredit these authors' conceptuo-phenomenological accounts. Two: ostensibly take their accusations on board, but insist on their blind-spots. Three: assume that treatment has changed since the period of 1970s–90s recounted in these two texts. As noted in my Introduction, but is salutary to recall here in full, in a recent literature review of 2017 by Seah et al. the following was reported.

> Twelve papers explored the attitudes of healthcare professionals toward working with patients with EDs. The majority of the studies reported negative feelings toward patients with EDs, while only two studies reported positive feelings.
>
> Four studies from the US reported negative emotions toward patients with EDs. Frustration was a commonly expressed emotion by 68.8%

86 This is the definition of 'clinician' given by the Merriam-Webster dictionary.

> of the residents who worked in an inpatient adolescent medicine unit (n = 82) [...]. However, another study (n = 124) on psychologists and psychiatrists from various units reported low levels of frustration, with these professionals instead expressing higher levels of boredom and anger, and feelings of failure and incompetency towards patients with EDs [...]. Feelings of helplessness and emotional distress were recorded in a study of healthcare professionals working in ED treatment centers (n = 298) [...] and in general units (n = 183) [...].
>
> Two studies conducted in Australia also revealed negative emotions of healthcare professionals. Patients with EDs were viewed as 'manipulative' and 'non-compliant', causing annoyance in healthcare professionals [...].
>
> Three studies explored the attitudes of different healthcare professionals. 68.8% of the residents (n =34) in a study expressed feelings of frustration, compared to 45.2% of the nurses (n =14) [...]. Psychiatrists were reported to have higher levels of anger and frustration, and feelings of aggression toward patients with EDs, than psychologists [...].[87]
>
> Patients with EDs face more stigmatizing attitudes than psychiatric patients suffering more general conditions, such as depression [...].[88]

Behind these intellectual blind-spots may well reside negative and unacknowledged affect (note the references to 'helplessness') on the part of healthcare professionals treating anorectics.

87 Seah et al. 2017: 132–33.
88 Seah et al. 2017: 134.

CHAPTER TWO

Bulimia Nervosa/Bulimarexia

Section 2.1

The sub-title's designation of Valérie Rodrigue's *La peau à l'envers. Le roman vrai d'une boulimique* (1989)[1] as a 'roman vrai' indicates that it is at the very least an autofiction, if not a fully autobiographical account. I use the term autofiction in its now commonly accepted sense of a text that blends fictional and autobiographical elements, but with a heavy weighting of the latter. Here, the autodiegetic narrator is named Julia, not Valérie; but while her surname is not supplied, we are told that it is Spanish sounding (p. 72), which clearly aligns it with the author's surname, Rodrigue.

The general tone of this testimony to bulimia nervosa/bulimarexia (hereinafter, I will refer only to bulimia nervosa, since the severe dieting connoted in 'bulimarexia' is limited in Julia's case) is wry and self-deprecating but also vigorously defensive, defiant, irreverent, and not infrequently humorous. That humour is often black, but humour it is – and I personally intuit such humour as an attempt by Rodrigue/her textual avatar Julia to preserve personal dignity by not appearing to be sympathy-seeking, despite the severity of her illness. Such wryness and black humour occur on the very first page: 'Regardez-moi au fond des yeux : ces petits lacs marécageux. Peut-être y verrez-vous des kilomètres de bouffe, des montagnes de lave alimentaire' [Look deep into my eyes: these little marshy lakes. Perhaps there will be kilometres of food, mountains of dietary lava] (p. 11). Beyond the comedy of the hyperbole in this metaphor lies the intensity of Julia's shame about her bulimia nervosa – a shame implicit in the very next sentence's likening

1 Rodrigue, Valérie, *La peau à l'envers. Le roman vrai d'une boulimique* (Paris: Robert Laffont, 1989).

of herself to two other socially stigmatised categories of human beings: drug addicts and leprosy sufferers (p. 11). Use of the noun 'toxico' signals addiction, one of the common motifs, as previously remarked, in my primary corpus.[2] The last sentence of this paragraph also deploys metaphor, this time not humorously but, rather, forcefully, figuring her relationship with food as a marriage that has turned out to be horrific: 'Ma vie est un mariage d'horreur avec la bouffe. Me gaver et me vider tout le temps' [My life is a horrific marriage with food. Force-feeding and emptying myself all the time] (p. 11).

The desire to remain a child, or to return to a childlike state so often ascribed to anorectics in the secondary literature, is here expressed overtly by a bulimic subject herself, who goes even further by implying that she wants to remain not just a child but a baby: 'Obsédée par mon poids, que je veux toujours riquiqui, je m'use dans une lutte acharnée pour ne pas grossir. Pour rester un bébé' [Obsessed with my weight, which I still want to be itsy-bitsy, I wear myself out in a fierce fight not to get fat. To remain a baby] (p. 11). The wish to remain a baby may imply a wish to return to infantile sealing within the family unit. This correlates with the enmeshment of the typical anorectic's (if not typical bulimic's), family, asserted by many secondary sources (largely psychoanalytic in orientation), which is also suggested in the next sentence: 'Prise en sandwich dans ma famille' [Sandwiched in my family] (p. 1). Linked to that lack of autonomy from her family, of a sense of having an individual identity, leads to her 'eating' (note the word-play, here linking the metaphorical eating to the physical eating that escalates into polyphagia, or in simpler language, bingeing) her existential anguish, and to not allowing other people to intrude in her inner, fragile, ill-defined self: 'A force de ne plus savoir qui je suis, je finis par bouffer l'angoisse de vivre qui m'angoisse, par refuser l'intrusion des autres' [Due to not knowing who I am, I end up eating the anxiety of living that anguishes me and refusing the intrusion of others] (p. 12). In the grip of her illness, that lack of a sense of individual identity reaches its zenith when, stocking up on food in supermarkets for a binge, she feels that she no longer exists at all (p. 12). The self-destructive impulses of the bulimic are dramatically conveyed in the metaphor of excessive food amounts as poison and her consumption of them as killing herself: 'Je rentre chez moi avec ce poison qui me pend à bout de bras avant de me tuer à bout portant' [I go home with this poison that keeps me at

2 See the sections on 'Addiction' in the Bibliographical Appendix.

arm's length before killing me at close range] (p. 12). Julia's despair is conveyed in another metaphor deployed to depict bulimia nervosa as the vomiting out of a life that is existentially painful: 'Pour ne pas grossir, je vais vomir. Aux W.-C., je vois le scénario en sens inverse et je dégueule ma vie' [To avoid getting fat, I'll throw up. In the bathroom, I see the scenario in the opposite direction and I puke up my life] (p. 12). And one other early example of effective use of metaphor is the image of bingeing as a wedding with food (in ironic contrast with the 'mariage d'horreur avec la bouffe' [horrific marriage with food] (p. 11) – albeit a wedding that takes place in complete privacy: 'La noce commence quand je me suis assurée une solitude totale : porte fermée à clef, téléphone débranché' [The wedding ceremony begins when I have ensured total solitude: locked door, unplugged phone] (p. 12). In Julia's need for absolute secrecy and the cutting of contact with the outside world just before embarking on a binge, there is a parallel with Loupias (one of my two case studies in Chapter 3).

The severity of Julia's bulimia nervosa is underlined in 'Je me lève la nuit, dix, vingt fois pour bouffer et vomir' [I get up ten or twenty times a night to eat and throw up] (p. 13). This leads to a sense of the bulimic's abjection, rendererered via contrast with the general public's perception of anorectics, who are, in her view, valorised:

> l'anorexique pèche par excès de perfectionnisme, elle joue avec la faim et met l'univers à ses pieds.
> La boulimique s'enlise dans une coulée alimentaire et abîme sa face externe, celle que l'on jette en pâture au jugement du monde. (p. 13)

> the anorectic sins through an excess of perfectionism, she plays with hunger and puts the universe at her feet.
> The bulimic is bogged down in a flow of food and spoils her outer face, the one that is thrown to the wolves for the judgement of the world.

The very next sentence re-introduces the common motif of addiction via use of the verb 'se shooter' [to shoot up/shoot oneself] (the discount items mentioned being food): 'Nous, les boulimiques, on se shoote aux promotions discount à deux balles en promotion' [We bulimics shoot up on discount promotions, we shoot ourselves with two discount bullets] (p. 13). Bulimia nervosa as a form of addiction akin to drug addiction is immanent in Julia's later use of the term 'overdose' to describe the excessive amount of food she buys for a planned binge (p. 132). The analogy is reinforced when Julia later homologises her addictive ED with the drug addiction of her friend Dominique (p. 135).

We have started in medias res, as does the text itself. To take a step back, what of the aetiology of Julia's illness? Her worries about food are located very precisely as having started when she was only 13 (p. 15). They first surface in a bizarre hyper-awareness of her father's mastication, which she perceives as obscene, in contrast with her usual idealisation of her father as a quasi-deity – 'Lui, l'être suprême' [Him, the supreme being] (p. 37) – and with her adoration of him – 'il est encore l'homme de ma vie' [he is still the man of my life] (p. 35). The father–daughter relationship turns out to be even more complicated by the fact that her father suffers from severely depressive episodes, with her reaction to these being extreme. After visiting him in hospital, she is, in her turn, severely traumatised: 'En quittant l'hôpital, j'ai l'impression que quelque chose en moi est mort ou malade' [Upon leaving the hospital, I have the impression that something in me is dead or sick] (p. 36). It is worth noting that the secondary literature stresses complex father–daughter relationships in the case of bulimics. That complexity is manifest not just in her ambivalent feelings towards him, but also in the phobic fantasy that he will end up eating her, implying a sense of his omnipotence over her. And indeed, he is depicted as a strict, authoritarian father. This strictness is accompanied by the setting of impossibly high standards for his children, leading to disappointment when Julia fails to be anything more than a mediocre student (p. 16).

Various predisposing/vulnerability factors in the development of bulimia nervosa asserted in the secondary literature are inscribed in the text. One is impulsivity,[3] which Julia ascribes implicitly to herself in the

3 For example, 'à l'image de la crise boulimique elle-même, la tendance à l'impulsivité et aux passages à l'acte est importante' [like the bulimic crisis itself, the tendency towards impulsivity and acting out is important] (Jeammet 2004: 23). See also the following: Johnson, C. and Connors, M.E., *The Etiology and Treatment of Bulimia Nervosa: A Biopsychosocial Perspective* (New York: Basic Books, 1987). More recently, it was reported: 'A recent trait-based risk model of BN highlights the impulsivity-related trait of negative urgency (i.e., the tendency to engage in rash acts when distressed) as an important transdiagnostic risk factor for the initial onset of BN.' Reas, Deborah L., 'Impulsivity-related traits distinguish women with co-occurring bulimia nervosa in a psychiatric sample', *International Journal of Eating Disorders*, 49, 12 (2016), 1093–96 (1093). 'Bulimia nervosa is very commonly associated with other 'adolescent' problem behaviors, such as experimentation with drugs or alcohol, smoking and sexual experimentation, which significantly increase the risk of this population.' Nicholson, J.

following once her illness has established itself, but which predates that establishment: 'De ma boulimie et de mes difficultés à vivre, ma famille n'a que la face externe : *mes rébellions, crises ado, fugues diverses*' [My family only sees the external face of my bulimia and my difficulties in living: my rebellions, teenage crises and running away] (p. 100; my emphasis). Another is, unsurprisingly, dissatisfaction with her body. At the age of 14, she dislikes her adolescent body, but not because of any fatness – quite the contrary, as seen in her claim on p. 41: 'je suis plutôt maigre' [I'm rather skinny]. In this respect she, like de Peretti (analysed in the second part of this chapter) is atypical of bulimics who, like her, will also go on to experience anorectic periods: '[t]he anorectic-bulimics also have a higher prevalence of premorbid obesity'.[4] Rather, Julia dislikes her body because of a perceived disharmony between its component parts: 'membres affreusement longs, tronc courtaud, silhouette transparente, allure passe-muraille' [horrifically long limbs, squat torso, transparent figure, the look of someone who can pass through walls] (p. 18). Significantly, she starts to find eating exhausting, and to perceive her body as alien (evoking the mind–body split/dualism that is such a prominent motif in the primary corpus). Julia personifies her body as a jailor with whom she refuses to come to terms. At this point, Julia's ideal is not of a thin body, but of a body she feels to be her own.

> Rien ne m'intéresse. Manger m'épuise. Étrangère à ce corps qui m'incarcère, je refuse de composer avec ses lois. Je ne serai pas assez mesquine pour sympathiser avec mon geôlier. Moi aussi, j'ai un idéal : le mien. Ronde, maigre, carrée, étirée, quelle importance ? C'est toujours un corps. On est fermé dedans quelle que soit sa forme. (p. 18)

> Nothing interests me. Eating exhausts me. A stranger to this body that incarcerates me, I refuse to deal with its laws. I will not be petty enough to sympathise with my jailer. I too have an ideal: mine. Round, lean, square, long, what's the difference? It's still a body. Whatever its form, we are still shut in.

The mind–body split/mind–body dualism is also present, along with the aspiration to 'purity' also widespread in the primary corpus, in the following, once Julia's bulimia nervosa has developed: 'Je voudrais tant

and Nicholls, D., 'Clinical and diagnostic characteristics of eating disorders in children and adolescents', in Latzer et al. 2011, 39–55 (47).

4 Halmi, Katherine, 'Current concepts and definitions', in Szmukler et al. 1996: 31.

être un tunnel filiforme, cylindrique et aseptisé. Avant d'atteindre le summum de perfection, il me faudra des années d'efforts pour nettoyer mon intérieur, le purifier à l'aide de puissants laxatifs' [I would like to be a filiform tunnel, cylindrical and sanitised. Before reaching the pinnacle of perfection, it will take years of effort to clean my interior, to purify it with powerful laxatives] (p. 97). The mind–body split/dualism is particularly salient in Julia's anguished self-interrogation : 'Jusqu'où va ma méprise? Mon horreur de la chair, de cet amas de matières mortelles? Est-il possible de devenir un jour un esprit évanescent et libre ? d'atteindre l'inquantifiable, l'inexistence sans mourir ?' [How far does my contempt go ? My horror of the flesh, of this mass of mortal matter ? Is it possible to one day become an evanescent and free spirit? To reach the unquantifiable, inexistence without dying?] (p. 97).

An additional predisposing/vulnerability factor commonly identified by the secondary literature for those who go on to become anorectic rather than bulimic, is an overly fusional relationship with her mother (in Julia's case, at the age of 14). The striking metaphor of coagulation expresses this overly fusional relationship, which she initially presents as a general truth than the particular truth of a child: 'coagulé par les attaches à sa mère. De menus cordons invisibles vous lient inévitablement à ses quatre volontés et il vous est impossible de lui échapper' [coagulated by attachments to her mother. Tiny invisible cords inevitably bind you to her every whim and you cannot escape her] (p. 19). More personalised is what immediately follows: 'Ma mère, il faudra qu'elle me rejette, qu'elle rompe nos liens si elle veut se débarrasser de moi, *car je vois par ses yeux* et pense si j'en ai l'autorisation' [My mother, she will have to reject me, to break our links if she wants to get rid of me, *because I see through her eyes* and wonder if I have permission] (p. 19; my emphasis). Later on, when she has fallen headlong into bulimia nervosa, she imagines her mother's contempt for and disowning of her – a projection of her own self-perception as a 'boudin loqueteux' [ragged fat lump] – and engages in a form of affective 'mimétisme' [mimicry], reacting to her mother's presumed hatred for her with murderous feelings/hatred for her mother. Yet the hatred is paradoxically juxtaposed with the possibility of excessive love for that same mother: 'Dans ces moments de violente empoignade, j'ai envie de tuer ma mère. Je ne sais plus si je l'aime trop ou si je la déteste' [In these moments of violent fighting, I want to kill my mother. I don't know if I love her too much or if I hate her] (p. 102). That paradoxical relationship with her mother, blending alienation and unhealthy identification, is also patent in the following remark: 'Je suis étrangère à ma maman parce que je ne lui ressemble pas assez pour me sentir femme et trop pour avoir ma propre identité' [I am a stranger to my mom because I don't resemble her enough to feel like a woman and too much to have my own identity] (p. 103). A final predisposing/vulnerability factor that is applied to both anorectics and bulimics in the secondary literature is people-pleasing, professed here by Julia: 'je ne sais pas dire non et je déteste par-dessus tout déplaire' [I don't know how to say no and above all I hate to displease people] (p. 31); cf. 'C'est drôle ce type : il m'indiffère. Seuls m'intéressent ses airs de Dame aux camélias. J'irai chez lui parce que je ne veux pas le décevoir' [He's funny, this guy: he's indifferent to me. I am only interested in his air of *Dame aux Camélias*. I'll go round to his place because I don't want to disappoint him] (p. 64). Finally, much later on in her testimony, another clue to the aetiology of her ED is limned as her sense of not knowing what to do with acute feelings (other than to block them out through bingeing, it is implied): 'Je n'ai jamais su quoi faire des sentiments, quand ils sont trop aigus : ils font mal comme un rasage de trop près' [I have never known what to do with feelings when they're too acute: they hurt like shaving too close] (p. 110).

Having examined predisposing/vulnerability factors in the development of Julia's bulimia nervosa, I now turn to the details of that development. The first sign of a desire to reduce her appetite, and by harmful means, comes at the age of 14 years: 'Par pur hasard, et de bonne heure, je découvre les vertus anorexigènes et subsersives du Neo Co en comprimés pris en dose massive et m'offre à profusion de scabreux délires artificiels grâce à cet opiacé' [Early on and by complete chance, I discover the appetite suppressing and subversive properties of Neo Co tablets taken in huge doses and give myself plenty of scabrous, artificial delusions thanks to this opiate] (p. 20). But rather than the anorexia nervosa that this discovery seems to portend, it is over-eating that begins. During the summer of her 14th year, afflicted by an undefined malaise, she begins to eat in order to make time pass more quickly. It is not irrelevant that apropos this malaise, a link between eating and language (a trope common in the primary corpus[5]) occurs in 'Pour ne pas périr d'ennui, je me mets à dévorer des mots, des lettres magiques que je vole de livre en livre' [To not die of boredom, I set to devouring words and magical letters that I steal from book upon book] (p. 38). The weight gain following her

5 See the section 'Language: EDs as a Form of Language' in the Bibliographical Appendix.

over-eating intensifies her sense of bodily discomfort and dis-ease: 'Au fil des jours, je me sens serrée dans mon corps, dont la peau se tend comme celle des tam-tams et comprends le sens d' « être mal dans sa peau »' [As the days go by, I feel tight in my body, whose skin is stretched like that of a tambourine, and understand the meaning of 'feeling uneasy in your own skin'] (p. 31). An abnormal mode of eating begins, namely eating alone in her bedroom (p. 33). In parallel, she is often told by her casual boyfriend after he has penetrated her that she has 'des grosses fesses' [a fat ass] (p. 41). But unusually, she soon afterwards expresses an awareness unusual for those who go on to develop bulimia/bulimarexia that she is, if anything, thin rather than fat: 'Et le type qui me traitait de gros cul alors que je suis plutôt maigre ?' [And the guy who said I had a fat butt even though I'm pretty skinny?] (p. 41).

Undiagnosed depression eventually leads to her using food as a tranquilliser and painkiller: 'Pour faire taire cette voix en détresse, je cherche un calmant suprême, un amnésique. Je me console avec la bouffe pour le plaisir animal de me sentir pleine' [To silence this distressed voice, I search for a supreme tranquilliser, an amnesiac. I console myself with food through the animal pleasure of feeling full] (p. 42). Again, immanent in this is the motif of addiction common in the primary corpus. Food becomes an anaesthetic that numbs anxiety and/or distress: 'Plus rien ne compte, que mes doigts dans ma bouche, le bruit régulier de mes mâchouillements' [Nothing matters except my fingers in my mouth, the regular noise of my chewing] (pp. 42–43). The last clause here ironically evokes the sound of her father's eating, which provokes antipathy in her, whereas the sounds of her own chewing are positively connoted, as part of a calming process. Another motif common in the primary corpus is 'le vide' [the emptiness]: she feels the need to fill by food what is not a physical but an existential emptiness. Equally significant is her framing of constant snacking as a regression to an infantile, indeed embryonic stage linked to incorporation in the maternal body: 'Je m'accroche au grignotage, à ce geste primaire comme si chaque déglutition me rapprochait davantage de l'eau maternelle, du sommeil d'avant la naissance' [I cling to the act of snacking, this primary gesture, as if each swallow would bring me closer to the maternal water, to a sleep before birth] (p. 42; cf. 'Pour rester un bébé' [To remain a baby] on p. 11).

This absorption in eating becomes a form of insulation from the threatening outside world, which converges with Balinksa's view of anorexia nervosa (although not bulimia nervosa) as a fear of the exterior world (see Chapter 1): 'Le reste du monde disparaît par enchantement, englouti avec ma nourriture' [The rest of the world magically disappears, swallowed up with my food] (Rodrigue, p. 42). With respect to the main title of Rodrigue's text, *La peau à l'envers*, [Skin Inside Out] 'l'envers' [inside out] connotes exteriority. This main title is alluded to and partly elucidated in a remark made after seeing a doctor who has made her aware of her communication problems: 'J'ai l'impression d'être montée à l'envers. Lisse au-dehors comme une chair privée de sensation' [I feel like I'm put together inside out. Featureless on the outside like flesh deprived of sensation] (p. 146). The motif of flesh deprived of the ability to feel is located as having begun when she was only eight years old, after having suffered sexual abuse by an uncle (which may also, clearly, count as a predisposing factor in developing an eating disorder). Her allegations against him having been discredited by his vehement denial, she is transformed from a child who has been victimised into a child who is condemned by her family as guilty of mythomania and neurosis (pp. 146–47). Julia's reaction is 'Vite, vite, que je grandisse, pour partir loin, que je devienne grosse et laide pour qu'il m'oublie' [Quick, quick, let me grow up so I can go far away, let me become fat and ugly so he forgets me] (p. 147). This initial desire to become fat and ugly in the hope – probably unconscious – that the rapist uncle would cease his minatory sexual pursuit of her is a desire diagnosed by the psychotherapist Susie Orbach who, as mentioned in Chapter 2, writes as a practising psychotherapist with long experience of treating eating-disordered patients:

> [T]he most frequently stated advantage women saw in being fat had to do with sexual protection. It is almost as though through the protective aspects of the fat, women are saying they must deny their own sexuality in order to be seen as a person.[6]

An additional 'benefit' of over-eating is conveyed in '[e]n mangeant, je prends du poids dans les deux sens du terme. Seule façon de m'ancrer au sol, de ne pas être à la merci d'un coup de vent ou de l'humeur des autres' [By eating, I gain weight in both senses of the word. It's the only way to anchor myself on the ground, to not to be at the mercy of a gust of wind or the mood of others] (p. 44). This facet of hyperphagia, or rather its result of becoming overweight (which inevitably happens to Julia, who

6 Orbach, Susie, *Fat is a Feminist Issue... How to Lose Weight Permanently – Without Dieting* (London: Arrow, 1988 [first published London: Paddington Press, 1978]), p. 70.

in two months gains 10 kilos: see p. 44), is also emphasised by Orbach: 'Fat is a way of saying "no" to powerlessness and self-denial.'[7] (This concords with one of the other primary texts, Karin Bernfeld's *Alice au pays des femelles* (2001).[8] Julia's own sense of powerlessness is replete in the fact that she feels she is 'à la merci d'un coup de vent ou de l'humeur des autres' (p. 44).

Let us return to commentary on the parallel with Balinksa and symptomal overlaps between different types of EDs, notwithstanding their obvious differences. Over-eating also serves for Julia as a buffer against a threatening outside world of other human beings, showing convergence with Balinksa's precept about anorexia nervosa, viz. that the anorectic fundamentally fears the exterior (see Chapter 1): 'On cesse d'être quand les autres commencent à bouger autour de vous. Car c'est l'un ou l'autre. Pendant que je mange, je suis persuadée d'exister vraiment [...] Comment alors exister dans le monde avec les autres sans être bouffée par le fait même de leur présence ? Imbroglio mental' [We stop being when others begin to move around us. Because it's one or the other. While I'm eating, I'm sure I really exist [...] How then can I exist in the world with others without being eaten by the very fact of their presence? Mental imbroglio] (Rodrigue, p. 43). The trope of EDs established by Balinksa – in her case, with respect to anorexia nervosa alone – as fundamentally a fear of and thus blocking out of the exterior, including other people, and that has also been inscribed previously by Rodrigue (see p. 42) is succinctly encapsulated in the last clause of Julia's following assertion: 'Au fond, le nœud du problème est là : je suis imperméable aux autres, les mots me roulent dessus sans jamais me marquer, je suis exilée en moi, et *vomis tout ce qui émane de l'extérieur*' [Basically, the crux of the problem is this: I am impervious to others, words roll off me without ever marking me, I am exiled within myself and *loathe everything that comes from outside*] (p. 144; my emphasis). In that last clause, the wordplay is adept, with 'vomir' [to loathe] referring here to loathing, but obviously having a literal meaning of vomiting, which is a central symptom of Julia's ED.

But the ephemeral 'benefits' of such over-eating inevitably have their negative downsides. One is that, as Julia's bingeing increases, in her quest for 'un état extatique où se confondent le jour, la nuit, le salé, le sucre' [an ecstatic state where night is confused with day and sweet

7 Orbach 1988: 43.

8 Bernfeld, Karin, *Alice au pays des femelles* (Paris: Balland, 2001), p. 100.

with savoury], she loses all sense of hunger and satiety – a loss typical of bulimics (p. 44). Another is stomach pains:

> J'ai peur du vide et du plein, et cherche à combler mon malaise en me remplissant. A ras bord, au-delà du possible… pour que mon estomac excessivement ballonné me fasse très mal… pour que cette douleur physique et identifiable me fasse oublier l'autre… ce vertige vide, plein, vide, plein… impalpable. (p. 44)
>
> I am afraid of emptiness and fullness and seek to satisfy my discomfort by filling myself. To the brim, beyond the possible… so that my excessively bloated stomach hurts a lot… so that this physical and identifiable pain makes me forget the other one… this empty vertigo, full, empty, full… impalpable.

Significant in this quotation are two other points. One is the motif of an existential 'vide' [emptiness] expressed by so many other eating-disorders subjects in the primary corpus. The other is that, in 'pour que cette douleur physique et identifiable me fasse oublier l'autre…' [so that this physical and identifiable pain makes me forget the other one…], there is a clear correspondence with the temporary relief from anguish experienced by self-harmers who, for instance, cut themselves (see Cairns 2015).

A statement is made by Julia about her weight gain that is both enigmatic (for she has the opposite of mastery of her body) and highly atypical of the bulimic she will go on to become, for bulimics in their vast majority are terrified of weight gain rather than seeking to augment it further (hence their purgation): 'Assez satisfaite d'avoir ainsi la maîtrise de mon corps, je décide de mettre les bouchées doubles pour enfler comme la grenouille au point d'exploser sur les murs de ma chambre' [Quite satisfied to have thus gained control over my body, I decided to work hard to swell like the frog to the point of exploding onto the walls of my room] (p. 45). Similarly atypical is her proclaimed satisfaction in publicly exhibiting her extra weight, even if this is done with a false gaiety that seems to be a function of her revolt against the exterior world: 'J'exhibe ma graisse au soleil de mon gros rire glorieux, rancunier et surtout malheureux' [I display my fat in the sun of my great big, glorious, resentful, and above all unhappy laughter] (p. 45). However, this satisfaction is only temporary. When, aged 18, she takes cognisance of her rapid weight gain by looking at herself properly in the mirror, she is highly distressed (pp. 45–46). Yet, paradoxically, her sense of mastering her body is reaffirmed, and even posited as a source of pride, partly in her caricaturing and defiance of what is most young girls' counter-ideal of bodily beauty:

> je suis une caricature de ce que n'importe quelle jeune fille souhaite ne jamais devenir. Ce constat n'est pas un aveu d'échec, mais une réalité dont j'ai une parfaite maîtrise. Cette vulgarité, cette baudruche, c'est mon œuvre, et j'en revendique tous les droits d'auteur. J'en suis fière [...]. (p. 46)

> I am a caricature of what any girl wants never to become. This observation is not an admission of failure, but a reality over which I have perfect control. This vulgarity, this balloon, it's my work, and I claim all the rights of authorship. I am proud of it [...].

But what follows compromises her adamant assertion of pride, by implying that it is the effect of the mind-altering drug that food has become for her: 'Sous l'emprise d'une euphorie nouvelle, je ne me vois ni réellement ni objectivement. La bouffe me maintient dans un état extatique comme un alcool trop fort, et occulte tout réalisme' [Under the influence of a new euphoria, I see myself neither realistically nor objectively. The food keeps me in an ecstatic state like an alcohol that's too strong, and obscures all realism] (p. 46; cf. Loupias in Chapter 3). Yet even here, there is a 'benefit' – the immunity it gives her to sensitivity about others, to the exterior world (cf. Balinksa again): 'Ma laideur est peut-être le prix à payer pour trouver la paix. Grâce à elle, je perds ma sensibilité au monde' [My ugliness is perhaps the price to pay in order to find peace. Thanks to it, I lose my sensitivity to the world] (p. 46).

Her euphoria and pride prove evanescent when, one morning, she suddenly realises that her inability to feel anything for others previously precious to her has left her wandering in 'une espèce de tunnel brumeux, tunnel sans fin, spirale inquiétante' [a sort of foggy tunnel, an endless tunnel, a worrying spiral] (p. 47). The metaphors are hard-hitting. Her conclusion, 'Je suis un mal de vivre' [I am a misery of life] (p. 47), provokes hysterical sobbing, an abrupt phenomenological transformation of her bingeing as beatitude into devil – 'ce diable qui m'entraîne dans la plus dingue des valses' [this devil who leads me into the craziest of waltzes] (p. 47) – and a lurch from one extreme to the other, from bingeing to drastic dieting (p. 47). The drastic dieting gets her to a weight of 45 kilos/7 stones, which for her height (1.61 metres/5 feet 3.3 inches: see p. 145) is underweight. At this new weight, she imagines she will 'contracter l'équilibre mental et tuer ainsi mes angoisses morbides' [contract mental balance and in doing so kill my morbid anxieties] (p. 47). This is a curious turn of phrase, for the verb 'contracter' [to contract] is commonly used to denote the contracting of an illness, perhaps the implication being that normatively defined mental balance is in fact a pathology. This would square with Julia's general cynicism about and defiance of the normative. Another exegesis would be that for Julia, normatively defined mental balance is unattractive in comparison to her previous euphoric highs induced by bingeing and their concomitant anesthetising of feelings, which made her invulnerable to others/the exterior world. In any case, she soon realises that something in her 'reste désespérément coincé' [remains desperately cornered] (p. 47) and becomes lucid about the fact that her desired low weight 'n'est pas un passeport pour le bien-être' [is not a passport to wellbeing] (p. 47).

The sense of her previous fat having been a protective cocoon and as having blocked unwelcome sexual attention from men – 'J'ai mal à la graisse manquante comme les amputés, cette ouate tissée tel un cocon protecteur. Et puis, pourquoi ces regards masculins plantés sur mes fesses moulées dans un jean taille 36 ?' [My missing fat hurts just like with amputees, that cotton wool spun like a protective cocoon. And what's more, why do I get male looks planted on my buttocks moulded into size 36 jeans?] (p. 48) – again converges with the theories of Orbach, who avers that 'many women first become fat in an attempt to avoid being made into sexual objects at the beginning of their adult lives'.[9] Despite missing this cocoon, she tries to retain her new lower weight, and in so doing, finds that an obsessional love hate relationship develops with food, which is at once highly coveted and demonised as a poison (p. 49). The obsession is greatly to her mental and physical detriment: 'Mes journées gravitent autour de ce dilemma : manger – ne pas manger. Les vertiges, crampes, assauts de bile sont des bornes qui jalonnent le chemin dingue que j'ai emprunté' [My days revolve around this dilemma: to eat – not to eat. Dizziness, cramps and sudden worrying are markers that punctuate the crazy path I have taken] (p. 49). But morbid mental enjoyment is experienced in this damage she is inflicting on her body: 'Je jouis de voir mon corps dévorer ses propres reserves, ronger ses capitons' [I enjoy watching my body devour its own reserves and gnaw on its cushioning] (p. 49). And, although this may be a retrospective realisation, awareness is expressed of the illusory nature of her bodily perception: 'Je crois toucher le bonheur en voyant dans le miroir la représentation imaginaire et idéalisée de moi-même se superposer à

9 Orbach 1988: 35.

mon image réelle' [I think I reach happiness by seeing in the mirror the imaginary and idealised representation of myself superimposed on my real image] (p. 49). Yet at the time, what is happening is a reversal from bingeing to starvation as a means of attaining emotional self-sufficiency: 'Je me sens chez moi dans ce corps famélique et engourdi. C'est le prix à payer pour vivre en autarcie sentimentale. En ne mangeant pas, je me situe hors d'atteinte des autres, physiquement autonome' [I feel at home in this starved and numb body. This is the price to pay for living in sentimental self-sufficiency. By not eating, I'm out of reach of others, physically autonomous] (pp. 49–50). Apprehension of her former sense of lacking personal integrity and space, of vulnerability to invasion by and conflation with others – lack of ego boundaries – is expressed in the succeeding statement: 'Ainsi, ils ne peuvent plus me détruire, me bouffer, m'attraper pour me confondre en eux' [That way they can no longer destroy me, eat me, catch me to blend me into themselves]. As stated in Chapter 1, my observations in a previous publication had noted personal space and space boundaries as a problematic concept in those afflicted by EDs.[10] It is interesting that the metaphor of this invasion and conflation is gustatory: eating as incorporation of the other.

Her mother's perception of her daughter as pretty now she has lost weight, and is in fact underweight, albeit not dramatically so (p. 51) is nefarious, and places that mother in the category the sociologist Muriel Darmon has named *incitateur* [inciter].[11] The unattainability of the anorexic ideal is incarnated in Julia's sense that she is still not thin enough, and in enunciation of an equally nefarious, famous saying that demonstrates the sociocultural influences on the development of EDs: 'On n'est jamais assez maigre' [We are never thin enough] (p. 51).[12] The morbidity of her attitude is patent in what she says about her bones in the succeeding clause: 'les os sont toujours trop gros. Va faire maigrir des os, et puis certains courbes s'obstinent à rester rondes ; impossible de perdre mes seins et mes fesses' [the bones are always too big. Go make the bones thinner, and even then some curves stubbornly stay round; it's impossible to lose my breasts and buttocks] (p. 51). This morbidity is equally obvious, particularly via use of the word dangereusement [dangerously], in Julia's reflection, 'Il faut maigrir encore pour voir saillir mes côtes,

10 Cairns 2015.

11 Darmon 2003: 112–13.

12 See the section 'Sociocultural Factors: Their Role in the Development of EDs' in the Bibliographical Appendix.

les os de mes hanches pointer dangereusement et délimiter ainsi ma place dans l'espace' [I have to lose more weight so I can see my ribs protruding and my hip bones pointing dangerously outwards, marking out my place in space] (p. 52). Also of salience here is the need she feels to mark the boundaries of the place she occupies in space (see again Cairns 2015). In retrospect, Julia recognises the mentally deleterious, indeed pathological, nature of the year she spent possessed by efforts to lose yet more weight (regularly using a tape measure to assess the size of multiple bodily sites – wrists, ankles, knees, neck, thighs, waist; weighing herself every quarter of an hour, applying so-called 'slimming' creams, etc.): 'Un an passé chez moi à me ramoner la cervelle pour trouver chaque jour un délire plus ou moins contraignant. Dans le dessein unique de passer le temps et maigrir encore' [A year spent at home scouring my brain every day to find a delirium that was more or less binding. With the sole single intention of passing time and continuing to lose weight] (p. 53). In addition to the pathological quest to lose yet more weight, there is also, in 'passer le temps' [passing time], the implication of the existential ennui evoked earlier. One of the other manifestations of this ennui, and also most probably of another method deployed to lose yet more weight, is the excessive walking in which she engages (hyperactivity is another common motif in the primary corpus[13]). Her own surmise regarding this engagement reveals her mental disorientation and sense of self-division or self-loss: 'Je marche longtemps, longtemps, peut-être à un coin de rue Julia rencontrera Julia' [I walk for a long, long time, maybe at a street corner Julia will meet Julia] (p. 54).

Eventually, her iron will cracks, her bodily needs take over, and she binges on multiple cakes. There is here a sense of self-dispossession, and, via simile, a sense of being possessed instead by a devil that reduces her to a puppet:

> Quand je passe à la caisse, je n'en crois pas mon porte-monnaie. Il me faudrait un an pour bouffer tous les gateaux. Une autre que moi m'ordonne dans ma tête de tout finir jusqu'à la dernière miette. Comme un diable qui fait de moi la marionnette de sa volonté. (p. 54)

> When I go to the cash register, I don't believe my wallet. It would take me a year to eat all the cakes. Someone other than me orders me in my head to finish everything right down to the last crumb. Like a devil who makes me the puppet of his will.

13 See the section 'Hyperactivity' in the Bibliographical Appendix.

Despite these disconcerting sensations, the binge has one 'benefit', previously registered above – an anxiolytic effect: 'l'angoisse a disparu' [the anxiety has disappeared] (p. 55). The trope of (over-)eating as a necessary anxiolytic is reinscribed shortly afterwards, and the hypothesis of bingeing as an addiction thereby reinforced:

> Je tue mon angoisse en mangeant. Parce que, au moment où je gloutonne, mon cerveau disjoncte, mes pensées se noient dans l'incohérence.
> Je m'affole à la vue de ce calmant à ma portée. (p. 61)

> I kill my anxiety by eating. Because, at the moment when I'm stuffing my face, a switch trips in my brain and my thoughts drown in incoherence.
> I freak out at the sight of this tranquilliser within my grasp.

The mental drive to devour food overrides any physical satiety, but that drive is nonetheless conveyed in ambiguously valorising terms, via simile, as something akin to love, albeit a demanding love: 'De bouchée en bouchée, le désir de dévorer s'accroît au lieu de s'estomper avec la satiété, se fait impérieux, obsédant, exigeant comme l'amour' [From bite to bite, the desire to devour increases instead of fading with satisfaction, it becomes imperious, obsessive and demanding like love] (p. 55). Love suggests an interpersonal relationship, and much later on, Julia's bulimia nervosa is personified as a partner with whom she has a sadomasochistic, destructive, but unbreakable relationship: 'Ma boulimie et moi, on forme un couple sado-maso, « ni avec toi ni sans toi »' [My bulimia and I, we form a sadomasochistic couple, 'neither with you nor without you'] (p. 124).

Yet while these qualities appear positive, Julia is aware of falling back into a trap, and determines to find an antidote to weight gain (p. 55). The register of love, or at least of eroticism, is reprised in Julia's use of a sexually connoted noun, 'orgie' [orgy] (p. 56), to denote a binge (cf. Loupia). Later, via a rhetorical question, a blunt and defiant parallel is drawn between her irresistible attraction to and orgasmic pleasure in the consumption of food and sexual attraction and orgasm: 'Si j'ai le point G sous la langue, personne ne s'étonnera, non ?' [If my G-spot were under my tongue, nobody would be surprised, would they?] (p. 124).[14] But the

14 See the section 'Addiction to Food/Bingeing/Compulsive Eating/Hyperphagia Specifically (Sometimes Likened during Consumption to Sexual *jouissance*)' in the Bibliographical Appendix.

flip-side to this erotic purview is use of sexual language to describe the opposite of the pleasure normally connoted by eroticism – self-disgust: 'Ce matin, le premier de l'été, suite à une orgie sans précédent, j'ai paniqué à la vue de mon estomac distendu comme un sac poubelle qu'on a oublié de descendre' [This morning, the first of the summer, after an unprecedented orgy I panicked at the sight of my distended stomach like a garbage bag that someone forgot to take out] (p. 56). Sexual language – 'baiser' [to fuck] – is also used with a negàtive charge to convey her disdain for her body when it resists the planned antidote to her binge, namely trying to make herself vomit up the food. After half an hour with no success, she persists, asserting her ambition for sovereignty over her body (note again the mind–body split/dualism): 'Attends un peu. Ne crois pas me baiser comme ça. Il n'y a pas plus monarque que le roi, et c'est moi qui gouverne chez moi' [Wait a bit. Don't think you can fuck me like that. There is no greater monarch than the king, and I'm the one who governs at home] (p. 57). Contrasting with the assertion of her own power ('c'est moi qui gouverne chez moi' [I'm the one who governs at home]), she denigrates herself with bitterly ironic humour:

> Je me fous deux doigts dans le tuyau du gosier. Les larmes me montent aux yeux. Rageuse, je garde les yeux ouverts pour ne rien perdre du spectacle. Mesdames, messieurs, bienvenue au cirque Barnum. Vous assistez à la grande première d'une boulimique accro'. (p. 57)

> I throw myself down with two fingers in the back of my throat. Tears come to my eyes. Angry, I keep my eyes open so as not to miss any of the show. Ladies and gentlemen, welcome to the Barnum Circus. You're attending the great premiere of an addicted bulimic.

Her tenacity finally pays off as she suddenly vomits copiously, and her reaction is one of pride, coupled with delight at the prospect of now being able to allow herself future 'orgies' with weight impunity: 'A nouveau vide, je pense avec délice aux orgies que je vais pouvoir m'offrir en toute impunité. J'ai trouvé le truc. Finalement, je ne suis pas si bête' [Empty once again, I think with delight of the orgies that I'm going to treat myself to with total impunity. I've cracked it. I'm not so stupid after all' (p. 58).

Thereafter a vicious circle of bingeing and vomiting sets in, involving secrecy and dissimulation in the family home. Again, due to the use of the present historic, it is unclear whether Julia was lucid at the time, or only in her retrospective narrative, about the illusory nature of her certainty of being in control: 'Je déjoue la nature pour avoir l'illusion de maîtriser ma vie. C'est ma seule certitude' [I thwart nature to have the illusion of controlling my life. This is my only certainty] (p. 59). While in the grip of bingeing her state is arguably one of borderline psychosis. This emerges in a paragraph on p. 61 condensing four important points: her inability to feel herself as a whole entity integrating mind and body (note again the mind–body split/dualism motif); a delusional sense of omnipotence when she is bingeing; a regressive wish not to grow up; and an almost schizophrenic self-estimation:

> Quand je bouffe, je ne suis plus qu'un ventre, car je ne sais pas être moi en entier. Rien ne me résiste. Je suis toute-puissante. J'ai trouvé la solution qui empêche de grandir. Je m'adore et me déteste à la fois. (p. 61)

> When I eat, I'm no more than a belly, because I don't know how to be entirely me. Nothing can resist me. I am all-powerful. I found the solution that stops me getting bigger. I adore and hate myself at the same time.

One of those points, the lack of mind–body integration, is reinscribed on the following page in the metaphor of combat – a duel between mind and body wherein the latter initially resists the former's resolve to vomit out food. She, driven by her mind, persists in those efforts: 'J'insiste jusqu'à ce que le duel cesse en ma faveur' [I insist until the duel ends in my favour] (p. 62).

However, Julia discovers that her so-called antidote to bingeing is in fact no antidote at all, for even though she vomits after bingeing, her weight still increases. She concludes that despite all her best efforts, she is not vomiting up all the food consumed, so lurches into a bizarre and unhealthy 'compromise':

> pour satisfaire ce besoin de porter des choses dans ma bouche, je continue à me préparer des encas à longueur de journée, mais bloque mes bouillies dans mes joues. Total : je n'avale rien. Donc ne grossis pas. Je mâche ces gâteaux sensuels, ces plats enchanteurs jusqu'à ce que mes gencives me fassent mal. (p. 62)

> to satisfy this need to have things in my mouth, I continue to prepare snacks all day long, but I hold the mush in my cheeks. End result: I don't swallow anything. So don't get fat. I chew those sensual cakes, those enchanting dishes, until my gums are sore.

This new obsessive–compulsive activity (which cannot be called 'eating', since she is swallowing nothing) also has detrimental effects on her body. One is bleeding of the lips (p. 63); the other is, unsurprisingly, weight loss, to a point where she again becomes underweight, although not life-threateningly so (44 kilos/6 stones 13 lbs, for a height of 1.61 metres/5 feet 3.3 inches) – a state of affairs in which, it is implied, she so revels that she does not care about the lip-bleeding (p. 63). The psychopathology clear in this disregard for the harm she is inflicting on her body is also reflected in a cognitive inability to recognise emotions: 'Je ne sais pas ce qu'est le chagrin ni la joie. Ni les sentiments en général' [I don't know what sorrow or joy is. Nor feelings in general] (p. 66). The psychopathology is also patent in the warped valorisation of her now underweight body. Although she does not have a distorted body image, insofar as she is able to see herself as extremely thin, the fact that she triumphs in this extreme thinness as a sign of strength and autonomy vis-à-vis her parents is morbid:

> cassante, pointue, volumes creusés, tendons saillants, ossature proéminente. Assez maigre pour affronter les parents, qui détestent tant l'opposition, la révolte, la rébellion. Assez fort moralement pour leur jeter au visage mon irréductible volonté : je suis désormais parisienne, majeure et maigre. Et votre avis m'est bien égal. (pp. 68–69)

> brittle, pointed, hollow cheeks, prominent tendons, protruding skeleton. Skinny enough to face my parents, who hate opposition, revolt and rebellion so much. Morally strong enough to throw my intransigent will back in their faces: I am now Parisian, adult and lean. And your opinion does not matter to me.

That desire for autonomy vis-à-vis her parents, in this case her mother, is conveyed when Julia moves to Paris at about the age of 20, and uses a telling metaphor to convey her unhealthily fusional relationship with her mother (discussion of which will follow below with respect to de Peretti's text): 'Un nouveau bout de vie commence pour moi, la petite fille pas terminée, encore collée à sa siamoise de maman' [A new stage of life begins for me, the unfinished little girl, still stuck to her Siamese mum] (p. 71). That new life is hardly satisfying. Having no qualifications apart from the *baccalauréat* to begin a fulfilling career (p. 74), Julia takes on, successively, a number of menial posts that provide no job satisfaction, such as shop assistant, from which she is asked to resign by her boss after four months (p. 75), and sales assistant on skates (p. 80). Further, the move from the family home does nothing to diminish her bulimia nervosa. The deleterious after-effects of a binge are rendered in grim detail, and applied to all bulimics:

> Le réveil est toujours pénible, pour nous, les boulimiques. Surtout les lendemains d'orgie. L'estomac embouteillé fait des bonds douloureux, la

> langue reste capitonnée de bave blanchâtre malgré le dentifrice, le menton se casse la gueule sur les glandes enflées. L'œil se noie sous la paupière qui bat de l'aile. (p. 77)
>
> Waking up is always painful for us bulimics. Especially the day after an orgy. The congested stomach churns painfully, the tongue remains padded with whitish drool in spite of the toothpaste, and the chin falls down onto swollen glands. The eye drowns under a fluttering eyelid.

One morning after a night's binge which she had not been able fully to evacuate by vomiting, she feels cheated by her body, particularly its digestive system (yet another exemplar of the mind–body split/dualism): 'C'est la première fois que je me fais avoir par le syndrome de la digestion' [This is the first time that I've been tricked by digestive syndrome] (p. 77). Food is constructed as an enemy insinuating itself into her corporeal cells, violating and torturing her, reducing her to a bodily 'wimp': 'Malgré moi, mon ennemie s'insinue dans mes cellules pour faire de mon corps une baudruche de chair mortelle. Elle se répand dans mes profondeurs, me viole et me torture' [In spite of myself, my enemy creeps into my cells to make my body a deadly balloon of meat. It spreads into my depths, rapes me and tortures me] (p. 77).

In this state of distress, it is unsurprising when, faced with her friend Marine's loving relationship with her boyfriend Anthony, Julia expresses a conviction that love is for others but not for her, as she is so (negatively) different from other human beings:

> Je ne supporte pas ce bonheur qui s'étend devant moi.
> L'amour, c'est pour les autres. (p. 82)
>
> I can't stand this happiness that lies in front of me.
> Love is for others.

Expression of her radical difference from other human beings had been made previously, wryly but with equal conviction – 'Je suis coupable d'un crime moral : la différence' [I am guilty of a moral crime: difference] (p. 39) – but this was at least partly due to her Jewish ethnicity. (See Chapter 1 for my comments on links between anorexia nervosa and Jewish ethnicity; while Julia is bulimic rather than anorectic in clinical terms, the word 'bulimarexic' in the title of the present chapter implies the frequent overlaps between the two, and as we have seen, Julia certainly does have periods of anorexia nervosa.) Her state of distress, in addition to convincing her that she is unlovable, also manifests itself in existential nihilism (cf. Valère), a sense that there is no meaning to her life, as if she were a surplus piece of merchandise in the fabrication of life. Wondering about the strangers she sees around her in Paris – 'Se demandent-ils seulement pourquoi ils vivent ?' [Are they just wondering why they are alive?] (p. 82) – she muses, 'Peut-être pas. Peut-être pas. Peut-être sont-ils dépassés par le sens de leur vie. C'est ce qui me manque, à moi. Un sens. C'est comme si j'étais un surplus' [Maybe not. Maybe not. Perhaps they are overcome by the meaning of their lives. That's what I lack. Meaning. It's as though I'm surplus to requirements] (p. 82). This impression of being surplus signals severe self-denigration, which reaches its nadir in the abjection of herself as bestial when she binges (cf. Loupias, studied in Chapter 3): 'D'habitude, j'agis en animal sauvage, je suis une bouche et des mains. Mon cerveau est ailleurs, perdu dans l'avalanche alimentaire' [I often act like a wild animal. I am a mouth and hands. My brain is elsewhere, lost in the avalanche of food] (p. 83). See also p. 121, where she casts herself as an animalistic and then potentially monstrous, sub-human creature: 'je lutte souvent très fort contre la pulsion animale qui m'ordonne de manger. Dans ces moments, il me faudrait une volonté d'acier pour lui résister, pour m'empêcher de me transformer en loup-garou' [I often fight very hard against the animal urge that orders me to eat. In these moments, I would need a will of steel to resist it, to stop myself from turning into a werewolf].

On one occasion, her generally impaired cognitive function improves as she starts to question her difference from others, which she interprets at least in her compulsive gorging as madness. This leads to an uncharacteristically positive insight that because she is conscious of being mentally ill, she can be cured. But on the very next page this new, hopeful insight is compromised by the metaphor of her vomiting as a shameful form of 'messe' [Mass] (p. 84), with the religious connotations evoking the ritual that constitutes the binge–vomit cycle. It is one with which, she asserts, she was born: for as a baby, she was always vomiting.

Other depredations of bulimia nervosa are starkly conveyed. One is the social handicap (cf. Balinksa's use of the noun 'handicap' [disability] as designating the effects of anorexia nervosa: Balinska p. 43) and isolation that the illness imposes. This is powerfully conveyed by the fact that fear of social interaction at a party induces a fear so acute it even, exceptionally, cuts her appetite: 'J'ai si peur de tous ces gens que j'en ai l'appétit coupé. Comment ai-je pu à ce point oublier les codes relationnels ? A croire que je ne sais plus parler qu'en terme de nourriture' [I am so afraid of all these people that my appetite has been cut. How could I forget relational codes to such an extent? Anyone would think that I can only speak in terms of food now] (p. 86). On the notion of handicap, the designation of her social and eating behaviour as 'paralysant' [paralysing] (p. 124) figures bulimia nervosa as a form of disability. A further depredation – given the illness's interference with normative sexual development – is her intense wish for lack of a sexed body: 'Moi, j'aurais donné dix ans de ma vie pour être ni homme ni femme' [I would have given ten years of my life in order to be neither man nor woman] (p. 89). This discomfiture with and disconnection, indeed alienation from, her body is reiterated in notation of her dislike of touching it, her never having masturbated, and her never having experienced an orgasm. When showering, she avoids touching her body (p. 95).

Yet another depredation of bulimia nervosa is the sense of degradation it induces in her. Julia hunts in the bin for discarded food, which is covered with cigarette ash (this parallels exactly with Loupias, discussed in Chapter 3). She feels that the degradation of the food she ingests is consonant with the degradation of her life in general:

> En fouillant ma poubelle, je trouve des biscuits ramollis par le detritus. Je ressors quelques rescapés et les nettoie des cendres de cigarettes qui se sont incrustrées dans la croûte. Ça pue un peu. Mais c'est comestible. Et ma vie ? Elle ne pue pas, ma vie ? (p. 96)

> While searching through my garbage, I find biscuits softened by the detritus. I take out some survivors and clean them of the cigarette ashes that are stuck to the crust. It stinks a little. But it's edible. And my life? Does my life not stink?

One perverse facet of bulimia nervosa, and what may seem like a paradox – namely, the stuffing down of food even when the bulimic no longer wants it all – is a common motif in testimonies of those who *have* suffered from it (including de Peretti, whose text is examined below). The explanation is simple in terms of the compensatory mechanism of vomiting: a moderate amount of over-eating may not allow vomiting, and very often a hugely excessive amount is required: 'Je me remplis à nouveau pour que la goutte d'eau fasse déborder le vase. En vertu du principe boulimique qui veut que l'on se remplisse à ras bord pour rendre ce qui reste dans le ventre' [I fill myself up again so that the drop of water makes the vase overflow. Following the bulimic principle that one fills oneself to the brim to bring up what remains in one's stomach] (p. 133). The vicious circle whereby food-deprivation will inevitably lead to another binge sooner or later is again ignored by Julia: after not being able to vomit everything up from one binge, she avows she will compensate by fasting the following day: 'Demain je jeûnerai pour rattraper' [Tomorrow I'll fast to make up for it] (p. 133).

Returning to the specifically somatic depredations of bulimia nervosa, certain unpleasant physical results of it are evoked: 'Et puis, ras le bol des aigreurs d'estomac, de cette haleine de putois, de ces glandes salivaires énormes qui me font un double menton' [And then, tired of the heartburn, this polecat breath and these huge salivary glands that give me a double chin] (pp. 124–25). Awareness of the serious damage she is inflicting on her body is expressed, but again without any particular concern, which is consonant with her alienation from, indeed loathing for, that body. Indeed, she deliberately seeks to harm it even further.

> Mon estomac commence à s'user. Il pue lui aussi. Il menace de se trouer. Quand j'avais dix-neuf ans, je m'étais promis un ulcère avant mon vingt-cinquième anniversaire. Pour détruire plus vite cet estomac exigeant, envahissant et vivace comme un félin sauvage tapi au coin du feu de mes entrailles, j'avale des verres de vinaigre à jeun, engloutis des tartines de moutarde assaisonnées de citron. Je cherche le produit décapant et amer apte à tuer cet organe monstrueusement présent. (pp. 96–97)

> My stomach begins to wear out. It stinks too. It's threatening to rip a hole in itself. When I was nineteen, I had promised myself an ulcer before my twenty-fifth birthday. To faster destroy this stomach that's demanding, invading and stubborn like a wild feline lurking at the fire of my innards, I gulp down glasses of vinegar on an empty stomach, followed by mustard sandwiches seasoned with lemon. I am looking for the right corrosive and bitter product to kill this monstrously present organ.

Of note here is the simile comparing her minatory stomach with a wild cat, which adds to the repertory of bestial parallels made to evoke her bingeing.

The fundamental reason for the immense difficulty in renouncing bingeing and bulimia nervosa is that they seem to have been the only aspects of her life experienced as belonging to her alone, her only weaponry against incursions into her personal space (p. 122; cf. Cairns 2015) and that, crucially, allow her to keep a distance from Others (this again shows isomorphism with Balinska's positing of fear of the exterior, including other people, as the root cause of her own abstinent anorexia without any episodes of bingeing):

> Avec la bouffe, ça va, tout va.
> C'est mon armure, ma tour d'ivoire, les Autres en sont exclus.
> C'est MA Boulimie
> MA Solitude
> MON Merdier
> C'est MA façon d'arrêter le temps, de faire taire ma sensibilité trop vulnérable, MA façon de ne pas subir les Autres.
>
> With food, it's fine, everything is fine.
> It's my armor, my ivory tower, the Others are excluded.
> It's MY Bulimia
> MY loneliness
> MY Shitheap
> It's MY way of stopping time, of silencing my overly vulnerable sensitivity, MY way of not suffering Others.

Barriers against any kind of emotional incursion into her personal space and affective integrity are implicit in the following rendering of her problems with interpersonal relationships:

> Ses compliments bien tournés m'agacent. Pourtant, je sais que c'est sincère, spontané, désintéressé. Mais ça m'énerve, comme si c'étaient des caresses dans le sens du poil. Je ne comprends ni l'amour ni les gentillesses, que je prends invariablement pour des attaques. Surtout, je n'admets pas qu'on puisse penser du bien de moi, qui me méprise tant. (p. 136)
>
> His well-turned compliments annoy me. Yet I know it's sincere, spontaneous, selfless. But it annoys me, as if it were rubbing me up the wrong way. I don't understand love or kindness, things that I invariably take for attacks. Above all, I cannot admit that anyone could think positively of me, me who despises myself so much.

The function of bulimia as a protective mechanism against the potential dangers of the exterior, of other people/Others, is foregrounded in her tentative steps much later on towards re-establishing friendships:

> Je reconnais au fond de moi-même que je ne peux pas vivre heureuse en jouant les bernard-l'ermite et que j'ai besoin d'amitié. Sans mon pare-chocs boulimique, je suis à vif. Incapable d'endurer le quart des souffrances qu'avant j'encaissais sans broncher. (p. 161)
>
> I recognise deep down that I cannot live happily while acting like a hermit crab and that I need friendship. Without my bulimic shock absorber, I'm on edge. Incapable of enduring a quarter of the sufferings that before I had endured without even flinching.

But set against the protection that bulimia nervosa seems to offer her from the invasiveness of others is a highly negative, oft noted byproduct of the illness: kleptomania.[15]

> Pourtant, je sais qu'un jour je devrai choisir entre la folie et la vie. Un jour, je ne supporterai plus ma solitude, ma kleptomanie envahissante. Ça me prend là, au bas du ventre, comme une envie urgente et intransigeante. J'ai soudain besoin de pénétrer par effraction dans le domaine d'autrui, d'accaparer les possessions des autres. L'envie de voler me domine en un éclair et prime sur tout le reste. Ça peut même ajourner une boulimie, c'est dire l'emprise de la kleptomanie sur moi. (p. 122)

> Yet I know that one day I will have to choose between madness and life. One day, I will not be able to bear my loneliness and my invasive kleptomania. It seizes me there, in the pit of my stomach, like an urgent and uncompromising desire. I suddenly need to break into the domain of others, to hoard the possessions of others. In a flash, the desire to steal dominates me and takes precedence over everything else. It can even postpone a bulimic episode, that's how strong a grip kleptomania has on me.

The last sentence is striking: the grip of kleptomania on her is so strong that it can even delay a binge. Further insight into the roots of this frequent symptom of bulimia nervosa is provided: theft is a rebellion against her sense of an injustice committed against her, of a general conspiracy against her; of the conviction that she has less than and is thus inferior to others, so needs to compensate herself by stealing from these others (p. 123). Of particular significance is that the objects she steals have not the slightest importance for her; what is important are the vertiginous sensations just before the act of stealing (p. 123). These sensations amount to a state of hyper-stimulation involving contradictory states – feeling hot and cold, drunk with fear and pride – but also, crucially, a delusory conviction of power, even of omnipotence: 'Tandis que je dissimule l'article dans ma manche, j'ai chaud et froid, je suis ivre de frousse et de fierté, je deviens le metteur en scène de cet instant, c'est moi qui domine l'univers' [While I hide the object up my sleeve, I'm hot and cold, I'm drunk with jitters and pride, I become

15 One example is Jeammet 2004: 23 (my emphasis): 'Enfin, à l'image de la crise boulimique elle-même, la tendance à l'impulsivité et aux passages à l'acte est importante, *tout comme la tendance à la cleptomanie*' [Finally, like the bulimic crisis itself, the tendency towards impulsivity and acting out is important, as is the tendency towards kleptomania].

the director of this moment, it's me who dominates the universe] (p. 123). Of particular note is the metaphor of her directing a theatrical performance.

But now something new and positive comes into the equation. We learn that Julia has always written tales and poems, and realise that while, typically, she denigrates her ability, writing at this turning-point becomes a form of solace and escape from her infernal ED (p. 105). The coincidence of EDs and writing is not infrequent[16] and the topos of scriptotherapy briefly mentioned in the Introduction will be considered more fully in the Conclusion; suffice it to recall here that Suzette A. Henke coined the term scriptotherapy to denote 'the process of writing out and writing through traumatic experience in the mode of therapeutic reenactment'.[17] For Julia, words and their arrangement into meaningful patterns seem to provide some mitigation of the pernicious ravages of her ED. Interestingly, via wordplay, both her particular ED (bulimia nervosa) and anorexia nervosa are yoked, albeit figuratively, in their relationship to writing and language generally: 'Entre deux boulimies, j'écris, noircis des pages. C'est difficile, comme de planter des choux sur des rochers. Je deviens anorexique des mots' (p. 119) [Between two bulimic episodes, I write, I blacken pages. It is difficult, like planting cabbages on rocks. I become anorectic from words]. Despite the difficulty, she persists, attempting to convey in writing the existential terror and the dark, omnipotent, all-invasive horror of bulimia nervosa:

> J'écris, ma bouffe infernale qui devient monstrueuse, insupportable comme une marée noire qui enfle, envahit, immerge le contient – le système solaire, les galaxies sont tapissés de noir. J'essaie de dire le mal, de le cerner par des mots précis, denses, touffus qui se bousculent à la porte de ma bouche, laquelle est malheureusement scellée, même le crayon ne veut rien savoir. (p. 119)

> I write, my infernal food becomes monstrous, unbearable like a black tide that swells, invades, immerses, contains it – the solar system, the galaxies are lined with black. I try to put the sickness into words, to define it by precise, dense, matted words that jostle at the door of my mouth, which is unfortunately sealed, even the pencil does not want to hear about it.

16 See the section 'Writing as Therapeutic for, Creative for, or Creative of, the Eating-disordered Subject' in the Bibliographical Appendix.

17 Henke, Suzette A., *Shattered Subjects: Trauma and Testimony in Women's Life-Writing* (London: Macmillan, 1998), p. xii.

The therapeutic effects of writing six pages about her 'vie de boulimique' [life of a bulimic] are foregrounded:

> J'ai décrit les symptômes, l'angoisse qui enfle et ne s'éponge qu'avec ma manie, ma vie d'ermite et ma fatigue. État général altéré, messieurs, mesdames, le cirque Barnum ferme ses portes plus tôt que prévu.
>
> Je me sens plus légère, comme si, par ces cris noir sur blanc, j'avais coupé l'herbe sous les pieds du diable, enrayé le processus évoluant inévitablement vers la folie. La Grande Folie. Celle dont on ne revient pas. La boulimie désormais est à côté de moi, encerclée par les carreaux de feuilles, emprisonnée dans les spirales du cahier. Je me suis déchargée d'elle. (p. 120)

> I have described the symptoms, the anguish that swells and can only be mopped up with my mania, my life as a hermit and my fatigue. General altered state, ladies and gentlemen, the Barnum circus is closing early.
>
> I feel lighter, as if, with these black cries on white paper, I have pulled the rug from under the devil's feet, stopped the process inevitably evolving towards madness. The Great Madness. The kind from which we do not return. Bulimia is now beside me, encircled by the grids on the pages, trapped in the spirals of the notebook. I have let it go.

Although the second sentence of the first paragraph here has, again, an ironic, self-derisive tone, the rest of the citation is robustly upbeat, asserting the liberatory effect of writing, whereby a process of imprisonment by bulimia nervosa is reversed, with it losing its power over her and indeed being imprisoned within her own written words. But the liberation is conditional upon others reading her text:

> Pour qu'elle desserre ses pinces et me laisse enfin respirer, il faudrait que ce texte soit lu, que cette sale boulimie soit mise à nu, disséquée par des milliers de gens, critiquée, jugée, salie.
>
> Pour qu'elle paie pour les années qu'elle a volées à ma jeunesse. (p. 120)

> So that it loosens its claws and finally lets me breathe, this text must be read, this dirty bulimia exposed, dissected by thousands of people, criticized, judged, dishonored.
>
> So that it pays for the years it stole from my youth.

Note the quasi-judicial tenor of Julia's demands, as if bulimia were a criminal charged with theft of her youth and needing to be tried by the figurative court of thousands of readers. The trope of a judicial system is also found in a more sociotropic statement, which begins with an expression of her readiness to accept publication by any woman's magazine:

> Le premier qui en voudra, je la lui cède.
> Qu'importe ! Il faut dire au monde qu'il y a des gens dingos, en liberté non surveillée. Qu'ils sont dangereux pour eux-mêmes, qu'ils peuvent mourir de leur angoisse. (p. 121)

> I'll give it to the first person who wants it.
> What does it matter! We must tell the world that there are nutcases who are unsupervised and free. That they are a danger to themselves and that they can die from their anguish.

Jubilation is experienced by Julia when her five-page article on bulimia nervosa, based on her lived experience of it, is accepted for publication. She optimistically anticipates that this publication will constitute a gruesome form of capital punishment – death – of her bulimia, cast here as a criminal human entitity (personified again): 'Je vais signer son arrêt de mort à la boulimie, la dépecer sur la place publique, au vu et au su de milliers de profanes interloqués ; non mais, qu'est-ce qu'elle écrit sur la bouffe, elle déconne cette pauvre fille' (p. 129) [I am going to sign bulimia's death sentence, dismember it in the public square, witnessed by thousands of dumbstruck laypeople; no, but what is she writing about food, this poor girl has got to be kidding]. Later on, the trope of writing as therapeutic is vividly reinscribed, with writing becoming a beatific experience enabling luminosity in a previously black life: 'Une semaine passe. Vouée à l'écriture, ce fil invisible et auréolé qui me mène à la naissance de la lumière, à la fontaine de jouvence dans laquelle mon âme n'a cessé de se baigner' [A week passes. Dedicated to writing, this invisible and halo-like thread that leads me to the birth of light, to the fountain of youth in which my soul has not stopped bathing] (p. 174).

Simultaneously, Julia is, at this breakthrough point, learning to overcome the mind–body split/dualism so endemic in eating-disordered individuals: 'J'apprends à réconcilier mon corps avec mon âme et mon âme avec la vie' [I am learning how to reconcile my body with my soul and my soul with life] (p. 174). Writing about her bulimia nervosa certainly seems to have been a form of productive scriptotherapy for Julia, for it has involved destruction of the sacred aura she previously attached to her illness, a destruction that symbolises the start of its decline: 'Écrire ma boulimie, en parler, désacraliser son existence symbolise pour moi le début de sa déchéance' [To write my bulimia, to speak about it and to take the mystique out of its existence symbolises for me the beginning of its decline] (p. 131). The key to this positive breakthrough via writing is the communication to others (hence her earlier insistence on the need to be read by others seen on p. 120) of the profound distress provoked by bulimia nervosa – which she qualifies as a form of madness. It is the breaking of a silence and thus of a secret that had previously chained her to the illness, all of which makes her feel she has escaped the enslavement imposed by it and instead discovered her own agency: 'En distribuant des bouts de ma folie aux autres, en l'exhibant ainsi, je romps le silence, le secret qui m'ont enchaînée à elle. Je lui échappe, je reconnais mes pouvoirs' [By distributing bits of my madness to others, by displaying it like this, I am breaking the silence and the secrecy that chained me to it. I am escaping it, I recognise my powers]. This hypothesis of writing as a form of scriptotherapy that has brought specific and substantial psychological benefits is abundantly confirmed later on in the statement:

> Donc, je dois absolument admettre mes limites et solliciter une aide médicale et psychologique.
>
> La chance de ma vie est d'avoir trouvé un exutoire dans l'écriture. (p. 138)

> So, I must absolutely recognise my limits and seek medical and psychological help.
>
> The biggest piece of luck in my life is to have found an outlet in writing.

Following the success of her first article on bulimia nervosa, Julia is asked by another magazine to conduct an enquiry into the illness (p. 138). She views this request as a good opportunity to meet clinicians treating those suffering from what is rightly designated as a pathology (p. 138). Although in many respects anorectics and bulimics share common problems and symptoms, the two groups are represented by Julia as mutually hostile, at least in the hospital meeting she has with them: 'On se regarde de travers sans mot dire, chacune épiant les manies de la voisine ; les deux camps (anorexiques et boulimiques) se détestent, les premières méprisent les secondes, qui les haïssent' [We look at each other suspiciously and without saying a word, each spying on her neighbour's mania; both sides (anorectic and bulimic) can't stand each other, the former despise the latter, who hate them back] (p. 142). The last two clauses here evoke the findings in some of the secondary literature, whereby bulimics are crudely viewed as 'failed anorexics'.

After researching and publishing her article, of which she is extremely proud, Julia also learns much. This is conveyed in her surprised discovery that 'normal' people could be alarmed or at least disturbed by the prospect of vomit, and her incomprehension that most of them find it repulsive is in its turn surprising to the reader (p. 149). This reinforces the impression of Julia's radical alienation from healthy relations with one's own body, in which vomit is normally a sign of the body rejecting something noxious or incongruent with its efficient functioning. Further learning occurs upon carrying out the instructions of her 'psy' (she does not specify if he is a psychiatrist, a psychotherapist, a psychoanalyst, or a psychologist) to keep a diary including her daily food intake. She finds that this 'discours écrit' [written speech], even when it includes details of binges, allows her to become logical, rational, and positive (p. 155). Again, scriptotherapy – although of a very different sort from her article, which explored the affective dimension of her bulimic suffering – proves to be of benefit:

> Le carnet m'aide énormément ; je suis mariée avec. Je suis littéralement asservie à ses feuillets, ce témoin de mes travers intimes. Crise ou pas, heureuse ou frustrée, je dois me décrire, hacher menu, disséquer, analyser chacune de mes réactions, cerner ma vie par des mots, surmonter les ennuis pour passer à autre chose. (pp. 155–56)

> The notebook helps me a lot; I am wedded to it. I'm literally in thrall to its pages, this testament of my intimate failings. Crisis or not, happy or frustrated, I must describe myself, finely chop, dissect, analyse each of my reactions, capture my life in words and overcome troubles in order to move on.

Note again the wordplay, this time on 'hacher menu' [finely chop], linking the literally non-alimentary to the food that is such a destructive and painful obsession for her.

The therapeutic effects of writing in general, even if it is only the obligatory written recording of her daily food intake, are underscored in the observation that this activity makes her feel safe and protected from excess – because it prevents her from getting her physical food intake out of mental proportion.

> Cette obligation me sécurise, car il est impossible de tricher avec le carnet, quand tout fait est rapporté noir sur blanc, dans les moindres détails. Je ne crains plus la démesure, puisque le carnet compte pour moi : si je mange un flan, il va être digéré dans mon estomac, hors de ma vue. Mais ce n'est pas pour cela qu'il va me trahir et se diviser en trente flans pour m'emmerder. Après l'avoir dégusté, je n'ai pas de raison d'angoisser, et de me mentir – « Oh, là, là, j'ai bouffé comme une poufiasse ! ». Le carnet est là pour confirmer, ou démentir, ce que j'ai mangé exactement. Ni plus ni moins. Donc, je suis rassurée. (p. 156)

> This obligation reassures me, because it is impossible to cheat with the notebook, when everything is reported in black and white, in the minutest detail. I no longer fear excess, since the notebook keeps track for me: if I eat a flan, it will be digested in my stomach, out of my sight. But that doesn't mean it will betray me and divide into thirty flans just to screw with me. After eating it, I have no reason to be anxious or to lie to myself – 'Oh my gosh, I have eaten like a fat slut!' The notebook is there to confirm, or deny, exactly what I ate. No more and no less. So, I am reassured.

While her binges have not ceased, writing has helped her to take a certain mental distance from them, because it gives an exact record of them in time, preventing her from mis-remembering and exaggerating their scope, and thus enabling her to put them into perspective (p. 156).[18] And soon, she even finds that reading her own writing in this food diary, with her comments on the most recent binge, has increased benefits, sometimes even preventing the next binge through a 'risk assessment' – a cognitive grasp of the damage that another binge will inflict (p. 156).

As we know from p. 145, Julia is 1.61 metres/5 feet 3.3 inches; while in treatment for bulimia nervosa and beginning to reduce considerably the frequency of her bingeing and vomiting, she weighs 54 kilos/8 stones 7 lbs (p. 157). At first, she resents the weight gain as unjust. But again, writing down her daily intake of food puts matters into perspective, and, as she states, it is only through inscribing her alimentary acts in writing that she becomes conscious of them – another manifestation of scriptotherapy:

> Mais il faut que mes actes soient rédigés sur le papier pour que je prenne conscience de leur existence.
>
> Je pensais aussi, à tort, me sous-alimenter, et trouvais injuste de grossir sans raison ; or, tout s'explique : mon carnet regorge de bonbons et de biscuits. Je ne pèse pas cinquante-quatre kilos par hasard. Sois je bâfre et je vomis, sans être sûre de régurgiter la totalité. Sois je fais attention à mon alimentation et mincis normalement. Au choix. (p. 157)

18 The treatment she is receiving, in its insistence on daily records of food intake, etc., appears to be CBT (cognitive behavioural therapy). CBT has often been found by researchers to be the most helpful treatment for bulimia nervosa. See Grilo 2006 for more information, particularly p. 110. See also Freeman, Christopher, *Overcoming Anorexia Nervosa: A Self-Help Guide Using Cognitive Behavioral Techniques* (London: Robinson, 2009 [first published 2002]).

> But my actions have to be written on paper for me to become aware of their existence.
>
> I also thought, wrongly, that I was underfeeding myself, and found it unfair that I was getting bigger for no reason; Now, everything is explained: my notebook is full of sweets and biscuits. It's no accident that I weigh fifty-four kilos. I can either gorge and vomit without being certain of regurgitating everything, or I can be careful with my diet and slim down normally. A choice.

The capital power of her writing and the cognitive breakthrough it enables are highlighted in two modes. One is recognising the irrationality of her eating patterns (p. 157). The second is enabling her to claim as an adult the right to eat normal, nutritionally balanced meals – accompanied, in parallel, with the aspiration to more 'normal' behaviour in social situations (p. 157).

Her writing-induced cognitive breakthrough soon reaps positive benefits that she regards as a comforting victory, with a reduction within one month in the frequency of her binges from two or three per day to one or two per week (p. 159). In keeping with the word 'victoire' [victory] (p. 159), one of whose uses is in the lexical field of war, a martial metaphor is deployed in the last clause of the following extract:

> Il me faut accepter cet étau qui se desserre et ce corps qui part à la dérive sans son abominable corset. Il faut qu'il trouve son équilibre, son aisance, qu'il communique avec mon esprit pour que, ensemble, ils jouissent de la vie au lieu de se faire la guerre. (p. 159)

> I must accept this loosening vice and this body that is beginning to drift without its abominable corset. It must find its equilibrium, its peace, in order to communicate with my spirit so that they can enjoy life together instead of waging war.

This extract also illustrates the lessening of the mind–body split/dualism in which her mind and body have been engaged, in (almost literally) mortal combat.

When Julia asks her doctor how, now that she has moderated her binges and regained some control over her eating, she can stop gaining weight, he replies, 'Vous devriez faire du sport pour extérioriser vos angoisses' ['You should do some sport to externalise your anxieties'] (p. 162). Her oral response to him ignores the essential point of his recommendation, instead focusing again on her body ideals, saying that exercise that would change the lower part of her body would suit her perfectly, since the upper part of her body has never been a problem for her. But inwardly, she admits that her reasoning is shaky, and that punishment of one's body, or separation/fragmentation of it into particular parts is unhelpful: 'En fait, c'est un raisonnement bancal : on ne développe pas harmonieusement un corps en le martyrisant, ou en séparant les parties qui le composent' ['Actually that's dubious reasoning: we don't develop a body harmoniously by torturing it or by separating the parts that make it up'] (p. 162). Stripped of the 'support affectif' [emotional support] (p. 162) of her binges, she wonders how she can fill her inner void in other ways, and, at that point, the method becomes noxious: consumption of sleeping pills and tranquillisers (p. 162). Note the renewed implied parallel between addiction to drugs and addiction to food/bingeing. The perceived affective support provided by her binges is conveyed via the metaphor of their absence leaving her without crutches – 'Sans béquilles' (p. 162) – without which she doesn't know how to walk. This absence leaves her feeling empty: note the link with the lexical field of food/eating (p. 163). That link is also found in the reference to one of her reasons for stuffing herself with 'médicaments' [meds] as being to 'feed' her imagination (p. 163). Another important cognitive breakthrough comes in response to an imperative issued by her 'psy', whereby she comes to realise that for many years she had been deluded in perceiving her father and mother as omnipotent (p. 163).

The metaphor implicit in the book's main title, which refers to skin, is alluded to here as Julia expresses how hard it is to be stripped of bulima nervosa as a 'coping' mechanism against threats from the exterior. In particular, she regrets the loss of its ability to 'protect' her, which here takes the metaphor of a tough military breastplate. This is an interesting and symptomatic recourse to corporeal imagery, so common in the psychological distress of eating-disordered individuals, and suggests, precisely, the protection of skin: 'Je regrette cette cuirasse coriace qui me maintenait dans un pseudo-monde parallèle et me permettait d'éviter les éceuils qui jalonnent tous les chemins' [I mourn this tough armour that kept me in a pseudo-parallel world and allowed me to avoid the pitfalls which punctuate every path] (p. 164). However, as her succeeding paragraph evinces, Julia is now aware that this putative protection was an escape from the reality of interrelationality, a form of anaesthesia against the general affective results thereof, some of which at least she admits may be positive, but the majority of which she regards as dangers inherent in truly relating to other human beings, the threatening exterior/Other: 'J'ai peur de ressentir les afflictions humaines, la joie, les affres de l'amour et les échecs à venir' [I am afraid to feel human afflictions, joy, pangs of love and failures to come] (p. 164).

Gradually, her fear of relationality diminishes, and the wordplay used in 'ne plus vomir' [no longer loathe/vomit] again taps into the lexical field of the alimentary, of the inside/out, or rather of expulsion of the inner to the outer, normally in disgust:

> J'ai appris à devenir une éponge, à assimiler la compagnie des autres, à comprendre qu'on peut aimer sans se tuer, simplement pour être bien. J'essaie de ne plus exister, leur présence, de me dessiner un bout de place parmi les vivants sous le soleil, les deux pieds sur la terre. (p. 165)

> I have learned to become a sponge, to assimilate the company of others, and to understand that one can love without killing oneself, simply to be well. I try to no longer exist in their presence, to outline a bit of space for myself among the living under the sun, with both feet on the ground.

She also learns, crucially, to take nutritional care of her body, and the metaphor of letting it breathe is revealing apropos her former figurative suffocation/suppression of it in bulimia nervosa: 'J'ai laissé souffler mon corps, je lui ai offert des protéines pour ses os, des légumes pour le fer, fait l'impasse sur les graisses à cause du cholestérol' [I let my body catch its breath, I gave it protein for its bones, vegetables for iron, did not eat fat because of cholesterol] (p. 165).

All is not, however, plain sailing in Julia's route to recovery. Another behavioural abnormality re-appears (recall her kleptomania, described on p. 122) that is not infrequently associated with EDs, particularly bulimia nervosa: shoplifting, in which Julia begins to engage impulsively[19] and compulsively (p. 166). The reasons she adduces again relate to the problematics of spatiality (see, for instance, Durand, Loupias, and in the secondary literature Cairns 2015). Previously she had jealously guarded her inner space, preventing its violation by others (no doubt stemming from her literal inner violation, or rape, by her uncle in childhood). Now, she appears to seek random revenge by violating the territory of others: 'Je volais, pour violer le territoire des autres' [I stole to violate other people's territory] (p. 165). Yet curiously, the shoplifting occurs at a highly positive transitional period, when she feels that she is finally becoming free of bulimia nervosa. The latter is personified and then, in the last sentence of the following, sinisterly dollified in a powerful metaphor: 'Impossible de retourner en arrière, la boulimie ne

19 See footnote 15 on impulsivity and rash acts in eating-disordered individuals, which would include theft.

veut plus de moi. J'ai lutté, le l'ai vaincue. Elle est morte. On dirait une vieille poupée désarticulée qui gît à mes pieds' [It is impossible to go back, bulimia does not want me anymore. I struggled and I conquered it. It is dead. It is like an old dismembered doll lying at my feet] (p. 166). The personification resumes on p. 167, with a dramatic simile ascribing vampiric and sadistic tendencies to her previous bulimia nervosa: 'Maintenant elle m'a laissée, brisée sur le sol, elle s'en va, assoiffée de chair fraîche, élire domicile pour se repaître, tel le vampire, de la sève d'une autre, téter l'angoisse d'une autre enfant malheureuse' [Now it has left me broken on the ground, it goes away, thirsty for fresh flesh, to take up home and feed like a vampire on another woman's sap, to suck the anguish from another unfortunate girl] (p. 167). Julia's previous infatuation with this quasi-human force (albeit a compromised infatuation, as had been evinced on p. 124 in 'Ma boulimie et moi, on forme un couple sado-maso, « ni avec toi ni sans toi »' [My bulimia and I, we form a sadomasochistic couple, 'neither with you nor without you'] is patent in 'J'essaie de t'oublier, boulimie adorée, à coups de cachetons, comme à l'adolescence, quand je ne te connaissais pas encore' [I'm trying to forget you with pills, beloved bulimia, just like in adolescence when I did not yet know you] (p. 167).With her recovery comes a new ability to let real human beings into her personal space, and she begins a relationship with a man named Maxime (p. 183).

At this point, the battle with bulimia nervosa is not one hundred per cent over. Julia does experience one very distressing relapse. This is relayed partly in the third person – perhaps a self-protective method of distantiation from its horror – as a scene from, precisely, a horror film in which she is at once the killer and the victim:

> Elle vit un film d'horreur déroulé en accéléré. Elle s'est vue dans la cuisine, s'empiffrant en ricanant bêtement. De frayeur, elle claque la porte, quittant le lieu du crime. Elle est bourreau et victime simultanément. Mais, ce matin, la course effrénée se révèle impuissante. IL FAUT DÉVORER. Me goinfrer, donc me purger. (p. 185)

> She saw a horror film played in fast-forward. She saw herself in the kitchen, stuffing herself with a stupid sneer. In terror, she slams the door, leaving the scene of the crime. She is both executioner and victim. But this morning, the frantic race turns out to be hopeless. I MUST DEVOUR. To stuff myself, and so purge myself.

However, the fact that only one relapse occurs is highly propitious. So too is her acceptance of the weight gain caused by cessation of vomiting.

What follows begins with a form of ekphrasis, a verbal rendering of her body as a painting, in which, despite the comic hyperbole of the painting, her accompanying reflections indicate final, almost amused acceptance of the womanly curves and flesh that are developing now she is eating normally and not vomiting:

> Je grossis : si j'étais une corbeille de fruits, ça donnerait le tableau suivant : deux pêches (joues), deux pastèques (fesses), deux melons (seins), une citrouille tranchée en deux pour les hanches. Adieu la ligne Barbie ! Ronde au-dehors, au-dedans, je m'assagis, renonçant à galoper tous azimuts... pour me poser dans le présent. [...] Aujourd'hui, le sujet ne me glace plus : je m'en fous ; comme si les kilos s'étaient infiltrés dans un autre corps que le mien. Je suis libre de paresser, telle une vahinée, enfouie dans une marée d'oreillers, corne de gazelle aux lèvres, doigts collants de miel : moi, une femelle ! (p. 186)

> I am putting on weight: if I were a basket of fruit, I would yield the following picture: two peaches (cheeks), two watermelons (buttocks), two melons (breasts), a pumpkin sliced in half for the hips. Say goodbye to the Barbie line! Round outside and in, I quieten down, no longer galloping all over the place... to settle down in the present. [...] Today, the subject does not make my blood run cold anymore: I don't care; as if the kilos had infiltrated a body other than mine. I'm free to laze about, like a Tahitian woman, buried among a tide of pillows, a gazelle horn at my lips and my fingers sticky with honey: me, a female!

That final acceptance is also clear in the following plea to an unspecified addressee:

> S'il vous plaît, laissez-moi me ressembler à moi-même. Mes rondeurs, mes chairs, mes os s'appartiennent, forment un tout compact, clairement limités dans l'espace. Je ne déborde pas sur le domaine des autres ; par conséquent, personne n'a le droit de piétiner mon territoire. (p. 187)

> Please, let me look like myself. My curves, my flesh, my bones all belong to one another, they form a compact whole, clearly demarcated in space. I don't overflow into the domain of others; consequently, no one has the right to trample on my territory.

Note again the emphasis on personal space, on interiority, exteriority, and on necessary boundaries. Pertinent here is a healthier attitude towards her formerly enmeshed family, with Julia's image of breaking the chains that bind her to her mother, allowing her (Julia) adult autonomy: 'Maman, Maman [...] Ne m'en veux pas si je romps nos chaînes, si je respire sans toi. Toi aussi, tu vas apprendre à vivre amputée de moi'

[Mom, Mom [...] Don't blame me if I break our chains, if I breathe without you. You too will learn to live amputated from me] (p. 187).

Writing is again mentioned as a means of aiding her complete recovery from bulimia nervosa. Reading her written notes, she realises both that she had spent vast amounts of money on food when bingeing, and that there are periods of the day when she is most tense. After the reading, she devises strategies to distract her from the temptation to binge:

> Dès 17 heures, j'évite absolument la solitude et l'oisiveté, je sors au ciné, à la bibliothèque, et depuis peu au cours de gym. Ayant récemment admis qu'un corps musclé est plus joli qu'un corps décharné ou mollasson. En tout cas, c'est mon esthétique. Et puis le sport est un excellent exutoire pour nerfs en pelote. (p. 189)
>
> From 5pm, I avoid loneliness and idleness at all cost, I go out to the movies, to the library, and recently to gym class. Having recently admitted that a muscular body is prettier than an emaciated body or a lethargic one. In any case, it's my aesthetic. And sport is also an excellent outlet for when you're all wound up.

The last three sentences indicate both a far healthier body ideal and the use of exercise not to lose weight but to release tension. At this point she weighs a healthy 54 kilos (8 stones 7 lbs) for a height of 1.61 metres (5 feet 3.3 inches) (p. 190). Accepting this weight is, in her view, heroic, as she wryly remarks to her readers, particularly addressing any among them who may be psychiatrists: 'Ne rigolez pas, surtout vous, docteur Psy, si vous me lisez : pour nous, ex-phobiques du poids, grossir est une épreuve douloureuse. A cinquante-quatre kilos, je suis héroïque' [Don't laugh, especially you, Doctor Shrink, if you read this: for us, ex-weight phobes, gaining weight is a painful ordeal. At fifty-four kilos, I am heroic] (p. 190). But the highly positive element here is her designation of herself as one of the recovered bulimics who are now 'ex-phobiques du poids' [ex-phobics of weight].

This testimony to the abyss of bulimia nervosa appears to have a genuinely happy ending (as has Balinska's to that of anorexia nervosa). Not only is Julia completely recovered from bulimia; she is finally able to trust the exterior world enough to allow herself to love her male partner, no longer needing the crutches that her illness appeared to represent, and now wants to fill herself with the pleasures of life rather than with excessive amounts of food. For she now views food simply as a means for her body to function and to be able to enjoy those pleasures of life:

> De toute façon, c'est finie la boulimie. Je n'ai plus besoin de béquilles, ni du carnet ni des thérapies. Je suis moi, soudée, forte, entière. J'ai envie de me remplir de plaisir, d'émotions, de paysages, de couleurs. La nourriture n'est qu'un moyen pour faire fonctionner mon corps. (p. 195)

> Anyway, the bulimia is over. I don't need the crutches, notebook or therapies anymore. I am me, mended, strong and whole. I want to fill myself with pleasure, emotions, landscapes and colours. Food is just a way to make my body work.

Section 2.2

Since its autodiegetic narrator is named Camille de Peretti (see p. 124), the author Camille de Peretti's *Thornytorinx* (2005) appears to be an autobiographical text. What might appear to be unnecessary caution on my part in saying 'appears to be' arises from the publisher's reference, in the paratextual material about de Peretti preceding the actual text, to 'Son premier roman' [Her first novel], but this is a noun in apposition, with 'Son premier roman' being immediately followed by '*Thornytorinx*, d'inspiration autobiographique' [*Thornytorinx*, inspired by her life]. So this paratextual material at the very least concedes, despite the publisher's use of the word 'roman' [novel], that it is inspired by the author's own life experience.

What is unequivocal is the text's status as a personal testimony to a grave ED, suffered by the author from her late teens into early adulthood. Camille suffers mainly from bulimia nervosa, but at a much later point this mutates into anorexia nervosa, albeit not nearly as serious a form of anorexia nervosa as the two cases studied in Chapter 1. The aetiology of her ED indisputably lies in a noxiously fusional[20] and psychopathological relationship with her mother – a classic feature in medico-clinico-theoretical texts about the role of the mother in anorexia nervosa, if not necessarily in bulimia nervosa. In saying this, I am absolutely not suggesting that this aetiology is universal; far from it. Indeed, I contend

20 In her otherwise very insightful analysis of *Thornytorinx*, Nathalie Morello underestimates the invasiveness of Camille's mother in her initial presentation of this mother as merely 'very attentive'. Morello, Nathalie, 'Anorexia, anger, agency: Investigating quests for self in three contemporary narratives in French', in Francesca Calamita, Petra Bagley, and Kathryn Robson (eds), *Starvation, Food Obsession and Identity: Eating Disorders in Post-1968 Women's Writing* (Oxford: Peter Lang, 2017), pp. 121–41.

that this quasi-doxa in (mainly earlier, particularly 1960s and 1970s) medico-clinico-theoretical texts about the key role of the mother in her daughter's anorexia nervosa is highly problematic, especially when it causes clinicians and medical academics both to side-line other causal factors and to stigmatise mothers of anorectics in general as pathogenic.

However, in Camille's particular case, it truly is undeniable that her mother lies at the root of her illness. This becomes patent as her narrative unfolds, as will be substantiated below. Significantly, de Peretti dedicated this book to her mother... As an incipit, it is important to register that de Peretti's mother herself had previously suffered from what is initially referred to by Camille as bulimia (p. 29) but is later described by her mother as bulimarexia: 'moi aussi j'ai été boulimique-anorexique' [I was also a bulimarexic] (p. 103). Some clinicians posit a hereditary factor in anorexia and bulimia nervosa.[21] One example is, 'It appears that anorexia nervosa and bulimia nervosa are disorders which run in families.'[22] Another is, 'The children of parents with an ED have been found to be much more at risk of developing a similar disorder than those whose parents had a healthy attitude toward food.'[23] It has also been pointed out, 'Des études actuelles montrent que le risque d'avoir un enfant anorexique est de 3 % si une personne apparentée en est atteinte, alors qu'il n'est que de 0,3% si ce n'est pas le cas' [Current studies show that the risk of having an anorectic child is 3% if a relative is affected by anorexia, whereas it is only 0.3% if this is not the case].[24] It is important to note the use of the present tense in 'une personne apparentée en est atteinte', because Camille's mother, despite her use of the past tense in her assertion 'moi aussi j'ai été boulimique-anorexique' [I was also a bulimarexic], clearly retains strong remnants of her 'former' ED. Of course, one could object that what appears to be genetic is actually mimetic – that the daughter who develops an ED is unconsciously imitating the eating-disordered behaviour of a parent or close relative, rather than having the predisposition to an ED in her genetic make-up.

While on the topic of familial factors, it is strange – perhaps symptomatic – that there is absolutely no mention of Camille's father

21 See the section 'Biological/Genetic/Hereditary Factors' in the Bibliographical Appendix.

22 Treasure, Janet and Holland, Anthony, 'Genetic factors in eating disorders', in Szmukler et al. 1995, pp. 65–81 (77).

23 Freeman 2009: 73.

24 Jeammet 2004: 46.

in the entire text. At one point she refers to her parents (p. 101), by which she means her mother and her step-father, but no reference is ever made to his predecessor, her biological father. With respect to the anorexic phase of Camille's illness, the following observation from the medical literature is pertinent: 'The anorexic young woman may well have experienced her father as a relatively distant figure, not in a close emotional contact with either his wife or his daughter'.[25] Emphasis is also placed on problematic father–daughter relationships in some of the secondary literature on bulimia nervosa.

Thornytorinx opens with a series of startlingly sordid statements that provocatively flout cultural taboos:

> J'ai vomi partout. Partout où j'ai pu. Autant que j'ai pu. N'importe où, n'importe quand. J'ai vomi avec mon index et mon majeur agrippés au fond de ma gorge. J'ai vomi à Paris et à Londres, j'ai vomi à Tokyo. J'ai vomi au réveil, sous le soleil et sous la pluie. En plein jour. Je me suis relevée jusque tard dans la nuit pour vomir. J'ai vomi dans les toilettes de la maison de ma mère, dans les toilettes des appartements de mes copines, dans celles de mon école et dans celles des boîtes de nuit. Puis les toilettes elles-mêmes sont devenues obsolètes. Alors j'ai vomi partout. Dans les rues.
>
> [...] Ça éclaboussait mes chaussures. (11)

> I vomited everywhere. Wherever I could. As much as I could. Anywhere, anytime. I vomited with my index finger and my middle finger stuck down the back of my throat. I threw up in Paris and London, I threw up in Tokyo. I vomited when I woke up, under the sun and in the rain. In broad daylight. I got up late into the night to vomit. I vomited in the toilets at my mother's house, in the toilets at my girlfriends' apartments, in those at my school and in nightclubs. Then the toilets themselves became obsolete. So I vomited everywhere. In the streets.
>
> [...] It splashed my shoes.

Some readers may find the assertions distastefully sensationalist, exhibitionist, even perversely triumphalist in the anaphora involving 'J'ai vomi' [I vomited]. Narration of a similarly severe vomiting episode brings censure from, for instance, Laura Jackson, who describes it as 'disgusting'.[26] Be that as it may, these assertions index the gravity of Camille's compulsion to purge food she has ingested. This compulsive

25 Dare, Christopher and Crowther, Catherine, 'Psychodynamic models of eating disorders', in Szmukler et al. 1995, pp. 125–39 (137).

26 Jackson 2014: 176.

vomiting is initially explained simply as a wish to be slim. But what is certainly not simple is her relationship to the vomit and indeed to her very 'self':

> Elle est là l'histoire. L'histoire d'une fille qui veut être mince et qui se fait vomir pour ça. Mais elle se fait tant vomir qu'à force elle ne sait plus ce qui la traverse, si elle est son propre vomi, si elle est étrangère à toute cette matière qui sort d'elle. Elle ne sait plus qui elle est. Elle est malade. (p. 12)
>
> That's where the story is. The story of a girl who wants to be thin and who makes herself vomit to that end. But she vomits so much that she doesn't know what is going through her, if she is her own vomit, if she is alien to all that matter coming out of her. She doesn't know who she is anymore. She is sick.

Within these reflections are two prominent elements: difficulty in mediating between bodily interiority and bodily exteriority, and a mind–body split/dualism (the latter being, as frequently remarked above, a common trope in the primary corpus). Also of note, in 'Elle ne sait plus qui elle est' [She doesn't know who she is anymore], is congruence with one of the comments on anorectics (including purgers, which Camille is) in Hilde Bruch's foundational study of 1978: 'These girls cannot experience themselves as unified or self-directed individuals.'[27]

Of significance in the Prologue is that Camille's distanced (third-person), retrospective admission that she was ill (p. 12) is countered by her vehement assertion (or what psychoanalysts would no doubt label her defence mechanism) that everyone is, in some sense, ill (p. 12) – and her meaning here is clearly that everyone is, in some sense, mentally rather than physically 'ill'. This assertion is also made in another French testimony to an ED (previously referred to): Durand's *Ma folie ordinaire: allers et retours à l'hôpital Sainte-Anne* (2006), in which Durand contests normative definitions of sanity and insanity. However, Camille's reasoning is less cogent than Durand's. For Camille follows the rhetorical question, 'Vous en connaissez, vous, des gens qui ne sont pas malades ?' [Do you know any people who aren't sick?], to which the implicit answer 'Non' [No] is sweeping, with rather reductive examples that fail to distinguish between on the one hand the sort of affective distress experienced by many individuals at certain points in their life, and genuine mental pathology on the other hand. Her examples

27 Bruch 1978: 55.

exaggerate and banalise mental suffering: 'La maladie, c'est toute notre vie, et c'est tellement banal. « Personne ne me comprend, personne ne me connaît. » Qui ne s'est jamais dit ça ?' [Illness is our whole life and it's really commonplace. 'Nobody understands me, nobody knows me.' Who has never said that?] (p. 12). And her denial that her illness was no worse than female epilation (p. 12) rings extremely hollow, since body-hair shaving or waxing do not pose the same grave health risks as bulimia nervosa.

Beyond the Prologue, it is not at all certain that in her main text de Peretti is trying in the writing present to render a distorted vision held by her in the past when her cognition was most seriously distorted by her illness, because her testimony ends on a jauntily toned assertion that she still vomits from time to time but is leading the life she wants to live (p. 149). Reverting to the Prologue, another unbalanced judgement within it from Camille is preceded by the positing of the author's present perspective at the time of writing, which suggests no change in outlook between that held in the writing present and that held when she was ill. Some readers may consequently infer that the author is both conceited and misguided in asserting that Camille was stronger than others:

> C'est l'histoire d'une fille qui se pose des questions. Elle a des angoisses et des tas de problèmes. Et elle souffre. Oh, elle sait souffrir, mais elle est plus forte que les autres et elle cache sa souffrance, parce que personne ne pourrait comprendre ça. (p. 13)

> It's the story of a girl who asks herself questions. She has anxieties and lots of problems. And she suffers. Oh, she knows how to suffer, but she is stronger than others and she hides her pain, because no one could understand that.

Admittedly, in the last two paragraphs of the Prologue to the text proper there are certainly signs that she has engaged in at least some self-questioning and self-critique and has acknowledged self-deception ('Il faut qu'elle comprenne qu'elle s'est trompée' [She needs to understand that she's made a mistake]).

> Aveugle et tordue de l'intérieur, elle se fait vomir au-dessus de la cuvette des chiottes parce que la vie est si horrible, et elle est fière que personne ne sache à quel point elle est un être d'exception.
>
> Ça la rassure, et pourtant elle a tort. Parce que pendant ce temps, elle vit dans la peur et dans le mensonge. Il faut qu'elle comprenne qu'elle s'est trompée. Toutes ces histoires de minceur, de balance et de calories, ce n'est pas ça le problème. C'est plus grave que ça. (p. 13)

> Blind and twisted from the inside, she makes herself vomit above the toilet bowl because life is so horrible, and she is proud that no one knows how much of an exceptional being she is.
> It reassures her, and yet she is wrong. Because during this time, she lives in fear and in lies. She needs to understand that she's made a mistake. All these stories of thinness, balance and calories, that's not the problem. It's more serious than that.

Yet the narrative and discursive jump-cuts in the text taken as a whole may lead the reader to consider Camille at worst an unreliable narrator, at best an epistemologically shape-shifting narrator. Doubt about the narrator's honesty, sincerity, and reliability, which has arisen several times already, revisits the reader (or at least, the reader with some knowledge of EDs) when Camille makes a disingenuous comment about forgetting to eat while spending her lunchtime break shopping (p. 95). Simply 'forgetting' to eat at normal mealtimes is very rare in eating-disordered subjects, who may very well abstain from the act at the socially normative times (breakfast, lunch, dinner), but will be hyper-conscious of their abstinence.

Turning now to close analysis of the text proper, the clinical profile of the academically high-achieving bulimic[28] is foregrounded in the very first sentence of the very first chapter: 'J'ai toujours été une bonne élève' [I have always been a good pupil] (p. 17). She does admit to having failed to gain admission to the highly prestigious École normale supérieure (p. 18), but this does not negate her claim to having been a good pupil, given the astronomically high academic standards required for admission to that institution (the British equivalent of Oxbridge). She goes on to state that she did a slapdash job in the entrance exams of the two other Grandes Écoles (HEIs with higher status than universities in France) to which she subsequently applied, ESSEC and HEC (p. 19), both of which specialise in business studies, but makes it plain that this was due to her ease in literary studies and ignorance of anything to do with figures/statistics. More important, though, are the reasons adduced

28 Among the numerous examples in the secondary literature attesting to this profile is the following: 'Despite the enormous amount of time and energy expended in bingeing and purging, many bulimarexic women manage to maintain high academic averages in college. By their own admission, they are overachievers.' Boskind-White, Marlene and White, William C., *Bulimia/Anorexia: The Binge/Purge Cycle and Self-Starvation* (New York/London: W.W. Norton & Company, 2000 [first edition 1983, second edition 1987]), p. 30.

for application to degree programmes for which she was not suited: to please her mother and her step-father, and to achieve any kind of (academic) success, of whatever sort, thus compensating for her failure to gain admission to the École normale supérieure, which had hurt her pride. The first reason is thoroughly consistent with the identikit image constructed by clinicians of the anorectic particularly, but also of the bulimarectic. The second reason also correlates with the very common symptom of over-investment in academic achievement so often reported in the secondary literature on anorectics/bulimarectics/bulimics.[29] The second reason also corresponds to her high self-confidence, which is atypical in ED sufferers. Camille seems to have had high self-confidence from a very early age, enjoying performing in front of others, and having grandiose ambitions.

> Pour les invités, j'enfilais mon long tutu blanc et j'esquissais trois pas de danse sur Giselle jusqu'à en faire pleurer les amies de maman. Une perle, une petite fille parfaite et tellement mature pour son âge. Alors il a fallu que je me décide très vite entre devenir président de la République – ô joie et sourire extasié des grandes personnes – ou star des étoiles scintillantes, princesse comme Sissi Impératrice, ma grande idole. (pp. 17–18)

> For the guests, I put on my long white tutu and I had a go at three dance steps to Giselle until my mom's friends started to cry. A pearl, a perfect girl and so mature for her age. So I had to decide very quickly between becoming President of the Republic – O joy and ecstatic smile of grown-ups – or star of sparkling stars, a princess like Empress Sisi, my great idol.

It is particularly telling that her great idol, 'Sissi Impératrice' [Empress Sisi], has herself been discussed in one of the secondary texts as an anorectic.[30] Further, and setting aside Camille's atypical self-confidence, her aspiration to princess-like status meshes with research findings 'of histrionic personality disorder or traits in patients with BN'.[31] One sign of Camille's histrionic tendency, and also of narcissistic attention-seeking, is her statement of pride at fainting easily (p. 27). This is in keeping with the fantasy-ideal she has constructed for herself, fuelled

29 See the section 'Hyperactivity/Hyperintellectuality/Over-investment in School or University Studies' in the Bibliographical Appendix.

30 Raimbault and Eliacheff 1989.

31 Smolak, Linda, Levine, Michael P., and Striegel-Moore, Ruth, *The Developmental Psychopathology of Eating Disorders* (Mahwah, NJ: Lawrence Erlbaum Associate, Publishers, 1996), p. 292.

by her mother, of a princess. (See also, for example, p. 111, where she attributes her frequent fainting to her being a princess, and p. 125.) Reiteration of her narcissistic attention-seeking occurs in 'tout ce qui comptait était de ne pas passer inaperçue' [all that mattered was not to pass unnoticed] (p. 27). This is followed by enigmatic expression of a perverse wish to be dissatisfied.

> Je n'ai jamais été satisfaite. Je pensais alors que j'étais une fille complexée parce que je voulais la perfection. J'avais tort. Je ne voulais pas la perfection, je ne voulais pas avoir plus ou moins de centimètres de tour de taille ou de poitrine, je voulais juste être mécontente, détester les centimètres, quels qu'ils fussent. (p. 27)

> I have never been satisfied. I thought I was a complex girl because I wanted perfection. I was wrong. I didn't want perfection, I didn't want my waist or chest to be a few inches wider or narrower, I just wanted to be unhappy, to hate the centimetres, whatever they were.

With careful precision, Camille establishes her 'case history' of weight and food-intake, and for somebody who is to become seriously bulimic/bulimarexic as a young adult the antecedents to her illness challenge the predominant findings of the secondary literature. As remarked above, one source in this literature affirms '[t]he anorectic-bulimics also have a higher prevalence of premorbid obesity',[32] which certainly does not apply to Camille. As a child, she had only a tiny appetite and was teased for looking like a skeleton by other children at primary school (p. 25). A highly significant datum is that when she was only six years old, a paediatrician told her mother that Camille presented an anorexic profile and that, consequently, the mother should never enter into conflicts with her daughter over food. This medical advice was scrupulously followed by her mother. Camille adds that her height increased more slowly than for other children and teenagers of her age, and that she did not start menstruating until the age of eighteen (p. 26) – a very late onset indeed, which is usually due to low body weight (for menstruation to commence, a girl must have accumulated a certain amount of body fat). At this early, pre-bulimarexic point, she records a desire to leave behind her child-like body (p. 26) that counters dominant psychoanalytically derived medico-clinical constructions of mainly anorexia nervosa but also of bulimia nervosa as essentially a fear of adult female sexuality. At that point she decides she does not like

32 Halmi, in Szmukler et al. 1995, pp. 29–42 (p. 31).

her body, due to its defiance of her (normative) expectations, in contrast to her mind, which, she claims, had always granted her wishes. What is crucial is the turn taken here, which correlates closely with many of the other primary texts on EDs, be they about anorexia nervosa, bulimarexia, bulimia nervosa, or binge eating disorder: namely, a mind–body split/dualism.[33]

> [...] je n'aimais pas mon corps, cet ingrat qui ne répondait pas du tout à mes attentes, alors que mon esprit, lui, avait toujours exaucé tous mes vœux. *J'ai séparé les deux entités à partir de ce moment-là* en plaçant clairement l'esprit en commandant général de toutes les opérations à venir, et le corps en boulet qui se doit d'obéir ou, au moins, de se cacher. (p. 26; my emphasis)

> [...] I did not like my body, this ingrate who did not meet my expectations at all, while my mind had always fulfilled all my wishes. *I separated the two entities from then on* by clearly making the mind the commander-in-chief of all future operations, and the body into a ball and chain that must obey or, at least, hide.

Note the martial metaphor deployed to convey the extremity of this mind–body split/dualism, with the metaphor of a military operation in which the mind subordinates and humiliates the body as if the body were a prisoner of war. On the mind–body split/dualism in de Peretti's text, Laura Jackson comments cogently:

> De Peretti's exhaustive documentation of the motion of crossing boundaries by eating and excreting focuses the narrative inside the body – on digestion, hunger, and physical pain – in order to make clear the violent and overwhelming struggle of an identity fractured between mind and body.[34]

Of significance is Camille's comment that it was when she started studying at ESSEC that she started to feel fat (p. 28), whereas she had never in her life actually been overweight – quite the contrary. However, she follows this up by adding that she had in fact gained weight, not huge amounts, but that her pelvis had got larger, she was taking the pill, was now eating more than just cucumber rounds, and was even experiencing hunger. All these facts she sums up as nothing but entirely normal, adding that the time had come for her to become an adult. But the final

33 See the section 'Mind–Body Split/Mind–Body Dualism' in the Bibliographical Appendix.

34 Jackson 2014: 172.

and single sentence in the chapter, separated from the more rational paragraph preceding it, is ominous: 'Et moi, j'ai voulu faire un régime' [And as for me, I wanted to go on a diet].

As the narrative progresses, the – albeit unintentionally – nefarious influence of her mother in the onset and persistence of Camille's ED is revealed as having been egregious. As remarked above, that mother had herself suffered from bulimia/anorexia in her youth, due to deep emotional problems. A psychic template for the pathological weight-obsession Camille will later develop had been set in childhood by the mother, whom she had witnessed weighing herself three times a day (p. 29). Camille had learnt that after having gained huge amounts of weight and then lost huge amounts, her mother had, thanks to the good advice of a psychotherapist, stabilised at a weight she (the mother) found reasonable (p. 29). But, crucially, Camille adds that her mother had never ceased to deprive herself of food, and that her mother's eating or not eating on a given day would depend entirely on whether the weight registered on her scales that day was still considered reasonable by the mother (p. 29). This implies that the mother's 'recovery' from bulimarexia, implied by that mother's use of the past tense in referring to the condition – 'moi aussi j'ai été boulimique-anorexique' [I was also a bulimarexic] (p. 103) – had certainly never been complete, from a psychological optic, as opposed to the optic of 'normality' based on cessation of purging, on attainment of a body weight that would at least have been sufficiently healthy for menstruation to resume (without which she would have been very unlikely indeed to conceive and give birth to her two daughters), and on long-term maintenance of that weight. Even here, there is evidence to suggest that the weight her mother found acceptable and at which she has been stable for many years is below the norm. For one of the reasons Camille gives for not liking her mother's body prior to the onset of her own illness is the fact that her mother's bones stuck out (p. 29). Thus, and significantly, as a child/young adolescent, Camille did not (yet) valorise thinness.

Nonetheless, the most damaging by-products of her mother's psychopathology are the horror all too evident to Camille at least that her mother harbours of her daughters becoming plump; the mother's conviction that one can never be too slim; and that, in fact, her mother never regretted Camille's morbid lack of appetite (pp. 29–30) in childhood. The only extenuating circumstances are that the mother never weighed Camille or her other daughter, only herself (p. 30). But even this concession is followed up by the observation that the mother could tell visually if her two daughters were too 'fat' or not – and thankfully, she never found either of them to be so. The mother's surveillance of her daughters' weight is reiterated in two recollections. First, before Camille's trip to Japan for work purposes, her mother gave her a new set of scales to take with her (p. 54): a poisoned present. Second, Camille recalls that while her sister (nine years younger) was able to eat a high-calorie diet (for example, including whole Nutella-spread baguettes for an afternoon snack) while remaining slim, their mother nonetheless reprimanded the sister and issued dire warnings that could very easily have provoked an ED in the sister too:

> Ma mère lui disait qu'elle mangeait trop, qu'un jour ou l'autre elle paierait le prix de ses excès. Elle était folle, ma mère, d'oser empêcher ma sœur de manger devant moi, elle ne se rendait pas compte, bien sûr, elle voulait que ces deux filles soient toujours des princesses magnifiques. (p. 94)

> My mother told her that she ate too much, that one day or another she would pay the price for her excesses. She was crazy, my mother, to dare to prevent my sister from eating in front of me, she did not realise, of course, she wanted these two girls to always be beautiful princesses.

The general mother–daughter over-enmeshment asserted in the secondary literature on anorexia nervosa at least is borne out inter alia by the notation that even when Camille is thousands of miles away in Japan, her mother phones her several times per day, and that Camille also phones her mother. The psychologically insalubrious effects of this enmeshed relationship are patent, and her mother's five-times' daily phone calls precipitate her into vomiting: an unequivocal linking of the mother's emotional demands upon Camille with the bulimia nervosa she has by now developed (p. 79). The serious psychological drain on her energy still exacted by her mother even when Camille is well into her twenties and has lived abroad for several months is made starkly obvious, despite Camille's ambivalent vacillation between condemnation and idealisation ('Une mère tyrannique et merveilleuse' [A tyrannical and marvellous mother]):

> Trop d'amour, peut-être, trop d'espoirs rassemblés sur la tête d'une seule enfant, sûrement, trop de souffrances à soulager pour avoir le temps de vivre ses propres maux. Une mère tyrannique et merveilleuse. Une mère qui pardonnerait tout à ses enfants pour mieux les culpabiliser. Impossible de lâcher cette mère-là. (p. 80)

> Too much love, perhaps, too many hopes gathered on the head of a single child, surely, too much suffering to relieve in order to have the time

> to live her own pains. A tyrannical and wonderful mother. A mother who would forgive her children everything to make them feel guilty. It's impossible to let go of that mother.

We have already noted Camille's tiny appetite as a child. Her premorbid weight was, if not dramatically low, then considerably lower than the female average for her height: from the age of 17 until she went to study at ESSEC, Camille weighed 50 kilos (7 stones 12 lbs) for a height of 1.7 metres (5 ft 7 inches). But a sea-change occurs when she undertakes higher studies. At ESSEC, her appetite suddenly soars, to the point where she experiences extreme hunger and begins to eat much more calorifically rich food outside of regular mealtimes (p. 30). Interestingly, this new hunger for food is accompanied by a hunger for life in general, particularly for sex with men, for alcohol, for high heels – for hedonism. The secondary literature often construes the 'typical' personality-type of bulimics as including (ab)use of alcohol and frequent sexual activity.[35] Her weight increases to 55 kilos (8 stones 9 lbs), for which her psychological intolerance is summed up lapidarily by one word: '[i]nadmissible' [inadmissible] (p. 30). Thus, she goes on her first-ever diet, a fateful move that eventually leads to a vicious circle of starving–gorging. The verb used to denote her mind being subordinated to her body, 'craquer' [to crack], has connotations in this particular usage (the denotation is simply 'giving in'/'not being able to resist') of mental breaking/breakdown:

> Je me privais, j'avais faim, je craquais. J'arrêtais ma voiture dans une station-service et j'achetais un paquet de cookies. N'ayant rien mangé depuis douze heures, je me l'empiffrais littéralement.
>
> "Craquer », mot emprunt de la plus atroce des culpabilités, où l'esprit se trouve à la merci du corps et, ce dernier une fois rassasié, on se sent terriblement faible. (p. 30)

> I deprived myself, I was hungry, I cracked. I stopped my car at a gas station and bought a packet of cookies. Having eaten nothing for twelve hours, I literally stuffed myself with them.
>
> 'Crack', a word borrowed from the most atrocious guilt, where the mind is at the mercy of the body and, once the latter is satisfied, you feel terribly weak.

35 Recall the statement from Nicholson and Nicholls 2011: 47: 'Bulimia nervosa is very commonly associated with other "adolescent" problem behaviors, such as experimentation with drugs or alcohol, smoking and sexual experimentation, which significantly increase the risk of this population.'

The mind–body split/dualism so endemic in testimonies to EDs is immanent in the second paragraph, and Camille expresses here the terrible sense of guilt at the supremacy of her body over her mind. Another example of this trope is Camille's reaction to the realisation that her body has consumed 700 calories more in a day than the amount her mind had set as a goal: 'J'avais pris sept cents de trop, mon corps devenait le débiteur de mon esprit' [I had taken seven hundred too many, my body became the debtor of my mind] (p. 35). That mind–body split/dualism is translated forcefully in Camille's succeeding reflections, in which the body is cast as low and bestial (cf. Rodrigue, and later on in this book Loupias), and placed in competition with the mind, to the point where a relationship of hatred grows between them. She does wryly concede that in fact, far from being like a dumb animal, the body is actually very canny, learning that if her mind is going to enforce fasting on it, it has to stock up on food (p. 31). The result is that despite the mortifications she inflicts on her body, and a generally low calorific intake even when including the gorging episodes, she gains weight – a slowing down of her metabolic rate that is a natural bodily reaction to alimentary privation, as attested in numerous texts in the secondary literature.[36]

The result is a neurotic obsession with weight: mirroring her mother, she starts to weigh herself several times per day (p. 31). It is telling, and symptomatic of anorectics' amply documented tendency to deny they are ill, that she describes this as a form of game, however neurotic, and thus downplays its actual pathology: 'Se peser plusieurs fois par jour est une sorte de jeu névrotique. On finit par si bien connaître son corps que l'on peut prédire à cent grammes près combien on pèse et combien on pèsera' [Weighing yourself several times a day is a kind of neurotic game. You end up knowing your body so well that you can predict, to the nearest hundred grams, how much you weigh and how much you will weigh] (p. 31). Unlike many sufferers from EDs, however, she does not engage in strenuous, calorie-burning exercise, and to this extent she again defies reports in the secondary literature (here she shares at least one trait with Balinska, who otherwise was a very differently eating-disordered individual: an anorectic restrictor type).[37] Camille's reasons for not over-exercising are partly what appears to be narcissistic

36 One early example is found in Palazzoli 1978: 14.

37 Occasionally the secondary literature states that not all anorectics/bulimics over-exercise, but such statements are extremely rare.

vanity – the self-myth of princess, which she later deconstructs, as will be demonstrated below – and partly the knowledge that exercise will intensify her hunger (pp. 31–32).

Camille's admission of her weight-neurosis is followed closely by another admission suggesting it is more extreme than mere weight-neurois and more akin to deep psychopathology. Realising that her calorific calculations had omitted certain foods ingested, she decides on a more scientific form of control, and in so doing declares that she has been possessed by a form of madness: 'C'est alors que j'allais voir le deuxième allié du *délire* qui s'était emparé de moi depuis quelque temps, la grande, l'illustre *Table des calories*' [That was when I would go and consult the second ally of the *delirium* that had seized me for some time, the great and famous *Calorie Table*] (p. 32; my emphasis). This book becomes, in her morbid mental state, a sacred text, whose sacrality she extends vaguely, but one can assume inferentially via the use of 'votre' [your], to other bulimarexics: 'Ce livre-là devient votre Bible' [That book becomes your Bible] (p. 34). On the same page the harmful nature of her neurosis and obsession/psychopathology is also rendered via the metaphor of imprisonment by it: 'votre névrose s'attribue bientôt des finesses que vous ne lui auriez pas soupçonnées. Les journées défilent prisonnières d'un décompte d'infinis possibles' [your neurosis soon develops ruses that you would not have suspected. The days pass by, prisoners of a countdown of infinite possibilities] (p. 34). Revealing the compulsive mental mechanisms that sustain EDs, she points out that while she has never been particularly good at remembering numbers, she rapidly becomes an expert on the calorific content of multiple forms of food (p. 33). The equally compulsive need to know the precise number of calories in all food ingested is underscored in the fearsome affect induced by the imprecision of calculating food consumed in restaurants. This fear is so intense that it produces bodily trembling (p. 34). Indeed, even at this early point in her testimony, compulsivity is emerging as a marked trait in Camille; and this is congruent with research findings on comorbidity in EDs, which demonstrate a higher correlation of obsessive compulsive disorder with such disorders. One example from the secondary literature is the following:

> Interestingly, two studies suggest that there may be links between obsessive–compulsive disorder and eating disorder. Rastam and Gilberg (1990) found a higher incidence of OCD personality amongst mothers of cases of eating disorders (4 versus 1 in the control group). Halmi

> and colleagues (1991) found a similar increase in obsessive–compulsive disorders in the mothers of patients with anorexia nervosa.[38]

Both Camille (who as mentioned above veers from bulimia to anorexia nervosa later) and her mother seem to suffer from OCD, in Camille's case again suggesting either heredity or unconscious mimeticism.

A classic symptom of anorexia, viz. the pressing of food on others while abstaining oneself in order to effect in those others what one most fears for oneself, namely weight gain (cf. Valère and her fellow anorectic patients in Chapter 1),[39] is fully present in Camille (p. 34). When she does over-eat, she vomits in order to eliminate the excess calories, admitting to herself that she has become 'une boulimique-anorexique' [a bulimarexic] (p. 35). She identifies the aetiology of her new state in her mother's former ED, as if the transmission of this disorder from mother to daughter were inevitable: 'Ça ne m'a pas plus choquée que cela. C'était une simple constatation, comme si j'avais toujours su qu'un jour ou l'autre je poserai sur moi le nom de cette maladie. Celle de ma mère' [It did not particularly shock me. It was a simple observation, as if I had always known that one day or another I would take on the name of this illness. My mother's illness] (p. 35). However, if Camille admits she has become 'une boulimique-anorexique' [a bulimarexic] (p. 35), she reveals ignorance of one aspect of anorexia nervosa: 'Une anorexique est maigre parce qu'elle a arrêté de manger. Et si elle a arrêté de manger, c'est parce qu'elle n'a plus faim, plus jamais' [An anorectic is skinny because she has stopped eating. And if she has stopped eating, it's because she isn't hungry anymore, ever again] (p. 36). Anorexia, meaning literally lack of appetite, is in fact a complete misnomer for the condition of anorexia nervosa. As both the primary and the secondary literature attest, anorectics *do* experience hunger, often intense, albeit

38 Treasure, Janet and Holland, Anthony, 'Genetic factors in eating disorders', in Szmukler et al 1995, pp. 65–81 (76). Their references are to Rastam, M. and Gilberg, G., 'The family background in anorexia nervosa: A population-based study', *Journal of American Academy Child Adolescent Psychiatry*, 31 (1991), 283–89, and Halmi, A.K., Eckert, E., Marchi, P., Sampugnaro, V., Apple, R., and Cohen, J., 'Comborbidity of psychiatric diagnoses in anorexia nervosa', *Archives of General Psychiatry*, 48 (1991), 712–18.

39 One notation of this trait in the secondary literature is the following: 'The anorectic is truly hungry but tries to displace her hunger. She plunges into anorexogenic activities. She may direct her attention to feeding others in the hope of diminishing her hunger. Any cook is aware that hunger wanes when a person spends a lot of time in the kitchen.' Sours 1980: 294.

variably and intermittently. As Susie Orbach remarks, 'Like the hunger striker, the anorectic is starving, she is longing to eat, she is desperate for food.' [40] More close to the mark is Camille's immediately following sentence – 'Son corps, lui semble-t-il, n'a plus besoin de rien' [Her body, it seems to her, no longer needs anything] – which, in the 'lui semble-t-il' [it seems to her] (p. 36), reveals the dubious grasp on reality, in fact the self-deception, of anorectics.

Camille contrasts these remarks with her description of the bulimarexic. The description starts with the statement 'Une boulimique-anorexique est un être hybride' [A bulimarexic is a hybrid being] (p. 37), which highlights the complexity of the bulimarexic's state compared to the anorectic's. Although her succeeding comments are more banal – that the bulimarexic is neither fat nor thin, is thought to be normal by others, and that her condition is thus very easy to hide – they are instructive for those with no or little understanding of the condition. And one comment is compelling: 'En France, une femme sur cinq est ou a été boulimique-anorexique, jugez donc de la banalité de la chose' [In France, one woman in five is or has been bulimarexic, so you can judge how commonplace that is] (p. 37).[41]

Anorexia-envy is expressed, a sad but not uncommon envy in those afflicted with both bulimia nervosa and bulimarexia, who often vilify themselves as 'failed' anorectics: 'En tant que boulimique-anorexique, je rêvais d'être une vraie anorexique' [As a bulimarexic, I dreamed of being a true anorectic] (p. 37). The following comments from the secondary literature explicate this envy:

> Anorexia brings with it the appearance and feeling of total control and almost total denial. This stimulates pride, and a sense of achievement, perfectionism and of being different (perhaps even better) than other people. Bulimia, on the other hand, brings with it a feeling of being completely out of control. It is shameful in its indulgent excesses, revolting in its final scenario (the vomit spattered toilet, the streaming eyes, the stench). This stimulates guilt and self-disgust.[42]

40 Orbach 1993: 82.

41 This figure is echoed in the US, according to one study in 1985: 'one out of every five women with a college education binges and purges regularly'; Wiley Emmett, Steven (ed.), *Theory and Treatment of Anorexia Nervosa and Bulimia: Biomedical Sociocultural & Psychological Perspectives: Biomedical, Sociocultural and Psychological Perspectives* (New York: Routledge, 1985), 194.

42 McCarthy and Thomson 1996: 10.

Such warped thinking is, though, sometimes mitigated by more rational thinking. The fluctuating cognitive precision spawned by EDs is transparent in this vacillation. Cognitive impairment in severely eating-disordered individuals is routinely asserted in the secondary literature, where it is usually ascribed to biochemical disturbances flowing from disturbed eating/malnutrition. One instance of such vacillation is the following.[43]

> En tant que boulimique-anorexique, je rêvais d'être une vraie anorexique, mais j'avais trop faim pour cela. Je me considérais comme une boulimique parce que j'estimais que je mangeais trop, que j'avais toujours mangé trop. Mais j'avais tort, je n'étais pas boulimique, je mangeais normalement, peut-être un peu plus que lorsque j'avais quatre ans et demi, certes, mais je n'étais pas boulimique. (p. 37)

> As a bulimarexic, I dreamed of being a true anorectic, but I was too hungry for that. I considered myself a bulimic because I felt that I ate too much, that I had always eaten too much. But I was wrong, I was not bulimic, I ate normally, maybe a little more than when I was four and a half, certainly, but I was not bulimic.

So, this erratic train of thought implicitly refutes identification either as an anorectic or as a bulimic, whereas she had started by identifying herself as a combination of the two: 'En tant que boulimique-anorexique' [As a bulimarexic] (p. 37). And what follows reinforces the grim complexity of bulimarexia, recording that she follows very strict diets, constantly calorie-counts, and is anguished at the idea of not being able to adhere to the very restricted calorie intake set as a goal. The pathological development of bulimarexia is lucidly charted:

> Et au départ, pour moi, il n'était question que de vomir ce que j'avais mangé « en trop ». Mais j'ai vite compris que ça ne servait à rien à rendre un biscuit. En plus, l'opération se révélait difficile et douloureuse. (p. 37)

> And initially, for me, it was only a question of vomiting what I ate 'in excess'. But I quickly realized that it was useless to bring a biscuit back up. In addition, the operation was difficult and painful.

The upshot is that paradoxically, and as with Rodrigue's Julia discussed above, in order to be able to vomit effectively the bulimarexic often

43 Hilde Bruch states, 'Binge eaters are also difficult candidates for psychotherapy. The whole illness is based on erroneous assumptions and misconceptions, and therapy aims at correcting the underlying psychological errors.' Bruch 1978: 10.

needs to eat a great deal more than she might actually want, otherwise her stomach will not empty itself.[44] Desperate to vomit, Camille finds a 'solution' to induce genuine nausea and 'successful' vomiting, albeit with the 'help' of finger-sticking deep into the throat: 'Sans même y penser vous foncez vers la cuisine, vous mangez le paquet entier dans un accès de désespoir en même temps que vous buvez du lait à petites gorges' [Without even thinking about it, you go to the kitchen and you eat the whole packet in despair while sipping milk at the same time] (p. 38). Perhaps what is most noteworthy is the sense of purification experienced afterwards (p. 38) – a common motif in testimonies of bulimarexics and bulimics, and one that coincides paradoxically with the sense of purity felt by anorectics through avoiding ingestion of food in the first place.

This discovery of how to vomit effectively is, Camille avers, the moment where she transitioned from bulimarexia into plain bulimia nervosa – and not, at least at the point of transition, without triumphal pleasure (p. 38). This new phase is toxically combined with an intensely active sexual life with her new boyfriend Jade during her studies at ESSEC, and a waning commitment to those studies, manifested by missing classes for the first time in her life (p. 41). Here again, Camille's case runs counter to the majority of the primary corpus and also to the secondary literature, which commonly posits overly conscientiously work on studies – though it is stressed more in the case of anorectics than of bulimics.[45] Her chaotic state of mind also manifests itself in perception of her body as enormously fat. Despite vomiting what she has binged in the evening, the next day she immediately consumes all the fast/junk food she can find in the student vending machines. While her perception of being enormously fat is absurdly inaccurate, illustrating the distortion typical of eating-disordered individuals' body-image found both in the primary corpus and in the secondary literature,[46] she does in fact gain weight during what she censoriously labels this 'vie dissipée' [dissipated

44 'In order to bring the food up again, larger and larger quantities have to be consumed' (see Bruch 1978: 84).

45 That over-conscientious stance towards study is encapsulated by mention of 'worry over school performance' in Smolak et al. 1996: 288.

46 For one early and succinct example in the secondary literature, which is limited to anorexia nervosa but holds true for bulimarexics, see Slade, P.D., 'Body image in anorexia nervosa', *British Journal of Psychiatry*, 153 (suppl. 2) (1988), 20–22.

life], going from 55 kilos to 58 kilos. In tandem, her obsession with weight increases, with her weighing herself three times a day – just as she had witnessed her mother doing in her childhood (p. 29), and again suggesting unconscious mimeticism.

Despite her claim 'je suis devenue une vraie boulimique' [I have become a true bulimic] (p. 38), her oscillation between bulimia nervosa and at least episodic anorexia nervosa is immanent in the fact that as she begins to vomit regularly, two or three times a week, she still believes in the virtues of food deprivation, with the latter meaning that she has little to regurgitate and thus the vomiting is difficult (p. 42). Again, awareness that in order to be able to vomit copiously she needs to eat more copiously resurfaces, and she starts, precisely, to eat a great deal more, resulting in more copious, more frequent, and more rapid vomiting (p. 43). The fact that she does not lose weight, staying at approximately 58 kilos, infuriates her each time she steps on the scales. The mind–body split/dualism resurfaces in the following, which indicates a sense of her body's mysterious and sly character: 'Mon corps mystérieux et sournois rendait une partie et stockait l'autre dans un va-et-vient dont le fonctionnement m'échappait' [My mysterious and devious body was bringing back up one bit and storing the other in a to and fro whose workings escaped me] (p. 43). The battle between the fragmented self, body and mind, is accentuated in 'Je continuais mes activités, espérant que mon corps allait finir par céder' [I continued my activities, hoping that my body would eventually give in] (p. 43).

Yet another fluctuation in her eating patterns occurs at the start of her job in Japan, when she loses three kilos in two weeks, due to the lower calorie eating habits common in Japan relative to France (p. 54). Despite her elation at this weight loss, she does admit her neurosis, and has a flash of lucidity in realising that the different bodily morphology of Japanese women relative to European women contributes to this neurosis: 'Il faut dire que les Japonaises entretenaient ma névrose. Elles sont très minces, très plates, elles n'ont ni fesses, ni taille, ni hanches, ni poitrine. Je rêvais de leur ressembler' [It must be said that Japanese women sustained my neurosis. They are very skinny and very flat, they have neither buttocks, nor waists, nor hips, nor chest. I dreamed of looking like them] (p. 54). But this is merely a flash, and the different bodily morphology of Japanese women results in an even more distorted body image: 'Impossible de ne pas se sentir obèse au Japon' [It's impossible to not feel obese in Japan] (p. 55), where the 'on' [we] erroneously and irrationally extends this body dysmorphic disorder to all Europeans, most of whom might have felt plumper but hardly obese in comparison to the Japanese. Her neurosis is stressed by the fact that she continues to vomit food even in this new country where she has already lost weight due simply to its different dietary norms (p. 57). The obsessionality of her thinking is reinforced by use of the adverbial locution 'avec acharnement' [with tenacity] (p. 58) to evoke the furious, relentless energy she puts into calorie-counting. In order not to offend her Japanese landlady, she eats the evening meals the latter prepares for her, but then silently vomits them out while taking a shower. The self-satisfied tenor of the detailed reflections on her expertise in efficacious vomiting, which she presents clinically as an operation, as if it were a military duty, simply reinforces the gravity of her psychopathology:

> L'opération devenait de plus en plus facile pour moi, je savais ce qui passait mal : la salade et les légumes par exemple, contrairement au riz et aux gâteaux qui, eux, se vomissent très bien. En règle générale, c'est toujours plus agréable de vomir sucré, tandis que l'ail est une des choses que je déconseille le plus fermement. (p. 58)

> The operation was becoming easier and easier for me, I knew what didn't work well: salad and vegetables for example, unlike rice and cakes, which can be vomited very easily. As a general rule, it is always more pleasant to vomit sweet, while garlic is one of the things I strongly advise against.

In terms of reader reception, most perturbing of all is the last clause, in which she is consciously (albeit not entirely seriously) offering advice to potential or actual bulimics about what not to try to vomit. Other inferable advice concerns waiting half an hour after eating before trying to vomit (p. 59). The simple fact of offering advice about efficacious vomiting is a noxious form of pedagogy for her readers. It is possible that the lexicon of advice is used wryly, even ironically; however, no textual evidence to support this hypothesis is found in the text. But despite the apparent self-satisfaction at such expertise, Camille in fact expresses lack of knowledge of her bulimarexic body.

> Le corps de la boulimique-anorexique est un vase communicant. Ça rentre et ça sort, on ne sait plus très bien pourquoi ni comment. À ce jeu-là on perd toute notion de ce qui nous a traversé, et alors la balance est maîtresse reine. (p. 59)

> The body of the bulimarexic is a communicating vessel. Things come in and out, we do not really know why or how. At this game we lose all sense of what has gone through us, and then the scales are lord and master.

The pathology of her thinking and behaviour is especially evident in one gruesome passage where she evokes in stomach-churning detail three successive episodes of vomiting, the contents of the vomit, and even the weight of the vomit, collected in a plastic bag and placed on the scales: 500 grams (p. 60). Similarly grotesque details are proffered to the reader in description of the aftermath of typical vomiting episodes in café toilets: 'Je me relevais, la main droite dégoulinante de bile avec des petits bouts de brioche comme autant de pustules jaunes sur mes doigts' [I picked myself up, my right hand dripping with bile and little bits of brioche like a load of yellow pustules on my fingers] (p. 84), with the simile of pustules figuratively evoking the poisoned nature of her condition. She herself admits, via the word 'folie' [madness], to the mental derangement provoking such behaviour: 'Je tirais la chasse d'eau et j'en profitais pour faire disparaître toutes les traces de ma *folie*' [I pulled the flush and used it to make every trace of my *madness* disappear] (p. 84; my emphasis).

There is a poignant punning in the repetition of the verb 'vomir' (p. 70), which action is axiomatically a key component of her bulimia nervosa/bulimarexia. On p. 70 it is first used in the sense of 'to loathe' (cf. Rodrigue's Julia, who says 'je [...] vomis tout ce qui émane de l'extérieur' [I [...] loathe everything that comes from outside, p. 144), then it segues into its physical meaning of 'to vomit'. By the end of four months in Japan Camille has started to loathe multiple facets of her life, and that loathing is expressed by anaphoric use of the charged and semantically mutating verb 'vomir'.

> Je vomissais ma solitude, je vomissais leur froideur, je vomissais les appels de Jade, je vomissais encore et toujours des pots de glace à la vanille de quatre cent cinquante millilitres, avalés en trois minutes, crachés en trois secondes, un long jet continu de glace à la vanille qui vous ferait presque croire que vous avez mangé deux fois le pot. (p. 70)

> I loathed my solitude, I loathed their coldness, I loathed Jade's calls, I vomited over and over again the four-hundred-and-fifty milliliter pots of vanilla ice cream, devoured in three minutes and spat out in three seconds, a long continuous jet of vanilla ice cream that would almost make you believe that you had eaten two pots' worth.

Her general distress and chaotic alimentary conduct are conveyed in the notations that her weight can vary from 52 to 55 kilos within the space of two days, that she vomits even when at work, resulting in a swollen face and blood-shot eyes, but in fact claims not to care about what her colleagues might think of such an appearance, since 'J'étais grosse et laide, peu m'importait les stigmates de mes vomissements' [I was fat and ugly, so the stigmata of my vomiting were not very important to me] (p. 70). The use of the noun 'stigmates' is ambiguous, connoting both simple physical marks of bodily disgrace and also Christ-like martyrdom. What is also significant is her recusant attitude and distorted perception of rights vis-à-vis her vomiting and its goal: 'Je voulais être mince, j'en avais bien le droit après tout' [I wanted to be thin, after all it was my right to be so] (p. 70).

Worsening of her pathology occurs as she turns to other purgative methods in addition to vomiting that have grave psychological consequences. Desperate to lose weight, she tries taking laxatives, but in typically excessive mode: a whole pack, which makes her very ill (p. 71). Although she never takes them again, it is from this point that she starts to have her first visual hallucinations. And very atypically for her particular personality configuration, here she admits, albeit litotically, to a sense of shame: 'Je n'étais pas très fière de moi' [I was not very proud of myself] (p. 71). Her landlady is so concerned that she takes her to hospital. And there, even while having hallucinations of mosquitoes and vomiting the bowl of rice given to her, she declares delight at having vomited in public: 'J'étais ravie de vomir en public' [I was delighted to have vomited in public] (p. 72). That delight appears entirely to annul her earlier, attenuated expression of shame, and to show an exhibitionist component in her bulimarexic syndrome (mentioned above in my comments on the opening of her testimony). Self-congratulation seems to be implied in 'Leurs toilettes étaient tout en marbre noir ; le premier jour, j'y ai été me faire vomir *délicieusement* après le déjeuner, étrennant ainsi ma venue dans ce nouveau monde' [Their toilets were all black marble; on the first day, I made myself vomit *deliciously* there after lunch, thereby christening my arrival into this new world] (p. 78; my emphasis). But again, it is difficult to discern whether there is irony in Camille's use of valorising lexis ('délicieusement' [deliciously]) to qualify her vomiting, this time in reference to its occurrence in a new workplace, in Paris.

That apparent pride and cavalier attitude towards her pathological behaviour could in fact be seen as a cover for her deep psychological fragility. When, having inadvertently blocked the shower drain due to vomiting under the shower, she confesses her bulimarexia to the boyfriend Jade with whom she is living, he takes her in his arms but says he doesn't want the vomiting to continue (pp. 81–82). They then have sex, but she feels like a stranger in his arms, since she had made a cry for help but feels that he didn't want to hear it – that the man she loved understood nothing. This failure of a bid for help provokes an increase in her obsession with food – 'Je pensais à la nourriture toute la journée' [I thought of food all day] (p. 82), in the amount of it she consumes, and in the rapidity of the consumption, with her stuffing pastries into her mouth quickly in public as she walks along the streets. Her increasing psychopathology is underscored by a perverse refusal to criticise the images of unnatural female thinness purveyed by (Western) society (p. 83). Her blinkered optic dismisses television programmes stimulating debate about the promotion of such unnatural thinness in some cases triggering anorexia nervosa as mere façades of 'democratic' correctness that simply cast women as victims. There are two flaws in her characteristically categorical judgement here. First, while the wish to appear democratic will obviously be one motivation in the commissioning of such programmes, to reject them wholesale on this sole basis is to throw the baby out with the bathwater. Second, while those suffering from EDs may well reject the label of victim in the interests of personal dignity, there is a strong case, and one that has been made frequently and compellingly,[47] that societal canons of unnatural thinness as perfection[48] do in fact make women (and some men) into victims, in the sense that they fall prey to anorexia nervosa (and indeed to other EDs) through no fault of their own because of their attempts to conform to these canons. The putative reasoning for her stance is that anorexia nervosa pre-dates late twentieth-century fashions, but while this is true, it casually ignores the rocketing increase in cases of the illness in the late twentieth century and early twenty-first. Partly mitigating the impression of arrogance and superficiality emitted by Camille here is her implicit recognition both of that arrogance and of her actual ordinariness, even the sad sordidness of her bulimic behaviour. Referring to teenaged girls' dreams of becoming media stars, she reflects, 'Être belle ou mince, peu importe, du moment que l'on est admirée. Et moi qui allais bientôt me mettre deux doigts au fond de la gorge pour me persuader que j'étais plus forte que les autres,

47 To take one example among many, but a particularly compelling one, see Bordo, Susan, 'Anorexia nervosa: Psychopathology as the crystallization of culture', in Irene Diamond and Lee Quinby (eds), *Feminism and Foucault: Reflections on Resistance* (Boston, MA: Northeastern University Press, 1988), pp. 87–117.

48 See the section 'Sociocultural Factors: Their Role in the Development of EDs' in the Bibliographical Appendix.

j'étais si banale' [It doesn't matter whether you're beautiful or slim, as long as we are admired. And I, who was about to put two fingers down the back of my throat to convince myself that I was stronger than the others, I was so unremarkable] (p. 83).

While Camille does by this point admit to herself that she is ill, she also asserts that she wants not to recover but simply to lose weight (p. 85). The absolutist and arguably schizoid nature of her bulimarexic ideation is thus exposed (p. 85). So too are: the relationship with food as one of enmity despite excessive consumption of it (p. 85); the sparking of a binge as an almost mechanical process – 'engrenage' [cycle] (p. 85) – over which no human agency is possible; and, paradoxically for those with no or little understanding of bulimia, the self-interdiction of pleasure in eating (for the non-cognoscenti, the obvious question is, 'Why eat excessively when one allows oneself no pleasure in eating?'); and, once again, the mind–body split/dualism in 'on n'aime pas que notre corps nous dise quoi faire' [we don't like that our body tells us what to do] (p. 85), conveying a hostile and conflictual relationship between the conscious mind's excessive needs and the body's normal alimentary needs. And things get even worse. Three years spent working for a bank during which she feels incompetent and deeply fearful lead to an exponential increase in her vomiting, in the workplace as well as at home (p. 90). Distorted cognition and affect are patent in her memory that vomiting was almost a relief because, to her mind, at least when she was vomiting she was doing something 'useful'. Also of concern are that she no longer finds the act disgusting, that she performs it with great ease, that her body has adapted to it in the sense that sticking her fingers down her throat hardly ever produces a sense of scratching her throat now.

However, in narrative retrospective, she does admit the serious damage she was unknowingly inflicting on her digestive system by frequent vomiting over a prolonged period. This is driven home by the fact that, when she is vomiting several times a day every day, her body is unable to digest anything (p. 95). Of salience is the adverb 'machinalement' [mechanically] to describe the mode in which she is vomiting, indicating no mental control over that mode. Her previously normal, indeed high, intellectual functioning is now illness-vitiated: her view of the damage she is inflicting on her body is deranged. Some readers at least may find distasteful (no pun intended) the pride she feels upon discovering that the plastic bag holding the contents of her most recent vomit weighs 1.5 kilos. They may also be confounded by the delusional certainty this gives her of having become 'une fille très organisée' [a very organised girl] (p. 96). Of course, this self-compliment may well be ironic, but once again there is no certainty for the reader, for no clues to irony are supplied by de Peretti. Camille's mental instability is reinforced by contradiction of her previous admission of being ill (p. 85) in a later claim that she is not (p. 97). It is also reinforced by her refusal to identify with the bulimic young women described on an Internet website she consults, even though she (Camille) provides a detailed symptomatology of the serious health problems caused by precisely her bulimia nervosa.

> Mes dents sentaient la vomissure [...] ma gorge me grattait, et puis quand je me brossais les dents le dentifrice devenait rose du sang de mes gencives. Bien sûr, j'avais mal partout, mes membres fous étaient en douleur, et la fatigue ne me lâchait plus. Je rêvais de m'endormir pour un mois et de me réveiller ayant perdu cinq kilos. Bien sûr, mon corps se déglinguait peu à peu. Il avait perdu l'habitude de digérer quoi que ce soit ; je saignais de partout. [...] Mon corps tirait la sonnette d'alarme. Je perdais mes cheveux. J'étais complètement détraquée hormonalement, d'autant plus que je prenais ma pilule avant de me coucher et qu'il m'arrivait de me relever dans la nuit pour vomir. (pp. 97–98)

> My teeth smelled of vomit [...] my throat was itchy, and then when I brushed my teeth the toothpaste got pink from the blood from my gums. Of course, I was in pain everywhere, my crazy limbs were in pain, and tiredness did not let me go. I dreamed of falling asleep for a month and waking up having lost five kilos. Of course, my body was slowly breaking down. It had lost the habit of digesting anything; I was bleeding everywhere. [...] My body was sounding the alarm. I was losing my hair. I was completely disordered hormonally, especially since I took my pill before going to bed and then got up in the night to vomit.

Finally, a crisis point occurs where she takes full cognisance of the gravity of her state. The mental breakthrough and its salutary effects are initially presented in both mildly comic and enigmatic mode – a single sentence opening a new chapter: 'Des pâtes m'ont sauvée' [Pasta saved me] (p. 99). The narrative that follows elucidates this breakthrough in terms of her horror at the effects of vomiting the pasta she had eaten before joining friends for an evening out. These effects are rendered in graphically gory detail, with the simile of white worms being particularly repugnant for this reader at least:[49]

49 Laura Jackson also expresses revulsion in referring to a 'particularly painful and disgusting episode of vomiting' (Jackson 2014: 175).

> Un soir de drame, j'avais mangé des tagliatelles et puis j'étais partie rejoindre des amis à une soirée. Comme à mon habitude, j'ai garé ma voiture et je me suis penchée en avant. Les pâtes avaient gardé leur forme initiale et sortaient douloureusement du fond de ma gorge dans l'ordre inverse où je les avais englouties. Alors je me suis surprise à aller les chercher. Je les tirais une à une du haut de mon gosier. [...] Je les jetais sur le trottoir, horrifiée. J'ai reculé, toute droite et crispée, les tagliatelles glissaient parfois, il ne fallait pas les laisser s'échapper. Je les sentais remonter le long de mon thornytorinx et s'offrir à mes petits doigts, qui les déroulaient lentement en faisant bien attention à ce qu'elles ne se cassent pas. Elles scintillaient au clair de lune sur l'asphalte comme des vermisseaux blancs. (p. 99).

> One tragic night, I had eaten tagliatelle and then gone to join some friends at a party. As usual, I parked my car and leaned forward. The pieces of pasta had kept their original shape and came out painfully from the back of my throat in the reverse order in which I had gobbled them. So I was surprised when I went to feel for them. I pulled them one by one from the back of my throat. [...] I threw them on the sidewalk, horrified. I retreated, straight and tense, the tagliatelle sometimes slipped, I couldn't let them slip away. I felt them go up through my thornytorinx and offer themselves to my little fingers, which unrolled them slowly, taking care that they did not break. They glittered in the moonlight on the asphalt like white worms.

When she comes round after having fainted, her self-disgust prompts the decision that such degrading behaviour must stop (p. 100). It is significant that the trigger to this sudden revolt against her bulimic behaviour is abhorrence at her perceived filth, with its implied aspiration to purity – the latter aspiration being a widespread trope in testimonies mainly to anorexia nervosa, but also to bulimia nervosa.

Unfortunately, it is into a drastically anorexic phase that the decision to cease vomiting leads her. The ostensible reason for her decision to eat literally nothing is that because her damaged digestive system now causes her involuntarily to bring up any food, she must avoid absorbing any food (p. 100). But at least complementing that reason, the informed reader infers, would be the fear of gaining weight through not purging any food consumed. When she begins to fast, the retrospective narration articulates points that again make it hard for the reader to discern if the writer looking back is attempting to convey past affect and cognition, or whether she is still at the time of writing caught up in such pathological affect and cognition. Thus we are unsure if the present-day narrator, who can for good reasons (see my introductory remarks above to Section

3.2) be closely associated with the author de Peretti, still feels proud about the great will-power and delight she proclaims in managing to eat absolutely nothing despite fainting episodes and feeling weaker than ever (p. 100). Many bulimarexics are secretive about their eating due to shame; so too is the anorectic, which Camille has now become. She does not want her family to realise she is fasting, so consents to eat some green beans at a family lunch that she cannot avoid, held just before going out shopping with her mother and sister (pp. 100–1). Even this derisory intake is more minimal than it appears, with her taking about ten green beans, spreading them out on the plate so that the quantity appears greater than it actually is. This is paradigmatic anorexic behaviour. The following statement expresses a wish not to annul the efforts put into eating nothing at all for three days: 'J'avais peur du regard de mes parents mais je ne voulais pas manger, c'était trop difficile, après tant d'efforts' [I was scared of the looks my parents gave me but I did not want to eat, it was too difficult after so much effort] (p. 101).

The physical (stomach pains) and psychological (delusional pride and manic behaviour) damage caused by her minimal eating is manifest in the consequences of three days of complete fasting followed by the formal family lunch at which she eats fewer than ten green beans (prompting her mother's disapproval – surprisingly, given the mother's previous concern about her daughter's over-eating rather than under-eating; see. p. 102, where the mother states, 'Tu ne manges rien, tu te pèses tout le temps, tu es ridicule à vouloir mincir comme ça' [You don't eat anything, you weigh yourself all the time, you're being ridiculous to want to slim down like that]).

> Mon ventre se tordait de douleur mais je n'allais pas vomir. J'étais forte. J'ai parlé sans m'arrêter tout le long du trajet. [...] J'étais à la limite de l'hystérie, le poulet, les haricots verts, la faïence, le pain, leur mastication, comme j'avais peur, je ne savais pas combien de temps j'allais pouvoir tenir sans manger. (p. 101)

> My belly was writhing in pain but I wasn't going to throw up. I was strong. I spoke without stopping the whole way. [...] I was on the verge of hysteria, chicken, green beans, earthenware, bread, their chewing, I was so scared, I didn't know how long I would be able to hold on without eating.

But despite the delusional pride and the manic talking, there is also some lucidity about the gravity of her self-alienation and about her mental imbalance, which are prompting suicidal ideation:

> Je ne savais pas comment faire pour recommencer à être moi. Je ne savais pas si j'étais devenue folle. Je repassais dans ma tête ces dernières semaines au-dessus de la baignoire avec mon sac en plastique, j'étais malade, mais forte, je voulais tout arrêter. J'avais envie de mourir. (p. 101)

> I didn't know how to start being me again. I didn't know if I had gone crazy. In my head I was running through these last weeks spent hunched over the bathtub with my plastic bag, I was sick, but strong, I wanted to stop everything. I wanted to die.

Following her mother's reprimand about fasting after saying during their shopping trip that she doesn't feel well (p. 102), she reaches a state of physical and mental crisis, indeed breakdown (the 'down' part of 'breakdown' being effectively rendered by 's'écroulait' [was collapsing]):

> Je ne pleurais pas, je hurlais de pleurs, tout s'écroulait à l'intérieur de moi, je sanglotais, je gémissais, je n'arrivais même plus à respirer, j'allais tomber à la renverse, m'écrouler sur le sol comme un veau à l'abattoir, les sons qui s'échappaient de moi m'effrayaient presque, je ne contrôlais plus rien. (p. 102)

> I didn't cry, I screamed tears, everything was collapsing inside me, I sobbed, I moaned, I couldn't even breathe, I was going to fall backwards, collapse on the floor like a calf at the slaughterhouse, the sounds that came out of me almost frightened me, I could no longer control anything.

The simile 'comme un veau à l'abattoir' [like a calf at the slaughterhouse] evokes both a sense of her victimhood and of her lack of human agency; it also taps into the lexical field of animality not uncommon in other French testimonies to EDs (such as Rodrigue's, as noted above in this chapter, and Loupias's, to be examined in Chapter 3).

Her mother's reaction is compassionate – taking Camille into her arms, asking her tenderly what's wrong (p. 103). But when Camille confesses to her mother that she is bulimarexic ('boulimique-anorexique', p. 103), has been vomiting every day for two years, wants to stop vomiting but is fearful of eating because this would lead to vomiting, the mother attempts to take control – 'Elle prenait la situation en main' [She took the situation in hand] (p. 103) – in categorically asserting that Camille must see a 'psy' [shrink]. It is at this point that she tells Camille she too had, previously, been bulimarexic ('boulimique-anorexique', p. 103), and that she is going to take her to see a doctor whom she deems to have been wonderful and who will give her good treatment. When Camille says she doesn't need anyone – a typical defence mechanism in eating-disordered individuals – her mother insists that Camille can get over her illness, but not alone, only with help.

The psychiatrist whom her mother insists she sees, Dr Lendonyos, appears entirely reasonable, saying that she must stop weighing herself (p. 108): the obsession with precise figures on the scales has to be broken before any bulimarexic can begin to recover. But her reaction is adamant resistance: 'Je lui ai répondu que c'était hors de question' [I told him that it was out of the question] (p. 108). He also prescribes Prozac (an antidepressant commonly prescribed for bulimia nervosa particularly among EDs), to which she does not seem to mount any resistance, and indeed is actually quite pleased about when he tells her that it has an appetite-depressing effect (p. 108) – another indication of her psychopathology. Further, he formally diagnoses her with obsessive compulsive disorder (OCD) (which as I remarked above has been linked in the secondary literature to EDs), saying that vomiting has become a drug to her, something she is unable to prevent. I have pointed several times above in this study to the addictive nature of EDs, as revealed by the primary corpus.[50] But when he wants her to take Xanax to treat this OCD, she is recalcitrant: 'Je me suis fermée comme une huître. Pas la peine d'insister, je n'en voulais pas' [I closed myself up like an oyster. It wasn't worth insisting, I didn't want it] (p. 108). Note in this simile the recurrent recourse to a lexis of animality/the non-human.

The stereotype of the invasive mother in anorexogenic families is reinforced in the following, as in many other parts of this text, which succeeds her notation on reduction of vomiting after the first few doses of Prozac:

> J'étais malgré moi secondée par ma mère qui, s'en voulant terriblement d'avoir été aveugle pendant deux ans, avait décidé de me surveiller inlassablement [...]. Elle me regardait avec des yeux angoissés chaque fois que je sortais de la salle de bains, et me demandait vingt fois par jour si tout allait bien. Certes, oui, j'allais bien, maintenant que j'avais enfin parlé, et je ne m'étais pas si bien portée depuis deux ans, et ma mère me croyait au plus mal. (p. 109)

> Despite my own wishes I was assisted by my mother who, blaming herself intensely for having been blind for two years, decided to watch me tirelessly [...]. She looked at me with anxious eyes every time I came out of the bathroom and asked me twenty times a day if everything was

50 Just one example is Szmukler, G.I. and Tantam, D., 'Anorexia nervosa: starvation dependence', *British Journal of Medical Psychology*, 57 (1984), 303–10.

> fine. Of course, yes, I was fine, now that I had finally talked, and I had not been this well in two years, and my mother thought I was in a very bad way.

Note in the last sentence here the beneficial effect Camille registers of having articulated in language her eating-disordered problems. Such benefit will be a key feature of the two case studies examined in the next chapter. However, the tendency to idealise a parent, and the prominence in her affective economy of the mother–daughter relationship (a salient trope in the other primary texts[51]), are revealed in her response to the psychiatrist's request that she talk to him about her mother: 'Il n'y a rien à dire sur ma mère. Je l'aime, ma mère chérie. Je l'aime, elle et son amour maternel à nul autre pareil' ['There is nothing to say about my mother. I love her, my darling mother. I love her and her motherly love like no other'] (p. 125).

The stereotype of the invasive mother in anorexogenic families is intensified in her comments to her psychiatrist Dr Lendonyos, and the supplement here is the illustration of her mother's vindictiveness – illustrative of the ambivalent, love–hate mother–daughter relationship upheld by some of the secondary literature.

> Elle pense que c'est sa faute, qu'elle m'a traumatisée d'une manière ou d'une autre. Mais elle s'en veut surtout parce qu'elle n'a rien vu. Je lui ai dit que j'étais une reine de la dissimulation et qu'il n'y avait aucun moyen pour qu'elle sache. Qu'elle n'y pouvait rien. Alors elle m'a répondu qu'elle était déçue, que je l'avais leurrée. [...] ça lui fait plaisir de participer à ma guérison, elle voudrait tout bien faire maintenant, alors quand je veux vomir je l'appelle. (p. 110)

> She thinks it's her fault, that she traumatized me one way or another. But she mostly blames herself because she didn't see anything. I told her that I was a queen of concealment and that there was no way for her to know. That she couldn't have done anything about it. So she replied that she was disappointed, that I had deceived her. [...] she enjoys playing a part in my recovery, she'd like to do everything right from now on, so when I want to vomit I call her.

Nonetheless, this particular mother–daughter relationship does sometimes have some localised benefits, as when phoning her mother while strongly tempted to vomit despite having eaten almost nothing

51 See the section 'Mother–Daughter Relationship: Fusion/ "Enmeshment"' in the Bibliographical Appendix.

for lunch does actually prevent her from the purge (p. 111). What is otherwise noteworthy in this passage is her notation that the temptation to vomit was more intellectual than physical: 'j'avais une envie terrible de me vider, c'était plus une tentation intellectuelle que physique' [I had such an enormous urge to empty myself, it was more of an intellectual temptation than a physical one] (p. 111). This, together with the use of the verb 'vider' [to empty], interlocks with the motif in many of the other primary texts of both 'le vide' [emptiness] and of aspiration to (putative) purity, or at least purification. It also evokes another motif in the primary texts, and one discerned several times above in Camille's case, viz. that of the mind–body split/dualism.

Due to eating very little indeed, rather than from vomiting, Camille's weight steadily declines (see, for example, pp. 111 and 114). The fact that she has a visual hallucination demonstrates one of the grave consequences of this semi-starvation (p. 117). However, the vomiting resumes due to a new source of emotional turmoil. When a man (César) whom she desires but is emotionally ambivalent about, given her long-standing relationship with another man (Jade), says she is the woman of his life, that he is going to marry her, and has a bouquet of flowers delivered to her, she experiences a relapse and starts eating but then purging.

> Nous sommes allés diner en famille dans un restaurant chinois de Belleville ce soir-là et je me suis fait vomir entre chaque plat avec un retour de cette rage effrayante qui m'avait quelque peu délaissée ces derniers temps. Prozac aidant. (p. 120)

> We went to dinner as a family at a Chinese restaurant in Belleville that night and I made myself sick between each dish with a return of this frightening rage that had somewhat deserted me lately. With the Prozac's help.

Three points are of interest here. First, the fact that the prospect of rupture with her long-term boyfriend and marriage to another man prompts the return to bulimic purging reflects research findings summarised by Freeman: 'There seems to be evidence that developmental mile-stones or phase-of-life events may serve as stressors for vulnerable women at any age, triggering AN as a maladaptive response'[52] – and AN (anorexia nervosa), as we know, can include episodes of purging (hence the hybrid noun 'bulimarexia'). Second, there is ambiguity in the lexical choice of 'rage', which can denote either 'rage' or 'mania'. If Camille means 'rage'

52 Freeman 2009: 67.

(as Morello believes),[53] this might express her angry reaction to a lack of control over her life, a common prompt to EDs; if she means 'mania', the extreme obsessionality by which bulimarexics are seized is underscored. Third, the fact that she registers the help of Prozac in having previously reduced her vomiting concurs with the numerous recent sources in the secondary literature on how this drug can help reduce bulimic symptoms.

Happiness with her new lover, whom she decides she will marry (p. 129), promotes a brief reprieve. On a three-week holiday with him, she only makes herself vomit once (p. 128), and her eating improves, even if she vastly overestimates its improvement, for she is certainly nowhere near over her illness (126). Self-deception is obvious in her affirmation that, despite her continued weight loss, she is cured, because she no longer vomits at all, is madly in love, and is no longer gripped by the previous, permanent obsession with food (p. 132). Her psychiatrist, however, is not duped. He asserts that she is not at all cured, opposes her wish to stop taking Prozac, and asks her if she would like to talk to him about her mother. Shortly before this, she had spoken to him of her mother in idealising idiom, and the following assertion to him illustrates vividly the overly fusional mother–daughter relationship, particularly in the metaphor 'elle est reliée à moi par un transmetteur intergalactique' [she's connected to me by an intergalactic transmitter], and in her ascription of magical powers to the bond with her mother:

> J'ai une mère magique, elle est reliée à moi par un transmetteur intergalactique. Ma mère était très angoissée à l'idée que je parte avec un inconnu. Elle m'avait fait jurer que je l'appellerais tous les deux jours pour lui confirmer que je n'avais pas été enrôlée dans un réseau de prostitution. (p. 129)

> I have a magical mother, she's connected to me by an intergalactic transmitter. My mother was very upset by the idea of me leaving with a stranger. She had made me swear that I would call her every other day to confirm that I had not been enlisted in a prostitution ring.

Her response to his later, direct request that she talk to him about her mother elicits the classical clinical portrait of the invasive mother of the anorexic daughter (and at this point Camille is in a decidedly anorexic phase of her illness) who consciously or unconsciously impedes her daughter's individuation: 'Ma mère est fière de moi. Même si elle a peur en ce moment, peur que je la déteste et que je me sépare d'elle' ['My mother

53 Morello 2017: 131.

is proud of me. Even though she's afraid at the moment, afraid that I hate her and that I'm separating myself from her'] (p. 132). Another facet of that portrait asserted in some of the secondary literature also emerges, viz. the mother's personal sense of underachievement/frustration, which goes in tandem with her controlling of and over-investment in her daughter. Despite Camille's mother having been a brilliant pupil, Camille's maternal grandmother 'a interdit à sa fille de faire des études secondaires et l'avait placée comme bonne chez le médecin du village, à quatorze ans. Alors elle s'est juré que ses enfants à elle iraient loin' [forbade her daughter from going to secondary school and got her a job as a maid for the village doctor at the age of fourteen. So she swore to herself that her own children would go far] (p. 132). Camille's mother's vicarious ambition for her own children resulted in the mother placing her under intense pressure to succeed academically (pp. 132–33). In this vicarious fulfilment of her own frustrated ambitions, Camille's mother is emblematic of one of the types of anorectics' mothers identified by psychiatrist Philippe Jeammet:

> De la part de la mère, l'usage du « nous » ou du « on » pour parler de sa fille est si fréquent qu'il ne peut être le seul effet du hasard. Cette intrication des générations répond à des situations affectives différentes, qui ne sont pas exclusives les unes des autres. Nous pouvons les schématiser ainsi :
>
> – *La fille, double narcissique de la mère.*
>
> Dans ce cas, plusieurs versions sont possibles. Une version admirative : « Ma fille, c'est moi telle que j'aurais pu être. »[54]

> On the part of the mother, the use of 'we' to talk about her daughter is so frequent that it cannot be pure coincidence. This interweaving of generations responds to different affective situations, which are not exclusive of each other. We can schematise them as follows:
>
> – *The daughter, a narcissistic double of the mother.*
>
> In this case, several versions are possible. A version centred on admiration: 'My daughter is me as I could have been.'

After her weight has continued steadily to drop and reaches 45 kilos (7 stones), her psychiatrist, having previously made no comment on this continuous loss, suddenly announces that if she falls to 44 kilos (6 stones 13 lbs, for a height of 1.7 metres/5 ft 7 inches, giving a BMI of 15.2) he will have her hospitalised (p. 135). When she opposes this and he says she will, then, have to eat, her reply illustrates another trope in

54 Jeammet 2004: 129.

the primary corpus – that of the euphoria produced by the anorectic's hunger that becomes addictive: 'Je n'ai pas faim. Je n'ai plus jamais faim et ça me rend euphorique' ['I'm not hungry. I'm never hungry anymore and that makes me euphoric'] (p. 135). Yet what she goes on to say reveals a quasi (if short-termist) logic to that euphoria – release from the tyrannical obsession with and feared desire for food that is all-consuming, guilt-inducing, and impedes ability to think of anything else: 'Après tous ces comptages, de lipides, glucides, après toutes ces privations, ces pensées gloutonnes et coupables. J'ai ma tête pour moi, j'ai tout mon temps pour réfléchir à des choses sensées' [After all this counting of lipids and carbohydrates, after all this deprivation and these gluttonous, guilty thoughts. I have my head to myself, I have all the time I need to think about reasonable things] (p. 135). In addition, this logic of sorts emphasizes how exhausting the parallel obsession with body shape is: 'Passer ses journées à vouloir évaluer la taille de ses fesses, c'est usant, vous savez' [Spending your days wanting to judge the size of your buttocks is exhausting, you know] (p. 135). Commenting on how she likes and finds herself pretty at 45 kilos, her following statement implies self-schism: 'Je me ressemble' [I resemble myself], with the 'Je' [I] and the 'me' [myself] implying two different selves. This is not identical but instead proximate to the mind–body split/dualism motif so common in the primary texts, a motif that becomes more evident in her sarcastic question to the psychiatrist: 'C'est si contradictoire que ça de vouloir se débarrasser de son corps et d'aimer la vie ?' [Is it so contradictory to want to get rid of your body and to enjoy life?] (p. 135).

Nonetheless, the psychiatrist's threat does result in her beginning to eat again, in order to escape hospitalisation and to marry César, with her wedding being an intensely happy experience (p. 136). From my perspective, however, what is more interesting is her evocation of this resumption of eating, which contains two if not antonymic then contrasting elements. The first is recognition that her starving had been regressive and pathological. The second is the profound sense of self-assault that anorectics may experience in eating against their personal will: 'Menacée, j'ai pris mon couteau et ma fourchette comme une grande personne saine de corps et d'esprit en m'imposant une violence atroce contre ce nouveau dégoût de la nourriture qui s'était emparée de moi' [Threatened, I took my knife and my fork like a grown-up, of sound mind and body, while forcing myself to commit atrocious violence against this new disgust of food that had seized me] (p. 136). What is also of note on p. 136 is the illustration of sociocultural forces, here the fashion industry, that may encourage anorexia nervosa: at a weight where she is being threatened with hospitalisation, her wedding-dress maker, though astounded, shows 'grande satisfaction' [great satisfaction] (p. 136) that Camille's waist size is only 56 centimetres/22 inches. Unfortunately, resumption of eating and the resultant weight gain prompt a disgusted sense of feeling fat that in turn prompts resumption of vomiting and of weighing herself compulsively – four times per day (p. 137). The mentally destabilising distress of her dilemma – gaining weight in order to stop having to see the psychiatrist, or losing weight in order to feel better in herself – is vividly conveyed via metaphor: 'Manger ou ne pas manger, je deviens folle, je voudrais être une bulle de savon' [To eat or not to eat, I am going crazy, I'd like to be a soap bubble] (p. 137). This metaphor renders a wish to become, like a soap bubble, insentient matter, untroubled by thoughts and emotions. But the particular choice of a soap bubble as metaphor also has connotations of weightlessness and cleanliness, with the latter relating to another of the common motifs in the primary literature: that of aspiration to purity.

Once more, the classical clinical view of the mother in the secondary literature on anorexia nervosa is mirrored in her mother's attitude towards her desired recovery – that the mother alone would effect it: 'Elle s'obstinait [...] à penser que ma guérison passerait par elle seule' [She persisted [...] in thinking that my recovery would happen through her alone] (p. 138). This indicates the 'typical' anorectic's mother's over-protectiveness but also her invasiveness and refusal to grant her daughter autonomy. However, the mother momentarily changes position after hearing a radio programme on France Inter about anorexic girls. This programme recapitulates the standard theory of the secondary/clinical literature, in a manner that Camille qualifies contemptuously as a popularisation of psychology seeking to give immediate answers. This theory is that anorexic girls think they will (metaphorically) 'kill' their mother if they seek individuation and autonomy, and that through fear of abandoning their mother, they refuse a woman's body, recovering a child-like body through weight loss: a form of self-infantilisation that can restore to the mother her original role as chief nourisher. The putative solution offered by the programme is for the mother to declare to the daughter that she no longer needs her, that while it is kind of the daughter to be so concerned for her, she needs her own life, and that while one can die through not eating, one will not die through disappointment in love. The mother declares she will implement this 'solution', telling Camille that she no longer needs her in order to live, that Camille is not indispensable, and that now Camille will be able to recover (p. 139). But flying in the face of all this, when Camille tells her mother the psychiatrist wishes to see her along with Camille, her mother 'a accepté avec joie' [joyfully accepted] (p. 139). Thus the chapter ends on a note of sardonic irony.

However, a new, positive evolution now starts whose first signs are Camille's eating pizzas with her sister, apparently in relaxed mode, and her sense that having verbally expressed her illness is a precursor to recovery: 'Le dire, casser mon image, devenir ce que j'étais. Cette fois-ci, j'ai su que ma guérison approchait' [Saying it, breaking with my image, becoming what I was. This time, I knew that my healing was approaching] (p. 141). The trope of smashing a self-image implicitly recognised as false via 'mon image' [my image] being followed by 'devenir ce que j'étais' [becoming what I was] reinforces this realisation that she has constructed a fallacious identity for herself in her pursuit of extreme thinness. Crucially, this positive evolution is accompanied by a newly critical attitude towards her mother after the latter's inconsistent response to the radio programme and to being invited to one of the psychiatrist's sessions along with Camille. This newly critical attitude is reflected in the aggressive expression used to denote her: 'Ma chienne de mère' [my bitch of a mother] (p. 142). The hostility also predisposes her to endorse precisely the theory in the radio programme that she had previously appeared to ridicule: that she needs, figuratively speaking, to cut the umbilical cord and achieve individuation from her mother. In the session that her mother attends, the psychiatrist confronts the mother directly with discourse also reflecting that theory, and the mother's responses indicate denial of her own incarnation of that (theoretical) anorexigenic mother:

> Le Dr Lendonyos lui a balancé :
> – Votre fille ne doit pas être votre mère, madame.
> Elle a nié.
> – Vous avez toujours tout partagé avec votre fille, y compris vos problèmes d'adulte.
> Elle a nié encore. (p. 142)

> Dr. Lendonyos told her:
> 'Your daughter must not be your mother, ma'am.'
> She denied it.
> 'You have always shared everything with your daughter, including your adult problems.'
> She denied it again.

The narrative that follows relays the mother's defensive and delusional, indeed virtually psychotic view of her daughter as never having been a child, as being exceptional, as always having understood everything, as being a real princess. Camille is thrown by this, and while her image of the axe in the citation below subtly posits a symbolic violence in her mother, nonetheless she initially appears to be back almost to square one in vowing never to stop loving that mother: 'Je me suis juré ce jour-là de ne jamais cesser de l'aimer' [I swore to myself that day to never stop loving her] (p. 142).

Yet this is not quite back to square one, and Camille's succeeding remarks demonstrate a new, objective grasp of the stifling, pathogenic quality of her mother's idealisation of her,[55] along with a critical distance indicated by reference to her mother as 'Cette femme' [that woman]: 'Cette femme a fait des erreurs, il ne fallait pas tant croire en moi, il m'étouffait, son amour admiratif, il me faisait peur. Toujours peur de la décevoir [...]' [That woman made mistakes, she should not have believed in me so much, her admiring love choked me, it scared me. Always afraid of disappointing her] (pp. 142–43). The fact that in striving to live up to her mother's impossibly high expectations of her Camille is motivated largely by fear of disappointing her, rather than by the apparently innate perfectionism typically found, according to the secondary literature, in 'pure' anorectics, correlates with research findings that perfectionism is more consistent in the latter than in bulimics.[56] Of course, as has been established several times, Camille does go through a period of anorexia, but her preceding period of bulimia nervosa lasts far longer. Further, and as recorded above, she has previously disavowed perfectionist tendencies (p. 27). In ruminating on what is necessary to achieve individuation and independence from her mother, Camille hints at a balanced goal of being able both to love and to judge her mother, but to love her as a separate person and no longer as part of a stifling symbiosis: 'L'aimer et la juger. L'aimer séparée' [To love her and to judge her. To love her separately] (p. 143).

55 Palazzoli 1978 emphasises the family's need to have a compliant, perfect child, which the child incorporates in her own self-perception. See Eisler, Ivan, 'Family models of eating disorders', in Szmukler et al. 1995: 155–76 (161; my emphasis).

56 'In general, the above studies show a consistent pattern of elevated levels of both maladaptive and achievement striving perfectionism among both AN and BN patients, although this pattern is most consistent for AN.' Bardone-Cone et al. 2007: 389.

The psychic breakthrough is clear in the clipped notation that concludes this narrative unit, indicating her lessened need for medication: 'Je suis passée à un demi-Prozac par jour' [I went down to half a Prozac per day] (p. 143). And in physical terms there is also progress, conveyed in the next, brief narrative unit, where it is revealed that she has increased her weight to 50 kilos (7 stones 12 lbs) and does not appear unduly distressed by this gain. Her anorexic ideation has, of course, not vaporised, for she entirely rejects the psychiatrist's notion of her going beyond 51 kilos (8 stones), and she is still underweight for her height of 1.7 metres (5 ft 7 inches). Yet she is now able to break out of the 'perfect' mould imposed by her mother by rebelling. This is exemplified through her shouting, sobbing, and swearing during a family meal at her half-brother's home, provoking a sense of scandal in her mother but jubilation in her 'nouvel état de rébellion' [new state of rebellion] (p. 143). This new ability to express emotions in front of others, which is not confined to her family alone, is approved by her psychiatrist:

> - Je suis fâchée.
> - C'est très bien.
> - Je me suis mise en colère contre toute ma famille, j'ai fait la toquée, j'ai pleuré devant tout le monde. J'ai même hurlé sur une automobiliste qui avait failli m'écraser, alors que je ne hurle jamais. Je traversais sans regarder, c'était ma faute.
> - C'est très bien. (p. 144)
>
> 'I'm angry.'
> 'That's very good.'
> 'I got angry with my whole family, I went nuts, I cried in front of everyone. I even yelled at a motorist who almost ran me over, even though I never yell. I crossed without looking, it was my fault.'
> 'That's very good.'

Her reaction to his approbation reveals the lingering ideal of the affect-censoring princess imposed by her mother and previously internalised as her own ideal, characterised by the excessive self-control so key to anorexic and bulimic aspirations: 'Mais les princesses ne disent pas de vulgarités, elles ne font pas des exagérations comme ça, elles se contrôlent, elles ne montrent rien sur leur visage de princesse' ['But princesses don't say rude words, they don't exaggerate like that, they control themselves, they don't let anything show on their princess faces'] (p. 144). When he answers, presumably ironically, with 'C'est une contradiction de la vie réelle qu'il va falloir affronter' ['That's a real-life contradiction that you'll have to face'], her response is ambiguous: 'Alors je veux bien être fâchée, mais je vous préviens que je ne marcherai jamais pieds nus' ['In that case I want to be angry, but I warn you that I'll never walk barefoot'] (p. 144). This statement could be interpreted as semi-healthy in embracing the right to be annoyed, and semi-negative in its clinging to the princess ideal. On the other hand, the resolve never to walk barefoot could be decoded more positively, dissociated from the princess ideal, as a metaphor for pride and dignity.

Renunciation of the obedience and censorship of anger that are parts of the princess ideal naturally poses a challenge: 'Être en colère. Mais c'est difficile quand on est une bonne élève de contester l'autorité. C'est difficile quand on est une princesse de jurer comme une poissonnière' [Being angry. But it's difficult to question authority when you're a good student. It's difficult to swear like a fishwife when you're a princess] (p. 145). Use of the present tense in 'on est une princesse' [you're a princess] suggests again her involuntary clinging to that ideal. Fear of renouncing the ideal is rendered in terms that reveal the basic reasons for clinging to it – a need to be liked or loved by everybody (recalling Julia's 'people-pleasing': Rodrigue pp. 31 and 64), and problems in accepting the right to accuse a mother who has been devoted to her: 'Quand on veut que tout le monde nous aime, comment ne pas faire plaisir ? Quand on a eu une mère dévouée comme la mienne, comment porter des accusations ?' [When you want everyone to like you, how can you not be nice? When you've had a devoted mother like mine, how can you make accusations?] (p. 145). However, another major cognitive advance inheres in the realisation that her vomiting was caused by inability to express anger (p. 145). As Morello astutely remarks apropos Camille's sessions with the psychiatrist, they allow her to 'understand that recovery involves being able to un/re/dis-cover the violence that she has never been able to express other than through her body'.[57] The new cognitive pathway Camille is forging towards psychic health still contains allusion to the princess ideal, but in the following this may well be a self-mocking allusion:

> Il ne faut dégueuler, pas tous les jours, pas dégueuler matin, midi et soir parce que ça fait mal dans le thornytorinx et que ça prend du temps. Question de logique. C'est sale et ça salit. Une princesse sent bon la rose et le jasmin. (p. 145)

57 Morello 2017: 135.

> Don't scream, not every day, don't puke morning, noon and night because that hurts your thornytorinx and it takes up time. It's a question of logic. It's dirty and it makes things dirty. A princess smells sweet like rose and jasmine.

The direct link between suppression of language expressing her emotions and somatic expression of those emotions through purging is plain in the following:

> Pourtant, je me souviens que j'étais lasse, perdue de tant de rage, de tant de cris, moi qui avais toujours vomi en silence. Trop de vomi, trop de paroles étouffées et recrachées telles quelles sous forme de jet baveux, trop de sourires et d'applications, certes, mais quelle fatigue. (p. 146)

> However, I remember that I was tired and lost in so much rage, so many cries, I who had always vomited in silence. Too much vomit, too many words muffled and spat out any old how, in the form of a drooling spray, too many smiles and cover-ups, certainly, but such weariness.

By the same token, EDs as a form of language, albeit metaphorical – one of the other salient motifs in the primary corpus – is starkly inscribed here, with a direct equivalence between vomit and suppressed words in their apposition ('Trop de vomi, trop de paroles étouffées et recrachées' [Too much vomit, too many words muffled and spat out]).

What may seem like a set-back is her mind's adoption of a new assault on her body:

> Mes jambes ont commencé à me gratter. On somatise comme on peut. Je me grattais jusqu'au sang, des démangeaisons insupportables. J'étais donc fâchée. Le courage d'aller crier après l'obscur objet de mon ressentiment me manquait. Je ne vomissais donc plus, je me grattais les jambes. Petite blague. Mon esprit avait trouvé un autre moyen de traumatiser mon corps. (p. 146)

> My legs started to itch. We somatise however we can. I would scratch until I drew blood, scratching at the unbearable itching. So I was angry. I lacked the courage to go and scream at the obscure object of my resentment. I wasn't vomiting anymore, I was scratching my legs instead. What a joke. My mind had found another way to traumatise my body.

But the fact that she is able to locate the reason for her mind's punishment of her body aids her ongoing recovery. That reason is mainly anger – at her husband César, her mother, her new mother-in-law (although it also includes, to a lesser degree, her fear of various events in her life). Once she has been able to pinpoint the sources of her anger, she stops scratching herself. Similar cognitive clarity is achieved when she recognises as somatisations of negative affect other new body-centred disturbances. These include neurotic fixation on the uncomfortable rubbing of socks on her feet, which she interprets as not wanting to progress – 'Et puis j'ai compris que mes pieds servaient à avancer de manière plus ou moins figurée et que je ne voulais pas progresser ce jour-là. Les frottements ont disparu' [And then I understood that my feet were used to move forward, more or less figuratively speaking, and that I didn't want to progress that day. The rubbing disappeared] (p. 147) – and buzzing in her ears, interpreted as not wanting to hear – 'Mes oreilles qui servent à entendre ont bourdonné' [My ears, which I use to listen, rang] (p. 147). Concrete progress, indeed victory, resides in the fact that she now only vomits in cases of extreme need, when the reasons for her anger are so deep she is unable to confront them (p. 147). Now she is hungry, not for food but for real living: 'J'attends avec impatience, moi, l'affamée, que la vie se manifeste' [I, the starving one, am waiting impatiently for life to show up] (p. 147).

The penultimate page (p. 148) before the two-page Epilogue of the text summarises Camille's entire narrative in the text proper: the story of a girl who makes herself vomit because she is angry, of herself as a fantasised princess who inflicts physical mortification on herself in order to meet the criteria of 'royalty' that she intuits her mother wishes her to fulfil. The metaphors deployed in this summary – princess, mortification, royalty – underscore the hyperbolically unrealistic standards set by her mother, and their fairy-tale connotations reinforce their unattainability. Interestingly, however, this summary also indicates that she mistakes her mother's standards as being universal – 'les yeux de sa mère, ce sont les yeux du monde entier' [The eyes of her mother, those are the eyes of the whole world] (p. 148); that her vomit is a form of self-expression whose verbal and behavourial expression she censors – 'du vomi pour s'exprimer' [vomit to express herself] (cf. p. 146, where the equivalence has already been implied); that her condition is, in fact, pathological – 'Elle est malade' [She is sick]; and that she sought to 'justify' her illness by another erroneous universalisation – 'Alors elle se dit non mais, sérieusement, vous en connaissez, vous, des gens qui ne sont pas malades ?' [So she says to herself no but, seriously, do you know any people who aren't sick?]. The last three clauses of the latter aggressive rhetorical question are an exact repetition of the question posed in the Prologue (p. 12), on only the second page of the entire text, thus creating an ominously circular effect. Absolutism and distorted cognition with respect to the body all emerge, and all are commonly recorded characteristics of anorexia nervosa in the secondary literature – and to a lesser extent of bulimia nervosa, which preceded her anorexia nervosa.

The second paragraph of the first page preceding the Epilogue extends the summary. Its first sentence reinforces her distorted cognition, or defence mechanism, and its second sentence implicitly acknowledges that distorted cognition in the 'quand même' [regardless]:

> Alors elle décide d'aller jusqu'au bout, elle le crie haut et fort : je suis une personne normale et vomir est un mode d'expression comme un autre. Dire que je suis surtout normale et surtout le penser, dire que je ne suis pas malade et vomir quand même. (p. 148)
>
> So she decides to go to the end, she shouts loudly: I am a normal person and vomiting is a mode of expression like any other. To say that I am – first and foremost – normal, and above all to believe it, to say that I am not sick and to vomit all the same.

But depressingly, the summary then vindicates the voluntarism of her abnormal fusion with and idealisation of her mother; the persistence, if now reduced, of the princess ideal inculcated by her mother; and the persistence of vomiting, albeit now only occasional:

> On a toujours le choix dans la vie et mon choix je l'ai fait : j'appelle ma mère tous les jours pour lui dire que je l'aime et qu'elle ne s'est jamais trompée. Je préfère être une princesse sous Xanax qu'une poissonnière qui croque des bonbons à l'eucalyptus. Je préfère aimer ma mère et vomir de temps en temps qu'aimer mon chien et aller faire du roller avec lui au bois de Boulogne pour me dire que je suis saine de corps et d'esprit. (p. 148)
>
> We always have a choice in life and I have made my choice: I call my mother every day to tell her that I love her and that she has never made a mistake. I prefer to be a princess on Xanax than a fishwife who crunches on eucalyptus candies. I prefer to love my mother and vomit from time to time rather than to love my dog and go rollerblading with him in the Bois de Boulogne to tell myself that I am healthy in body and in mind.

With respect to the first sentence of this extract from p. 148, Morello contends, 'Camille chooses not to abide by the psychiatric *doxa* of needing to "kill" the all-powerful mother as a necessary condition for full recovery.'[58] While Morello's contention is correct, her apparent approval

58 Morello 2017: 136.

is questionable in Camille's case, given the second sentence of the extract from p. 148. The penultimate sentence of p. 148 appears to continue the delusional self-justification – 'Le sport, c'est pas une mortification physique, peut-être ?' [Is sport perhaps just physical mortification?], but the final sentence has some philosophical depth and possible credibility to it, one of its implications being that at least in some cases, relentless exercise may be caused by psychic pain and guilt: 'Tout passe par la douleur et la culpabilité' [Everything passes through pain and guilt] (p. 148).

The first paragraph of the last page of the narrative proper (149) appears to continue the summary of her former psychopathology, reinforcing in more flagrant form her distorted cognition – denial of (any remnants of) her illness – and morbidly enmeshed relationship with her mother:

> Je ne suis pas malade, je n'ai pas de troubles alimentaires compulsifs, et si parfois j'en ai quand même, je ne vais hurler pour m'en débarrasser. S'il fallait faire un effort et si je décidais de détester ma mère, vous me donneriez quoi en échange ? Le sentiment de satiété ? Non, merci. (149)

> I'm not sick, I don't have a compulsive eating disorder, and if sometimes I do have one, I'm not going to yell to get rid of it. If I had to make an effort and if I decided to hate my mother, what would you give me in return? The feeling of fullness? No thanks.

Morello's interpretation is well worth citing: 'Her choice to be "normalement malade" [normally ill] (149) rather than achieve what is conventionally considered full recovery is based on the fear of destroying the bond sustaining both mother and daughter'.[59] Although I aver that there are other reasons for this 'choice to be "normalement malade"' [choice to be 'normally ill'] (such as the surmise that Camille may not actually have been sufficiently free of psychopathological ideation to make a genuine 'choice'), I agree that it is one of the reasons. Signs of persistently psychopathological ideation include the fact even Camille's brief flashes of semi-lucidity – 'et si parfois j'en ai quand même' [and if sometimes I do have one]; 'S'il fallait faire un effort et si je décidais de détester ma mère' [If I had to make an effort and if I decided to hate my mother] – are compromised in the first case by minimisation ('parfois' [sometimes]) and in the second case by Manicheanism, as if there were no happy medium between excessive love and simple hatred for the mother.

59 Morello 2017: 137.

Indeed, the final page of the narrative proper, which moves into the diegetic present of writing as opposed to the diegetic past of the summary, betrays something of a cognitive regression, isomorphic with something of a physical regression.

> Aujourd'hui, je vomis, de temps à autre, je vomis encore, mais je ne suis pas triste, et je ne suis pas une victime. Je ne l'ai jamais été.
>
> Je crois en Dieu et en la vie éphémère. Je suis le vent qui crie et l'herbe qui flotte. Je suis la princesse des bulles de savon. J'ai quatre ans et demi. [...] Je suis amoureuse, je suis une forcenée. J'ai peur du vide et de m'ennuyer. Mais jamais je ne m'ennuie.
>
> Je ne suis pas guérie, on ne guérit pas de cette colère. Ma balance trône toujours dans ma salle de bains. Je monte dessus matin et soir. Et alors ? Au moins je ne suis plus sous Prozac. Je suis une personne normalement malade. J'aime un fou qui m'aime et qui me comprend. Et je suis une bonne élève. Je suis en deuxième année au cours Florent, je vais devenir une grande actrice. Je fais ce que je veux, je fais ce qui me plaît. Je danse dans la nuit, je pleure en croyant que je suis Bérénice. Je suis une femme mariée. Oui, je me pèse et j'ai peur de grossir. J'ai peur de vieillir aussi. Je suis mince. Et alors quoi ? Je mène ma vie comme je l'entends pour une fois. Se faire vomir n'a jamais empêché quiconque d'aimer et d'être aimée. Une femme sur cinq. Je ne suis pas seule, et je ne me cache pas.
>
> Au fond, on ne guérit jamais d'une pareille absurdité. (p. 149)

> Today, I'm vomiting from time to time, I'm still vomiting, but I'm not sad, and I'm not a victim. I never have been one.
>
> I believe in God and in ephemeral life. I am the howling wind and the floating grass. I am the soap bubble princess. I am four and a half years old. [...] I'm in love, I'm a maniac. I am afraid of emptiness and of getting bored. But I'm never bored.
>
> I'm not cured, this anger cannot be cured. My scales still have pride of place in my bathroom. I get on them morning and evening. So what? At least I'm no longer on Prozac. I am a normal sick person. I love a crazy man who loves me and who understands me. And I am a good student. I am in my second year at the Cours Florent, I'm going to become a great actress. I do what I want, I do what I like. I dance at night, I cry, believing that I'm Bérénice. I am a married woman. Yes, I weigh myself and I'm afraid of putting on weight. I'm afraid of getting old too. I am thin. And so what? For once I'm living my life how I want to. Making yourself vomit never stopped anyone from loving and being loved. One in five women. I'm not alone, and I'm not hiding.
>
> Basically, such an absurdity can never be cured.

The physical regression is inscribed in 'Aujourd'hui, je vomis, de temps à autre, je vomis encore [...] Ma balance trône toujours dans ma salle de bains. Je monte dessus matin et soir [...] je me pèse et j'ai peur de grossir' [Today, I'm vomiting from time to time, I'm still vomiting [...] My scales still have pride of place in my bathroom. I get on them morning and evening [...] I weigh myself and I'm afraid of putting on weight] and the cognitive regression in 'Je suis la princesse des bulles de savon. J'ai quatre ans et demi' [I am the soap bubble princess. I am four and a half years old], where she slips back into self-infantilisation, with 'bulles de savon' [soap bubbles] recurring to a previously deployed metaphor of weightlessness, here ascribed to princess-like status (p. 137). The significance of weightlessness for EDs is obvious. Note also the motif of 'le vide' [the emptiness] that is a common motif in the primary corpus: 'J'ai peur du vide' [I'm afraid of emptiness].

Nonetheless, this last page does also relay some positive signs. At least she has a mutually loving relationship with her husband, is optimistic about her acting training, and takes pleasure in leisure activities like dancing. In negative counterpart, the Epilogue of the text rather gloomily demonstrates that her mother remains, as it were, incurably anorexigenic. On a family holiday, she reprimands Camille for making her sister eat her own leftovers, proclaiming: 'Tu m'as très bien comprise, Camille, arrête de lui refiler tes restes. Tu ne vois pas qu'elle est assez grosse comme ça ? Elle ne mangera pas une frite de plus !' ['You understood me very well, Camille, stop giving her your leftovers. Can't you see that she's fat enough as it is? She'll not eat one more chip!'] (p. 152). And this despite the opposition of César, Camille's husband, who retorts 'Mais elle n'est pas grosse du tout, elle est trop mince au contraire' ['But she's not fat at all, on the contrary she's too skinny'] (p. 152). Camille, rather ominously, remains silent on the subject, and the autobiographical novel ends simply with her stating, 'On attend un souffle de vent' [We're waiting for a breeze]: an evasive and cryptic remark that fails to concur in César's efforts to neutralise the mother's anorexigenic influence.

Conclusion

Rather than disappointment in the lack of a 'happy ending' that affirms complete recovery, which contrasts with Rodrigue's *La peau à l'envers. Le roman vrai d'une boulimique*, the reader would perhaps be better advised to recognise that Camille's partial recovery in *Thornytorinx* reflects an empirical reality, viz. that a not-negligible proportion of those with EDs may never make a full recovery.[60] (Indeed, many mortalities are associated with EDs.)[61] This should come as no surprise, given the socio-cultural pressures that continue to promote unnaturally thin body 'ideals'. It is also not nugatory that Camille, in admitting that she has not recovered fully, identifies the problem as persisting anger, rather than an ED, which at least shows awareness of the source of that ED. In a sense she has reached a stasis where she is no longer in physical danger by losing weight, and her vomiting is only occasional. The differences between the endings of these two personal accounts of bulimia nervosa/ bulimarexia may also have to do with two other factors. One is Camille's failure entirely to break the umbilical cord with her mother, unlike Rodrigue's Julia. Another is the moot point of whether there was a genetic component to Camille's ED, as is suggested by her testimony. If indeed there was, her poorer outcome was quasi-foretold.

60 I have only been able to find data in the secondary literature on chronicity in anorexia nervosa, not for other EDs. But since both Rodrigue's Julia and de Peretti's Camille go through anorexic periods, and may therefore be qualified as bulimarexics, this data is not irrelevant, and is worth quoting. 'Even with intensive treatment, studies generally find that fewer than 50% of patients with AN recover, roughly one-third improve, and 20% show a chronic and disabling life course (Steinhausen, 2002; Zipfel, Lowe, Reas, Deter, & Herzog, 2000). [...] Even among AN patients who appear to achieve a full recovery, roughly one-third relapse (Herzog et al., 1999; Strober et al., 1997). Among patients who no longer meet criteria for AN, lifelong struggles continue with relatively low weight and substantial body image psychopathology as well as with certain psychological features (e.g., perfectionism and obsessiveness) that often persist despite some improvement in the AN itself (Sullivan, Bulik, Fear, & Pickering, 1998). Follow-up studies of patients with AN also found high rates of additional psychiatric disorders (Steinhausen, 2002). Very high rates of depression, anxiety, and alcohol use disorders are found in patients with AN over life course (Sullivan et al., 1998). AN is associated with substantially elevated mortality (Crisp, Callender, Halek, & Hsu, 1992; Keel, Dorer, Eddy, Franko, Charatan, & Herzog, 2003), which is estimated at 5.6% per decade (Sullivan, 1995).' Grilo 2006: 41.

61 'Eating disorders, along with substance use disorders, have the highest mortality rates of all psychiatric disorders (Keel et al., 2003). Most deaths result from starvation, cardiac events, or suicide.' Grilo 2006: 41.

CHAPTER THREE

Binge Eating Disorder

Section 3.1

La Tortue sur le dos: ma lutte contre la boulimie (2001)[1] by Annick Loupias (who was born in France in, we infer, 1950 and only moved to Quebec in 1981 aged 31) is an autobiographical account of the intense and life-threatening struggle of a French teenager aged 15, then woman up to the age of 37, with a severe ED (p. 11). However, designation of her ED as bulimia in the subtitle of her book is contestable. With all due respect to the author in her choice of title, I found that careful reading of her testimony reveals what she actually suffered from first of all was bulimia nervosa, but that this mutated into binge eating disorder – the difference being that she largely ceased to purge after bingeing, contrary to her previous compensatory practice of (ab)using vast amounts of laxatives. One way of describing binge eating disorder is the following.

> Loss of control (LOC) is defined as the feeling of not being able to stop eating or control what/how much one is eating, and is a requisite characteristic of binge eating disorder (American Psychiatric Association, 2013). LOC eating is prevalent during the developmental period of adolescence, with rates ranging between 9% and 30% in community samples (Tanofsky-Kraff, 2008), and even higher rates (e.g. about 9% and 30% in over-weight, treatment-seeking samples (Decaluwe, Braet, & Fairburn, 2003).[2]

1 Loupias, Annick, with Louise Lambert-Lagacé and Annette Richard, *La Tortue sur le dos: ma lutte contre la boulimie* (Quebec: Les Éditions de l'homme, 2001).

2 Ranzenhofer, L., Engel, S.G., Crosby, R.D., Haigney, M., and Tanofsky-Kraff, M., 'A pilot study of attachment style and emotional experience in adolescent girls with loss of control eating', *Advances in Eating Disorders: Theory, Research and Practice*, 4, 3 (2016), 250–63 (250–51).

Carlos Grilo's asseveration supports my view of Loupias's ED as becoming, after bulimia nervosa with anorexic periods, binge eating disorder: 'The research diagnosis of BED requires recurrent episodes of binge eating. It is important to note that the fifth criterion is that the person does not regularly use inappropriate weight compensatory behaviors.'[3] Although for some time Loupias (ab)uses laxatives, after a certain point she largely ceases such 'inappropriate weight compensatory behaviors'. During the 22 years of her illness Loupias transitions gradually from bulima nervosa/bulimarexia to hyperphagia with very little or no purgation – in other words, to binge eating disorder. Although during those 22 years she does continue on occasion to undertake draconian (but short-lived) diets (see, for example, pp. 36, 41, 71), does occasionally vomit after a binge (see pp. 87 and 92), but far prefers the purgative method of excessive laxative consumption, as the years go by she practically ceases to purge after bingeing (although sometimes her body involuntarily sicks up the excessive food, but that is not self-induced purgation: see, for example, 'je m'écroule dans mes vomissures. Je n'ai pas eu le temps de me rendre à la salle de bains. Mon corps refuse toute nourriture… Il n'en peut plus et moi non plus' [I collapse into my vomit. I didn't have time to go to the bathroom. My body refuses all food… It can't take it anymore and neither can I], pp. 102–3). This cessation of a process central to bulimia nervosa, viz. purgation after bingeing, is occluded by Lambert-Lagacé's description on p. 124 of the bulimia nervosa that she clearly believes is *the* condition that afflicted Loupias. Further, Lambert-Lagacé observes on p. 124 that bulimic women 'maintiennent un poids normal ou légèrement au-dessous de la normale' [maintain a normal weight or one slightly below normal], an observation also made by Jeammet,[4] but Loupias does actually become distinctly overweight at various points: see, for instance, p. 52, where three young men in the street insult her as being fat; p. 55, where it is recorded that she is 30 kilos overweight, and a stranger says she shouldn't be doing hard manual work in her

3 Grilo 2006: 17. By 'inappropriate weight compensatory behaviors', Grilo refers to self-induced vomiting, abuse of laxatives, diuretics, enemas, over-exercise, etc.

4 'En effet, même si des conduites boulimiques sont parfois diagnostiquées chez des patientes obèses ou ayant une surcharge pondérale modérée, dans la très grande majorité des cas, les patientes gardent un poids normal, et même un peu en dessous de la norme, qui n'a toutefois rien d'alarmant' (Jeammet 2004: 2).

physical state, which he assumes to be pregnancy; and p. 108, where she states that her weight is 83 kilos (13 stones). However, overweight *is* common in an individual with binge eating disorder – an individual Loupias becomes.

By way of introduction to Loupias's book, it is apt to sum it up thus. It is a highly moving personal narrative that engages readers on a deep affective level, and has great potential to educate both general readers and also many in the health-care professions about some of the causes of, subjective experience of, and promising treatments for the illness against which she battled so long and that she finally conquered fully. The pedagogical aspects reside thoroughly in the author's charting of how she finally made a complete recovery, but are supplemented in the sections following her phenomenological narrative by her psychologist Annette Richard and her dietician Louise Lambert-Lagacé, without whom this genuinely 'happy ending' would almost certainly never have been achieved. In a previous publication, part of which analysed *La Tortue sur le dos: ma lutte contre la boulimie*, I summarised the text thus:

> Loupias's *La Tortue sur le dos* is a triptych. The first section, by far the longest at 111 pages, is authored by Loupias, the subsequent seventeen pages by her dietician, Louise Lambert-Lagacé, and the last forty-eight by a psychologist, Annette Richard. Loupias's section, which forms the bulk of the triptych, charts her harrowing struggle, from the age of fifteen to thirty-seven, with catastrophically disordered eating, alternating between mild anorexia and extreme bulimia, the distress of which prompts two other forms of self-harm – self-beating and alcohol abuse – and even two suicide attempts. It also contains analeptic sequences focusing on her troubled childhood, references to several heterosexual relationships in adult life, and narrative of her path towards a complete recovery.[5]

It will be clear from the first paragraph of the present chapter that careful reconsideration since that previous publication has changed my mind about Loupias's ED having become 'extreme bulimia'. I now consider her to have slid into binge eating disorder, a diagnostically discrete condition. Other than that, however, the summary remains valid.

Picking up on the word 'distress' in the quotation from my 2015 article, it should be acknowledged that such distress is widely ignored in popular perceptions of EDs in general, which are often viewed as

5 Cairns 2015: 496.

either attention-seeking and/or self-indulgent. This view myopically disregards the complex psychological mechanisms EDs involve. Far from attention-seeking and self-indulgence, Loupias's testimony to her own ED stresses the self-disgust and resulting self-abjection provoked by her repetitive bingeing. For instance, she uses a bestial simile to convey that self-abjection: 'Je mange comme un animal, à pleines mains' [I eat like an animal, by the handful] (p. 24). She also conveys one of the causative mechanisms of her repetitive bingeing: to stifle fear, in the case below fear of a man's attraction to her:

> Pourquoi ai-je aussi peur ? Je ne connais qu'une seule manière de faire taire ce sentiment : l'étouffer, le recouvrir de monceaux de nourriture, ne pas lui laisser la moindre chance de prendre possession de moi. [...] il me suffit d'ouvrir la bouche, de me gaver comme on gave les oies. (p. 58)

> Why am I so scared? I know only one way to silence this feeling: to smother it, to cover it with heaps of food, not to give it the slightest chance of taking possession of me. [...] it is enough for me to open my mouth, to force-feed myself like geese are force-fed.

Cathy Caruth observes 'the way that the experience of a trauma repeats itself, exactly and unremittingly, through the unknowing acts of the survivor and against his very will'.[6] And Loupias's long-term illness is intensely traumatic.

Part of the intense trauma of Loupias's illness is the affective agony ('affres') it induces, conveyed via an infernal metaphor: 'Le premier volet est donc un témoignage, le mien. Il pourra paraître pénible et parfois incroyable aux personnes qui n'ont pas connu les affres de ce voyage en enfer qui a beaucoup à voir avec l'obsession de la minceur' [The first part is a testimony: mine. It may seem gruelling and at times unbelievable to people who have not experienced the horrors of this trip to hell that has much to do with the obsession with thinness] (p. 12). Like Balinska (as a former anorectic, restrictor type, at the opposite end of the ED spectrum), Loupias's intention in publishing her testimony to this illness is sociotropic: 'Mais aux autres, à toutes ces femmes qui vivent dans la noirceur et se gavent jour après jour pour ne plus avoir mal, j'ose espérer que ce livre saura redonner confiance en la possibilité bien réelle de guérir' [But to the others, to all those women who live

6 Caruth, Cathy, *Unclaimed Experience: Trauma, Narrative, and History* (Baltimore, MD/London: The Johns Hopkins University Press, 1996), p. 2.

in darkness and stuff themselves day after day to no longer feel pain, I hope that this book will restore confidence in the very real possibility of healing] (p. 12). Of relevance is that she refers only to women. As observed in my Introduction, although males also suffer from EDs, the incidence is dramatically lower than for females. And there is also a gendered motivation for bingeing implied in 'se gavent jour après jour pour ne plus avoir mal' [stuff themselves day after day to no longer feel pain] that echoes the arguments made by psychotherapist and psychoanalyst Susie Orbach in her *Fat is a Feminist Issue* (1988).[7]

That 'mal' [pain], or suffering, along with its deleterious effects on her interpersonal relationships, become evident on the very first page of Loupias's testimony:

> Ce matin, avec fracas et colère, j'ai refermé la porte sur ma souffrance. J'ai chassé l'homme que j'aime, parce qu'il n'est pas assez présent. Je le déteste de ne pas me tenir la main, de ne pas me prendre en charge. Je le déteste autant que moi-même, femme terrorisée et incapable de marcher seule. J'ai peur. Mon vide intérieur est toujours aussi vide. L'amour de cet homme ne m'a pas changée. Je sais depuis longtemps que personne ne peut m'aider, que personne ne peut me calmer. Seule la nourriture m'apaise. Elle m'est d'une totale fidélité. Patrick a disparu de ma vie, je l'ai décidé. À sa place, il reste un trou béant, je ne suis plus rien… À ce moment précis, j'ai un énorme besoin de manger. (p. 13)

> This morning, with a crash and in anger, I closed the door on my suffering. I sent away the man I love because he's not present enough. I hate him for not holding my hand, for not taking charge of me. I hate him as much as I hate myself, a woman terrified and unable to walk alone. I am scared. My inner emptiness is still just as empty. The love of this man did not change me. I have known for a long time that no-one can help me, that no-one can calm me down. Only the food appeases me. It's totally loyal to me. Patrick disappeared from my life, I decided it. In its place, there is a gaping hole, I'm nothing… At this moment, I have a huge need to eat.

Regarding '[m]on vide intérieur' [my inner emptiness], as we have seen in previous chapters, 'le vide' [emptiness] is a salient topos in the primary corpus, traversing all the different types of EDs examined in my book. With Loupias it is inscribed several times; for instance, '[c]haque fois que je m'éloignerai de ma mère, je remplirai ce vide de nourriture, je me remplirai… à ma façon' [every time I grow apart from my mother,

7 Orbach 1988.

I will fill this emptiness with food, I will fill myself... my way] (p. 28). In this particular example, her bingeing is her only way of stifling an upsetting emotion, here prompted by separation from a loved one; the binge is a symbolic attempt to fill the affective void by literal filling of her body. The suffering, arising from self-hatred, takes the form not just of disordered eating but also other forms of self-abuse, such as hitting herself both while not bingeing and while bingeing: 'Je perds le contrôle et me frappe le visage violemment. Je me déteste. Je me frappe jusqu'à ne plus supporter la douleur. Pendant mes orgies alimentaires, je répéterai souvent ces gestes d'automutilation. Ma haine de moi est lourde et solidement ancrée' [I lose control and hit my face violently. I hate myself. I hit myself until I can't stand the pain anymore. During my food orgies, I will often repeat these gestures of self-harm. My hatred of myself is heavy and firmly anchored] (p. 15).[8] (The sexually connoted noun 'orgie' [orgy] in eating is also found in Karin Bernfeld's *Alice au pays des femelles* [2001]).[9] The secondary literature has commented on such self-injurious behaviour in eating-disordered women: 'Most patients injured themselves by means of cutting (46.2%, N=60), *hitting* (38.5%, N=50), or scratching (34.6%, N=45).'[10]

The self-hatred ('Ma haine de moi' [My hatred of myself], p. 15) leads to a self-division: 'Je ne sais plus qui est cette femme qui mange sans aucune retenue et qui ne sait pas pourquoi. Nous sommes deux. Celle qui est grosse m'est totalement étrangère' [I no longer know who she is, this woman who eats with no restraint without knowing why. We are two. The fat one is a complete stranger to me] (p. 15). This abuts onto, although is not absolutely identical to, another salient motif in the primary corpus, namely the mind–body dualism/split, but becomes identical in the remark apropos her state in the days following this period of massive bingeing: 'Mon corps sort d'une lutte sans merci pour résister à mes assauts' [My body comes out of a merciless struggle to resist my assaults] (p. 15). This motif recurs several times. One example is '[d]epuis des années, mon corps est un accordéon qui joue la gamme de mes émotions' [for many years, my body has been an accordion that plays the scale of my emotions] (p. 16), her body is invested

8 This was pointed out in Cairns 2015.

9 Bernfeld 2001: 101.

10 Paul, Thomas, Schroeter, Kirsten, Dahme, Bernhard, and Nutzinger, Detlev O., 'Self-injurious behaviour in women with eating disorders', *American Journal of Psychiatry*, 159, 3 (March 2002), 408–11 (409; my emphasis).

via an interesting musical metaphor with malicious power over her emotions, the latter deemed to arise from the mind. Another example is '[j]e vidange mon corps comme on vidange une voiture. Il me faut le nettoyer après l'avoir gavé' [I drain my body like you drain the oil from a car. I need to clean it after stuffing it] (p. 17), which deploys a simile reversing the power stakes, with her – her mind, and its agency – dictating an emptying of a body construed as a machine that is alien to her true 'self'.

Loupias's suffering is conveyed in multiple other modes. As well as metaphor and simile, Loupias uses personification (which could of course be considered a metaphor in itself), as when she casts what she calls her bulimia as a possessive woman, indeed quasi-lover, who plugs an affective deficit – the sense of not being loved – and acts as an anaesthetic against her suffering:

> la boulimie attend toujours derrière ma porte. Elle me connaît bien, elle sait qu'après de longues périodes d'anorexie, elle reprendra sa place. [...] Elle remplace tout l'amour absent, elle me punit de n'être rien à mes yeux, elle est le seul moyen mis à ma disposition pour anesthésier ma douleur de vivre. (p. 16)

> bulimia is still waiting at my door. She knows me well, she knows that after long periods of anorexia, she will take her place. [...] She replaces all the absent love, she punishes me for being nothing in my eyes, she is the only means at my disposal to anesthetise my pain of living.

The last sentence is replete with paradox: bulimia replaces the love she lacks, but it also punishes her, and then once more it becomes a positive force insofar as it numbs her existential pain. An anaesthetic is a form of drug, and indeed Loupias frequently refers to food and compulsive, excessive consumption of it as a drug. One early example is, 'Je me pose cette question dans mes moments de lucidité, quand j'arrive à me voir telle que je suis, quand ma drogue ne m'anesthésie pas' [I ask myself this question in moments of lucidity, when I am able to see myself as I am, when my drug isn't numbing me] (p. 68).

As with the other case studies analysed so far, it is important to try to establish the aetiology of the ED in question. In Loupias's case, parental relations feature starkly and darkly. They are not the only factors: chronic lack of self-confidence in all domains, not just the corporeal, is another, as revealed in her feelings before a job interview: 'J'ai le trac. Je ne me sens pas à la hauteur. Toujours le même sentiment d'incompétence, de dénégation. Je n'ai aucune confiance en moi' [I'm nervous. I don't feel up to it. Always the same feeling of incompetence, of denial. I have no confidence in myself] (p. 51). This chronic lack of self-confidence is not matched by introversion, though. Her statement that she is the opposite of shy (p. 60) concords with much of the secondary literature's character-profiling of bulimics, who are presented as far less introverted than anorectics, and often as extremely sociable despite their serious psychological problems. Thus, for example, Jeammet observes the following.

> L'anorexique est réservée, souvent sombre et introvertie, de contact difficile. Avare de ses mots, elle a un discours laconique, dépourvu d'adjectifs, qui se limite aux faits et à leur description, comme pour mieux éviter les émotions.
>
> Au contraire, le premier contact avec la boulimique fait volontiers illusion. Le plus souvent charmante, vive, affichant une réussite scolaire, professionnelle, voire familiale tout à fait satisfaisante, elle fait preuve d'une disponibilité affective, d'un allant et d'une capacité de séduction qui font qu'on peut la qualifier d'« hystérique ». Mais ce masque avenant et enjoué sert à cacher un véritable « enfer quotidien ».[11]

> The anorectic is reserved, often gloomy, introverted and difficult to connect with. Unforthcoming with her words, she has a terse way of speaking, devoid of adjectives and limited to the facts and their description, as if to better avoid emotions.
>
> On the other hand, the bulimic, at first, keeps up appearances. Most often charming, lively, boasting success in academic, professional and even family spheres, she demonstrates emotional availability, an energy and a capacity for seduction that could be described as 'hysterical'. But this cheerful and appealing mask serves to hide a real 'daily hell'.

But with respect to aetiology, certainly her problematic relationships with her parents are predominant. A significant parallel with Calife (to be examined in Section 3.2) is implicit in the link between hyperphagia and lack of verbal communication within the sufferer's family (p. 88). In the case of both Maud (based on Calife herself) and Loupias, the parents, and thus their children, never talk about anything that matters affectively, and thus they censor emotions. Silence for Loupias had been a form of imprisonment during her childhood that had far-reaching effects in her adolescent and adult life, aptly conveyed by imagery of tentacularity. In reference to her parents, she reflects thus.

11 Jeammet 2004: 26–27.

> Je ne peux oublier que le silence a verrouillé toute mon enfance, il s'est étendu sur ma vie, comme des tentacules. Silence des mots, silence du cœur : la mort doit ressembler à cette négation des sentiments, à ces bouches ouvertes et muettes. Peur de dire, peur de s'exposer, peur de se révéler… (p. 88)

> I can't forget that silence has locked away my entire childhood, it has spread over my life, like tentacles. Silence of words, silence of the heart: death must be like this negation of feelings, these open, mute mouths. Afraid to say, afraid to expose oneself, afraid to reveal oneself…

Symptomatically, she also comments that as an adult, during a visit to her parents after a period of alimentary moderation, she is overcome by a desperate need to eat, in order, she states, to replace the missing words: 'Toujours ce silence. […] J'ai envie de tout briser, de partir, de ne plus revenir… et de manger, comme toujours, comme avant. Pour remplacer les mots…' [Always this silence. […] I want to break everything, to leave, to not come back… and to eat, as always, as before. To replace the words…] (p. 88). The quotation above also recalls an earlier statement when, after recounting a typical binge on only the second page of her testimony, Loupias diagnoses such uncontrolled eating as 'ma seule façon de dire mon désespoir' [my only way of expressing my despair] (p. 14). Both quotations illustrate the common trope in the primary corpus of EDs as a form of language.[12]

The following observations from the secondary literature are of relevance to Loupias's parental relations and their part in the aetiology of her ED:

> most bulimics have experienced some form of significant emotional deprivation in their early life.[13] […] Whatever the cause, the child typically early on turns to food as a means of solace, of filling the void left by parental inattentiveness or implicit abandonment. On the surface, however, she typically cultivates a positive façade, an appearance that she 'can manage.' Underneath, though, she feels needy, childlike, and dependent, feelings of which she is deeply ashamed. Under no circumstances does she permit herself to reveal her primitive feelings of

12 See the section 'Language: EDs as a Form of Language' in the Bibliographical Appendix.

13 See, for example, Swift, W.J. and Letven, R., 'Bulimia and the basic fault: A psychoanalytic interpretation of the binging-vomiting syndrome', *Journal of the American Academy of Child Psychiatry*, 23 (1984), 489–97; Johnson and Connors 1987: chapter 6.

> abandonment, sadness, and rage. These are discharged in episodes of bingeing and purging.[14]
>
> Retrospective reports from adult patients with BED describe the subjective experience of being neglected and overlooked in their families of origin (Wilfley, 1989). As a result, these individuals report feeling that they were cheated from getting the love and nurturing to which they felt entitled. They describe feeling that they did not have sound, positive attachments, and they continue to long for the nurturing they never got as children.[15]

Loupias certainly felt emotional deprivation and neglect by her father. The particularly problematic relationship of a bulimic daughter to her father identified in some of the secondary literature is reflected in her father paying her little attention, except to show anger, or in the most dramatic of circumstances, such as when she has just made a suicide attempt. He is also an authoritarian figure, most definitely master of the family, who prizes scholastic achievement highly, and whom she disappoints in this respect (p. 25). Insofar as he tries to discipline her, the following observation from the secondary literature is relevant at least for the bulimic phase of her ED: 'paternal overprotection was particularly important, which provides evidence against the anecdotal picture of fathers of anorexics and bulimics as ineffectual [...]'.[16] Further on (p. 72), the secondary literature's findings also gel with the fact that she falls madly in love with and does everything possible to please a man, Jean, who is almost a carbon copy of her father, suggesting an unconscious desire to attain the paternal love and approval of that father in an ersatz of him. This desire, unconscious when she first falls for Jean, becomes clear in retrospect, and certainly by the time of writing her testimony: 'je ne me rends pas compte que j'ai choisi cet homme parce qu'il est exactement comme mon père : un modèle de contrôle

14 Gordon, Richard A., *Anorexia and Bulimia: Anatomy of a Social Epidemic* (Oxford: Blackwell, 1990; second edition published 2000), p. 108. Note his 'filling the void', which echoes the motif of 'le vide' on whose commonality in the primary corpus I have frequently commented.

15 Smolak et al. 1996: 386. The reference is to Wilfley, D.E., 'Interpersonal analyses of bulimia: Normal weight and obese' (unpublished doctoral dissertation, University of Missouri, Columbia).

16 Calam, Rachel, Waller, Glenn, Slade, Peter, and Newton, Tim, 'Eating disorders and perceived relationships with parents', *International Journal of Eating Disorders*, 9 (1990), 479–85 (483–84).

et de perfection' [I don't realise that I've chosen this man because he's exactly like my father: a model of control and perfection] (p. 76). The sentence immediately succeeding this belated insight poetically implies the noxious nature of this fixation on her father: 'Insidieusement, les vieux fantômes réapparaissent' [Insidiously, old ghosts reappear] (p. 76). And the ominous nature of this sentence is vindicated when the violence of the father and of his ersatz emerge, disturbingly, for the first time: 'Et comme mon père que je poussais à bout et qui réagissait violemment, Jean éclate. [...] Ce jour-là, j'arrive au travail avec un œil au beurre noir' [And like my father who I pushed to the limit and who reacted violently, Jean exploded. [...] That day, I arrive at work with a black eye] (p. 78). Cf. also p. 80, where she compares Jean's exultation at her success in new studies with that of her father's when she passed her *baccalauréat*, with both men's positive attitude towards her being dependent on external achievements rather than her inner qualities as a human being.

As for the mother–daughter relationship, such a prominent aspect of the secondary literature on EDs, this too was highly problematic. Although Loupias adored her mother, she also ascribes direct blame for her pathological problems to her. Referring to her suffering ('douleur' [pain], p. 18) at professional problems due to her ED and the self-hatred the latter provokes, she asserts of her mother, 'Elle ne sait pas à quel point elle en est la cause, à quel point nous sommes liées toutes les deux' [She doesn't know the extent to which she's the cause of it, the extent to which we're both linked] (p. 18). This is elaborated later in Loupias's narrative, but at this early point a crucial statement is made: 's'est glissé en moi ce besoin de remplacer l'amour d'une mère par la nourriture, comme un sein maternel, comme un deuxième soi' [the urge slipped into me to replace my mother's love with food, like a maternal breast, like a second self] (p. 19). Despite adoring her mother, she was never secure in the sense of her mother's love for her, with intense attachment anxiety leading to her insecurity in adult, heterosexual relationships. One early example recounts her feelings aged 13 of anxiety, indeed fear, as a child when her mother is absent:

> Je suis seule à la maison, maman est sortie. Je n'aime pas quand elle s'absente, j'ai peur. Plus je grandis, plus j'ai besoin d'être près d'elle. [...] Quand elle part, je suffoque, mes doigts s'engourdissent, j'ai l'impression que mon cœur va sortir de ma poitrine, je deviens de plus en plus oppressée. Aujourd'hui, c'est pire que d'habitude. Je pourrais en mourir. (p. 20)

> I'm alone at home, mom is out. I don't like it when she's away, I'm scared. The more I grow up, the more I need to be close to her. [...] When she leaves, I suffocate, my fingers grow numb, I feel like my heart will come out of my chest and I become more and more stressed. Today is worse than usual. I could die from it.

Crucially, it is at this point, when she feels bereft of her mother's presence, that she has her first experience of over-eating – eating when she is not physically but emotionally hungry, and discovering the calming effects of over-eating, as if food were an anxiolytic drug:

> Alors j'ouvre le placard où se trouvent les provisions de biscuits. Je prends un paquet et je mange debout, vite. Le goût du sucre m'apaise, dès les premières bouchées je me calme. Sans m'en rendre compte, j'engloutis la boîte de biscuits. Je me sens plus détendue, comme engourdie. Je viens d'avoir treize ans. Je viens de me rendre compte du pouvoir de la nourriture... (p. 20)

> So I open the cupboard where the cookies are kept. I take a packet and I eat quickly while standing up. The taste of sugar appeases me and after the first few bites I calm down. Without realizing it, I swallow the box of cookies. I feel more relaxed, like I'm numb. I have just turned thirteen. I have just realized the power of food...

As an addendum to this discussion of her parents' role in the genesis of her ED, it is relevant to mention her state of infantilisation in the presence of her parents even when she is an adult: 'Je suis là, assise en face d'eux, et j'ai cinq ans. Si je pouvais, je leur dirais que je ne veux qu'une chose : rester près d'eux, que je n'ai pas grandi, que je ne sais pas comment m'y prendre' [I'm here, sitting in front of them, and I'm five years old. If I could, I would tell them that I want just one thing: to stay close to them, that I have not grown up, that I don't know how to go about it] (p. 62). The wish to remain with them indicates regression, and inability to achieve autonomy from her parents – a finding often recorded in the secondary literature.

Before Loupias develops binge eating disorder, as a teenager she oscillates between extreme over-eating and extreme under-eating, with the result that her relationship with the act of eating in general becomes Manichean and pathological:

> Pour ne pas devenir grosse, je me mets au régime entre mes crises de boulimie. Ces prises de nourriture incontrôlées ne durent pas longtemps, un ou deux jours, au pire une semaine. Ensuite j'arrête de manger. Je ruse pour que personne ne s'en aperçoive. Je m'affame et j'augmente ma

> quantité de cigarettes et de café. [...] Je ne mange pas plus de cinq cents calories par jour, et cela les bonnes journées. Quand il n'y a pas d'école, je jeûne. Finalement, je perds les quelques kilos pris très rapidement au cours de mes orgies. Ainsi naît dans mon esprit la hantise du poids, de la graisse et de l'imperfection. Désormais, manger signifie perdre du pouvoir et ne pas manger, être performante et maîtresse de moi. (p. 26)
>
> I go on a diet between my bulimia crises so I don't get fat. These uncontrolled food binges don't last long, one or two days, at worst one week. Then I stop eating. I do this subtly so no one will notice. I starve myself and I increase my quantity of cigarettes and coffee. [...] I don't eat more than five hundred calories a day, and that's on the good days. When there's no school, I fast. Eventually, I lose the few pounds that I put on very quickly during my orgies. That's how the fear of weight, fat and imperfection is born in my mind. From then on, eating signifies a loss of power and not eating signifies efficiency and self-mastery.

A brief reprieve during the summer holidays from boarding school – 'J'ai retrouvé un certain équilibre auprès de ma mère. Les nuages noirs de la boulimie s'effacent tout doucement, le calme revient' [I found some balance close by my mother. The black clouds of bulimia fade slowly, calm returns] (p. 27) – vanishes as soon as she has to leave her mother to return to school. At school her anguish returns, this time taking the proportions of a hysterical fit (p. 27), recalling the suggestion of a certain histrionic tendency mooted above. Eventually she is sent to a psychiatric hospital (p. 31) where she is simply stuffed with sedative drugs for three weeks. At the end of these three weeks, she realises that she is still addicted to food, still dependent on the need to fill herself, symbolically and literally.

With respect to the formulation 'je suis toujours droguée à la nourriture' [I have always been a food addict], this book has previously referred both to the salient trope in the primary corpus of food/eating as a form of addiction akin to drug or alcohol addiction, and to some of the secondary literature on the topic. Other examples of Loupias's addiction to food as a drug abound. She herself names the excessive foods she is about to consume 'ma drogue' [my drug] (p. 33), where, after starting to eat a bar of chocolate, 'Pour un instant, le calme m'envahit' [For a moment, I am overwhelmed with calm] (p. 33) – again stressing the anxiolytic effects of food/eating on her; she states of this chocolate consumption, 'je me rends compte que je suis toujours droguée à la nourriture, toujours dépendante de ce besoin de me remplir' [I realise that I have always been addicted to food, always dependent on this need to fill myself up] (p. 33) (here the topos of emotional emptiness/alimentary filling again common in the primary corpus emerges); on p. 33, her impatient waiting for her daily walk from hospital to a grocery to stock up on food is likened via simile to a drug addict awaiting their dose of heroin; on p. 34 she reiterates, 'La bouffe est devenue ma drogue' [Food has become my drug]; on p. 53 she refers to the large quantities of food demanded by her body and mind as 'leur drogue, leur calmant' [their drug, their sedative]; on p. 68 she refers to food/compulsive eating as 'ma drogue' [my drug]; on p. 83 she states after a particularly stressful experience, 'j'ai besoin de ma drogue, je dois me calmer. Sous la pluie battante, je marche en mangeant des gâteaux trempés' [I need my drug, I need to calm myself. I walk under the pounding rain while eating soaking wet cakes]; on p. 98 she notes tersely, 'Arrêt au dépanneur pour aller chercher ma drogue' [Stop at the convenience store to go look for my drug]; on p. 102 she comments with some pathos, and inflecting the presentation of excessive food as a tranquilliser with qualification of it as almost the opposite, viz. self-punishment, 'Je laisse la nourriture remplir son rôle, celui de calmant, celui de punition, c'est selon. J'ai toujours un bon prétexte pour manger…' [I let the food fulfil its role, that of calming or that of punishment, it depends. I always have a good excuse to eat…]; on p. 102, p. 98 is echoed in 'Puis je cours au dépanneur : je n'ai plus assez de drogue. Jambon, fromage, crème glacée, chocolat, biscuits…' [Then I run to the convenience store: I don't have enough of my drug left. Ham, cheese, ice cream, chocolate, cookies…]; on p. 114 she refers to the chocolate she has just bought as 'Ma drogue' [my drug]; and on p. 116, again she refers to food in general as 'ma drogue' [my drug].

But despite the temporary relief provided by her drug 'of choice' (a misnomer here if ever there were one, for she has no control over her hyperphagia), her sense of isolation, and inability to express her distress in language, are so great from an early stage that she makes her first suicide attempt aged 15:

> Je suis de plus en plus mal dans ma peau d'adolescente, je ne sais pas à qui en parler ni, surtout, comment le dire. On ne parle jamais à la maison, ou alors de la pluie et du beau temps. Jamais des sujets qui me préoccupent, jamais des garçons, encore moins de ces envies qui me font me caresser la nuit. Je suis très seule, tout le temps, dans ma tête. Alors le suicide sera ma manière inconsciente d'aller chercher de l'attention. Dans ma quinzième année, je ne trouve comme paroles que ce geste définitif, excessif, à l'image de ce que je suis. Après le déjeuner, je dérobe les

> somnifères de mon père, puis je monte dans ma chambre. Avant d'avaler les médicaments, j'écris un court mot : « Puisque je vous embête, adieu ! » Je me réveille à l'hôpital après un lavage d'estomac, toute la famille autour du lit, l'air totalement atterré. Mon désir d'attirer l'attention de maman est satisfait, elle m'aime vraiment... Pour une fois, je suis passée avant tout le monde, avant mon père, mon frère et ma grande sœur. (p. 21)
>
> I am getting more and more uneasy in my teenager's skin, I don't know whom to talk to about it nor, more than anything else, how to say it. We never talk at home, just make small talk. Never about topics that worry me, never boys, even less about those desires that make me touch myself at night. I am very lonely, all the time, in my head. So suicide could be my unconscious way of getting attention. In my fifteenth year, the only word I can find is this definitive and excessive gesture, in the image of what I am. After lunch, I steal sleeping pills from my father, then I go up to my room. Before I swallow the medicine, I write a short note: 'Since I'm bothering you, goodbye!' I wake up in the hospital after having my stomach pumped, the whole family around the bed, looking totally aghast. My desire to attract mom's attention is satisfied, she really loves me... For once, I took priority over everyone else, over my father, my brother and my big sister.

Note again the motif of EDs as a form of language, reflected in a suicide attempt that is an element of the psychopathology of her escalating ED: 'je ne trouve comme paroles que ce geste définitif' [the only word I can find is this definitive gesture] (p. 21). Note also that this first suicide attempt is more a bid for her mother's attention, whereas the second attempt, later on in her 22 years of disordered eating, will be a genuine attempt to put an end to her mental suffering via death. Two other points bear flagging up with respect to this first suicide attempt. One is the impulsivity of her act, and the fact that, as already noted with respect to de Peretti and Rodrigue, the secondary literature often construes the 'typical' personality-type of bulimics (at this point Loupias has not crossed over from bulimia nervosa to binge eating disorder) as including impulsiveness, along with sensation- or novelty-seeking, (ab)use of alcohol, frequent sexual activity, and even shop-lifting.[17] Loupias certainly engages at various points during her 22-year illness in abuse of alcohol, as we will see below, and if not in shop-lifting, then in theft of food while working in a hotel (p. 55) and later in a restaurant (p. 78). The second point relates to the first: her attention-seeking suicide attempt

17 See note 15, Chapter 2 on impulsivity in bulimia nervosa.

(if it is a genuine suicide attempt) suggests a tendency to excess and to behavioural self-dramatising ('ce geste définitif, excessif, à l'image de ce que je suis' [this definitive and excessive gesture, in the image of what I am]). This is absolutely not to deny her deep suffering; rather, I am stressing her inability to articulate that suffering in language. This, arguably, corresponds to the following statement from the secondary literature already cited in relation to de Peretti in Chapter 2 (although in Loupias's case I would not endorse the moral censure connoted by the adjective 'histrionic' – unlike Camille in de Peretti's text, Loupias experiences no pride in what viewed from the outside is histrionic conduct and ideation): '[a]uthors have noted the presence of histrionic personality disorder or traits in patients with BN'.[18] Later on, her desperate need for her mother's attention induces behaviour that goes beyond the self-dramatising to the dangerously violent, and arguably to the psychopathic (p. 35). Craving for her mother's undivided attention leads her to a brutal physical attack on her sister, leaving the latter's jaw broken, and to locking her mother in a room for a whole day. In the midst of her anger and pain, she wants to be anaesthetised and to die, but instead consumes the entire contents of her father's biscuit box – thus further reinforcing the earlier metaphor of binge-eating as a symbolic anaesthetic (p. 35).

After the first suicide attempt, she is given her first tranquillisers, but her eating nonetheless becomes even more disordered, and she begins to fear its compulsivity:

> Manger devient un acte solitaire qui prend de plus en plus d'importance. Régulièrement, je vole dans les provisions de maman, puis je m'arrange pour faire les commissions à sa place et j'en profite pour m'acheter du chocolat ou des biscuits. Je commence alors à avoir peur de ce comportement compulsif. (p. 22)

> Eating becomes a solitary act that takes on more and more importance. Regularly, I steal from my mom's groceries, then I offer to do the shopping for her and I take the opportunity to buy chocolate or cookies. I begin to be afraid of this compulsive behaviour.

That compulsive quality is emphasised by the almost trance-like state into which she enters when on the threshold of a binge: 'Je suis dans un état second, incapable de me raisonner. Rien ni personne ne va m'arrêter. Il me faut manger, maintenant, pour ne plus penser, pour ne plus rien sentir' (p. 23). Also emphasised in the last two clauses here is the earlier reference

18 Smolak et al. 1996: 292.

to bingeing as a form of cognitive and affective anaesthetic. The chemical metaphor is extended when food is, once more, mediated as a drug: 'Il me faut manger, tout de suite. Je grimpe les escaliers en courant et entre dans ma chambre tout essoufflée. Une fois la porte fermée à clé, je sors ma drogue de sa cachette' [I have to eat right now. I run up the stairs and enter my room short of breath. Once the door is locked, I take my drugs out from their hiding place] (p. 24). But while excited about the imminent food consumption, she is also hyper-anxious (p. 24).

After the practically psychopathic incident of physical assault on her sister, all relations with her family end; she moves from the family home into a flat (p. 35), and her ED worsens to the extent that she attempts suicide a second time. This time there is no doubt it is a serious attempt to kill herself: 'Au fond de mon sac se trouvent ma libération et ma guérison : mes médicaments. Je franchis cette sortie de secours *en espérant ne plus jamais revenir dans ce monde que je déteste'* [At the bottom of my bag is my release and my healing: my medication. I break through this emergency exit *hoping never to return to this world that I hate*] (pp. 36–37; my emphasis). She wakens up in a hospital bed, having had her stomach pumped. Judged too serious a psychiatric case, she is referred to a high-security hospital where she is strapped to her bed and given an injection (p. 38). Only when her mother signs her discharge papers is her freedom restored (p. 39). She then falls back into the vicious circle of trying to lose weight through severely restricted calorie consumption: less than 800 calories per day. The resulting weight loss brings about a temporary spell of happiness and self-confidence during which she even finds herself 'belle, désirable, et... guérie' [beautiful, desirable and... cured] (p. 42). The belief that she is cured proves erroneous. Beginning a relationship with a man named Patrick (to whom her book is dedicated, and with whom she will reunite after full recovery, many years later), she eats normally in his presence, but the rest of the time reverts to semi-starvation and laxative abuse. For a while, she does not gain weight, but then starts to do so, because when she eats with Patrick, she loses control and over-eats (p. 43).

Patrick later tells her he was well aware of her dramatic fluctuations in weight, but her situation of being permanently on a diet is, disturbingly, accorded a quasi-normality among French women. As a married man, he is unable to see her as much as she wants; and, tellingly, her binges increase in proportion with her need for his greater love and presence (p. 44). Again, the desperate need for love when not fulfilled, as seen most obviously vis-à-vis her mother, provokes compensatory comfort in over-eating in order to fill her affective void. Oscillation between over-eating and under-eating sets in once more, but the last sentence of the following extract, while expressing anorexigenic thinking, more positively indicates a new awareness that she cannot accept being on a diet for life.

> Pour être aimée et pour m'aimer, je paie très cher : je m'affame régulièrement et je cache mon obsession. Et je remarque qu'elle s'amplifie. Je ne supporte plus un gramme de graisse, plus je suis mince plus je veux maigrir, ce n'est jamais assez. […] *Je sais que je vais passer le reste de mes jours au régime et je n'arrive pas à l'accepter.* (p. 45; my emphasis)

> To be loved and to love myself, I pay dearly: I get hungry regularly and I hide my obsession. And I notice that it is growing. I cannot stand a gram of fat anymore, the slimmer I am, the more I want to lose weight, it is never enough. […] *I know I'm going to spend the rest of my days on a diet and I cannot accept it.*

The vicious cycle whereby drastic dieting slows down the metabolic rate (amply attested to in the clinical literature) provokes aggressivity towards others – a projection of her self-aggression (p. 47). And once again, another period of bingeing kicks in. While aware of the vicious cycle – 'Je constate que plus je suis des régimes, plus ma boulimie prend de l'ampleur et plus je grossis' [I find that the more I diet, the more my bulimia grows and the fatter I get] (p. 49) – she is as yet unable to act constructively upon that awareness.

One glimmer of hope is the fact that, when absorbed in and fulfilled by a new job, her sitomania (meaning either an obsession with food or an abnormal craving for food) and her bingeing diminish (p. 51). But her parents are negative about her new job, and indeed the business for which she works does finally fail – after which her binges once more increase. The lexicon of hell (cf. 'ce voyage en enfer' [this voyage into hell] to describe her experience of her ED on p. 12) is again mobilised to evoke her despair: 'Une fois de plus, l'enfer recommence. Je tourne à vide' [Once again, hell recommences. I am unable to think straight] (p. 52). (That lexicon is also found on p. 79, to evoke yet another onset of intense bingeing: 'ma descente aux enfers' [my descent into hell].) Note in the last sentence in the quotation from p. 52 the play on words: 'Je tourne à vide' literally means 'I'm unable to think straight', but use of this particular idiom containing the word 'vide' [emptiness] also connotes her figurative emptiness, contrasting with her physical filling of herself in a binge. Other prompts to bingeing include inchoate fear :

'De qui ai-je peur ? Pourquoi ai-je aussi peur ? Je ne connais qu'une seule manière de faire taire ce sentiment : l'étouffer, le recouvrir de monceaux de nourriture' [Who am I afraid of? Why am I so afraid? I know only one way to silence this feeling: to smother it, to cover it with heaps of food] (p. 58).

Parental disapproval again manifests itself as a trigger to bingeing, this time when they disapprove her plans to move to Germany with Philippe, her new boyfriend. Having stocked up on food, she drives away from her parents' home in a state of dissociation: 'Puis je pars vers Montpellier, sans savoir qui je suis, où je vais vraiment, ni ce que je fais' [Then I leave for Montpellier, without knowing who I am, where exactly I'm going nor what I'm doing] (p. 64). This state is not unfamiliar to her, and its anguish is only calmed by eating: 'Cela m'arrive souvent de vivre dans une autre peau, d'être totalement une autre. Aujourd'hui, ce sentiment d'étrangeté est très fort. Plus ma main se porte à ma bouche, plus l'angoisse diminue' [I often find myself living in another skin, being a completely different person. Today, this feeling of strangeness is very strong. The more my hand goes to my mouth, the more the anxiety diminishes] (p. 64). (Note the interesting coincidence of the metaphor 'peau' [skin] with one of the words, also used metaphorically, in the title of Rodrigue's text on bulimia nervosa; see Chapter 2.) Other psycho-behavioural abnormalities are physical aggression towards others. This has already been apparent in the assault on her sister leading to the latter's broken jaw. It now leads to her viciously punching the man who loves her and whom she sees as a lifeline ('Philippe est ma bouée' [Philippe is my lifeline], p. 62): 'Je l'agresse à un point tel qu'il a peur. Je veux l'estropier, je veux le castrer. Je suis une bête enragée qui a mal et qui attaque' [I attack him so much that he is afraid. I want to cripple him, I want to castrate him. I am a rabid beast who is in pain and attacks] (p. 67). Of significance is the reprise of self-comparison with an animal (cf. p. 24, commented on above), which degrades her to the status of the sub-human – entirely consonant with her self-abjection and self-disgust. The latter are also evoked in a viscerally grotesque metaphor to mediate her sense of being wounded and infected from within.

> Mon désespoir vient de loin. Je suis impuissante parce que je n'en connais pas la cause. Alors je camoufle les effets, je recouvre momentanément mes plaies, que ce soit par de l'amour, par de la bouffe ou par la fuite. Mais immanquablement le pus refait surface, il pousse derrière la croûte, il me contamine… (p. 68)

> My despair comes from far away. I am helpless because I don't know the cause of it. Then I camouflage the effects, I temporarily cover up my wounds, whether with love, food or avoidance. But inevitably the pus reappears, it rises up underneath the scab, it contaminates me...

And still she is unable to act upon her awareness of the vicious circle commented on above. While waiting for her visa for a move to Quebec, she follows the Scarsdale diet (p. 72), but as usual, is excessive even in this, carrying on beyond the fortnight of dieting recommended, feeling she is never slim enough (p. 72). For the first time since her teens, she reaches the weight of fifty kilos (p. 72). In a moment of lucidity, she again recognises her systematic oscillation between yo-yo dieting/bingeing and of its nefarious effects on her metabolism (p. 74). The strain on her physiological system of this punishing oscillation is evident when she goes swimming: 'Après quatre-vingts longueurs – je réussis même à transpirer dans l'eau ! – et un sauna, je frise la crise d'apoplexie' [After eighty lengths – I even managed to sweat in the water! – and a sauna, I come within an inch of a stroke] (p. 74). Yet this flash of lucidity is annulled by an attempt to 'normalise' her alimentary yo-yoing: 'Je me rends bien compte que j'engloutis les fins de semaine mais, au fond, bien des femmes font la même chose' [I am well aware that I stuff myself at weekends but, when it comes down to it, many women do the same thing] (p. 75).

After an initially idyllic period with Jean in Quebec, and as always after a period of alimentary privation, she intuits that once more, food will get the better of her, due to her permanent sense of inner void. This is rendered by an architectural metaphor:

> Mon déséquilibre est grand, trop profond pour que je puisse bâtir quoi que ce soit. Je n'ai aucune fondation, mon sous-sol est fait de trous béants, de crevasses sans fond. Jean, pas plus que Philippe, ne peut les remplir. La nourriture ne va pas tarder à reprendre sa place. (p. 77)

> My imbalance is big, too profound for me to build anything. I have no foundation, my basement is made of gaping holes, bottomless crevices. Jean, no more than Philippe, cannot fill them. Food will soon take its place once again.

This metaphor is paralleled by one in Calife's testimony to binge eating disorder (to be examined as the second case study of this chapter), in which even at the age of 10, before her ED begins, Maud feels unstable and insecure: 'L'étrange sentiment d'être... une maison sans fondation' [The strange feeling of being... a house with no foundation] (Calife

p. 22). Further isomorphism with Calife's testimony is the personification of food and the force compelling her to over-consume it as a canny and tyrannical woman:

> La nourriture ne va pas tarder à reprendre sa place. Je l'ai tenue éloignée un moment, mais cette compagne ne me laisse jamais tranquille, elle attend son tour patiemment, elle sait qu'elle va finir par gagner et me terrasser. Elle sait que je ne peux pas me passer d'elle. (Loupias, p. 77)
>
> Food will soon take its place once again. I kept her away for a moment, but this companion never leaves me alone, she waits patiently for her turn and she knows that she'll eventually win and knock me down. She knows I cannot make do without her.

It is significant that this impression of being dominated and driven by a tyrannical, anthropomorphised force exterior to the self is found not just in accounts of binge eating disorder but also in those of anorexia nervosa and bulimia nervosa, suggesting again certain traits common to very different EDs with otherwise very different symptomatologies.

Loupias's emotional instability, greatly aggravated if not necessarily caused by her ED, soon results in yet another failure in a heterosexual relationship, followed by a resumption of bingeing: 'Le grand amour est déjà terminé. Du jour au lendemain, je craque. Mes orgies de bouffe recommencent. Hors de tout contrôle, je dévore, j'engloutis' [The great love is already over. Overnight, I crack. My food orgies begin again. Out of control, I devour, I swallow] (p. 78). An indirect explanation of this serial failure in relationships, not just amorous ones, is the self-attribution of cannibalism to convey her tendency figuratively to devour people:

> Totalement désemparée, je demande à mon entourage de comprendre, de me tendre la main. Pas grand monde ne le peut, le risque est trop grand de basculer avec moi. Je dévore les gens comme la nourriture, je les prends en otage, je pompe toutes leurs énergies. (pp. 78–79)
>
> Totally helpless, I ask those close to me to understand, to reach out to me. Not many people can, the risk of toppling over with me is too great. I devour people like food, I take them hostage, I pump all their energies.

There is a renewed period of naked desperation in desperate bingeing, with the bingeing revealing another form of self-abjection: 'À son retour du travail, Jean me trouve dans le lit de la chambre d'amis au milieu de déchets et de pots de crème glacée vides. Ses yeux traduisent du dégoût et de la souffrance mêlés' [On his return from work, Jean finds me in the bed of the guest room surrounded by garbage and empty pots of ice cream. His eyes betray a mixture of disgust and suffering] (p. 81). A toxic dynamic develops between her and Jean, as he reacts to her hurt aggression and physical violence with more dangerous physical violence (p. 85).

A life-changing event now intervenes in this infernal spiral. When her mother unexpectedly dies, despite her immense pain, Loupias retrospectively constructs this death as her own birth (p. 92). But this new birth, to an eventually happier and healthier life, is of course not immediate. Indeed, the image of a mirror – echoing in inverted form the famous trope in Lewis Carroll's *Alice's Adventures in Wonderland* (1865) (also alluded to by Balinska: see Chapter 1) – is used to evoke how close she came to passing into an entirely other realm – of irremediable despair or even psychosis – after her mother's death and Jean's departure from her life: 'À partir de cet instant, je décroche et commence à m'enfoncer dans le désespoir. Je perds tout point de repère. Les six mois suivants vont être cruciaux. Il aurait suffi de peu pour que je traverse le miroir' [From that moment on, I switch off and start to sink into despair. I lose any point of reference. The next six months will be crucial. It would have taken very little to make me go through the mirror] (p. 98). Although the psychotherapist she is now seeing, Annette, provides unstinting support (p. 98), her bingeing continues, and is worsened by alcohol- and prescription drug-abuse (p. 98). The secondary literature has commented on not infrequent polyconsumption of food, alcohol, and drugs in those with EDs. One example focusing particularly on binge eating disorder is '[b]inge-eating disorder is also associated with high rates of lifetime co-occurring substance abuse'.[19]

With her increasing dependence on alcohol and prescription drugs, she gradually reaches a state where even bingeing fails to quell her anguish, which is both mental and physical torture:

> L'angoisse ne me quitte pas. J'ai beau me gaver de nourriture et de pilules, je ne retrouve plus ma route. À dix heures du matin, direction Le Lux : frites et vin rouge. Mon cœur est déchaîné, je le sens palpiter. Que m'arrive-t-il ? Je reviens à la maison. La propriétaire me regarde, inquiète. J'ai, paraît-il, l'air blafard et le visage torturé. Je presse mes mains, je bouge sans arrêt et j'ai de la difficulté à respirer. (pp. 98–99)

> The anxiety does not leave me. It's no good gorging myself with food and pills, I cannot find my way anymore. At ten o'clock in the morning, I got

19 Yager et al. 2006: 35.

> to Le Lux: fries and red wine[20]. My heart is unleashed, I feel it pounding. What is happening to me? I'm coming back home. The owner looks at me, worried. I have, it seems, a pallid look and a tortured face. I wring my hands, I move constantly and I have trouble breathing.

Her visible illness is followed by incarceration in another psychiatric hospital, where she is again forcibly restrained, but this time reacts with manic violence:

> je suis à l'hôpital Saint-Luc en psychiatrie. Une image me hante encore : pendant qu'on m'attache sur le lit, je hurle et je crache au visage des infirmiers. Ils me laissent seule. Hors de moi, je déplace le lit à la seule force de mes mouvements de rage : j'ai réussi à traverser toute la chambre. Je n'en peux plus. Je me mets à pleurer. Ce sera ma dernière crise de violence. J'ai expulsé toute ma rage et mon désespoir. (p. 99)

> I am at Saint-Luc Hospital in psychiatry. An image still haunts me: while I am tied to the bed, I scream and spit in the face of the nurses. They leave me alone. Beside myself, I move the bed with the sheer force of my rage-fuelled movements: I have managed to cross the whole room. I cannot stand it anymore. I start crying. This will be my last violent fit. I expelled all my rage and despair.

After discharge from the hospital, her bingeing continues, despite her psychotherapeutic treatment by Annette. An unexpected telephone call from her father tellingly provokes a particularly abject ('je m'écroule dans mes vomissures' [I collapse into my vomit]) binge, catalysed by memories of her sense of abandonment as a teenager, of child-like fear, and a psychic regression to that state (pp. 102–3).

However, her abysmal despair leads to a momentous decision that will, finally, initiate the path to recovery: the decision to consult a dietician (Louise Lambert-Lagacé) with a sense that if this doesn't relieve her suffering she will take her own life. That decision is conveyed in the wordplay of deciding to change her skin: 'Comme un propriétaire décide un jour de vendre sa maison parce qu'elle ne lui convient plus, j'ai décidé aujourd'hui de changer de peau. Et si ça ne marche pas, ma vie s'arrêtera là, un point c'est tout' [As a homeowner decides one day to sell their house because it no longer suits them, I decided today to turn over a new leaf. And if it doesn't work, my life will stop there,

20 Le Lux was an all-night commercial complex which opened in 1984 and became one of the favourite hang-outs of cool Montreal night life (http://memoire.mile-end.qc.ca/en/lux).

end of discussion] (p. 106). This is an interesting and apposite stylistic device given that, although 'changer de peau' is a common locution in French meaning 'to turn over a new leaf' [literally 'to change one's skin'], in her case skin is part of the body she detests and is the source of so much suffering: I have already noted above this pregnant lexical choice on p. 64: 'Cela m'arrive souvent de vivre dans une autre peau, d'être totalement une autre. Aujourd'hui, ce sentiment d'étrangeté est très fort. Plus ma main se porte à ma bouche, plus l'angoisse diminue' [I often find myself living in another skin, being a completely different person. Today, this feeling of strangeness is very strong. The more my hand goes to my mouth, the more the anxiety diminishes] – along with the interesting coincidence of the metaphor 'peau' [skin] with one of the words in the title of Rodrigue's text, whose whole title connotes a sense of being 'inside-out', or abnormal, particularly in a corporeal sense.

The dietician Louise gives the crucial advice that Loupias must learn to nourish herself, to enjoy eating, and not to eat less than the prescribed amounts of the well-balanced meal she (the dietician) prescribes (p. 109). Loupias is initially fearful that once she starts eating these meals she will not be able to stop eating. But the equally crucial statement made by Louise is 'Si vous vous faites plaisir en mangeant, vous n'éprouverez pas le besoin de vous gaver' [If you enjoy eating, you won't feel the need to stuff yourself] (p. 110). And Louise is proven right. Having followed Louise's advice, eating normal, nutritionally balanced (and not low-calorie) meals in normal quantities, Loupias does not binge, her mood improves, and she discovers on her second appointment with Louise that she has actually lost weight (p. 110). The result is that she starts genuinely to believe that she can recover from her ED (p. 111). And that recovery is indeed in operation: for three months, she does not have a single binge (p. 113), and she ascribes this to the simple but hyper-important fact that the dietician had asked her to take pleasure in eating (rather than constantly trying to lose weight and ending up bingeing). The road to recovery is, predictably, not entirely smooth. Fearing a relapse into bulimia after a punishing exercise regime, she is engulfed by anxiety so intense she feels as if she has moved into a different plane of existence: 'Au volant de ma voiture vers la Rive-Sud, je conduis dans un état second, en proie à une terrible angoisse et à la peur de l'échec' [At the wheel of my car headed towards the Rive-Sud, I drive in a daze, in the grip of a terrible anxiety and fear of failure] (p. 114). Fortunately, the support of a friend helps her away from this mental precipice. Congruence with de Peretti (see de Peretti p. 70) is found in their joint use of a pun employing the verb 'vomir', which in its sense of 'to vomit' is, as I remarked in Chapter 2, of course a key facet of bulimia nervosa. Although Loupias vomited far, far less than de Peretti, and eventually seemed to cease doing so altogether, both play on the other meaning of the verb 'vomir', when used transitively: 'to loathe'. With Loupias, the pun occurs in the last clause of a tentatively positive sentence, as she is beginning to recover from her illness:

> Ça doit être ça, guérir. Ne pas pousser la porte de l'épicerie quand on est triste, ne pas ouvrir la porte du frigidaire quand on se sent nulle, ne plus se gaver pour se punir, ne plus vomir ce que l'on est… (p. 116)

> That's what healing must be. To not go in the door of the grocery store when you are sad, to not open the door of the refrigerator when you feel bad, to no longer gorge yourself as a punishment, to no longer loathe what you are…

Final, full recovery is at long last achieved, as the following uplifting statements evince: 'Côté nourriture, tout va bien. Je n'ai pas revu Louise depuis un an, en juin, date anniversaire de notre première rencontre, il y a déjà sept ans' [As for food, everything is fine. I haven't seen Louise for a year this June, and June also marks the anniversary of our first meeting, already seven years ago] (p. 119); 'je suis définitivement guérie de ma boulimie' [I am cured of my bulimia for good] (p. 120); 'Manger est un vrai plaisir, les repas entre amis sont des fêtes gourmandes' [Eating is a real pleasure, meals with friends are food lovers' parties] (p. 121). This full recovery leads to her blossoming in two other key dimensions to a fulfilling life – the professional and the interpersonal: 'Et puis je pratique l'un des plus beaux métiers du monde : je joue avec les mots, ceux des autres… Je suis réviseure, passionnée et amoureuse de mon travail' [And what's more I do one of the most beautiful jobs in the world: I play with words, those of others… I am a reviewer, passionate and in love with my work] (p. 121); note the attachment to language, one of the salient motifs in the primary corpus, although here it applies to a recovered eating-disordered individual; 'Et comme si mon bonheur n'était pas encore assez grand, l'amour m'a donné rendez-vous un matin de février, il y a un peu plus d'an an. L'homme marié que j'ai mis à la porte il y a trente ans est venu me rechercher' [And as if my happiness was not already great enough, I had a rendezvous with love on a February morning, a little over a year ago. The married man I kicked out thirty years ago came to look for me] (p. 121). This is highly inspiring for those reading her testimony and suffering from the same mental and physical torture that it so graphically and potently documents.

Thus concludes Loupias's account on an authentically 'happy ending' (like Balinksa's and Rodrigue's). Before closing this section on Loupias, however, it is worth considering two points from the end texts written by her psychologist and dietician, for their pedagogical purposes and for the additional help they can thus provide to those still suffering from uncontrollable bingeing. As seen above, I disagree with Loupias's dietician Louise Lambert-Lagacé's conviction that Loupias's condition was bulimia nervosa as opposed to binge eating disorder – although it is interesting to note that this dietician does describe binge eating disorder on p. 149 of her end text. However, Lambert-Lagacé is certainly correct in asserting the inefficacity for any individual who binges uncontrollably, be their ED classed bulimia nervosa or binge eating disorder, of trying to lose weight by taking laxatives or diuretics: 'L'utilisation de laxatifs ne fait pas perdre de poids, puisque les calories sont absorbées avant d'arriver au colon. [...] Les diurétiques, tout comme les laxatifs, ne font pas maigrir, ils provoquent cependant une déshydratation [...]' [The use of laxatives does not cause weight loss, since calories are absorbed before arriving at the colon. [...] Diuretics, like laxatives, do not cause weight loss, but they do lead to dehydration [...]] (p. 132).

As for the end text of Annette Richard, Loupias's psychologist, it makes a highly apt parallel between Loupias's and the novelist Marie Cardinal's need[21] to verbalise the distress they had previously somatised, albeit in very different modes; this recalls the salient tropes of verbal and written language in the primary corpus.

> Et pourtant, « je suis de plus en plus mal dans ma peau d'adolescente », dit-elle, « et je ne sais pas à qui en parler et surtout comment le dire » (p. 21). Elle mettra presque quarante ans pour trouver, à la suite de Marie Cardinal, « les mots pour le dire », et elle le fait de façon très touchante dans ce récit. (p. 160)

> And yet, 'I am getting more and more uneasy in my teenager's skin,' she says, 'I don't know whom to talk to about it nor, more than anything else, how to say it' (p. 21). She will take almost forty years to find, following Marie Cardinal, 'the words to say it', and she does so very touchingly in this story.

21 This need becomes apparent in the eponymously entitled book *Les Mots pour le dire* by Marie Cardinal (Paris: Grasset, 1976). For more information on *Les Mots pour le dire*, see my monograph *Marie Cardinal: Motherhood and Creativity* (Glasgow: University of Glasgow French and German Publications, 1992).

A further insight of Richard's is her interpretation of Loupias's reaction to her father's unique focus on his career success and her mother's sadness: 'Elle réagit en rejetant son père et en se collant à sa mère, à qui elle tente probablement d'apporter les rares moments de joie de sa vie' [She reacts by rejecting her father and clinging to her mother, to whom she probably tries to bring rare moments of joy in her life] (p. 168). This is an interesting reflection of both the problematic father–daughter dynamic and the overly fusional mother–daughter relationship so oft posited as a model in the secondary literature. And in Loupias's case, I would argue that it is an accurate model. Finally, Richard's reference to a psychoanalyst specialising in EDs, Susan Sands, is also thought-provoking. Sands, she reports,

> parle même d'un "soi boulimique" pour bien symboliser ce clivage vertical du sens de soi de la personne en deux parties qui alternent dans la conscience du sujet. Le « soi ordinaire et habituel » est possédé, submergé et souvent saboté par les comportements boulimiques compulsifs, donc par le « soi boulimique ». (p. 170)

> even speaks of a 'bulimic self' to symbolise this vertical division of the person's sense of self into two parts that alternate in the consciousness of the subject. The 'ordinary and habitual self' is possessed, submerged and often sabotaged by compulsive bulimic behaviours, in other words by the 'bulimic self'.

These comments evoke not the mind–body dualism/split so common in the primary corpus, but rather, a dualism within the mind, or even an ontological dualism, that afflicted Loupias when she became a 'non-soi, comme une personne autre que soi, clivée' [non-self, like a person other than oneself, split up]. But not, happily, for always, as her complete recovery attests.

Section 3.2

The last paragraph of the previous section stressed inter alia Loupias's need, in order to recover, to verbalise the dis-ease and distress she had for so long somatised. In Anne Calife's *Meurs la faim* (first published in 1999),[22] whose author states that her autodiegetic narrator Maud

22 Calife, Anne, *Meurs la faim* (The Menthol House, 2010; previously published under the name of Anne Colmerauer, *Meurs la faim* (Paris: Gallimard, 1999)).

is based entirely on herself (p. 293), vocalised language too finally becomes the key to the autodiegetic narrator's recovery from a long and harrowing illness – binge eating disorder: 'Maud a guéri en… parlant. Tout simplement' [Maud healed simply through… speaking] (p. 293).

Calife inscribes a more straightforward case of binge eating disorder[23] than does Loupias, for in Maud's case the disorder is not preceded by dieting, and consists simply of an apparently inexplicable cynorexia (or in other words, insatiable desire for food). Only when she is well in the grip of binge eating disorder does she attempt a diet, which after four days simply ends in a binge (pp. 128–48). Relevant here is one finding from the secondary literature: 'About half of individuals with BED recall that their binge eating was not preceded by dieting.'[24] Once mired in her illness, Maud does occasionally go on other diets, but they always terminate in binges (p. 206), sometimes after weight loss (see, for example, p. 218) but then, eventually, further weight gain. However, her binge eating disorder becomes so severe that it leads to a period of hospital treatment where, without any choice or agency in the matter, she is put on a severe weight-reducing diet that, as it reaps rapid results, starts to become anorexogenic, with her wishing to lose more weight than is necessary or healthy. Ultimately, and again, she ends up regaining all the weight lost, and then gains even more than at the outset of the hospital treatment. This is a classic outcome of draconian weight-loss diets generally, not just among individuals with EDs, particularly when they are not accompanied by any kind of psychotherapeutic help in enabling the person concerned to understand why they had become overweight in the first place. This lacuna is all the more regrettable in psychopathologically disturbed patients like the chief protagonist Maud, suffering from binge eating disorder, as opposed to obese patients who do not binge. It is also relevant to note that the target weight set by the hospital may have been too low for Maud's individual physiology. Helen Malson's observations on this point are highly relevant:

23 As quoted in connection with Loupias, but well worth repeating in Calife's, Carlos Grilo of the Yale University School of Medicine observes, 'The research diagnosis of BED requires recurrent episodes of binge eating. It is important to note that the fifth criterion is that the person does not regularly use inappropriate weight compensatory behaviors and does not meet current criteria for anorexia nervosa or bulimia nervosa' (Grilo 2006: 17). By 'inappropriate weight compensatory behaviors', Grilo refers to self-induced vomiting, abuse of laxatives, diuretics, enemas, over-exercise, etc.

24 Smolak et al. 1996: 190.

> Nisbett (1972), for example, proposed that each person has an individually determined, homeostatically defended 'set point' or ideal weight. Consequently, it is argued, societal emphasis on thinness may result in normatively, but not physiologically, overweight people attempting to suppress their weight. Thus, dieting is equated with biological deprivation, resulting in a number of behavioural responses such as increased responsivity to external cues to eat as a physiological attempt to regain the set point (Ruderman, 1986).
>
> It follows from this that restrained eating will increase the likelihood of bingeing because binge eating may be understood as an attempt by the body to restore a more biologically appropriate weight (Polivy and Herman, 1985). And there is considerable evidence that bingeing and dieting co-occur (see Polivy and Herman, 1987).[25]

To return to the start of her ED, Maud is between 12 and 13 years old when she starts bingeing, during which she feels possessed by an alien (significantly, female) tyrant who dictates her compulsive eating: 'Qu'elle est tyrannique celle-là, jamais elle ne me laissera en paix' [She's so tyrannical, that one, she'll never leave me in peace] (p. 141). I have commented above in this book on the frequent personification of EDs in the primary corpus, most often as tyrannical female figures. In Maud's case, the ED is not just personified, but also, much later on, metaphorically animalised via the noun 'griffes' [claws]: 'Elle a bondi, déchirant de ses ongles griffus la toile grise de mon univers' [She jumped, tearing her clawed nails into the gray canvas of my universe] (p. 241). Her potency forces Maud into degrading behaviour, as attested when Maud lacks the money to buy more food: 'Elle me fait fouiller les poubelles des commerçants, attrapant ici un fruit moisi, là du pain rassis' [She makes me search through the shopkeepers' trash, grabbing a mouldy fruit here and some stale bread there] (pp. 249–50). During the binge, Maud describes herself, as does Loupias, as being in 'un état second' [a daze] (p. 146).

As for the aetiology of her ED – and without wishing to fall into the all-too common trap of simplistically blaming all parents for their child's ED – it is at least indubitable that Maud's parents certainly do not help her establish a stable and confident sense of self that might have been a protective factor against her later illness. While Maud's mother is not materially neglectful, she does not appear to demonstrate love overtly towards her daughter. And she displays the same invasiveness as is frequently ascribed in the secondary literature to mothers of anorectics,

25 Malson 1998: 90.

summed up by Maud in the second lapidary sentence in the following (the reference to the 'tache brune' [brown stain] is the sign of menstrual blood signalling Maud's menarche): 'Ma tache brune ne m'appartient plus ni ma puberté. Tout appartient à ma mère' [My brown stain didn't belong to me, nor did my puberty. Everything belonged to my mother] (p. 56). Reinforcement of this invasiveness, and of the destructive effects it has on Maud's building of any sense of autonomous thought and independent existence, is present in the following:

> Ma mère possède l'étrange faculté d'assassiner toutes chaudes mes envies et ensuite de me rallier à son point de vue. Elle balaye mon cerveau comme elle balaye la cuisine, rapidement et efficacement. Après, je ne sais même plus ce que je voulais. Ni même qui je suis. (p. 75)

> My mother has the strange ability to murder all my burning desires and then make me agree with her point of view. She sweeps my brain like she sweeps the kitchen, quickly and efficiently. After, I do not even know what I wanted. Not even who I am.

This invasiveness is also discernible in Maud's remark about her mother's minute knowledge of her school day: 'Elle connaît mon emploi du temps par cœur : il est collé dans son agenda. [...] Dans sa journée, elle me suit minute par minute' [She knows my timetable by heart: it's pasted into her diary. [...] During her day she follows me minute by minute] (pp. 101–2). The stifling quality of her mother's 'protectiveness' and surveillance of her and her sister is evinced in the last clause of 'elle nous enveloppe, nous protège, nous étouffe' [she envelopes us, protects us, suffocates us] (p. 104). Invasiveness is accompanied by possessiveness in Maud's mother. After a happy outing at a friend's house, Maud remarks of her mother, 'Elle n'aime pas que je quitte le foyer. Surtout, elle n'aime pas que je sois heureuse ailleurs' [She doesn't like me leaving the house. Above all, she doesn't like me being happy elsewhere] (p. 84). When her mother hassles her with questions about the loss of that friend, Maud feels compelled to answer, but reflects 'je perds encore un peu de moi-même' [I lose a little bit of myself again] (p. 103), reiterating the maternal block to her building an autonomous identity. That block is reinforced by the reflection on her mother's unrealistic aspirations for her (recalling those of Camille's mother for Camille in de Peretti's text): 'Sa fille doit redevenir lisse, nacrée comme un coquillage' [Her daughter must become smooth and pearly again, like a shell] (p. 105). To this aspiration, Maud acquiesces inwardly, all the while conveying via an aqueous metaphor what troubled waters lie beneath the false smooth surface: 'Oui maman, voilà, voilà, je m'efforce d'être un étang à la surface lisse. Tant pis si l'eau stagne. Tant pis si elle est de plus en plus trouble, si elle devient glauque' [Yes mom, that's it, I'm trying so hard to be a pond with a smooth surface. Never mind if the water stagnates. Never mind if it's more and more troubled, if it becomes murky] (p. 105). By this point Maud's ED has already begun, so it is more appropriate to refer to maternal maintenance rather than causation of the disorder.

As for Maud's father, he exhibits an egregious lack of love and nurturing towards her. His treatment of her is emotionally icy and often physically violent. The absorption within his work and alienation from his child chimes with the following observations from the secondary literature about anorectics:

> The fathers of anorexics are often absent from the day-to-day life of the family: both physically absent as a result of working abroad, or a hundred miles away and emotionally distant. Typically they are austere, demanding, engrossed in their work and stern in their criticism.[26]

To take the last point first, Maud's father is more than stern in his criticism – he is cruelly degrading: when she fails to answer a maths question he has asked her, 'il saisit une pile de biscottes beurrées, qu'il m'envoie une à une au visage' [he grabs a load of buttered crispbreads which he throws at my face one by one] (p. 116). Turning to another point in the quotation above, that of paternal emotion, this is conveyed succinctly by 'Mon père a l'étrange particularité d'être là et pas là, en même temps' [My father has the strange quality of being there and not being there at the same time] (p. 10). Four other examples are her rueful comment, when he has just mocked her developing breasts, 'Pour une fois qu'il remarque quelque chose' [For once he notices something] (p. 54); 'Depuis un certain temps, il ne cesse de me fuir. J'entre dans une pièce, il en sort' [For quite some time he has continuously avoided me. I go into a room and he leaves it] (p. 61); 'Mon père me manque' [I miss my father] (p. 65); and the fact that for four whole months, he does not speak a single word to her (p. 72). The latter example is particularly ominous in the last sentence of the following extract.

> Peu à peu, mon père s'éloigne doucement.
> Peu à peu, je ne le vois pas.
>
> C'est à partir de là que j'ai eu faim, je crois. (p. 72)

26 Duker and Slade 1988: 108.

> Little by little, my father slowly distances himself.
> Little by little, I don't see him.
>
> It was from then on that I got hungry, I believe.

In the sequencing and association of these three sentences here, from the last sentence we can extrapolate a direct link between her father's hurtful distancing of himself from Maud and the onset of her ED.

Such emotional neglect is bad enough; but the father's physical violence towards Maud is deeply perturbing. Several examples demonstrate this violence forcefully. As a five-year-old child, while her father is absorbed in writing, Maud puts a hand on his knee; his response is aggressive and potentially harmful: 'Je reçois une tape sur la tête et me cogne à un angle' [I got a whack on the head and hit myself against a corner] (p. 11). So too is the following physical abuse, where he does not even have the pseudo excuse of anger at having his work disturbed: still only a child, when Maud asks her father twice where her toys are, he gives her a savage and again potentially dangerous slap: 'Une gifle monumentale s'abat sur le haut de mon crâne. Immobile, oreilles bourdonnantes, je ne remue plus' [A monumental slap hits the top of my skull. Motionless and with my ears ringing, I stop moving] (p. 15). Another example of his physical abuse of Maud is that, while she is helping him with painting and a pot of paint falls over due to a gust of wind coming through the windows – hardly her fault – he slaps her in the face so hard that a mark is left (p. 28). The lack of any justification whatsoever for what are in fact frequent slaps inflicted on daughter by father is conveyed by Maud, along with the lack of verbal communication between them: 'C'est bien beau de ne jamais nous parler, l'ennui c'est quand on reçoit une gifle : on ne sait jamais pourquoi' [It's all well and good never talking to each other, but that means when you get a slap you never know why] (p. 41). This link between his physical violence towards her and verbal communication (or censorship thereof) is reiterated later, when she states, 'Le regard de mon père est chargé de colère contenue. Si je dis un mot, un seul mot, il va me gifler à toute volée' [My father's stare is loaded with suppressed anger. If I say a word, a single word, he'll slap me] (p. 85).

Given this, it is significant that her recovery from her illness, as previously stated, comes through verbal expression (p. 293) – not to him, sadly, but to a psychiatrist (p. 292). His violent treatment of her may be causally related to what Maud asserts of him more generally once she reaches puberty (when yet another example of his physical violence is his kicking her for having failed to remove the halyards of his precious sailing boat: see p. 213): 'mon père n'aime pas les femmes et que m'en voilà une. À la place de ses deux filles, déjà, il voulait des garçons' [my father doesn't like women and here I am, a woman. In place of his two daughters, he already wanted boys] (p. 58). In puberty, he is disgusted by her (p. 61). All of this stands in poignant contrast with Maud's conception of happiness as a child when she craved affection from her father: 'je crois bien que le bonheur, ce serait un papa poilu, avec des pantoufles à carreaux, dans un fauteuil en velours, *sa petite fille sur les genoux*' [I really think that happiness would be a hairy dad, with checkered slippers, in a velvet armchair, *his little girl on his knee*] (p. 44; my emphasis). Also of pathos is her acute distress at puberty, prompting his exacerbated avoidance of her, leading to her daily weeping and sobbing, which he hears but simply ignores (p. 64). This distress is so acute that it leads to self-abuse: 'Dans ma chambre, je me roule par terre en sanglotant, *me lacère le visage*. Là-haut, il entend. Il sait. Il augmente le volume de sa chaîne stéréo pour ne pas entendre' [In my room, I roll on the floor sobbing *and lacerate my face*. Up there, he can hear. He knows. He turns up the volume of his stereo so as to not hear] (p. 64; my emphasis).

While on the role of the family of the eating-disordered patient, it is relevant to note the following from the secondary literature: 'Problems with attachment have long been suspected to play a role in the aetiology of disordered eating. [...] Attachment anxiety refers to the degree to which an individual expects separation, abandonment, or insufficient love.'[27] Clearly, Maud received insufficient, indeed no love from her father, and was emotionally abandoned by and thus emotionally separated from him. Also of relevance to Maud's case are the following observations.

> Retrospective reports from adult patients with BED describe the subjective experience of being neglected and overlooked in their families of origin (Wilfley, 1989). As a result, these individuals report feeling that they were cheated from getting the love and nurturing to which they felt entitled. They describe feeling that they did not have sound, positive attachments, and they continue to long for the nurturing they never got as children.
>
> Related empirical data are consistent with these clinical reports, suggesting that problems in self-development are characteristic of individuals with BED.[28]

27 Ranzenhofer et al. 2016: 251.

28 Smolak et al. 1996: 386.

Still on the question of aetiology, it is useful to bear in mind certain factors beyond the familial. Already at the age of ten, Maud feels unstable, and the metaphor deployed in her terse but tense prose here (already cited above in a different discursive context) to express this feeling maps on to the phenomenology of spatiality found in a not-negligible number of the other 44 texts in my primary corpus bearing witness to EDs: 'Dix ans. [...] Les malaises surgissent partout. L'étrange sentiment d'être... une maison sans fondation' [Ten years. [...] Uneasiness arises everywhere. The strange feeling of being... a house with no foundation] (p. 22). (p. 24) Migration as a young child from Quebec to France (p. 10), and moving home frequently, again part of the phenomenology of spatiality (literally changing one's location in space) is both hated by her – 'Je déteste les déménagements' [I hate moving house] (p. 15) – and psychologically destabilising to her during her childhood (as it was also to Balinska): 'Quoi ? Quoi ? Déménager ? Encore ? Je me rétracte. Je fais une boule. De toutes mes forces, je refuse' [What? What? Moving house? Again? I'm withdrawing myself. I'm making a ball. With all my strength, I refuse] (p. 24). It is relevant to consider this dislocation as a possible predisposing/vulnerability factor to developing an ED, in the light of remarks from the secondary literature: 'In earlier works Katzman and Katzman and Lee have argued that EDs may be precipitated by problems with transition, dislocation, and oppression that produce solutions in manipulations of weight, diet and food.'[29] Finally on the issue of spatiality, Maud's ED, like Loupias's, seems if not to have been caused by, then to have been aggravated by a lack of personal space, created by familial invasiveness (p. 218).[30]

Next, even before the onset of her ED she lacks any self-esteem, feeling worthless: 'se regarder dans la glace, se dire qu'on n'est pas jolie du tout, qu'on ne vaut rien' [looking at yourself in the mirror, saying to yourself that you're not pretty at all, that you're worthless] (p. 31; the last clause is echoed later on, on pp. 67–68, when she condemns

29 See Katzman, Melanie A., 'Eating disorders: Global marker of change', in Latzer et al. 2011: 84. Her references are to Katzman, M.A., 'Feminist approaches to eating disorders: Placing the issues in context', in P. Bria, A. Ciocca, and S. De Risio (eds), *Psychotherapeutic Issues on Eating Disorders: Models, Methods and Results* (Rome: Società Editrice Universo, 1998), pp. 19–26. See also Katzman and Lee 1997: 387, 392.

30 See again Cairns 2015.

herself as 'incapable' and unable to inspire love in others. This may be the reason why she either finds it hard to make friends or chooses deliberately to isolate herself from other children: 'Dans la cour, je suis souvent seule' [In the playground, I'm often alone] (p. 38). (This inability to make friends or self-isolation is echoed when, in adolescence, she feels condemned to a path 'sans espoir, sans père, sans amis' [without hope, without a father, without friends] [p. 73].) In addition, she seems again even before the onset of her ED to be afflicted by a self-schism, or self-alienation, attested by her vacillation between the predominant first-person pronoun 'Je' [I] and its grammatical cognates on the one hand, and numerous uses of the proper name 'Maud' along with third-person pronouns and their grammatical cognates (see pp. 18, 21, 42, 43, 94, 105, 113, 117, 119, 125, 133, 134, 136, 139, 141, 144, 145, 146, 147, 148, 152, 154, 157, 159, 163, 164, 173, 185, 187, 223, 227, 228, 235, 254, 259, and 275). (Such vacillation is also found in, for example, and as Kathryn Robson remarks,[31] Geneviève Brisac's *Petite* (1994)[32] and Lou Delvig's *Jours sans faim* (2001).)

This self-schism, or self-alienation, may be tangentially linked to the mind–body split/dualism motif so preponderant in the primary corpus. Further, Maud is perfectionist in her schoolwork (p. 68), a common feature, as I have previously commented, in both the primary literature and in the secondary literature on ED symptomatology (although the secondary literature ascribes this to anorexia nervosa particularly, and also, to a slightly lesser degree, to bulimia nervosa, as opposed to binge eating disorder). Finally, disgust at sexual organs, and horror of menstruation – thus, rejection of two defining elements of an adult female body – is felt by Maud as early as the age of 11, when her feminist mother decides to gives her a sexual education: 'Avec ses organes génitaux, elle m'écœure. [...] Mon Dieu, faites que j'aie mes règles le plus tard possible' [With her genitals, she disgusts me. [...] My God, make me have my period as late as possible] (p. 46). Other signs of puberty, such as the growth of black pubic hair (along with hair growth under her armpits), also disgust her; and her sense here that her body is betraying her (p. 53) reveals once more the mind–body split/dualism so prominent in the primary corpus already coming into play. While this rejection of the adult female body is far more commonly treated in the secondary literature as a predisposing factor for anorexia nervosa, in Maud's case

31 Robson 2016: 110.

32 Brisac, Geneviève, *Petite* (Paris: Éditions de l'olivier, 1994).

of binge eating disorder it is a strong index of dislike for her developing female body, a body that in all healthy girls naturally increases in fat proportion at puberty.

That dislike, which involves lack of self-respect, is reflected in Maud's account, here in the form of a letter posted to herself,[33] which issues strict instructions to impose self-discipline in her schoolwork, hygiene, orderliness, and eating. The instruction relating to eating is to cease eating bread, due to what has been perceived as (it is unclear whether by herself or somebody else) a roll of fat on her stomach (p. 50). But against the spirit of this letter, she starts before receiving the letter to eat more bread. She also sends herself another letter in which, significantly, the only instructions relate to reducing her food intake (p. 128). In the mental pain of her self-dislike, again like Loupias she engages in self-harm: 'je me roule par terre en sanglotant, me lacère le visage' [I roll on the floor sobbing and lacerate my face] (p. 64). That pain is aggravated by her father's alienation from her, leading to the sense of void[34] so prevalent in the rest of the primary corpus:

> Mon père me manquait. La cavité grandit en moi. Le trou s'étire, prend toute la place nécessaire à son épanouissement.
> [...]
> Je me remplis de *vide*.
> Je suis du *vide* avec de la peau autour. (p. 65; my emphasis)

> I miss my father. The cavity grows in me. The hole widens, takes all the space necessary for its growth.
> [...]
> I fill myself with *emptiness*.
> I am *emptiness* covered in skin.

Albeit tangential, a link with this sense of void is that when a minor binge in the company of her friend Caroline induces a sense of shame, she feels that eating should be a solitary pleasure (p. 94) – a pleasure empty of the presence of other human beings. This contradicts the time-honoured recommendation of eating as commensality, which brings people together and enhances relationships. And when Caroline

33 Note the motif of writing prominent in many of the other primary texts. See the section 'Writing as Therapeutic for, Creative for, or Creative of, the Eating-disordered Subject' in the Bibliographical Appendix.

34 See the section '"Vide", Physical and Metaphysical' in the Bibliographical Appendix.

abandons her without explication, she does indeed binge in secret (pp. 111–13), losing all sense of time and memory, in a trance-like state (cf. p. 23 of Loupias). Notation of that trance-like state had been preceded by notation of a sense of floating while bingeing (p. 93), which is redolent of the effects of drug abuse; and as we have seen, addiction to food was integral to Loupias's illness. Loupias frequently refers to food as a tranquilliser, and similarly, Maud refers to eating '[p]our me calmer' [to sedate myself] (p. 114). Further, after another binge Maud experiences both the previous loss of memory while bingeing mentioned above and also a sense of self-loss/self-alienation: 'Sous la coquette, les miettes me grattent. Que s'est-il passé ? Je ne sais pas. Qui était là dans la cuisine ? Qui est sous la coquette ? Je ne sais pas' [Beneath the coquette, the crumbs scratch me. What happened? I don't know. Who was there in the kitchen? Who is beneath the coquette? I don't know] (p. 149). This is another, and serious, index to the psychopathology of Maud's ED. Another is that she binges when angry, here at her father (p. 98), thus using eating as a form of language to express difficult emotions rather than verbalising them.

Taking cognisance of her inevitable weight gain, she weeps, swamped by self-hatred (p. 121), a sentiment reinforced by the lapidary denigration of herself as 'Folle, grosse, incapable' [Crazy, fat, incapable] (p. 123). The mind–body split/dualism already immanent in several previous narrative units is reprised forcefully in self-blame for what her body, as opposed to her 'self' (which she associates with her mind), has done to her, as if her body were an autonomous agent: '*Crescendo allegro* ira ton corps, pour une escalade vertigineuse vers le sommet du gras' [Your body will go *crescendo allegro*, for a dizzying escalation to the fatty summit] (p. 125). The mind–body split/dualism is also reprised in 'Mon corps, ce sale corps, m'agresse encore, ses larges cuisses, sa lourde poitrine' [My body, this dirty body, is attacking me again, its big thighs, its heavy chest] (p. 143), as if her body were separate from its victim, her 'self', or mind. Admittedly, at one point she does refer to her 'cerveau-estomac' [brain-stomach] (p. 148), in what appears to be a reversal of the mind–body split/dualism, because here her mind and body are conflated – but only one part of that body, the stomach; that part thar sends signals to the brain, or mind, of the need or desire for food, and is thus an entity separate from the mind. Her sense of self, never secure before her ED began, is further weakened by this general ontological confusion, as is illustrated in a whimsical passage whereby she metaphorically conflates herself with the food she is euphorically consuming:

> Tour à tour, je passe à l'état de pain, de sauce dégoulinante, de saucisson. Me voilà brune et oblongue, barre de chocolat toute de riz croustillante. Puis, je mue en épais emmental fleurant l'étable chaude ; enfin, je me métamorphose en légère pétale de chips s'envolant au moindre souffle de vent. (p. 158)

> In turn, I go through the states of bread, of dripping sauce and of sausage. Here I am brown and oblong, a bar of crispy rice chocolate. Then, I transform into thick emmental smelling like a warm stable; finally, I metamorphose into a light petal of chips, blowing away with the slightest breeze.

That euphoria is, as ever, transient, lasting only for the duration of the binge. The distressing aftermath is hatred of her ever-enlarging body, which leads to further psychopathological conduct – renewed self-abuse: 'Entre mes deux mâchoires, j'attrape la peau fine du poignet. Je mords-mords. Se dessine la dentelle précise des incisives, bientôt colorées par le sang qui perle' [Between my two jaws, I grip the thin skin of my wrist. I bite and bite. The precise pattern of the incisors is imprinted, soon coloured by the blood that starts to bead] (pp. 143–44). But binge eating disorder has its contradictions, and despite the self-hatred and self-abuse caused by her bingeing, she states that the only respite she gets, the only happiness she experiences, is in eating: 'Piocher dans la corbeille à pain à volonté. C'est mon seul Bonheur, laissez-le-moi' [Digging through the bread basket as I please. It's my only happiness, let me keep it] (p. 152). Note the address to an unknown 'vous' [you], which reifies through personification society's pressures to restrain eating. Personification is also deployed to depict food, 'Elle' [She] (p. 154), and the use of capital letters suggests one step further from personification to quasi deification of food, consonant with the following prayer-like passage – which also has sexual connotations that evoke the not infrequent trope in the primary corpus of eating as a form of *jouissance*[35] [enjoyment]:

> Peu importe la quantité de Nourriture. Seul compte l'instant. Que la Nourriture soit toujours avec moi, qu'Elle ne me quitte plus, que je ne La quitte plus. Que je l'Etreigne, La baise à chaque seconde de mon existence. Tant pis si le baiser est mortel. [...] Dans la nuit, je l'embrasserai encore, ma Nourriture à moi, ma Nourriture chérie, en croquant des biscottes dérobées. (pp. 154–55)

35 See the section 'Addiction to Food' in the Bibliographical Appendix.

> The quantity of Food does not matter. Only the moment counts. May the Food always be with me, let Her leave me no more, let me leave Her no more. Let me Embrace her, kiss Her every second of my life. Too bad if the kiss is deadly. [...] At night, I'll kiss her again, my own Food, my darling Food, crunching on stolen crispbreads.

The personification is extended via metaphor to convey a faithful companion found in food, during whose consumption Maud experiences well-being and a corresponding, if illusory, sense of stability (the stability recurring to Loupias's view of food as a tranquilliser), and a fusional relationship with it:

> Désormais, ma fidèle compagne ne me quitte plus. [...]
>
> Maud se sent bien avec Elle. Maud a trouvé sa voie, ne se pose plus de questions, ne se tourmente plus. La terre est enfin stable. Les remous ont cessé.
>
> J'ai toujours quelque chose en main ou en bouche. Salé, sucré, acide, pourvu que ça puisse s'avaler. Je n'établis pas de limite entre Elle et moi. La fusion est totale. Nous sommes soudées jusqu'à la fin de mes jours. (p. 157)

> From now on, my faithful companion doesn't leave me anymore. [...]
>
> Maud feels good with Her. Maud has found her way, no longer asks herself questions, no longer torments herself. The ground is finally stable. The turmoil has stopped.
>
> I always have something in my hand or in my mouth. Salty, sweet, sour, as long as it can be swallowed. I don't set any limits between Her and me. The fusion is total. We are united until the end of my life.

The sexual dimensions of her relationship with food seen in the extract from p. 154 to p. 155 above intensify so much that she declares it is in eating when she experiences her first orgasm (p. 158).

The ineluctable downsides to this putatively idyllic relationship are a sense that life when not eating is horrendous, and unhealthy weight gain (p. 159). Once more the mind–body split/dualism is invoked: 'Plus mon esprit aspire à disparaître, à se diluer dans l'air, plus mon corps s'épaissit et s'alourdit' (p. 164). Self-splitting emerges in a remark on her self-abjecting behaviour, prompted by her sitomania, such as rummaging in the dustbins of neighbours to find more food (p. 189) and stealing her grandmother's biscuits (p. 189): 'Ce n'est pas moi, et c'est moi' [This isn't me and this is me] (p. 189). As for the unhealthy weight gain, she initially ignores it in favour of the insulating effect against pain provided by food. One example of such insulation is affective immunity to the menacing presence of her father:

> La Nourriture a tout absorbé, même ma famille.
>
> Le premier à disparaître fut tout naturellement mon père. Je n'entends plus ses pas pesants dans l'escalier. [...]
>
> Il n'y a plus qu'Elle qui trône, Princesse altière dans sa robe chatoyante. Fière d'être l'unique centre d'intérêt de la soirée, Elle me tend sans cesse la corbeille de pain, le plat de légumes. Pour honorer ma toute Belle, je puise sans répit dans le Frigidaire. Je Lui baise les mains en léchant mon assiette. Je m'agenouille à ses pieds achevant le dernier yaourt. (pp. 165–66)

> Food has absorbed everything, even my family.
>
> The first to disappear was naturally my father. I no longer hear his heavy steps on the stairs. [...]
>
> No one but She takes centre stage, the haughty Princess in her shimmering dress. Proud to be the only centre of interest of the evening, She always gives me the bread basket, the dish of vegetables. To honour my Beautiful one, I relentlessly draw upon the Fridge. I kiss Her hands while licking my plate. I kneel at Her feet as I finish the last yoghurt.

As well as extending the metaphor of an amorous relationship with food, this extract also, not unlike the previous quasi-deification (pp. 154–55), confers aristocratic qualities on the companion into which she has personified food. What is troubling is that Maud is wrapped up in a fantasy world to the extent that she communicates with no real human being: 'Au collège, je n'échange de paroles avec personne. Elle, fidèle, reste toujours là, à mes côtés. Je Lui voue un attachement si profound que je ne désire voir personne d'autre' [In college, I exchange words with nobody. She, faithful, always remains there by my side. I vow to Her such a great attachment that I don't want to see anyone else] (p. 172). Arguably, she is borderline psychotic in her belief in this amorous relationship with an insentient entity, food, to which she even ascribes mad jealousy when she (Maud) does, on one rare occasion, converse and spend time with a pleasant neighbour: 'Évidemment, l'Autre, folle de jalousie, tambourine dans ma tête. Elle ne consent à me partager avec personne' [Needless to say, the Other, crazy with jealousy, pounds in my head. She doesn't agree to share me with anybody] (p. 173). That detachment from reality is also manifest in her ignoring the continuing weight gain of which she is aware through outgrowth of her clothes, having to buy men's clothes because her extra centimetres mean no women's sizes now fit her, and in her never now weighing herself (p. 169). This all-consuming (no pun intended) fantasy relationship with food even leads to theft of food (p. 176). As noted in the section on Loupias, the secondary literature often construes the 'typical' personality-type of bulimics as including impulsiveness, sensation- or novelty-seeking, (ab)use of alcohol, frequent sexual activity, and even shoplifting.[36] Although Maud's theft is from her parents' or her grandmother's (p. 189) stock of food, not from shops, it is still theft.

Finally, at the age of about 15, Maud becomes aware of the negative nature of her relationship with food, even though she does not express it in such technical terms: 'Oui, je l'avoue. Elle commence à me causer bien plus de souffrances que de satisfactions' [Yes, I admit it. She's starting to cause me more suffering than satisfaction] (p. 179). Stretchmarks on her thighs due to immense weight gain contribute to this wake-up call (p. 179). Hatred of and alienation from her mutating body leads to a conceptual fragmentation of that body: 'Depuis ces vergetures, le champ de mon corps se rétrécit dangeureusement. Je n'en accepte plus que mes mains, mes pieds et ma triste figure' [Since these stretchmarks, the scope of my body is narrowing dangerously. I now only accept my hands, my feet and my sad face] (p. 183). Significantly, neither of her parents seems to notice or mention her flagrantly obvious pathology (p. 181), again reinforcing the impression of parental neglect. Her attitude towards the force compelling her to over-eat (which, as we have seen above, she personifies in borderline-psychotic mode as a female human being) changes from adoration, indeed quasi-deification, to fear. The reason she insists on going to a new day-school in Marseille, quite far away from home, is because she won't meet others she knows there – above all, this purportedly human force (p. 200). This force does not, of course, disappear in Marseille, for it resides within her head, and operates implacably on her body: 'Maud, tu as cru pouvoir en finir avec Elle, mais Elle te suit à la trace. Dimanche, j'avais déjà vidé les placards' [Maud, you thought you could end it with Her but She's tracking you. Sunday, I had already emptied the cupboards] (p. 227).

36 It is worth reproducing here the following from the secondary literature, already quoted in Chapter 2, since even though the focus in on bulimia nervosa rather than binge eating disorder, the two diagnostically discrete conditions obviously share one key factor, viz. bingeing. 'A recent trait-based risk model of BN highlights the impulsivity-related trait of negative urgency (i.e., the tendency to engage in rash acts when distressed) as an important transdiagnostic risk factor for the initial onset of BN' (Reas 2016: 1093). 'Bulimia nervosa is very commonly associated with other "adolescent" problem behaviors, such as experimentation with drugs or alcohol, smoking and sexual experimentation, which significantly increase the risk of this population' (Nicholson and Nicholls in Latzer et al. 2011: 47). Johnson and Connors (1987).

A newly positive turn is taken when Maud falls in love with another girl, a schoolmate named Claire, which results in reduction of her (Maud's) food consumption. Unfortunately, this is but a brief respite: when Claire falls in love with a boy, Maud's bingeing resumes on a massive scale (see pp. 239, 241, 242, 243, 244, 245). Before Claire falls in love with a boy, the reason for the reprieve, namely being in love with another girl, stands in contrast with the failure of men to interest her enough to distract her from compulsive eating: 'Que vaut un homme, son désir, face à la furie qui me commande de dévorer des kilos de nourriture ? Rien ou si peu' [What is a man worth, his desire, when faced with the fury commanding me to devour kilos of food? Nothing or very little] (p. 216). Although she does not explicitly state she is in love with Claire, she does admit of the possibility (p. 231), and various details reveal her amorous and sensual attraction towards Claire. One example is comparison of the profound attractions for Maud of food (in a synecdoche where 'crémerie' [dairy shop] represents the dairy foods sold within such a shop) with Claire's beauty: 'Une crémerie, c'est doux, rond et chaud. Presque autant que le cou blanc de Claire' [A dairy shop is soft, round and warm. Almost as much as Claire's white neck] (p. 236). During this brief reprieve, food loses some of its imperious grip on her: 'Au lycée, je m'abstiens encore. Claire me maintient la tête hors de l'eau' [At high school I abstain again. Claire keeps my head above water] (p. 227); and, referring to the chips she is tempted to eat once she has withdrawn money from a cash dispenser, she says, metaphorically anthropomorphising the chips, 'Mes coquines, sales petites coquines. Je louche affreusement vers le distributeur d'argent. Mais le câble invisible de Claire me retient encore' [My beauties, my dirty little beauties. I look lustfully at the cash machine. But Claire's invisible cable still holds me back] (p. 236). While she does not actually enter into a relationship with Claire (Claire is firmly heterosexual), Maud's feelings are clearly lesbian. This coalesces with another set of research findings, but is at variance with another. The first set is from 1990: 'Striegel-Moore, Tucker, and Hsu (1990) [...] did find a nonsignificant trend indicating lesbians diet less and binge more than heterosexual women, but the incidence of purging was too infrequent in their sample for analysis.'[37] This suggests that lesbians

37 Siever, M.D., 'Sexual orientation and gender as factors in socioculturally acquired vulnerability to body dissatisfaction and eating disorders', *Journal of Consulting and Clinical Psychology*, 62, 2 (1994), 252–60 (253). The study referred

suffer more from what is now called binge eating disorder than do heterosexual women. The second set of research findings is from 1996: 'Lesbian women show less body dissatisfaction and vulnerability to eating disorders than do heterosexual women (Brand, Rothblum, & Solomon, 1992; Siever, 1994).'[38] Clearly, this second set of research findings is not true of Maud's case.

Thrown back into the infernal spiral of bingeing after Claire, too absorbed by her new boyfriend, drops her, Maud's condition worsens gravely (p. 250). She hardly goes to school any longer, not having enough time to do so when her behaviour is dictated by the personified, omnipresent force 'Elle' [She] that tracks her every day, compelling her to spend vast amounts of time eating vast amounts of food. The sense of possession by this force segues into one of morbid fusion, whereby 'Elle' becomes part of her own body (and brain: 'cervelle'):

> Elle est là, partout.
> Tous les jours.
> Elle ruisselle sous mes pieds, dans le ciel. Elle s'infiltre dans mes narines, dans mon nombril. Elle tisse dans ma cervelle sa place noire et humide. Mon sang La traverse et me traverse comme un seul corps ; chaque jour, grandissant davantage.
>
> She is there, everywhere.
> Every day.
> She flows under my feet and in the sky. She infiltrates my nostrils and my belly button. She weaves her black and wet space into my brain. My blood passes through Her and then into me like a single body; growing more every day.

Convinced, finally, that she is bordering on madness – 'Je flaire la folie' [I smell madness] (p. 250) – Maud asks her mother to have her hospitalised (p. 251). Her mother agrees, still amazingly blind to her daughter's ED, fearing instead a hormonal imbalance (p. 253) After an initial hospital consultation, in which Maud eventually avows her vast binges (pp. 255–56), it is decided that she will need to go on a strict diet

to by Striegel-Moore, Tucker, and Hsu was published as 'Body image dissatisfaction and disordered eating in lesbian college students', *International Journal of Eating Disorders*, 9 (1990), 493–500.

38 Smolak et al. 1996: 286–87. The references given here are to the following. Brand, P., Rothblum, E., and Solomon, L., 'A comparison of lesbians, gay men, and heterosexuals on weight and restrained eating', *International Journal of Eating Disorders*, 11 (1992), 253–59; and Siever 1994.

of 1,350 calories per day (p. 258), keep a diary of what she eats and how she feels (p. 258), and be seen by a psychiatrist, with the latter prospect horrifying her (p. 257).

From p. 261 to p. 287, the narrative structure turns into diary form, representing the diary the doctor had asked her to keep. However, the doctor soon stops reading it (p. 266), and after a certain point she decides that *nobody* is going to read it, above all not the doctor (p. 271). This is because, one infers, the feelings that she inscribes in it are too personal and private, and because she has had enough invasion in her life already. Inter alia, this diary reveals the following. She is given anxiolytic medication that calms her and reduces her appetite (p. 261). This helps her adhere to the strict diet, and she is willingly hospitalised at Christmas to avoid the risk of breaking her diet with the temptation of abundant festive meals (p. 263). While faithfully adhering to the diet, she dreams every night of tempting foods (p. 262). Three months into her dieting, rapid weight loss leads to amenorrhea (p. 265), normally seen as a sign of severe underweight, even though she is still overweight, albeit much less so now due to the dieting. This is not uncommon in the early stages of EDs generally: as seen in footnote 49 of Chapter 1, which focused on anorexia nervosa (restrictor type), one source in the secondary literature states, 'The early loss of periods may reflect a non-specific endocrine response to weight loss in that group of individuals who only function normally at the upper part of a normally distributed weight range.'[39]

Another cross-over between different EDs is that, while not underweight, Maud starts to develop anorexogenic thoughts. Although she reaches her target weight of 52 kilos (p. 267), she still thinks she is too fat (p. 268) and wishes to lose further weight, in order, she says, to have a safety margin (p. 268). The dramatic change in her thinking is evinced by her labelling of food stuffs she previously adored and with which she literally stuffed herself, such as jam, chocolate and mayonnaise, as 'horribles' [horrible] (p. 267). These food items are meant to be included in moderate quantities in the weight-stabilisation diet prescribed by the dietician now that she has reached her target weight, but Maud vows not to follow this diet including such foods, declaring she no longer experiences hunger and would like to weigh 49 kilos instead of her present 52 kilos. This distorted thinking may possibly be because she has lost too much weight, given that different individuals have different 'set points' of weight at which they are

39 Andersen in Szmukler et al. 1995: 373.

healthy and do not need to diet to maintain that weight; perhaps 52 kilos is too low for Maud's individual physiology. Because we do not know what her highest weight was, it is difficult to draw a definitive conclusion, but what we do know is that she had lost a very large amount of weight – 25 kilos – in eight months, which is roughly half of the 52 kilos at which she is now. The following assertion from the secondary literature would suggest that this would have been dangerous:

> The threshold where emaciation becomes physically dangerous is reached when a person's weight falls to between 65–60 per cent of her/his AEBW,[40] or to 50 per cent of an obese original weight, whichever comes first. For example, the person who originally weighed 16 st., but whose AEBW is 10 st. will already have reached a critical point when his or her weight falls to 8 st. (50 per cent). It is *this* that is the significant calculation, and *not* the 6 st. 7 lb. that would be 65 per cent of their 10 st. AEBW.[41]

That the transformation in her thinking into the anorexogenic may well have been caused by excessive weight loss is supported by the following from the secondary literature.

> From a small sample it would appear that for obese people communication difficulties occur around 80 per cent of their original obese weight, if weight loss has been swift. This means that if person B (whose AEBW is 9 st. 7 lb.) has been an overweight 15 st. for the last eight years and then this weight falls to 12 st. in five months, B at this point will have the same altered thinking as A at the point where A's weight has fallen from A's 8 st. to 80 per cent of this (i.e. 6 st.6 lb). B's [p. 81] thinking will be altered even though, at 12 st., B is still 2 st. 7 lb. *above* her or his AEBW.[42]

However, Maud's anorexogenic thinking rapidly disappears, and she falls back into bingeing. It is of key significance that this relapse occurs after her father has slapped her for the most trivial of faults: forgetting while on the phone about a pot of eggs she had set to boil, and their eventually exploding (p. 269) The motif of writing as therapeutic or at least palliative, which is common in the primary corpus, is discernible here, when, immensely distressed by this relapse, she writes in her diary:

> J'ai touché le fond. Il faut que j'attrape les impressions là autour de moi, et que je les couche sur le papier. C'est trop horrible, c'est trop affreux. Il

40 AEBW stands for Average Expected Body Weight.

41 Duker and Slade 1988: 77.

42 Duker and Slade 1988: 80.

> faut que je le décrive quelque part, et c'est juste sur ce sale cahier que je tombe (p. 269)
>
> I've hit rock bottom. I must catch the feelings around me and lay them on the paper. It's too horrible, it's too awful. I have to describe it somewhere and it's just that I fall upon this dirty notebook.

In only two months, due to constant bingeing, she regains the 25 kilos that it had taken her eight months to lose (p. 270). Of capital importance is the comment that, paradoxically, given the distress provoked by this huge and astonishingly rapid weight gain, she has in fact instigated it deliberately, in order to hurt and destroy herself: 'Le pire, c'est que j'ai fait exprès. De me faire du mal, de me détruire' [The worst thing is that I did it on purpose. To hurt myself, to destroy myself] (p. 270). This indicates the painful depths of her self-hatred, reanimated by her father's violence towards her. Her morbid alimentary behaviour and psychological imbalance lead to 'des sortes de crises, on dirait des crises de convulsion' [all sorts of fits, what seem like convulsive fits] (p. 273), involving weeping in class, then muscle tensing and fist-clenching, full-body trembling, and even shouting in front of her classmates and teacher (p. 273). The reason she proffers is, 'C'est que je n'en peux plus de moi, de ce corps, de ma tête, de ce que j'ai fait de moi' [It's just that I cannot bear myself anymore, this body, my head, what I've done to myself] (p. 273). Her pathology is not just psychological, but also has noxious physical effects: severe dental problems due to over-eating and not brushing her teeth (p. 284).

A crisis point is reached when Maud believes she has gone mad (p. 276), with an aggravating factor being the impossibility of her family talking to her about her state. She stresses how silence about anything untoward reigns in this family (p. 276), whose members she qualifies negatively as 'bourgeois' (p. 277), with connotations of avoiding topics of conversation deemed to be not in 'good taste' (no pun intended). Immured in despair, she attempts to commit suicide, taking a packet of sleeping pills (p. 279), but all that happens is that she is asleep for three days (p. 280). Incredibly, her parents appear not to have checked on her during those three days. At the first meal she takes with them after the abortive suicide attempt, 'Personne n'a abordé le sujet' [Nobody broached the subject] (p. 280). This alludes analeptically to the 'Postface' (p. 293), where she asseverates 'Finalement, rien n'est pire que le silence' [Finally, nothing is worse than silence], which is followed, in the very last words of the 'Postface', by the positive obverse: 'Maud a guéri en... parlant. Tout simplement' [Maud healed simply by... speaking] (p. 293).[43]

But to return to the main text, the failure of her attempted suicide does not prevent further suicidal ideation. Such is her hatred of and contempt for herself after bingeing that she asserts, 'Mourir, c'est la seule solution' [Dying is the only solution] (p. 281). Systematically, she considers all the possible methods of suicide, and attempts two of them: walking straight into oncoming traffic, and throwing herself off a high building. In the first case the drivers of the oncoming vehicles manage to stop in time before hitting her, and in the second case, the high building she chooses is closed at the top for security reasons (p. 282). So she returns to her original method of overdosing on sleeping pills, but this time supplements them with a variety of other pills and half a litre of vodka. This second suicide attempt is again abortive: she simply wakens up the following morning with a bad headache and slight stomach pains (p. 283). One suicide attempt via walking into an oncoming vehicle does cause damage when the vehicle hits her, but only to her left leg, and certainly does not kill her (p. 283). Realisation that killing oneself is actually very difficult to achieve prompts further ratiocination, which ends in a momentous decision that turns out to be the beginning of Maud's long road to complete recovery. That momentous decision is to consult of her own volition a psychiatrist (p. 286).

For the first few weeks, Maud talks only of food to her (female) psychiatrist (p. 291). Then, aware that food and Maud's pathological relationship with it are symptoms under which lie grave affective and interpersonal problems, the psychiatrist asserts that all this does not interest her, and asks Maud to talk about other things (p. 292). Initially disconcerted, not knowing what lies buried beneath the weight of food (her pun), beneath her sitomania, Maud complies, and begins to tell the psychiatrist about her life from the age of five (p. 292). So, on this final page of the book proper, the narrative ends with a form of *mise en abyme*, as Maud starts to tell the psychiatrist what we realise is the book we ourselves have been reading. Thus there is a symmetry to Califе's book, or a cyclical quality: her narration to the psychiatrist of her illness from its predisposing factors in childhood through to its suicidal nadir mirrors our reading of that same narrative. In fact, the very last words

43 Familial silence, or refusal verbally to communicate, is also indicated as one of the causative factors of the chief protagonist's anorexia nervosa in Sandra Tohorah's *La mort patiente* (Cestas: Élytis Editions, 2005).

reprise verbatim the first paragraph of the book, with one very significant change, to the last sentence of the paragraph. In the opening paragraph of the book, the last sentence had been, 'Et tout le silence qui rend le soleil plus fort' [And all the silence that makes the sun stronger] (p. 9); in the closing paragraph of the book, the last sentence of the reprised paragraph has become, 'Et ce silence qui rend le silence plus fort…' [And this silence that makes the silence stronger…] (p. 292). The minatory role given to silence in the final sentence of the book reflects the assertion in the 'Postface': 'Finalement, rien n'est pire que le silence' [Finally, nothing is worse than silence] (p. 293). Her parents had maintained an intransigent silence over her illness, thus seriously worsening it. And, as is stated in the 'Postface', it is the breaking of this silence about her illness, her verbal articulation of her traumatic past and present, that eventually cures her (and let us recall that Calife identifies herself entirely with Maud, so the 'guéri' indicates a genuinely happy ending in real life): 'Maud a guéri en… parlant. Tout simplement' [Maud healed simply by… speaking] (p. 293). This evokes what Annette Richard, Loupias's psychologist, had said of another French woman's – Marie Cardinal's – similar experience of eventual recovery from affective and mental illness through 'talking therapy', recounted in her aptly entitled *Les Mots pour le dire* (1975). As a coda to this analysis of *Meurs la faim*, we might speculate whether Calife's writing of it has served as a supplement to the talking therapy: the supplement of scriptotherapy. Further attention to scriptotherapy will be paid in my next and final chapter, the Conclusion to this book.

Conclusion

The foregoing chapter has analysed two testimonies to binge eating disorder. As acknowledged in the opening part of Section 3.1, the diagnostic status of Loupias's ED was not so clear-cut as that of Calife. Loupias herself chose to classify her ED as bulimia nervosa in the very title of her book, and her dietician Louise Lambert-Lagacé concurred in that classification. But careful reading of Loupias's text reveals a condition more akin to binge eating disorder, and there are multiple convergences between the symptomatologies of Loupias and Calife, with the latter suffering unequivocally from binge eating disorder.

Beyond such nosological questions, however, one essential factor needs to be stressed: the immense suffering provoked by the ED to which both Loupias and Calife fell prey. That suffering was arguably even more intense than the suffering experienced by Valère and Balinska from anorexia nervosa (restrictor type) and Rodrigue and de Peretti from bulimia nervosa, for in the case of Loupias and Calife their suffering led to multiple suicide attempts. Although Valère committed suicide at the age of 21, this was a long time after her hospitalisation for anorexia nervosa, and although according to Clerc 1987 she remained underweight, she did not appear to be nearly as ill as when hospitalised. Further, while Valère's text demonstrated suicidal ideation, and she consciously identified her self-starvation as an attempt at suicide, starving oneself over a long period of time is not the same as a concrete, immediate suicide attempt. That the two case studies of binge eating disorder studied in this chapter reveal this ED prompted many concrete, immediate suicide attempts proves that binge eating disorder is certainly as dangerous an ED as anorexia nervosa and bulimia nervosa. That binge eating disorder is so under-recognised and so under-treated relative to the latter two conditions is of deep concern, and more research is urgently required – literally to save lives.

Conclusion

This Conclusion has several discrete sections. First, it provides a synthesis of the foregoing chapters that endeavours to identify *the* key point(s) emerging from them rather than falling into mere summary. Second, it considers and critiques the fairly brief pronouncements of the only three French philosophers who, to my knowledge, have written on topics germane to this book, viz. anorexia nervosa and food: Gilles Deleuze, Julia Kristeva, and Jacques Lacan. These pronouncements are limited in Lacan's case to infantile anorexia rather than anorexia nervosa in adolescents and adults, and in Kristeva's case to food, particularly the conception of food in certain cultural contexts as impure. Third, it engages with theorists who are less renowned than Deleuze, Kristeva, and Lacan but who for me are, on the whole, and not withstanding exceptions I will pinpoint, far more insightful in their thinking on EDs: feminist theorists. This third section will acknowledge the influence on poststructuralist feminism of another renowned French philosopher: Michel Foucault. Fourth, it offers a supplement to the hypothesis articulated at the end of my *French Studies* article of 2015 on EDs and spatiality. Fifth, it assesses the concept of scriptotherapy with respect to EDs, previously mentioned in relation particularly to Rodrigue (Chapter 2) and Calife (Chapter 3), and defined by Suzette A. Henke as 'the process of writing out and writing through traumatic experience in the mode of therapeutic reenactment'.[1]

1 Henke 1998: xii.

Section 1: Synthesis

Although only 6 of the 45 texts in my primary corpus have been analysed in depth, as case studies they are representative of most of the other 39 in placing emphasis above all on the acute suffering involved in the phenomenological experience of an ED; and the suffering is more often mental than physical. This is something of a paradox, given the medical corps's overwhelming attention to the physical risks of EDs. This medical bias is understandable to the extent that in the most extreme of ED cases doctors have a duty to preserve life, and also because unless they are psychiatrists, they will not have the training required adequately to deal with mental suffering. However, this simply underscores the need for physical treatment to be accompanied by psychotherapy.

There are two other outstanding features of the primary corpus. One is the very frequent recourse to metaphor (usually ontological metaphor). In the Introduction to this book, I asserted reasons for the importance of paying attention to metaphor in narratives of EDs:

> One is the axiomatic difficulty of those with anorexia nervosa and bulimia nervosa/bulimarexia especially in accurately and objectively conceptualising their body size and body shape, as opposed to merely 'feeling' it, usually as objects of hatred – metaphors work by evoking images and sensations rather than by conscious, reasoned conceptualisation.

An additional reason is that EDs are usually so unfathomable to those who have never fallen prey to them that imaginative methods of conveying their phenomenology need to be found, methods involving implied comparisons with experiences and phenomena that *are* more likely to be familiar to the non-ED-afflicted reader. The second outstanding feature of the primary corpus is the mind–body split/mind–body dualism. Again, as remarked in my Introduction, James Geary, in *I Is an Other. The Secret Life of Metaphor and How it Shapes the Way We See the World* (2011), states, 'Through metaphor, body and mind are inextricably linked.'[2] I responded to this with, 'Ostensibly, this inextricability of body and mind is the complete antithesis of the mind–body split/dualism trope, but the use of conceptual metaphor may be a way of overcoming that split/dualism.' As an addition to these musings in my Introduction, I would add what may seem like a rather self-evident point, but one that is worth making. In an ED, the sufferer is

2 Geary 2011: 93.

pitting her mind, which wishes drastically to reduce normal food intake (in anorexia nervosa and bulimia nervosa) or to consume abnormal amounts of food (in binge eating disorder) against her body, which in the case of anorexia nervosa and bulimia nervosa needs the food it is being denied, and in the case of binge eating disorder demands abnormally large quantities of food.

The foregoing comments have focused on thematic concerns. One brief remark on form: the vast majority of the 45 primary texts are narrative in structure, albeit sometimes with intercalations of poems or diary extracts. However, a very small number are more discursive. One obvious example is Dominique Buffet's *Nestor, la bouffe et moi* (2016), which, while intimately based on its author's own experience of an ED, is also a form of 'self-help' guide for readers afflicted by the same ED. In an annex to Buffet's book, four panegyrics are provided by three medical pundits and also by one celebrity, Patrick Poivre d'Arvor (whose daughter had suffered from bulimarexia and committed suicide).[3] Their praise stresses the pedagogical value of the testimony, as do the series of equally enthusiastic panegyrics from lay readers who had either suffered from the same illness or been close to a sufferer of the same illness.

Section 2: French Philosophers on Anorexia Nervosa and Food

As indicated in my opening paragraph, Lacan's first published reference to 'anorexia nervosa' was not in fact to anorexia nervosa as we conceptualise it today, but rather to infantile anorexia nervosa: 'Dans l'anorexie mentale, ce que l'enfant mange, c'est le rien. Vous saisissez par ce biais comment l'objet du sevrage peut venir à fonctionner au niveau de la castration, comme privation' [In anorexia nervosa, what the child eats is nothing. In this way, you understand how the objective of weaning can come to work at the level of castration, as deprivation].[4] In another publication, he pursued this line of thought.

3 See his own testimonies to his daughter's illness: d'Arvor, Patrick Poivre, *Lettres à l'absente* (Paris: Albin Michel, 1993) and *Elle n'était pas d'ici* (Paris: Albin Michel, 1995).

4 Lacan, Jacques, *Les quatre concepts fondamentaux de la psychanalyse, Livre XI* (Paris: Seuil, 1973), p. 96. The section transcribed here comes from 'Du regard comme objet petit a', 'VIII: La ligne et la lumière'. The date given at the end of this section is '4 mars 1964'.

> Je vous ai déjà dit que l'anorexie mentale n'est pas un *ne pas manger*, mais un *ne rien manger*. J'insiste – cela veut dire *manger rien*. Rien, c'est justement quelque chose qui existe sur le plan symbolique. Ce n'est pas un *nicht essen*, c'est un *nichts essen*. Ce point est indispensable pour comprendre le phénomène de l'anorexie mentale. Ce dont il s'agit dans le détail, c'est que l'enfant mange rien, ce qui est autre chose qu'une négation de l'activité. De cette absence savourée comme telle, il use vis-à-vis ce qu'il a en face de lui, à savoir la mère dont il dépend. Grâce à ce rien, il la fait dépendre de lui.[5]
>
> I have already told you that anorexia nervosa is not about *not eating*, but about *eating nothing*. I insist – it means *eating nothing*. Nothing is in fact something that exists on the symbolic plan. It's not a *nicht essen*, it's a *nichts essen*. This point is essential to understanding the phenomenon of anorexia nervosa. Specifically, what is involved is that the child eats nothing, which is something different from a negation of the activity. From this absence which is savoured as such, he wears out vis-à-vis whatever he has in front of him, namely the mother on which he depends. Thanks to this nothing, he makes her depend on him.

My exegesis of this is that the infantile anorectic wishes actively to embrace nothingness by rejecting the food offering of the mother and thus seeking power over that mother in its otherwise powerless, utterly dependent state. Isabelle Meuret, in her *L'anorexie créatrice*, comments thus on Lacan's asseverations (with 'la' [it] in the third clause referring to 'l'anorexie' [anorexia]):

> Lacan, pour sa part, la définit non pas comme *ne pas manger*, mais comme *manger rien*, signifiant par là que l'anorexie n'est pas une négation, mais plutôt affirmation d'un manque, la présence d'un vide accablant qui mène à la dépendance maternelle (Lacan, 1994: 184–185). En plaçant le sujet 'dans l'histoire du désir et dans la relation à l'Autre', Lacan apporte des éléments essentiels quant à l'aliénation dont souffre l'anorexique (Bidaud, 1997: 29).[6]
>
> Lacan, in turn, defines it not as *not eating*, but as *eating nothing*, meaning by this that anorexia is not a negation, but rather an affirmation of a lack, the presence of an overwhelming emptiness that leads to maternal dependence (Lacan, 1994: 184–185). By placing the subject 'in the history

5 Lacan, Jacques, *Le Séminaire, Livre IV: La Relation d'objet* (Paris: Seuil, 1994) [Texte établi par Jacques-Alain Miller], pp. 184–85.

6 Meuret 2006: 16–17.

> of desire and in relation to the Other', Lacan brings essential elements with regards to the alienation suffered by the anorectic.

Meuret's analysis is interesting in its mention of 'l'aliénation dont souffre l'anorexique' [the alienation suffered by the anorectic], which is attested in many of the primary texts in my corpus. In sum, however, Lacan's theory may well be valid in cases of infantile anorexia nervosa, but infantile anorexia is very different from the anorexia nervosa of adolescents and adults inscribed in my primary corpus. Other reservations about Lacanian theory on anorexia nervosa are found in Maurice Corcos's *Le corps insoumis: psychopathologie des troubles des conduites alimentaires* (2011 [first published 2005]).[7] Thus Corcos's rather snide 'Voilà les lacaniens avec leur accrochage à l'étymologie du mot désir (*désirare* = manquer de)' [There we have the Lacanians with their clinging to the etymology of the word desire (*désirare* = lack)] (p. 284), whereby he implies Lacanians are disciples obsessed by the notion of lack, which they try to yoke to desire. The only relevance of this for my primary corpus is that the rebellion of the infant against the mother, and its perception of her as omnipotent, may sometimes linger in adolescence or even adulthood, contributing to if not causing an ED. Corcos also rejects Lacan's annulment of the real in favour of the symbolic in his (Lacan's) views on anorexia:

> Il y a une vérité organique et émotionnelle de l'anorexie (un corps anatomique et affecté et pas seulement un corps imaginaire) qui doit s'opposer à toute dérive intellectuelle lacanienne ou romanesque qui lui confectionnerait un visage symbolique écrasant, jusqu'à l'annuler, le réel.[8]

> There is an organic and emotional truth of anorexia (an anatomical and affected body and not just an imaginary body) that must oppose any Lacanian or fanciful intellectual slide that would make it an overwhelming symbolic face, to the point of cancelling out the real.

I concur fully in this statement. So, Lacan, it seems to me, brings only restricted understanding of anorexia nervosa, partly because he discourses only on infantile rejection of food, not anorexia nervosa in adolescents and adults, and partly because his purview is fixated upon the psychoanalytic dogma of the symbolic. Yet his 'l'anorexie mentale

7 Corcos, Maurice, *Le corps insoumis: psychopathologie des troubles des conduites alimentaires* (Paris: Dunod, 2011 [first published 2005]).

8 Corcos 2011: 289–90.

n'est pas un *ne pas manger*, mais un *ne rien manger*' [anorexia nervosa is not about *not eating*, but about *eating nothing*] does provoke perhaps fruitful thought that can be applied to adolescent and adult anorectics.

Deleuze, in my view, offers very rocky ground for sowing seeds of understanding about anorexia nervosa. His comments on the condition are at least partly based on the case of his wife Fanny, who suffered from it herself.

> Hommage à Fanny : cas de l'anorexie. Il s'agit de flux alimentaires, mais en conjonction avec d'autres flux, flux vestimentaires par exemple (l'élégance proprement anorexique, la trinité de Fanny : Virginia Woolf, Murnau, Kay Kendall). L'anorexique se compose un corps sans organes avec des vides et des pleins. Alternance de bourrage et de vidage : les dévorations anorexiques, les absorptions de boissons gazeuses. Il ne faudrait même pas parler d'alternance : le vide et le plein sont comme les deux seuils d'intensité, il s'agit toujours de flotter dans son propre corps. Il ne s'agit pas d'un refus du corps, il s'agit d'un refus de l'organisme, d'un refus de ce que l'organisme fait subir au corps, Pas du tout régression, mais involution, corps involué. Le vide anorexique n'a rien à voir avec un manque, c'est au contraire une manière d'échapper à la détermination organique du manque et de la faim, à l'heure mécanique du repas. Il y a tout un plan de composition de l'anorexique, pour se faire un corps anorganique (ce qui ne veut pas dire asexué : au contraire devenir-femme de tout anorexique).[9]

> Homage to Fanny: a case of anorexia. It is a question of food fluxes, but combined with other fluxes, clothes fluxes, for example (specifically anorectic elegance, Fanny's trinity: Virginia Woolf, Murnau, Kay Kendall). The anorectic consists of a body without organs with voids and fullnesses. The alternation of stuffing and emptying: anorectic feasts, the drinking of fizzy drinks. We should not even talk about alternation: void and fullness are like two demarcations of intensity; the point is always to float in one's own body. It is not a matter of a refusal of the body, it is a matter of a refusal of the organism, of a refusal of what the organism makes the body undergo. Not regression at all, but involution, involuted body. The anorectic void has nothing to do with a lack, it is on the contrary a way of escaping the organic constraint of lack and hunger at the mechanical mealtime. There is a whole plane of construction of the anorectic, making oneself an anorganic body (which does not mean asexual: on the contrary, woman-becoming of every anorectic).

9 Deleuze, Gilles and Parnet, Claire, *Dialogues* (Paris: Flammarion, 1977), p. 132.

I remain unconvinced – and my primary corpus supports me in this – about the combination of food fluxes with 'd'autres flux, flux vestimentaires par exemple (l'élégance proprement anorexique [...]' [other fluxes, clothes fluxes, for example (specifically anorectic elegance [...]). There is absolutely no empirical evidence, either in my primary corpus or in the secondary literature, to suggest that the anorectic, once in the grips of her illness, prizes clothes and elegance. Deleuze seems to extrapolate from his wife Fanny's case to all anorectics – an erroneous move. And what does 'Il ne faudrait même pas parler d'alternance : le vide et le plein sont comme les deux seuils d'intensité, il s'agit toujours de flotter dans son propre corps' [We should not even talk about alternation: void and fullness are like two demarcations of intensity; the point is always to float in one's own body] actually mean? To me at least, it is conceptually elusive, indeed conceptually inaccessible. For our purposes the only relevant point in this long quotation is '[l]e vide anorexique n'a rien à voir avec un manque, c'est au contraire une manière d'échapper à la détermination organique du manque et de la faim, à l'heure mécanique du repas' [the anorectic void has nothing to do with a lack, it is on the contrary a way of escaping the organic constraint of lack and hunger at the mechanical mealtime]. As my foregoing chapters have demonstrated, 'le vide' [the void/emptiness] is a common motif in the primary corpus. Yet this sentence from Deleuze remains rather hermetic. How is '[l]e vide anorexique' [the anorectic void], exactly, 'une manière d'échapper à la détermination organique du manque et de la faim, à l'heure mécanique du repas' [a way of escaping the organic constraint of lack and hunger at the mechanical mealtime]? Here Deleuze seems to conflate 'manque' [lack] with hunger; if by 'manque' [lack] he means lack of hunger, this is the logical opposite of hunger.

Much more credible, however, is a further assertion by Deleuze regarding the anorectic:

> il trahit l'aliment, parce que l'aliment est traître par nature (idée de l'anorexique, que l'aliment est plein de larves et de poisons, vers et bactéries, essentiellement impur, d'où [*sic*] nécessité d'en choisir et d'en extraire des particules, ou d'en recracher).[10]

> they betray food, because food is treacherous by nature (the anorectic thinks that food is full of grubs and poisons, worms and bacteria, hence the need to select and extract particles from it, or to spit it back out).

10 Deleuze and Parnet 1977: 133.

Here, he abuts onto Kristeva's pronouncements: 'Lorsque la nourriture apparaît comme objet polluant, elle ne l'est comme objet oral que dans la mesure où l'oralité signifie une frontière du corps propre. Une nourriture ne devient abjecte que d'être un bord entre deux entités ou territoires distincts' [When food appears as a polluting object, it is as an oral object only to the extent that orality means a boundary of one's own body. A piece of food only becomes abject in order to be a border between two distinct entities or territories];[11] 'Il reste néanmoins que toute nourriture est susceptible de souiller' [It remains, however, that all food is liable to contaminate].[12] For the eating-disordered person, particularly the anorectic, purity is felt only in the absence of food within the body, as if a border between the pure – viz. the empty body – and the impure – viz. the food-occupied body – must be maintained. This obviously interrelates with the motif of the mind–body split/dualism widespread in my primary corpus, since in effect the boundary crossed is also that between the body, which needs food to survive, and the mind, which in the anorectic and the bulimarexic attempts at all costs to limit food intake or else eliminate it entirely.

Another more credible assertion by Deleuze on anorexia is one with which many feminist critics would agree:

> L'anorexie est une politique, une micro-politique : échapper aux normes de la consommation, pour ne pas être soi-même objet de consommation. C'est une protestation féminine, d'une femme qui veut avoir un fonctionnement de corps, et pas seulement des fonctions organiques et sociales qui la livrent à la dépendance.[13]

> Anorexia is a political system, a micro-politics: to escape from the norms of consumption in order not to be an object of consumption oneself. It is a feminine protest, from a woman who wants to have a function of the body and not simply organic and social functions that make her dependent.

This provides a smooth segue into the next section.

11 Kristeva 1980: 90.
12 Kristeva 1980: 91.
13 Deleuze and Parnet 1977: 132.

Section 3: Feminist Perspectives

More convincing for me at least than Deleuze and Lacan in their writings on anorexia nervosa are certain feminist analyses of EDs (even if these analyses are not infrequently limited to anorexia nervosa, to the detriment of the other EDs examined in this book). Prominent texts here are Bordo's[14] and Brumberg's[15] (although the former distances her stance from the latter's), and Susie Orbach's.[16]

But before opening up my purview to the wide and varied set of feminist perspectives, allow me to pick up on an element of the previous section: Deleuze's writings. Notwithstanding the deficiencies I personally perceive in Deleuze's theorisation of anorexia nervosa, many poststructuralist feminists have drawn on wider, non-ED-specific Deleuzian theory in their own investigations of EDs (again, generally of anorexia nervosa). Indeed, one French studies scholar, Amaleena Damlé, utilises wider Deleuzian theory in her chapter on two of the texts in my primary corpus, Amélie Nothomb's *Robert des noms propres* (2002) and Lou Delvig/Delphine de Vigan's *Jours sans faim* (2001).[17] Poststructuralist feminist Branca Arsic writes the following of her article.

> The paper discusses Deleuze's concept of the feminine through the exploration of the questions of eating, cooking, and specifically anorexia, as well as an 'anorexic relation' to fashion and dressing. It argues that anorexia should be understood as a micro-political experimentation in fashioning one's own body on its flight to becoming woman.[18]

The second sentence is, for me, perturbing in its romanticising valorisation of anorexia as an agentic choice, and in its implication that the anorectic achieves freedom from normative strictures surrounding womanhood. First, the primary corpus reveals that, although the prodromic diet with which anorexia nervosa usually begins (diets are of course undertaken by millions of girls and women, but do not lead to EDs for the majority) may have been a putative choice, that 'choice' soon becomes no choice at all, but rather an overwhelming compulsion, driven by severe affective/

14 Bordo 1988: 87–117.

15 Brumberg, Joan Jacobs, *Fasting Girls: The History of Anorexia Nervosa* (Cambridge, MA/London: Harvard University Press, 1988).

16 Orbach 1988; Orbach 1993 [1986].

17 Damlé 2013.

18 Arsic, Branca, 'The experimental ordinary: Deleuze on eating and anorexic elegance', *Deleuze Studies*, 2 (2008), 34–59 (34).

existential problems, to reduce food intake more and more. Any such 'choice' soon vanishes as the illness starts to control the anorectic. As psychiatrist Philippe Jeammet accurately observes:

> L'anorexique peut avoir malgré tout le sentiment que son comportement correspond à un choix – contrairement à la boulimique qui doit toujours le subir – mais au fond d'elle-même elle sent confusément que ce choix n'en est pas un et se voit obligée d'en nier les effets.[19]

> Despite everything, the anorectic may feel that she behaves like this by choice – unlike the bulimic who must suffer regardless – but deep down inside she feels confusedly that this is not really a choice and feels obliged to deny its effects.

Furthermore, although in her unwomanly because emaciated body, the anorectic does achieve a type of freedom from socially imposed corporeal templates for womanhood, that freedom comes at a very high price. For its cause is a serious, sometimes fatal illness, which while it certainly does not always end in death, involves intense mental suffering and can do permanent physical damage to the body. To be fair to Arsic, she does make the following concession: 'In thinking about anorexia I don't intend to recommend it.'[20] But what immediately follows is disturbingly morbid: 'It is up to everybody to invent their own micro-politics of pain.'[21] Why encourage a 'micro-politics of pain' in the first place? She then returns to a more reasoned stance with the following caveat:

> Needless to say, the experimentation called anorexia can be dangerous, indeed lethal. The anorexic has to be able to guide the experiment without being guided by it. She has to experiment without ending in the failure of experimentation, the point at which the experiment turns against the experimenter and becomes deadly. The point is to keep the experiment going and thus to keep whoever experiments alive, even if not within the same banal everyday conception of what life is.[22]

Nonetheless, this caveat, coming only at the end of Arsic's article, still to some extent promotes a potentially deadly illness as a potentially productive, tight-rope-walk form of resistance provided the anorectic who 'experiments' does not go too far. 'The anorexic has to be able to guide the experiment without being guided by it' is highly problematic. Quite

19 Jeammet 2004: 86.

20 Arsic 2008: 57.

21 Arsic 2008: 57.

22 Arsic 2008: 58.

simply, as I have already argued, basing my argument on evidence from the large number of published testimonies of those who have suffered from anorexia nervosa, the anorectic is not in a position of mental control sufficient to safeguard against the putative experiment that may 'guid[e]' her not towards productive resistance, but instead towards possible death ('The standardised mortality ratios in AN are between 5 to 10 times greater than in normal controls', research demonstrates),[23] or at least towards severe illness entailing possibly irreversible damage to her mind and body. Instead, Arsic mediates anorexia nervosa as an agentic endeavour, arguably as a curiosity-driven scientific endeavour ('experiment'). And as I suggest above, there is no agency in the onset of the anorectic's falling prey to this illness. To recall what was stated in my Introduction, anorexia nervosa, like other EDs, is often figured metaphorically as alien, despotic, outside forces forcing the subject into self-destructive behaviour. To conclude my brief consideration of markedly poststructuralist-theory-oriented feminists, it is worth noting the statement below of Helen Malson, whose idiom 'technology of the self' suggests a Foucauldian influence (to which I will return in relation to Debra Ferreday's words about Megan Warin later in this section), and who adopts a measured position:

> 'Anorexia', I have argued, can be read as a multiple and ambiguous technology of the self whose meanings are multiple, shifting and contradictory. It can be read as a discursive (and material) practice which is paradoxically both self-productive and self-destructive.[24]

The 'self-productive' nature of 'anorexia' mentioned here meshes with one of the salient tropes in the primary corpus: the creation of a (new) self in eating-disordered behaviour. However, it has to be said that this new self is by no means always a positive one.

I quoted above Helen Malson's use of the idiom 'technology of the self', suggesting a Foucauldian influence. In some respects, this influence has been productive. 'Feminist analyses have interpreted anorexic symptoms from a Foucauldian perspective as signifying "an avoidance of the disciplinary gaze" that seeks to define and regulate the female body' (Malson and Ussher 49).[25] Further Foucauldian feminist poststructuralist

23 Latzer et al. 2011: 3.

24 Robertson, Matra, *Starving in the Silences: An Exploration of Anorexia* (Sydney: Allen and Unwin, 1992), p. 186.

25 Kemp 2016: 56. Kemp's reference is to Malson, Helen M. and Ussher, Jane M., 'Beyond this mortal coil: Femininity, death and discursive constructions of the anorexic body', *Mortality*, 2, 1 (1997), 43–61.

perspectives are contained in the following comments from researchers referring to interviews with anorexic women:

> This construction of 'anorexia' as a fading away, as 'not wanting to be seen' can be read as an avoidance of the disciplinary gaze that Foucault describes a part of a micro-physics of power that both controls and produces the individual.[26]

So far, so good. However, in her review article of social anthropologist Megan Warin's *Abject Relations: Everyday Worlds of Anorexia* (2010),[27] Debra Ferreday remarks that Warin questions 'the Foucauldian approach that has come to dominate recent academic work, particularly feminist academic work, on eating disorders'.

> Warin begins with a list of those theorists who have directly or indirectly drawn on Foucauldian frameworks to 'explain' eating disorders. The list is an impressive one, encompassing Bordo, Bartky, Malson, Naomi Wolf, Diamond and Quinby, and many others. She argues that Bartky and Bordo, in particular, have been instrumental in setting the tone for feminist research on anorexia as an essential part of the critique and deconstruction of femininity. Susan Bordo's germinal text *Unbearable Weight* (2003) is perhaps the most influential recent work in this area. In this model, anorexia speaks to the contradictory nature of patriarchal discourses of femininity such that it becomes 'a way of simultaneously resisting and complying with these ideals' (Warin, 2010: 10). Such a reading positions anorexic subjects as 'caught in a web of discursively produced hierarchical positions in which they are always dominated and disadvantaged' (2010: 11) Power is thus always imagined as domination.[28]

Warin's book has the value of detecting the blind-spots of discursive approaches to anorexia based on Foucauldian premises:

> The particular use of Foucault's discourse has rendered the gendered body malleable, one that 'locates the generative forces outside the immediate, lived reality of the lifeworld' (Jackson 1996, 21; see also McNay 1999).
>
> This passivity of the body is in part a result of the way in which these writings locate discourse and its operations of power and knowledge solely in specific institutional practices – in hegemonic and dualist structures

26 Malson and Ussher 1997: 49.

27 Warin, Megan, *Abject Relations: Everyday Worlds of Anorexia* (Piscataway, NJ: Rutgers University Press, 2010).

28 Ferreday, Debra, 'Anorexia and abjection: A review article', *Body & Society*, 18, 2 (2012): 139–55 (149–50).

> that allow little space for agency, embodiment, and the everyday. This is in spite of the theoretical shift in Foucault's own understanding of power from institutions to the self.[29]

The 'passivity of the body' mentioned in the above quotation is also a factor in the social constructivist approaches to EDs referred to by Nathalie Morello.

> Challenging the medical approach that tends to reduce eating disorders to individual pathology, many commentators point to the influence of media and fashion representations, and the relentless pressure orchestrated by the beauty industry to conform to normative models of thinness – an interpretation that feminist cultural theorists have investigated since the late 1980s, particularly in Anglo-Saxon countries.[30] From a social constructivist perspective, eating disorders can be understood as submission to, or resistance to, normative aesthetic models, and decreasing their incidence means exposing how the female body is constantly scrutinised and objectified. Rather than considering a cure, the focus is more on critiquing the damaging effects that patriarchal capitalist societies have on women's mental and physical health as well as investigating and fostering their agency, a concept that in psychological terms is generally understood to mean the ability to define one's goals and act upon them in a reflected and intentional way, and that encompasses both a state of being – to experience a sense of agency – and doing – to exercise agency.[31]

The moot concept of the ED sufferer's agency is also resonant in Maree Burns's observations on anorexia, which point to the arguably 'masculine'-connoted freighting of such agency.

> In addition to representation of anorexia as the embodiment of a more traditional femininity characterized by abstinence, restraint, and passivity, self-starving is also paradoxically privileged as a signifier of those qualities that have historically been associated with 'masculinity',

29 Warin 2010: 11.

30 See Bordo, Susan, *Unbearable Weight: Feminism, Western Culture, and the Body* (Berkeley, CA: University of California Press, 1993); Faludi, Susan, *Backlash: The Undeclared War Against American Women* (New York: Crown Publishing Group, 1991); French, Marilyn, *The War Against Women* (New York: Summit Books, 1992); MacSween, Morag, *A Feminist and Sociological Perspective on Anorexia Nervosa* (London: Routledge, 1995); Orbac 1986; Wolf, Naomi, *The Beauty Myth: How Images of Beauty Are Used Against Women* (New York: William Morrow, 1991).

31 Morello 2017: 125.

> such as self-control, persistence, transcendence of the (labile feminine) body, and strength.[32]

Burns continues by presenting a contrasting perspective on 'anorexia as the embodiment of a more traditional femininity'[33] (recurring to findings of her 'Extracts 6, 7 and 8', which come from interviews she conducted with eating-disordered women):

> Due to the problematic nature of construing the (potentially) dying anorexic woman positively (see Malson and Ussher, 1997), we see in Extracts 6, 7 and 8 that a woman who restricts no longer exemplifies the characteristics of a desirable femininity. She becomes, as Becca describes, a 'horrifying skeleton'. To engage in practices that potentially invite death cannot be incorporated within dominant discourses of femininity characterized by selflessness and care-giving. Furthermore, unlike a woman with bulimia who is able to remain an object of the heterosexual male gaze, a woman with anorexia undermines the 'gendered performance criteria' and becomes a 'spectacle stripped of pleasure for the public spectator' (Spitzack, 1993: 3). In other words, her body dramatically exceeds the slender ideal.[34]

One final valuable insight from Burns is eminently worthy of consideration:

> by separating and listing personality characteristics and behaviours in the diagnostic criteria sets for anorexia and bulimia (thereby constructing these as deviant), psychiatry and psychology participate in the promulgation of dichotomizing cultural assumptions about what is and is not acceptable womanhood.[35]

Moving from explicitly poststructuralist feminist analyses to other more general feminist analyses that focus more simply on gender as a role in EDs, Matra Robertson, in her *Starving in the Silences: An Exploration of Anorexia* (1992), makes the important statement that '[f]eminism has challenged the medical profession for its lack of understanding of the gender issues in anorexia nervosa and has attempted to set up an

32 Burns 2004: 284. By 'anorexia as the embodiment of a more traditional femininity', Burns is making a comparison with bulimia nervosa.

33 Burns 2004: 284.

34 Burns 2004: 284. Her references are to Malson and Ussher 1997: 43–61, and Spitzack, C., 'The spectacle of anorexia nervosa', *Text and Performance Quarterly*, 13 (1993), 1–20.

35 Burns 2004: 285.

alternative explanation of the condition'.[36] Later, she insists, 'We must be careful not to get caught in the juggernaut of speaking for the woman being treated for anorexia, who is seldom the originator of the discourse, but is instead its silent object.'[37] My book has sought precisely to give a voice to women, via quotations from their testimonies, who are suffering or have suffered not just from anorexia nervosa – Robertson's focus – but from other EDs also. Unfortunately, in order to maintain coherence, I have had to restrict my primary corpus to texts written by metropolitan French women. A feminist take is provided below on anorexia nervosa outside the Western world, and outside the parameters of the Western *DSM*'s criterion of intense fear of fat for diagnosis of the condition:

> [...] in the case of Miss W., a Chinese non-fat phobic anorexic patient with a familial history of distance and abuse, Lee (1995) describes her loss of interest in eating as 'symbolizing a loss of voice in a social world perceived to be solely oppressive' (p. 31) – a quote which out of context could surely be attributed to a white female feminist.[38]

Returning to transnational approaches, restricted neither to the non-West nor the West, let us consider the central problem involved in examining eating disorders from an ethical or political perspective. This includes concepts previously mentioned such as passivity and agency, as well as, at the end of the quotation below, the mind–body split/dualism motif so common in my primary corpus.

> On the one hand, as feminists, we want to recognize that the personal is political and that eating disorders cannot be explained at the level of individual pathology. An adequate account needs to address the social or ideological domain of representation that in some way helps produce such disorders. This recognition has led to the critique of a representational domain variously described as phallocentric, phallogocentric, or patriarchal. On the other hand, there is a reluctance to locate women as passive victims in some point of innocence outside representation. Thus, the task for feminists has been conceived of as constructing autonomous women's representations, and this task has appealed to an articulation of the female body. The body is, then, considered as that which has been belied, distorted, and imagined by a masculine representational logic. At the same time, the body has been targeted as the redemptive opening for a specifically feminine site of representation. In terms of

36 Robertson 1992: 45.
37 Robertson 1992: 54.
38 Katzman and Lee 1997: 388.

> eating disorders, this ambivalence surrounding representation might be cashed out as follows: the anorexic is the victim of representation, trapped in embodiment through stereotypical and alienating images – but at the same time only representation can cure this malaise; only a realistic, nonrepressive and less regulative form of representation will allow women to see themselves as autonomous subjects. We argue that this tension surrounding representation actually sustains the Cartesian mind/body dualism that it ostensibly criticizes.[39]

That 'Cartesian mind/body dualism' is also explored by Helen Malson.

> I have explored how this discourse of Cartesian dualism constitutes the body as threatening, eruptive and alien to the mind/self. And, in constituting the body as potentially disruptive, it produces the necessity of controlling/denying the body. Dualistic discourse, I have argued, produces both the problem – the need to control and ultimately to eradicate the (female) body – and the (fictional) solution – the construction of a disembodied and hence gender-neutral subjectivity signified by the very thin 'anorexic' body. Within this discourse the thin/anorexic body is constituted as a controlled body and as the signifier of a powerful, disembodied and ostensibly genderless subjectivity. Yet the body of dualistic discourse is also figured as a female body. Ideological constructions of 'woman' as bodily and of 'the female body' as alien and dangerous have a long history and are deeply embedded in contemporary Western culture. The discourse of Cartesian dualism consolidates the negative figure of 'woman' as bodily, alien and dangerous, of 'woman as excess'. It produces the desire to control, deny and ultimately to eradicate the body, particularly the female body. That so many girls and women now engage in this process of bodily destruction through self-starvation is clearly an overly determined cultural practice. In this chapter I have sought to illustrate how this discourse of Cartesian dualism forms a significant part of the cultural discourses and the discursive practices of bodily destruction in which 'anorexia' is currently constituted.[40]

I concur fully with Malson's analysis here, and find it an enriching supplement to my own analyses in previous chapters.

39 Bray, Abigail and Colebrook, Claire, 'The haunted flesh: Corporeal feminism and the politics of (dis)embodiment', *Signs: Journal of Women in Culture and Society*, 24, 1 (1998), 35–67 (35).
40 Malson 1998: 141.

Section 4: Spatiality

In my 2015 article for *French Studies*, I maintained the following.

> Yet, despite the ostensibly divergent aetiologies found in Loupias and Durand's texts, there is one striking convergence: a lack of space granted to the female child. In Loupias's proxemics, the lack of space was figurative, given her claustrophobically close relationship with her mother. In Durand's, it was literal: she had no room of her own, having to sleep in her doctor father's consulting room within the family home, and was thus permanently exposed to the gaze of others:
>
>> J'ai souvent fait le lien entre errer ainsi dans l'appartement sans savoir vraiment où me poser avec mes troubles de la personnalité. Je n'avais pas d'endroit où me réfugier, où me construire. Je n'avais pas de base solide, pas de murs protecteurs à l'abri du regard des autres. Même mon corps était à la portée de tous. Il ne me restait que ce que j'avais dans la tête. Ça, personne ne pouvait y toucher, personne ne pouvait me violer. (p. 152)
>>
>> I have often made the link between wandering in the apartment without really knowing where to sit down and my personality disorders. I had no place to take refuge, where to build myself. I did not have a solid base, and no protective walls to hide from the eyes of others. Even my body was within everyone's reach. All I had left was what was in my head. Nobody could interfere with that, nobody could violate me.
>
> Just as in the same way that literally filling herself with food offered Loupias relief from her figurative void, so with Durand first her anorexia, then her self-harm, and most obviously her numerous overdoses offered a form of temporary mental escape from the basic primal wounds of sexual and scopic violation.[41]

I would like briefly to extend those earlier musings on the role of spatiality in EDs first through some further thoughts of my own on the matter, and then by presenting relevant insights from other critics. So, my own further thinking on the matter is that if the lack of space experienced by the eating-disordered individual is figurative, it may link to the fear of relationships with other human beings – viz., the fear of other human beings invading one's inner space – harboured by many ED sufferers, particularly anorectics (a fear observed repeatedly in the secondary literature). This fear, often stemming from early familial patterns, is of

41 Cairns 2015: 499–500.

such interpersonal relationships becoming intrusive and obliterating the self or else preventing the formation of the pre-anorectic's autonomous self-identity, fear of these relationships fostering in an ED sufferer an over-dependence on the other person, which would again restrict or abolish 'personal' or 'interior' space. Finally, it is axiomatic that the anorectic, and some bulimics, literally occupy less physical space in the world through becoming emaciated. What is less well known by the non-initiate is that the anorectic, and some bulimics, often feel (due to poor or non-existent self-esteem) they have no right to the same space accorded to other, 'normal', human beings.

So much for my own further thinking on the role of spatiality in EDs. What have other critics had to say on the subject? Space limits to this book preclude my giving only more than a few representative examples. Dina Birksted-Breen, for her part, avers apropos her work with an anorexic patient:

> I am using the term 'father' here as one talks about 'the breast' not the actual organ or the person, but the father as representing the Other, and the space between mother and infant the space without which there will be no symbols, no words. I am suggesting, therefore, that there is in anorexia nervosa a disturbance in the area of symbolization connected with this lack of space.[42]

Maurice Corcos's observation meshes with Birksted-Breen's, even if he expresses matters slightly differently: 'l'adolescent a manqué et manque d'espace (psychique) ce qui altère la construction et la reconstruction de son moi corporel et psychique' [teenagers lacked and lack (psychic) space which alters the construction and reconstruction of their bodily and psychic self].[43] Both imply arrested psychic development in the anorectic due to a lack of the space that should gradually open up between mother and infant in order for the latter to enter into the Symbolic order. Why this would lead to anorexia nervosa remains opaque. More limpid is a passage at the end of Birksted-Breen's article.

> I have discussed anorexia nervosa, in this paper, from the point of view of the anorexic's wish for and fear of fusion with her mother. I have described some of the feelings which are being defended against by this state of fusion, as well as some of the consequences, in particular

42 Birksted-Breen, Dana, 'Working with an anorexic patient', *The International Journal of Psychoanalysis*, 70 (1989), 29–40 (30).

43 Corcos 2011: 21.

> the lack of a 'transitional space' and what this means for mental development.[44]

What Birksted-Breen's says here does in fact resonate with some of the texts in my primary corpus, such as de Peretti's, although as we know de Peretti's Camille, based on the author herself, only developed anorexia nervosa after bulimia nervosa.

Birksted-Breen and Corcos obviously write from a psychoanalytic perspective that not all readers will find convincing. Personally, I find that the psychoanalytic fixation on early parent–infant relations to 'explain' anorexia nervosa is extremely limited in purview (de Peretti's Camille continues the fusional relationship with her mother well beyond early childhood, into early adulthood), and that it ignores other, sociocultural factors that may well contribute to the onset of the illness. More attention to those factors is paid by Helen Malson, who seems to imply the status of the underweight body itself as a 'site' (if only a site of struggle) – and a site obviously encompasses space.

> As we have seen, talk about 'the thin body' can be viewed as a site of struggle over the multiplicity of its meanings. It can, for example, be 'read' as signifying non-woman as well as 'perfect femininity'. It resists as well as embodies patriarchal gender identities. And one way in which the femininity of 'the thin body' is most clearly resisted is in its discursive construction as androgynous or boyish.[45]

The end of this section on spatiality bridges onto my final section, which explores the 'space' of the writing act, and of its possibly beneficial effects for ED sufferers.

Section 5: Scriptotherapy

As observed in my analysis of Rodrigue's text (Chapter 2), Suzette A. Henke coined the valuable term 'scriptotherapy', which she defined as 'the process of writing out and writing through traumatic experience in the mode of therapeutic reenactment'.[46] The parallelism of Henke's formulation 'writing out and writing through' with the psychoanalytic formulation 'acting out and working through' highlights the potentially

44 Birksted-Breen 1989: 39.

45 Malson 1998: 114.

46 Henke 1998: xii.

beneficial effects of writing in overcoming traumatic experiences, such as eating-disordered illness. Rodrigue in particular benefited from the therapeutic effect of writing about the trauma of her bulimia nervosa. In addition, and from a transnational optic, there is another example of such benefit in a text not included in my primary corpus because it was written by a Swiss rather than a French woman, and my corpus comprises only texts by French women writers. However, this text is written in French, and is highly relevant to the question of scriptotherapy and its benefits for eating-disordered individuals. It is Alice Bairoch's *Voyage en anorexie* (2007),[47] and recounts the author's experience – despite the title – of bulimarexia (anorexia and bulimia with vomiting following binges). One particular extract demonstrates these benefits.

> Heureusement, l'écriture de ce récit a eu des conséquences plutôt positives sur moi ; cela m'a démontré l'absurdité des raisonnements que je tenais à l'époque et m'a définitivement dégoûtée de revivre une telle aventure. De plus, j'ai réussi à mieux comprendre le pourquoi de cette maladie, à me rendre compte des raisons qui m'y ont amenée et à essayer donc de tout mettre en œuvre pour que cela ne se reproduise plus jamais.
>
> Ce travail a été réellement bénéfique pour moi. Il m'a permis de mieux me connaître et m'a donné une vision différente de l'anorexie que celle que j'avais avant d'écrire mon récit.[48]

> Fortunately, the writing of this story has had rather positive consequences for me; it showed me the absurdity of the reasoning I held at the time and definitely put me off reliving such an episode. In addition, I have been able to better understand the cause of this sickness, to realize the reasons that steered me towards it and to try to do everything possible to ensure that it never happens again.
>
> This work has been really beneficial to me. It allowed me to get to know myself better and gave me a different vision of anorexia from the one I had before writing my story.

In considering scriptotherapy, we need to ask whether it has perhaps been if not central to then of ancillary help in the recovery process of the eating-disordered narrators or chief protagonist in the primary texts. For other traumas, its efficacy has been proven transnationally, as was plain in a quotation made in my Introduction (Smyth and Pennebaker 1999: 75, 80, 84, 85). And in relation to other illnesses or debilitating medical

47 Bairoch, Alice, *Voyage en anorexie* (Sainte-Croix [Switzerland]: Les Presses du Belvédère, 2007).

48 Bairoch 2007: 156–57.

conditions, one study asserts, 'These results confirm the hypothesis that writing about emotionally traumatic experiences reduced symptoms in individuals with chronic illness.'[49] This study also asserts the following:

> Thus, writing may become a helpful process, quite like a therapy, even more so if the subjects of the text are traumatic experiences – which both authors explain as the motivation to write their accounts. For them, it was an attempt to cope with their traumatic experiences. As empirical research has shown, writing may have a structuring, ordering, clearing, relieving, conquering, and curative effect.[50]

The last sentence here gives some insight into quite why and how scriptotherapy may be beneficial.

One French studies scholar, Kathryn Robson, observes: 'Many narratives of anorexia explicitly figure writing, and storytelling, as part of the experience of anorexia and of recovery, including Amélie Nothomb's account of writing as a substitute for anorexia and a means of reconstituting the body in *Biographie de la faim*.'[51] But Robson also observes contrarily of Lou Delvig/Delphine de Vigan, author of *Jours sans faim* (2001), '[h]er writing does not constitute scriptotherapy (she understands that "l'écriture n'y peut rien" [writing can't do anything about it] [Delvig 55]'.[52]

So far, apart from Robson's comments on *Jours sans faim,* all appears to confirm the beneficial effects of scriptotherapy for traumatised individuals such as the eating disordered. I have been able to find only one other critic who goes against this grain.

> Thus, Swiss author, Adolf Muschg (1981), estimates that in certain cases writing about traumatic experiences even intensifies or amplifies the trauma when he states: 'Writing has not relieved my life. It only has made the rip obvious that goes through my history'. [...] The reason for that may be that during the writing process, authors remain within

49 Smyth, J.M., Stone, A.A., Hurewitz, A., and Kaell, A., 'Effects of writing about stressful experiences on symptom reduction in patients with asthma or rheumatoid arthritis', *Journal of the American Medical Association*, 281, 14 (1999]), 1304–9 (1307).

50 Stirn, A., Overbeck, G., and Pokorny, D., 'The core conflictual relationship theme (CCRT) applied to literary works: an analysis of two novels written by authors suffering from anorexia nervosa', *The International Journal of Eating Disorders*, 38, 2 (2005), 147–56 (154).

51 Robson 2016: 110.

52 Robson 2016: 112.

> themselves. There is no intervening or correcting therapist. In writing, authors spend a lot of time by themselves and with the symbolized object-relationships (the implied reader) as well as with the mute objects of the text.[53]

Given that this one counter-example of the benefits of scriptotherapy is belied by so many other researchers, I strenuously assert these benefits – and not just because of the numerical factor regarding the secondary texts; it is the primary corpus examined in this book that confirms those benefits, and that primary corpus should surely be given greater weight than the views of any researcher, since it comprises authors who have themselves experienced EDs and such benefits of scriptotherapy.

53 Muschg, A., *Literatur als Therapie? Ein Exkurs über das Heilsame und das Unheilbare* [Literature as therapy? About the healable and unhealable] (Frankfurt: Suhrkamp, 1982).

Bibliographical Appendix

Commonalities – Salient Points, Tropes, and Motifs in Different Eating Disorders Emerging from the Primary Texts, and References Thereto from the Secondary Literature (Clinical, Medically Research Based, and Critical Theory)

As its title indicates, this appendix charts (in alphabetical, not hierarchical order) salient and recurring points, tropes, and motifs in different EDs that have emerged from the 45 primary texts. These primary texts are published testimonies from French women inscribing personal experience of different EDs: anorexia nervosa, restrictor type; anorexia nervosa, purger type (or, in a nosological variant, bulimarexia); bulimia nervosa; and binge eating disorder. Despite the extremely obvious differences between these different EDs, there are also a great number of commonalities, as the sheer length of many of the lists below indicates. This chapter also supplies detailed page references to these points, tropes, and motifs as examined in the secondary literature (clinical, literary-critical, and medically research based).

Addiction: Inter Alia, to Hunger/Self-starvation/Over-exercise/Food, as Pathological Dependencies (Sometimes Paralleled with Addiction to Alcohol, Drugs, etc.)

References in Secondary Literature

Balasc, Christiane, *Désir de rien* (Paris: Aubier, 1990), pp. 10, 11

Brumberg, Joan Jacobs, *Fasting Girls: The History of Anorexia Nervosa* (Cambridge, MA/London: Harvard University Press, 1988), p. 30

Corcos, Maurice, *Le corps insoumis: psychopathologie des troubles des conduits alimentaires* (Paris: Dunod, 2011 [first published 2005]), pp. 21, 128, 230

Duker, Marilyn and Slade, Roger, *Anorexia Nervosa and Bulimia: How to Help* (Milton Keynes/Philadelphia: Open University Press, 1988), pp. 1, 22, 27

Fichter, M. M. and Pirke, K. M., 'Starvation models and eating disorders', in George Szmukler, Chris Dare, and Janet Treasure (eds), *Handbook of Eating Disorders: Theory, Treatment and Research* (Chichester/New York/Brisbane/Toronto/Singapore: John Wiley & Sons, 1995; reprinted 1996), pp. 83–107 (p. 90)

Freeman, Christopher, *Overcoming Anorexia Nervosa: A Self-Help Guide Using Cognitive Behavioral Techniques* (London: Robinson, 2009 [first published 2002]), pp. 2–3

Gordon, Richard A., *Anorexia and Bulimia: Anatomy of a Social Epidemic* (Oxford: Blackwell, 1990; second edition published 2000), pp. 158–60

Guillemot, A. and Laxenaire, M., *Anorexie mentale et boulimie. Le poids de la culture* (Paris: Masson, 1997 [second edition]), pp. 113, 114

Jeammet, Philippe, 'Vers une clinique de la dépendance. Approche psychanalytique', in R. Padieu et al. (eds), *Dépendance et conduites de consommation. Questions en santé publique* (Les Éditions Inserm, 1997), pp. 10, 33–56

Jeammet, Philippe, *Anorexie Boulimie. Les paradoxes de l'adolescence* (Paris: Hachette Littératures, 2004), pp. 10, 59, 69, 81–108, 178, 194

Szmukler, George and Tantam, Digby, 'Anorexia nervosa: Starvation dependence', *British Journal of Medical Psychology*, 57 (1984), 303–10

Venisse, J.L., 'Pertinence du concept d'addiction dans les troubles du comportement alimentaire', in Michel Reynaud (ed.), *Traité d'Addictologie* (Paris: Flammarion, 2006), pp. 650–54

Venisse, J.L., 'Editorial: Le scandale des addictions sans drogue', *Synapse*, 226 (June 2006), 2–3

Addiction to Hunger Specifically (Sometimes as Akin to Sexual *Jouissance*)

References in Secondary Literature

Kestemberg, Évelyne, Kestemberg, Jean, and Decobert, Simone, *La Faim et le Corps. Une étude psychanalytique de l'anorexie mentale* (Paris: Presses Universitaires de France, 1972), pp. 8, 95, 157, 158, 187, 188, 194, 200, 213

Meuret, Isabelle, 'L'anorexie ou l'expression d'une faim en soi', *Revue des Lettres et de Traduction*, 8 (2002), 373–80

Meuret, Isabelle, *L'anorexie créatrice* (Paris: Klincksieck, 2006), pp. 17, 18

Addiction to Food/Bingeing/Compulsive Eating/Hyperphagia Specifically (Sometimes Likened During Consumption to Sexual *Jouissance*)

References in Secondary Literature

Beitscher-Campbell, Harriet, Blum, Kenneth, Febo, Marcelo, Madigan, Margaret A., Giordano, John, Badgaiyan, Rajendra D., Braverman, Eric R., Dushaj, Kristina, Li, Mona, and Gold, Mark S., 'Pilot clinical observations between food and drug seeking derived from fifty cases attending an eating disorder clinic', *Journal of Behavioral Addictions*, 9 (August 2016), 1–9 (1, 5)

Berridge, Kent C., '"Liking" and "wanting" food rewards: Brain substrates and roles in eating disorders', *Physiology & Behavior*, 97 (2009), 537–50 (545, 547)

Boskind-Lodahl, Marlene, 'Cinderella's stepsisters: A feminist perspective on anorexia and bulimia', *Signs: Journal of Women in Culture and Society*, 2 (1976), 342–56 (351, 352)

Corcos, Maurice, Lamas, Claire, Pham-Scottez, Alexandra, and Doyen, Catherine, *L'anorexie mentale: déni et réalités* (Rueil-Malmaison: Doin, 2008), p. xi

Eichenbaum, Luise and Orbach, Susie, *Outside In... Inside Out. Women's Psychology: A Feminist Psychoanalytic Approach* (Harmondsworth: Penguin, 1982), p. 90

Guillemot, A. et Laxenaire, M., *Anorexie mentale et boulimie. Le poids de la culture* (Paris: Masson, 1997 [second edition]), pp. 113, 114

Hilker, Ines et al., 'Food addiction in bulimia nervosa: Clinical correlates and association with response to a brief psychoeducational intervention', *European Eating Disorders Review* (September 2016); DOI: 10.1002/erv.2473

Vries, Sarah Kristin de, 'Food addiction and bulimia nervosa: New data based on the Yale Food Addiction Scale 2.0', *European Eating Disorders Review* (2016); DOI: 10.1002/erv.2470

Biological/Genetic/Hereditary Factors

References in Secondary Literature

Beitscher-Campbell, Harriet, Blum, Kenneth, Febo, Marcelo, Madigan, Margaret A., Giordano, John, Badgaiyan, Rajendra D., Braverman, Eric R., Dushaj, Kristina, Li, Mona, and Gold, Mark S., 'Pilot clinical observations between food and drug seeking derived from fifty cases attending an eating disorder clinic', *Journal of Behavioral Addictions*, 9 (August 2016), 1–9 (1, 5)

Berridge, Kent C., '"Liking" and "wanting" food rewards: Brain substrates and roles in eating disorders', *Physiology & Behavior*, 97 (2009), 537–50 (545, 546, 547)

Eviatar, Zohar and Latzer, Yael, 'Hemispheric asymmetry in eating disorders', in Yael Latzer, Joav Merrick, and Daniel Stein (eds), *Understanding Eating Disorders: Integrating Culture, Psychology and Biology* (New York: Nova Science Publishers, 2011), pp. 169–80 (p. 176)

Frank, Guido K.W. and Jappe, Leah M., 'The neurobiology of eating disorders', in Yael Latzer, Joav Merrick, and Daniel Stein (eds), *Understanding Eating Disorders: Integrating Culture, Psychology and Biology* (New York: Nova Science Publishers, 2011), pp. 157–68 (157, 165, 176)

Freeman, Christopher, *Overcoming Anorexia Nervosa: A Self-Help Guide Using Cognitive Behavioral Techniques* (London: Robinson, 2009 [first published 2002]), p. 53

Halmi, Katherine, 'Current concepts and definitions', in George Szmukler, Chris Dare, and Janet Treasure (eds), *Handbook of Eating Disorders: Theory, Treatment and Research* (Chichester/New York/Brisbane/Toronto/Singapore: John Wiley & Sons, 1995; reprinted 1996), pp. 29–42 (29)

Jansen, A., 'Eating disorders need more experimental psychology', *Behaviour Research and Therapy*, 8 (2016), 2–10 (4, 6)

Jeammet, Philippe, *Anorexie Boulimie. Les paradoxes de l'adolescence* (Paris: Hachette Littératures, 2004), pp. 46, 47

Latzer, Yael, Merrick, Joav, and Stein, Daniel (eds), *Understanding Eating Disorders: Integrating Culture, Psychology and Biology* (New York: Nova Science Publishers, 2011), pp. 4–5

Lewis, B. and Nicholls, D., 'Behavioural eating disorders', *Paediatrics and Child Health*, 26, 12 (December 2016), 519–26 (519, 520, 521)

Nunn, K., Frampton, I., Gordon, I. and Lask, B., 'The fault is not in her parents but in her insula: A neurobiological hypothesis of anorexia nervosa', *European Eating Disorders Review*, 16, 5 (2008), 355–60 (passim)

Raveneau, G., Feinstein, R., Rosen, L.M., and Fisher, M., 'Attitudes and knowledge levels of nurses and residents caring for adolescents with an eating disorder', *International Journal of Adolescent Medicine and Health*, 26, 1(2014), 131–36 (135)

Treasure, Janet and Holland, Anthony, 'Genetic factors in eating disorders', in George Szmukler, Chris Dare, and Janet Treasure (eds), *Handbook of Eating Disorders: Theory, Treatment and Research* (Chichester/New York/Brisbane/ Toronto/Singapore: John Wiley & Sons, 1995; reprinted 1996), pp. 65–81

Uher, R., Murphy, T., Brammer, M.J., Dalgleish, T., Phillips, M.L., Ng, V.W., Andrew, C.M., Williams, S.C.R., Campbell, I.C., and Treasure, J., 'Medial prefrontal cortex activity associated with symptom provocation in eating disorders', *American Journal of Psychiatry*, 161 (2004), 1238–46 (1238, 1239, 1244, 1245)

Vandereycken, Walter, 'Food for thought: Gerald Russell's writings on eating disorders', in George Szmukler, Chris Dare, and Janet Treasure (eds), *Handbook of Eating Disorders: Theory, Treatment and Research* (Chichester/New York/Brisbane/Toronto/Singapore: John Wiley & Sons, 1995; reprinted 1996), pp. 403–4 (403–4)

Woolf, Emma, *An Apple a Day: A Memoir of Love and Recovery from Anorexia* (London: Summersdale, 2012), p. 235

Creativity/Creation of (New) Self in Eating-disordered Behaviour

References in Secondary Literature

Corcos, Maurice, *Le corps insoumis: psychopathologie des troubles des conduits alimentaires* (Paris: Dunod, 2011 [first published 2005]), pp. 88, 290

Darmon, Muriel, *Devenir anorexique. Une approche sociologique* (Paris: La Découverte, 2003), p. 223

Eichenbaum, Luise and Orbach, Susie, *Understanding Women* (London: Penguin, 1985) [This is a new expanded version of *Outside In… Inside Out. Women's Psychology: A Feminist Psychoanalytic Approach* (Harmondsworth: Penguin, 1982)], pp. 172, 173

Jeammet, Philippe, *Anorexie Boulimie. Les paradoxes de l'adolescence* (Paris: Hachette Littératures, 2004), p. 69

Meuret, Isabelle, *L'anorexie créatrice* (Paris: Klincksieck, 2006), passim

Meuret, Isabelle, *Writing Size Zero: Figuring Anorexia in Contemporary World Literatures* (Brussels/Belgium/New York: Peter Lang, 2007), pp. 13, 39, 64, 105

Distorted Body Image/Over-estimation of Body Size

References in Secondary Literature

Chernin, Kim, *Womansize: The Tyranny of Slenderness* (London: The Women's Press, 1983 [first published as *The Obsession: Reflections on the Tyranny of Slenderness* [New York: Harper and Row, 1981]), pp. 6, 9, 18, 62

Duker, Marilyn and Slade, Roger, *Anorexia Nervosa and Bulimia: How to Help* (Milton Keynes/Philadelphia, PA: Open University Press, 1988), p. 22

Freeman, Christopher, *Overcoming Anorexia Nervosa: A Self-Help Guide Using Cognitive Behavioral Techniques* (London: Robinson, 2009 [first published 2002]), p. 11

Grilo, Carlos M., *Eating and Weight Disorders* (Hove/New York: Psychology Press, 2006), p. 6

Halmi, Katherine, 'Current concepts and definitions', in George Szmukler, Chris Dare, and Janet Treasure (eds), *Handbook of Eating Disorders: Theory, Treatment and Research* (Chichester/New York/Brisbane/Toronto/Singapore: John Wiley & Sons, 1995; reprinted 1996), pp. 29–42 (31)

Malson, Helen, *The Thin Woman: Feminism, Post-Structuralism and the Social Psychology of Anorexia Nervosa* (London/New York: Routledge, 1998), p. 83

Orbach, Susie, *Hunger Strike: The Anorectic's Struggle as a Metaphor for our Age* (London: Penguin, 1993 [first published by Faber and Faber, 1986]), pp. 134, 135

Raimbault, Ginette and Eliacheff, Caroline, *Les indomptables. Figures de l'anorexie* (Paris: Odile Jacob, 2001 [first edition: 1989]), pp. 44, 53

Slade, Peter, 'Body image in anorexia nervosa', *British Journal of Psychiatry*, 153, 2 (1988), 20–22 (20)

Sours, John A., *Starving to Death in a Sea of Objects: The Anorexia Nervosa Syndrome* (New York/London: Jason Aronson, 1980), p. 232

Whitehouse, A.M., Freeman, C.P.L., and Annandale, A., 'Body size estimation in anorexia nervosa', *British Journal of Psychiatry*, 153, 2 (1988), 23–26 (23, 25)

Hyperactivity/Hyperintellectuality/Over-investment in School or University Studies

References in Secondary Literature

Bordo, Susan, 'Anorexia nervosa: Psychopathology as the crystallization of culture', in Irene Diamond and Lee Quinby (eds), *Feminism and Foucault: Reflections on Resistance* (Boston, MA: Northeastern University Pres, 1988), pp. 87–117 (94)

Bruch, Hilde, *The Golden Cage: The Enigma of Anorexia Nervosa* (London: Open Books Publishing Ltd, 1978), pp. 5, 12, 46

Corcos, Maurice, *Le corps insoumis: psychopathologie des troubles des conduits alimentaires* (Paris: Dunod, 2011 [first published in 2005]), p. 129

Corcos, Maurice, Lamas, Claire, Pham-Scottez, Alexandra, and Doyen, Catherine, *L'anorexie mentale: déni et réalités* (Rueil-Malmaison: Doin, 2008), p. xi

Darmon, Muriel, *Devenir anorexique. Une approche sociologique* (Paris: La Découverte, 2003), p. 198

Duker, Marilyn and Slade, Roger, *Anorexia Nervosa and Bulimia: How to Help* (Milton Keynes/Philadelphia, PA: Open University Press, 1988), p. 27

Fichter, M.M. and Pirke, K.M., 'Starvation models and eating disorders', in George Szmukler, Chris Dare, and Janet Treasure (eds), *Handbook of Eating Disorders. Theory, Treatment and Research* (Chichester/New York/Brisbane/Toronto/Singapore: John Wiley & Sons, 1995; reprinted 1996), pp. 83–107 (p. 90)

Jeammet, Philippe, *Anorexie Boulimie. Les paradoxes de l'adolescence* (Paris: Hachette Littératures, 2004), pp. 14, 15, 25, 59, 103

Kestemberg, Évelyne, Kestemberg, Jean and Decobert, Simone, *La Faim et le Corps. Une étude psychanalytique de l'anorexie mentale* (Paris: Presses Universitaires de France, 1972), p. 96

Orbach, Susie, *Fat is a Feminist Issue… How to Lose Weight Permanently – Without Dieting* (London: Arrow, 1988 [first published London: Paddington Press, 1978]), p. 181

Palazzoli, Mara Selvini, *Self-Starvation: From Individual to Family Therapy in the Treatment of Anorexia Nervosa* (New York/London: Jason Aronson, 1978 [first published in English translation from the Italian original: London: Human Context Books, Chaucer Publishing Co. Ltd, 1974]), pp. 127, 153

Sours, John A., *Starving to Death in a Sea of Objects: The Anorexia Nervosa Syndrome* (New York/London: Jason Aronson, 1980), p. 274

Language: EDs as a Form of Language

References in Secondary Literature

Balasc, Christiane, *Désir de rien* (Paris: Aubier, 1990), p. 9

Clerc, Isabelle, *Valérie Valère: un seul regard m'aurait suffi* (Paris: Perrin, 1987), p. 54

Corcos, Maurice, *Le corps insoumis: psychopathologie des troubles des conduits alimentaires* (Paris: Dunod, 2011 [first published 2005]), p. 290

Guillemot, A. et Laxenaire, M., *Anorexie mentale et boulimie. Le poids de la culture* (Paris: Masson, 1997 [second edition]), p. 129

McEachern, Patricia A., *Deprivation and Power: The Emergence of Anorexia Nervosa in Nineteenth-Century France* (Westport, CT/London: Greenwood Press, 1998), p. 5

McEachern, Patricia A., *Deprivation and Power: The Emergence of Anorexia Nervosa in Nineteenth-Century France* (Westport, CT/London: Greenwood Press, 1998), p. 175

Merleau-Ponty, Maurice, *Phénoménologie de la perception* (Paris: Gallimard, 1945), p. 191

Meuret, Isabelle, 'L'anorexie ou l'expression d'une faim en soi', *Revue des Lettres et de Traduction*, 8 (2002), 373–80 (274, 375, 376, 377, 380)

Meuret, Isabelle, *L'anorexie créatrice* (Paris: Klincksieck, 2006), p. 115

Meuret, Isabelle, *Writing Size Zero: Figuring Anorexia in Contemporary World Literatures* (Brussels/Belgium/New York: Peter Lang, 2007), pp. 13, 54

Orbach, Susie, *Hunger Strike: The Anorectic's Struggle as a Metaphor for our Age* (London: Penguin, 1993 [first published by Faber and Faber, 1986]), pp. xviii, xxii, 3, 4, 44, 48, 83

Orbach, Susie, *Fat is a Feminist Issue… How to Lose Weight Permanently – Without Dieting* (London: Arrow, 1988 [first published London: Paddington Press, 1978]), pp. 23–24

Raimbault, Ginette and Eliacheff, Caroline, *Les indomptables. Figures de l'anorexie* (Paris: Odile Jacob, 2001 [first edition: 1989]), p. 268

Vice, Sue, 'The well-rounded anorexic text', in Tim Armstrong (ed.), *American Bodies: Cultural Histories of the Physique* (New York: New York University Press, 1996), pp. 196–203 (197, 196, 199, 200, 201)

Metaphor – Particularly Conceptual/Cognitive Metaphor, to Express Embodied Distress

References in Secondary Literature

Chernin, Kim, *The Hungry Self: Women, Eating, and Identity* (London: Virago Press, 1986), p. 115

Duker, Marilyn and Slade, Roger, *Anorexia Nervosa and Bulimia: How to Help* (Milton Keynes/Philadelphia, PA: Open University Press, 1988), p. 22

Geary, James, *I Is an Other: The Secret Life of Metaphor and How it Shapes the Way We See the World* (New York: HarperCollins, 2011), p. 93

Senkbeil, Karsten and Hoppe, Nicola, '"The sickness stands at your shoulder…": Embodiment and cognitive metaphor in Hornbacher's *Wasted: A Memoir of Anorexia and Bulimia*', *Language and Literature*, 25, 1 (2016), 3–17 (passim)

Warin, Megan, *Abject Relations: Everyday Worlds of Anorexia* (New Brunswick/New Jersey/London: Rutgers University Press, 2010), pp. 143, 174

Mind–Body Split/Mind–Body Dualism

References in Secondary Literature

Bordo, Susan, *Unbearable Weight: Feminism, Western Culture and the Body* (Berkeley, CA/Los Angeles, CA: California University Press, 1993)

Boskind-Lodahl, Marlene, 'Cinderalla's stepsisters: A feminist perspective on anorexia and bulimia', *Signs: Journal of Women in Culture and Society*, 2 (1976), p. 352

Bray, Abigail and Colebrook, Claire, 'The haunted flesh: Corporeal feminism and the politics of (dis)embodiment', *Signs: Journal of Women in Culture and Society*, 24, 1 (1998), 35–67, p. 52

Bruch, Hilde, *The Golden Cage: The Enigma of Anorexia Nervosa* (London: Open Books Publishing Ltd, 1978), pp. 5, 55

Cameron, Elspeth, 'Famininity, or parody of autonomy: Anorexia and *The Edible Woman*', *Journal of Canadian Studies/Revue d'Études canadiennes*, 20, 2 (summer 1985), 45–69 (58)

Chernin, Kim, *Womansize: The Tyranny of Slenderness* (London: The Women's Press, 1983 [first published as *The Obsession: Reflections on the Tyranny of Slenderness* [New York: Harper and Row, 1981]), pp. 2, 47, 57, 62, 63, 151

Clerc, Isabelle, *Valérie Valère: un seul regard m'aurait suffi* (Paris: Perrin, 1987), pp. 34, 163

Corcos, Maurice, *Le corps insoumis: psychopathologie des troubles des conduits alimentaires* (Paris: Dunod, 2011 [first published 2005]), p. 285

Garfinkel, Paul E. and Garner, David M., *Anorexia Nervosa: A Multidimensional Perspective* (New York: Brummer/Mazel, 1982), p. 289

Havercroft, Barbara, 'Paper thin: Agency and anorexia in Geneviève Brisac's Petite', in Valerie Raoul et al. (eds), *Unfitting Stories: Narrative Approaches to Disease, Disability, and Trauma* (Waterloo, ON: Wilfred Laurier University Press, 2007), pp. 61–69 (p. 61)

Jackson, Laura, 'Purging the self: Transcribing the divided, anorexic subject in Geneviève Brisac's Petite and Camille de Peretti's Thornytorinx', in Adrienne Angelo and Erika Fülöp (eds), *Protean Selves: First-Person Voices in Twenty-First-Century French and Francophone Narratives* (Newcastle: Cambridge Scholars Publishing, 2014), pp. 166–79 (166, 168, 172)

Kristeva, Julia, *Powers of Horror: An Essay on Abjection* (New York: Columbia University Press, 1982), p. 75

Malson, Helen, *The Thin Woman: Feminism, Post-Structuralism and the Social Psychology of Anorexia Nervosa* (London/New York: Routledge, 1998), p. 141

Orbach, Susie, *Hunger Strike: The Anorectic's Struggle as a Metaphor for our Age* (London: Penguin, 1993 [first published by Faber and Faber, 1986]), pp. 28, 132, 133

Palazzoli, Mara Selvini, *Self-Starvation: From Individual to Family Therapy in the Treatment of Anorexia Nervosa* (New York/London: Jason Aronson, 1978 [first published in English translation from the Italian original: London: Human Context Books, Chaucer Publishing Co. Ltd, 1974]), pp. 72, 74, 81, 86, 87, 92, 143, 148, 150, 151, 233

Root, M.P.P. and Fallon, P., 'The incidence of victimisation experiences in a bulimic sample', *Journal of Interpersonal Violence,* 3 (1988), 161–63 (162)

Senkbeil, Karsten and Hoppe, Nicola, '"The sickness stands at your shoulder...": Embodiment and cognitive metaphor in Hornbacher's *Wasted: A Memoir of Anorexia and Bulimia*', *Language and Literature*, 25, 1 (2016), 3–17 (8, 10, 11)

Smolak, Linda, Levine, Michael P., and Striegel-Moore, Ruth, *The Developmental Psychopathology of Eating Disorders* (Mahwah, NJ: Lawrence Erlbaum Associate, Publishers, 1996), p. 124

Warin, Megan, *Abject Relations: Everyday Worlds of Anorexia* (New Brunswick/ New Jersey/London: Rutgers University Press, 2010), pp. 58, 73, 76, 77

Witzum, Eliezer, Latzer, Yael, and Stein, Daniel, 'A historical background to current formulations of eating disorders', in Yael Latzer, Joav Merrick, and Daniel Stein (eds), *Understanding Eating Disorders: Integrating Culture, Psychology and Biology* (New York: Nova Science Publishers, 2011), p. 62

Mother–Daughter Relationship: Fusion/'Enmeshment'

References in Secondary Literature

Bachar, Eytan and Samet, Yekutiel, 'Self psychology in the treatment of anorexia nervosa and bulimia nervosa', in Yael Latzer, Joav Merrick, and Daniel Stein (eds), *Understanding Eating Disorders: Integrating Culture, Psychology and Biology* (New York: Nova Science Publishers, 2011), pp. 181–95 (pp. 186, 187)

Balasc, Christiane, *Désir de rien* (Paris: Aubier, 1990), p. 94

Barcai, A., 'Family therapy in the treatment of anorexia nervosa', *Amer. J. of Psychiat.*, 128 (1971), 286

Birksted-Breen, Dana, 'Working with an anorexic patient', *The International Journal of Psychoanalysis*, 70 (1989), 30–40 (30, 38)

Blitzer, R., Rollins, N., and Blackwell, A., 'Children who starve themselves: Anorexia nervosa', *Psychosom. Med.*, 23 (1961), 368–83

Boskind-Lodahl, Marlene, 'Cinderella's stepsisters: A feminist perspective on anorexia and bulimia', *Signs: Journal of Women in Culture and Society*, 2 (1976), 347–48

Bruch, Hilde, 'Conceptual confusion in eating disorders', *J. Nerv. Ment. Dis.*, 133 (1961), 46

Bruch, Hilde, 'Perceptual and conceptual disturbances in anorexia nervosa', *Psychosom. Med.*, 24 (1962), 187–94

Bruch, Hilde, 'Hunger and instinct', *J. Nerv. Ment. Dis.*, 149 (1969), 91

Bruch, Hilde, 'Children who starve themselves', *The New York Times Magazine* (10 November 1974), p. 70

Bruch, Hilde, *The Golden Cage: The Enigma of Anorexia Nervosa* (Cambridge, MA: Harvard University Press, 1978), pp. 12, 25, 26, 27, 29, 40, 41, 67, 69

Brumberg, Joan Jacobs, *Fasting Girls: The History of Anorexia Nervosa* (Cambridge, MA/London: Harvard University Press, 1988), p. 29

Cameron, Elspeth, 'Famininity, or parody of autonomy: Anorexia and *The Edible Woman*', *Journal of Canadian Studies/Revue d'Études canadiennes*, 20, 2 (summer 1985), 45–69

Chernin, Kim, *Womansize: The Tyranny of Slenderness* (London: The Women's Press, 1983 [first published as *The Obsession: Reflections on the Tyranny of Slenderness* [New York: Harper and Row, 1981]), pp. 102, 103, 107, 133, 134, 143, 147, 148, 151, 152, 153, 167

Chernin, Kim, *The Hungry Self: Women, Eating, and Identity* (London: Virago Press, 1986) [Copyright Kim Chernin 1985], pp. 37, 42, 43, 56, 57, 60, 66, 77, 93, 95, 99, 117, 118, 119, 120, 124, 125, 130, 136, 137, 155, 201

Clerc, Isabelle, *Valérie Valère: un seul regard m'aurait suffi* (Paris: Perrin, 1987), pp. 26, 27, 31, 68, 98, 125

Colahan, Mireille and Senior, Rob, 'Family patterns in eating disorders: Going round in circles, getting nowhere fast', in George Szmukler, Chris Dare, and Janet Treasure (eds), *Handbook of Eating Disorders: Theory, Treatment and Research* (Chichester/New York/Brisbane/Toronto/ Singapore: John Wiley & Sons, 1995; reprinted 1996), pp. 243–57 (246, 247)

Corcos, Maurice, *Le corps insoumis: psychopathologie des troubles des conduits alimentaires* (Paris: Dunod, 2011 [first published 2005]), pp. ix, x, 21, 61

Dally, P. and Gomez, J., *Anorexia Nervosa* (n.p.: William Heinemann Medical Books, Ltd., 1979), chapter 4

Eichenbaum, Luise and Orbach, Susie, *Understanding Women* (London: Penguin, 1985) [NB This is a new expanded version of *Outside In... Inside Out. Women's Psychology: A Feminist Psychoanalytic Approach* (Harmondsworth: Penguin, 1982)], p. 173

Eisler, Ivan, 'Family models of eating disorders', in George Szmukler, Chris Dare, Chris and Janet Treasure (eds), *Handbook of Eating Disorders: Theory, Treatment and Research* (Chichester/New York/Brisbane/ Toronto/Singapore: John Wiley & Sons, 1995; reprinted 1996), pp. 155–76 (159)

Gordon, Richard A., *Anorexia and Bulimia: Anatomy of a Social Epidemic* (Oxford: Blackwell, 1990; second edition published 2000), p. 109

Hepworth, Julie *The Social Construction of Anorexia Nervosa* (London/ Thousand Oaks, CA/Delhi: Sage, 1999), p. 55

Jeammet, Philippe, *Anorexie Boulimie. Les paradoxes de l'adolescence* (Paris: Hachette Littératures, 2004), pp. 128, 129, 200, 201, 207

Kestemberg, Évelyne, Kestemberg, Jean, and Decobert, Simone, *La Faim et le Corps. Une étude psychanalytique de l'anorexie mentale* (Paris: Presses Universitaires de France, 1972), pp. 8, 32, 33, 38, 131

King, A., 'Primary and secondary anorexia nervosa syndromes', *Brit. J. Psychiat.*, 109 (1963), 471, 472, 475, 476

Lawrence, Marilyn, *The Anorexic Mind* (London: Karnac, 2008), pp. 56, 88–91

Leclaire, Serge, 'L'obsessionnel et son désir', *Évolution psychiatrique*, 3 (1959), 383–411 (387, 388)

MacSween, Morag, *Anorexic Bodies: A Feminist and Sociological Perspective on Anorexia Nervosa* (London/New York: Routledge, 1993), pp. 39, 55–59, 61, 63, 76–78, 80, 82, 84–86, 197–98

Meyer, C. and Weinroth, L.A., 'Observations on psychological aspects of anorexia nervosa', *Psychosom. Med.*, 19 (1957), 395

Meuret, Isabelle, *L'anorexie créatrice* (Paris: Klincksieck, 2006), pp. 17, 24, 35, 137, 139, 154

Meuret, Isabelle, *Writing Size Zero: Figuring Anorexia in Contemporary World Literatures* (Brussels/Belgium/New York: Peter Lang, 2007), pp. 107, 182, 183

Nemiah, C., 'Anorexia nervosa, fact and theory', *Amer. J. Dig. Dis.*, 3 (1958), 249, quoted in V. Taipale, O. Tuomi, and M. Aukee, 'Anorexia nervosa: An illness of two generations?', *Acta Paedopsychiat.*, 38 (1971), 21

Orbach, Susie, *Fat is a Feminist Issue... How to Lose Weight Permanently – Without Dieting* (London: Arrow, 1988) [first published London: Paddington Press, 1978], pp. 36, 40, 41, 42, 43,180

Orbach, Susie, *Hunger Strike: The Anorectic's Struggle as a Metaphor for our Age* (London: Penguin, 1993 [first published by Faber and Faber, 1986]), pp. 23, 27, 59, 61, 62, 63, 141, 142, 141, 142

Palazzoli, Mara Selvini, 'The families of patients with anorexia nervosa', in J. Anthony and C. Koupernik (eds), *The Child in His Family* (New York: Wiley, 1970), pp. 323–27

Palazzoli, Mara Selvini, *Self-Starvation: From Individual to Family Therapy in the Treatment of Anorexia Nervosa* (New York/London: Jason Aronson, 1978 [first published in English translation from the Italian original: London: Human Context Books, Chaucer Publishing Co. Ltd, 1974]), pp. 39, 40, 63, 68, 77, 87, 88)

Raimbault, Ginette and Eliacheff, Caroline, *Les indomptables. Figures de l'anorexie* (Paris: Odile Jacob, 2001 [first edition: 1989]), p. 43

Sayers, Janet, 'Anorexia, psychoanalysis, and feminism: Fantasy and reality', *Journal of Adolescence*, 11 (1988), 361–71

Sceats, Sarah, *Food, Consumption and the Body in Contemporary Women's Fiction* (Cambridge: Cambridge University Press, 2000), p. 64

Sours, John A., *Starving to Death in a Sea of Objects: The Anorexia Nervosa Syndrome* (New York/London: Jason Aronson, 1980), pp. 6, 7, 223, 323, 325, 375

Spignesi, Angelyn, *Starving Women: A Psychology of Anorexia* (Dallas, TX: Spring Publications, 1983), pp. 24, 39, 40, 41, 42, 43, 44, 45, 46, 49, 51

Taipale, V., Tuomi, O., and Aukee, M., 'Anorexia nervosa: An illness of two generations?', *Acta Paedopsychiat.*, 38 (1971), 24

Thoma, H., *Anorexia Nervosa* (New York: International Universities Press, 1967), p. 261

Purity/Transcendence of the Flesh/Transcendence of the Need for Food That Sustains that Flesh

References in Secondary Literature

Bordo, Susan, 'Anorexia nervosa: Psychopathology as the crystallization of culture', in Irene Diamond and Lee Quinby (eds), *Feminism and Foucault: Reflections on Resistance* (Boston, MA: Northeastern University Press, 1988), pp. 87–117 (94) [An earlier version of this essay was published in the *Philosophical Forum*, 17, 2 (Winter 1985–86), 73–104]

Boskind-White, Marlene and White, William C., *Bulimia/Anorexia: The Binge/Purge Cycle and Self-Starvation* (New York/London: W.W. Norton & Company, 2000) [First edition 1983, second edition 1987]

Bruch, Hilde, *The Golden Cage: The Enigma of Anorexia Nervosa* (London: Open Books Publishing Ltd, 1978), p. 15

Clerc, Isabelle, *Valérie Valère: un seul regard m'aurait suffi* (Paris: Perrin, 1987), p. 37

Jeammet, Philippe, *Anorexie Boulimie. Les paradoxes de l'adolescence* (Paris: Hachette Littératures, 2004), pp. 16, 52

Kristeva, Julia, *Powers of Horror: An Essay on Abjection* (New York: Columbia University Press, 1982), p. 75

Orbach, Susie, *Hunger Strike: The Anorectic's Struggle as a Metaphor for our Age* (London: Penguin, 1993 [first published by Faber and Faber, 1986]), p. 84

Raimbault, Ginette and Eliacheff, Caroline, *Les indomptables. Figures de l'anorexie* (Paris: Odile Jacob, 2001 [first edition: 1989]), p. 267

Warin, Megan, *Abject Relations: Everyday Worlds of Anorexia* (New Brunswick/New Jersey/London: Rutgers University Press, 2010), pp. 1, 2, 11, 12, 76, 81, 94, 116, 129, 131, 132, 134, 171, 172, 176, 186

(Self-)Surveillance: Foucauldian Analyses

References in Secondary Literature

Bordo, Susan, *Unbearable Weight: Feminism, Western Culture and the Body* (Berkeley, CA/Los Angeles, CA: California University Press, 1993), p. 27

Darmon, Muriel, *Devenir anorexique. Une approche sociologique* (Paris: La Découverte, 2003), p. 341

Malson, Helen M. and Ussher, Jane M., 'Beyond this mortal coil: Femininity, death and discursive constructions of the anorexic body', *Mortality*, 2, 1 (1997), 43–61 (49, 51)

White, Michael, 'Deconstruction and therapy', *Dulwich Centre Newsletter*, Part 3 (1991), 21–40

Sexual and/or Self-abuse: History of or Present Engagement with Eating-disordered Individuals (Particularly Bulimics)

References in Secondary Literature

Bordo, Susan, *Unbearable Weight: Feminism, Western Culture and the Body* (Berkeley, CA/Los Angeles, CA: California University Press, 1993), p. 179

Bulik, C.M., Sullivan, P.F., and Rorty, R., 'Childhood sexual abuse in women with bulimia', *Journal of Clinical Psychiatry*, 50 (1989), 460–551 (passim, but particularly 460)

Cachelin, Fary, Schug, Robert, Juarez, Laura, and Monreal, Teresa, 'Sexual abuse and eating disorders in a community sample of Mexican American women', *Hispanic Journal of Behavioral Sciences*, 27, 4 (2005), 533–46 (passim, but see particularly 535)

Connors, M.E., 'Developmental vulnerabilities for eating disorders', in L. Smolak, M. Levine, and R. Streigel-Moore (eds), *The Developmental Psychopathology of Eating Disorders: Implications for Research, Prevention and Treatment* (Mahwah, NJ: Lawrence Erlbaum Associates, 1996), pp. 285–310 (297, 300, 301)

Connors, M.E. and Morse, W., 'Sexual abuse and eating disorders: A review', *International Journal of Eating Disorders*, 13, 1 (1993), 1–11 (1, 2, 3, 4, 8, 9)

Corcos, Maurice, *Le corps insoumis: psychopathologie des troubles des conduits alimentaires* (Paris: Dunod, 2011 [first published 2005]), pp. xi, 91, 149, 150

Duker, Marilyn and Slade, Roger, *Anorexia Nervosa and Bulimia: How to Help* (Milton Keynes/Philadelphia, PA: Open University Press, 1988), pp. 46, 47

Eisler, Ivan, 'Family models of eating disorders', in George Szmukler, Chris Dare, and Janet Treasure (eds), *Handbook of Eating Disorders: Theory, Treatment and Research* (Chichester/New York/Brisbane/Toronto/Singapore: John Wiley & Sons, 1995; reprinted 1996), pp. 155–76 (p. 158)

Fallon, Patricia, Katzman, Melanie A., and Wooley, Susan C. (eds), *Feminist Perspectives on Eating Disorders* (New York/London: The Guildford Press, 1994), pp. 177, 179, 181, 182, 185, 186, 187, 443

Freeman, Christopher, *Overcoming Anorexia Nervosa: A Self-Help Guide Using Cognitive Behavioral Techniques* (London: Robinson, 2009 [first published 2002]), pp. 84–85

Gordon, Richard A., *Anorexia and Bulimia: Anatomy of a Social Epidemic* (Oxford: Blackwell, 1990; second edition published 2000), pp. 103–4

Jeammet, Philippe, *Anorexie Boulimie. Les paradoxes de l'adolescence* (Paris: Hachette Littératures, 2004), pp. 23, 53, 54, 75, 76, 77, 79

Lawrence, Marilyn, *The Anorexic Mind* (London: Karnac, 2008), p. 76

Luna, Elizabeth, *Palabra y Praxis: Creative Writing, Personal Narrative, Spoken Word and the Art of Healing* (a Master of Arts thesis submitted at California State University, 2016), pp. 152, 153, 154

Malson, Helen, *The Thin Woman: Feminism, Post-Structuralism and the Social Psychology of Anorexia Nervosa* (London/New York: Routledge, 1998), p. 84

Paul, Thomas, Schroeter, Kirsten, Dahme, Bernhard, and Nutzinger, Detlev O., 'Self-injurious behaviour in women with eating disorders', *American Journal of Psychiatry*, 159, 3 (March 2002), 408–11 (408, 409, 411)

Root, M.P.P. and Fallon, P., 'The incidence of victimisation experiences in a bulimic sample', *Journal of Interpersonal Violence*, 3 (1988), 161–63

Warin, Megan, *Abject Relations: Everyday Worlds of Anorexia* (New Brunswick/New Jersey/London: Rutgers University Press, 2010), pp. 139, 140, 141, 142, 143, 174, 175

Sociocultural Factors: Their Role in the Development of EDs

References in Secondary Literature

Allen, Jodie, 'The spectacularization of the anorexic subject position', *Current Sociology*, 56, 4 (2008), 587–603 (passim)

Barlow, D.H. and Durand, V.M., *Abnormal Psychology: An Integrative Approach*, 2nd edition (Boston: Brooks/Cole, 1999), p. 237

Bray, Abigail and Colebrook, Claire, 'The haunted flesh: Corporeal feminism and the politics of (dis)embodiment', *Signs: Journal of Women in Culture and Society*, 24, 1 (1998), 35–67. See p. 35.

Chernin, Kim, *Womansize: The Tyranny of Slenderness* (London: The Women's Press, 1983 [first published as *The Obsession: Reflections on the Tyranny of Slenderness* [New York: Harper and Row, 1981]), pp. 2, 8, 19, 22, 32, 33, 45, 61, 62, 88, 93, 94, 96, 98, 108, 109, 110, 115, 116, 117, 119, 120, 124, 125, 131, 132, 147, 148, 154, 155

Chernin, Kim, *The Hungry Self: Women, Eating, and Identity* (London: Virago Press, 1986), pp. 17, 19, 25, 36, 103, 104, 125, 186, 188, 201

Godin, Laurence, 'Saisir l'anorexie par le corps: de la subjectivité anorexique à la diversité des experiences', *Recherches féministes*, 27, 31–47 (passim).

Gordon, Richard A., *Anorexia and Bulimia: Anatomy of a Social Epidemic* (Oxford: Blackwell, 1990; second edition published 2000), p. vi

Guillemot, A. et Laxenaire, M., *Anorexie mentale et boulimie. Le poids de la culture* (Paris: Masson, 1997[second edition]) pp. 70, 77, 85, 96, 97, 98, 128, 129

Malson, Helen and Ussher, Jane, 'Body poly-texts: Discourses of the anorexic body', *Journal of Community and Applied Social Psychology*, 6 (1996), 267–80 (passim)

Orbach, Susie, *Fat is a Feminist Issue… How to Lose Weight Permanently – Without Dieting* (London: Arrow, 1988 [first published London: Paddington Press, 1978]), pp. 17, 183, 184

Orbach, Susie, *Hunger Strike: The Anorectic's Struggle as a Metaphor for our Age* (London: Penguin, 1993 [first published by Faber and Faber, 1986]), pp. xiii, xvii, xviii, 9, 10, 28, 85, 133.

Raimbault, Ginette and Eliacheff, Caroline, *Les indomptables. Figures de l'anorexie* (Paris: Odile Jacob, 2001 [first edition: 1989]), pp. 53, 55, 57

Robertson, Matra, *Starving in the Silences: An Exploration of Anorexia* (Sydney: Allen and Unwin, 1992), p. 52

Schmidt, Ulrike, Tiller, Jane, and Morgan, H. Gethin, 'The social consequences of eating disorders', in George Szmukler, Chris Dare, and Janet Treasure (eds), *Handbook of Eating Disorders: Theory, Treatment and Research* (Chichester/New York/Brisbane/Toronto/Singapore: John Wiley & Sons, 1995; reprinted 1996), pp. 259–70 (p. 261)

Sours, John A., *Starving to Death in a Sea of Objects: The Anorexia Nervosa Syndrome* (New York/London: Jason Aronson, 1980), pp. xiv, 322

Szmukler, G. I. and Patton, G., 'Sociocultural models of eating disorders', in George Szmukler, Chris Dare, and Janet Treasure (eds), *Handbook of Eating Disorders. Theory, Treatment and Research* (Chichester/New York/Brisbane/Toronto/Singapore: John Wiley & Sons, 1995; reprinted 1996), pp. 177–92 (p. 178)

Spatiality

References in Secondary Literature

Birksted-Breen, Dana, 'Working with an anorexic patient', *The International Journal of Psychoanalysis*, 70 (1989), 29–40 (30)

Cairns, Lucille, 'Bodily dis-ease in contemporary French women's writing: Two case studies', *French Studies*, 69, 4 (October 2015), 494–508 (499, 500, 508)

Corcos, Maurice, *Le Corps insoumis* (Paris: Dunod, 2011 [first published in 2005]), p. 21

Malson, Helen, *The Thin Woman: Feminism, Post-Structuralism and the Social Psychology of Anorexia Nervosa* (London/New York: Routledge, 1998), 114

Warin, Megan, *Abject Relations: Everyday Worlds of Anorexia* (New Brunswick/New Jersey/London: Rutgers University Press, 2010), pp. 5, 8, 9, 48

'Vide', Physical and Metaphysical

References in Secondary Literature

Balasc, Christiane, *Désir de rien: de l'anorexie à la boulimie* (Paris: Aubier, 1990), p. 56

Bruch, Hilde, *The Golden Cage: The Enigma of Anorexia Nervosa* (London: Open Books Publishing Ltd, 1978), p. 144

Chernin, Kim, *Womansize: The Tyranny of Slenderness* (London: The Women's Press, 1983 [first published as *The Obsession: Reflections on the Tyranny of Slenderness* [New York: Harper and Row, 1981]), pp. 188, 189

Chernin, Kim, *The Hungry Self: Women, Eating, and Identity* (London: Virago Press, 1986), pp. 16, 20, 155

Clerc, Isabelle, *Valérie Valère: un seul regard m'aurait suffi* (Paris: Perrin, 1987), pp. 68, 69, 149

Duker, Marilyn and Slade, Roger, *Anorexia Nervosa and Bulimia: How to Help* (Milton Keynes/Philadelphia, PA: Open University Press, 1988), pp. 114, 203

Geist, R., 'Self psychological reflections on the origins of eating disorders', *The Journal of the American Academy of Psychoanalysis*, 17, 1 (1989), 5–27 (10, 11, 13, 14, 15, 16, 21, 35)

Guillemot, A. et Laxenaire, M., *Anorexie mentale et boulimie. Le poids de la culture* (Paris: Masson, 1997 [second edition]) (passim)

Jeammet, Philippe, *Anorexie Boulimie. Les paradoxes de l'adolescence* (Paris: Hachette Littératures, 2004), pp. 75, 102, 128, 139, 141

Orbach, Susie, *Hunger Strike: The Anorectic's Struggle as a Metaphor for our Age* (London: Penguin, 1993 [first published by Faber and Faber, 1986]), pp. 86, 88, 89, 93

Palazzoli, Mara Selvini, *Self-Starvation: From Individual to Family Therapy in the Treatment of Anorexia Nervosa* (New York/London: Jason Aronson, 1978 [first published in English translation from the Italian original: London: Human Context Books, Chaucer Publishing Co. Ltd, 1974]), pp. 87, 153

Raimbault, Ginette and Eliacheff, Caroline, *Les indomptables. Figures de l'anorexie* (Paris: Odile Jacob, 2001 [first edition: 1989]), p. 9

Spignesi, Angelyn, *Starving Women: A Psychology of Anorexia* (Dallas, TX: Spring Publications, 1983), p. 35

Warin, Megan, *Abject Relations: Everyday Worlds of Anorexia* (New Brunswick/New Jersey/London: Rutgers University Press, 2010), pp. 129, 132, 139, 172

Writing as Therapeutic for, Creative for, or Creative of, the Eating-disordered Subject (Linked Tangentially to this, Devouring of Books and Words rather than of Food by a Number of the Anorexic Subjects in the Primary Texts)

References in Secondary Literature

Clerc, Isabelle, *Valérie Valère: un seul regard m'aurait suffi* (Paris: Perrin, 1987), pp. 7, 38, 114, 115, 136, 149

Henke, Suzettte A., *Shattered Subjects: Trauma and Testimony in Women's Life-Writing* (London: Macmillan, 1998), p. xii

Jackson, Laura, 'Purging the self: Transcribing the divided, anorexic subject in Geneviève Brisac's Petite and Camille de Peretti's Thornytorinx', in Adrienne Angelo and Erika Fülöp (eds), *Protean Selves: First-Person Voices in Twenty-First-Century French and Francophone Narratives* (Newcastle: Cambridge Scholars Publishing, 2014), pp. 166–79 (166, 167, 177)

Jurga, Antoine and Planche, Jean-Christophe, *Ecritures autobiographiques* (Calais: CRDP du Nord, 1997), pp. 71–72

Luna, Elizabeth, *Palabra y Praxis: Creative Writing, Personal Narrative, Spoken Word and the Art of Healing* (Master of Arts thesis, California State University, 2016), pp. 4–5

Malson, Helen, *The Thin Woman: Feminism, Post-Structuralism and the Social Psychology of Anorexia Nervosa* (London/New York: Routledge, 1998), p. 159

Meuret, Isabelle, 'L'anorexie ou l'expression d'une faim en soi', *Revue des Lettres et de Traduction*, 8 (2002), 373–80 (375)

Meuret, Isabelle, *L'anorexie créatrice* (Paris: Klincksieck, 2006), pp. 24, 25, 28, 115, 138, 145, 158, 182, 186, 187, 188

Meuret, Isabelle, *Writing Size Zero: Figuring Anorexia in Contemporary World Literatures* (Brussels/Belgium/New York: Peter Lang, 2007), pp. 13, 98, 151, 265

Meuret, Isabelle, 'L'Anorexie: Entre aliénation 'mentale' et revendication d'altérité: Le Cas des écrivaines algériennes', *International Journal of Francophone Studies*, 12, 1 (2009), 19–35 (30)

Olson, Greta, *Reading Eating Disorders: Writings on Bulimia and Anorexia as Confessions of American Culture* (Frankfurt am Main: Peter Lang, 2003), pp. 122, 123, 144

Robson, Kathryn, 'Voicing abjection: Narratives of anorexia in contemporary French women's (life)writing', *L'Esprit Createur*, 56, 2 (Summer 2016), 108–20 (110)

Smyth, J.M. and Pennebaker, J.W., 'Sharing one's story: Translating emotional experiences into words as a coping tool', in C.R. Snyder (ed.), *Coping: The Psychology of What Works* (New York/Oxford: Oxford University Press, 1999), pp. 70–89 (pp. 75, 80, 84, 85)

Vice, Sue, 'The well-rounded anorexic text', in Tim Armstrong (ed.), *American Bodies: Cultural Histories of the Physique* (New York: New York University Press, 1996), pp. 196–203 (pp. 197, 196, 199, 200, 201)

Vitiello, Joëlle, 'Le double meurtier chez Sabrina Kherbich', in Frédérique Chevillot and Colette Trout (eds), *Rebelles et criminelles chez les écrivaines d'expression française* (Amsterdam: Rodopi, 2013), pp. 129–45

Weinberger-Litman, Sarah, Latzer, Yael, and Stein, Daniel, 'A historical, cultural and empirical look at eating disorders and religiosity among Jewish women', in Yael Latzer, Joav Merrick, and Daniel Stein (eds), *Understanding Eating Disorders: Integrating Culture, Psychology and Biology* (New York: Nova Science Publishers, 2011), pp. 109–22 (p. 110)

Bibliography

Primary Texts

Liliane Atlan, *Les Passants* (Paris: Payot, 1989)

Othilie Bailly, *L'Enfant qui se laissait mourir* (Paris: le Grand livre du mois, 1992)

Marta Aleksandra Balinska, *Retour à la vie: quinze ans d'anorexie* (Paris: Odile Jacob, 2003)

Emmanuelle Bayamack-Tam, *Une fille du feu* (Paris: P.O.L., 2008)

Karin Bernfeld, *Alice au pays des femelles* (Paris: Balland, 2001)

Karin Bernfeld, *Apologie de la passivité* (Paris: J.-C. Lattès, 1999)

Karin Bernfeld, *Les Portes de l'espérance* (Paris: Flammarion, 2003)

Marie Bertin, *Journal sans faim* (Paris: Rageot, 2000)

Alice Blot, *Témoignage d'une anorexique ou Une vie à la dérive* (Paris: Editic, 1994)

Audrey Bohan, *Ma vie… Ma boulimie. La souffrance, le silence, la honte… puis le chemin vers soi, le chemin du bien-être* (Paris: Lulu.com, 2013)

Geneviève Brisac, *Petite* (Paris: Éd. de l'olivier, 1994)

Dominique Buffet, *Nestor, la bouffe et moi* (Monaco: Éditions du Rocher, 2016)

Anne Calife, *Meurs la faim* (The Menthol House, 2010 [previously published under the name of Anne Colmerauer, *Meurs la faim* (Paris: Gallimard, 1999)])

Isabelle Caro, *La petite fille qui ne voulait pas grossir* (Paris: Flammarion, 2008)

Noëlle Châtelet, 'La belle et sa bête', *Histoires de bouches* (Paris: Mercure de France, 1986), pp. 153–70

Noëlle Châtelet, 'La femme-papyrus', *Histoires de bouches* (Paris: Mercure de France, 1986), pp. 55–69

Delphine Danieau, *Je voulais redevenir enfant: une adolescence anorexique* (Chantonnay: Mosée, 2001)

Sophie Delorme, *Maigrir à en mourir. Témoignage recueilli par Dorothée Noblet* (Paris: Édition n°1, 1996)

Lou Delvig (this was a pseudonymous name for the author now known as Delphine de Vigan), *Jours sans faim* (Paris: Éd. France loisirs, 2001)

Marie Dupont, *Maman, pourquoi tu ne manges pas? Mon combat contre l'anorexie* (Paris: Philippe Rey, 2007)

Emilie Durand, *Ma folie ordinaire: allers et retours à l'hôpital Sainte-Anne* (Paris: Les Empêcheurs de tourner en rond, 2006)

Claudine Galea, *Jusqu'aux os* (Rodez: Éd. du Rouergue, 2003)

Florence Hache, *Vivre pour manger* (Paris: Thélès, 2003)

Nancy Huston, *La Virevolte* (Paris: Actes Sud, 1994)

Justine (avec la collaboration de Marie-Thérèse Cuny), *Ce matin j'ai décidé d'arrêter de manger* (Paris: Oh! Editions, 2007)

Ysabelle Lacamp, *Une jeune fille bien comme il faut* (Paris: Éd. J'ai lu, 1993)

Annick Loupias, with Louise Lambert-Lagacé and Annette Richard, *La Tortue sur le dos: ma lutte contre la boulimie* (Quebec: Éditions de l'homme, 2001)

Mathilde Monaque, *Trouble tête. Journal intime d'une dépression* (Paris: Éditions des Arènes, 2006)

Amélie Nothomb, *Biographie de la faim* (Paris: A. Michel, 2004)

Amélie Nothomb, *Robert des noms propres* (Paris: A. Michel, 2002)

Vittoria Pazalle, *Anorexie et boulimie: journal intime d'une reconstruction* (Escalquens: Editions Dangles, 2007)

Camille de Peretti, *Thornytorinx* (Paris: Belfond, 2005)

Brigitte Peskine, *Chantages* (Paris: l'Ecole des loisirs, 1990)

Véronique Poivre d'Arvor, *À Solenn* (Paris: Albin Michel, 2004)

Audrey Raveglia, *Jeûne fille* (Paris: Balland, 2002)

Valérie Rodrigue, *La peau à l'envers. Le roman vrai d'une boulimique* (Paris: Robert Laffont, 1989)

Sonia Sarfati, *Comme une peau de chagrin* (Montreal: Les Éditions de la courte échelle, 1995)

Corinne Solliec, *Le petit corps* (Paris: Gallimard, 2006)

Janine Teisson, *L'enfant plume (*Paris: le Grand livre du mois, 2000)

Sandra Tohorah, *La mort patiente* (Cestas: Élytis Editions, 2005)

Valérie Valère, *Le Pavillon des enfants fous* (Paris: Stock, 1978)

Nadine Vasseur, *Le Poids et la voix* (Cognac: le Temps qu'il fait, 1996)

Marie-Sophie Vermot, *Pouvoir se taire, et encore* (Paris: T. Magnier, 2002)

Maroussia Vossen, *L'amie jalouse: entre danse et anorexie* (Paris: L'Harmattan, 2004)

Fawzia Zourai, *Ce pays dont je meurs* (Paris: Ramsay, 1999)

Secondary Texts

Abraham, Nicolas and Torok, Maria, *L'Ecorce et le noyau* (Paris: Flammarion, 1978)

Al-Dakhiel Winkler, Laura, Stampe Frølich, Jacob, Schulpen, Maya, and Klinkby Støvling, René, 'Body composition and menstrual status in adults with a history of anorexia nervosa – At what fat percentage is the menstrual cycle restored?', *International Journal of Eating Disorders*, 50, 4 (2017), 370–77

Altmann, Esther, 'Anorexia and bulimia are amongst the most emotionally and physically devastating disorders affecting young Jewish women', http://www.myjewishlearning.com/article/eating-disorders-in-the-jewish-community

Andersen, Arnold A., 'Sequencing treatment decisions: Cooperation or conflict between therapist and patient', in Szmukler et al. 1995, pp. 363–79

Arnold, Carrie, 'Anorexia: You don't just grow out of it', *The Guardian*, 29 March 2016, http://www.theguardian.com/society/2016/mar/29/anorexia-you-dont-just-grow-out-of-it

Arsic, Branca, 'The experimental ordinary: Deleuze on eating and anorexic elegance', *Deleuze Studies*, 2 (2008), 34–59

Bairoch, Alice, *Voyage en anorexie* (Paris: Presses du Belvédère, 2007)

Bar-On, Dan, et al., 'Multigenerational perspectives on coping with the Holocaust experience: An attachment perspective for understanding the developmental sequelae of trauma across generations', *International Journal of Behavioral Development*, 22, 2 (1998), 315–38

Bardone-Cone, A.M., Wonderlich, S.A., Frost, R.O., Bulik, C.M., Mitchell, J.E., Uppala, S., and Simonich, H., 'Perfectionism and eating disorders: Current status and future directions', *Clinical Psychology Review*, 27 (2007), 384–405

Bernfeld, Karin, *Écriture du corps et discours clinique dans les autobiographies d'anorexie-boulimie* (unpublished doctoral thesis, Université Paris Diderot – Paris 7, 2013)

Beumont, P.V.J., Russell, J.D., and Touyz, S.W., 'Psychological concerns in the maintenance of dieting disorders', in Szmukler et al. 1995, pp. 221–41

Birksted-Breen, Dana, 'Working with an anorexic patient', *The International Journal of Psychoanalysis*, 70 (1989), 29–40

Bordo, Susan, 'Anorexia nervosa: Psychopathology as the crystallization of culture', in Irene Diamond and Lee Quinby (eds), *Feminism and Foucault: Reflections on Resistance* (Boston, MA: Northeastern University Press, 1988), pp. 87–117

Bordo, Susan, *Unbearable Weight: Feminism, Western Culture, and the Body* (Berkeley, CA: University of California Press, 1993)

Boskind-White, Marlene and White, William C., *Bulimia/Anorexia: The Binge/Purge Cycle and Self-Starvation* (New York/London: W.W. Norton & Company, 2000 [first edition 1983, second edition 1987])

Brand, P., Rothblum, E., and Solomon, L., 'A comparison of lesbians, gay men, and heterosexuals on weight and restrained eating', *International Journal of Eating Disorders*, 11 (1992), 253–59

Bray, Abigail and Colebrook, Claire, 'The haunted flesh: Corporeal feminism and the politics of (dis)embodiment', *Signs: Journal of Women in Culture and Society*, 24, 1 (1998), 35–67

Brom, Danny, Kfir, Revital, and Dasberg, Haim, 'A controlled double-blind study on children of Holocaust survivors', *Israel Journal of Psychiatry*, 38, 1 (2001), 47

Brotman, A.W., Stern, T.A., and Herzog, D.B., 'Emotional reactions of house officers to patients with anorexia nervosa, diabetes and obesity', *International Journal of Eating Disorders*, 3 (1984), 71–77

Bruch, Hilde, *Eating Disorders* (London: Routledge and Kegan Paul, 1973)

Bruch, Hilde, 'Developmental considerations of anorexia nervosa and obesity', *The Canadian Journal of Psychiatry*, 26, 4 (1981), 212–17

Bruch, Hilde, *The Golden Cage: The Enigma of Anorexia Nervosa* (Cambridge, MA: Harvard University Press, 1978)

Brumberg, Joan Jacobs, *Fasting Girls: The History of Anorexia Nervosa* (Cambridge, MA/London: Harvard University Press, 1988)

Burns, Maree, 'Eating like an ox: Femininity and dualistic constructions of bulimia and anorexia', *Feminism and Psychology*, 14, 2 (2004), 269–95

Cairns, Lucille, 'Bodily dis-ease in contemporary French women's writing: Two case studies', *French Studies*, 69, 4 (October 2015), 494–508

Cairns, Lucille, '*Dissidences charnelles*: The female body in revolt', in James Baldwin, James Fowler, and Shane Weller (eds), *The Flesh in the Text* (Oxford: Peter Lang, 2007), pp. 205–25

Cairns, Lucille, *Marie Cardinal: Motherhood and Creativity* (Glasgow: University of Glasgow French and German Publications, 1992)

Cairns, Lucille, *Post-War Jewish Women's Writing in French* (Oxford: Legenda, 2011)

Calam, Rachel, Waller, Glenn, Slade, Peter, and Newton, Tim, 'Eating disorders and perceived relationships with parents', *International Journal of Eating Disorders*, 9 (1990), 479–85

Campbell, P.G., 'What would a causal explanation of the eating disorders look like?', in Szmukler et al. 1995, pp. 49–64

Caruth, Cathy, *Unclaimed Experience: Trauma, Narrative, and History* (Baltimore, MD/London: The Johns Hopkins University Press, 1996)

Chesler, Betty E., 'Implications of the Holocaust for eating and weight problems among survivors' offspring: An exploratory study', *European Eating Disorders Review*, 13, 1 (January 2005), 38–47

Clerc, Isabelle, *Valérie Valère: un seul regard m'aurait suffi* (Paris: Perrin, 1987)

Corcos, Maurice, *Le corps insoumis: psychopathologie des troubles des conduites alimentaires* (Paris: Dunod, 2011 [first published 2005])

Corcos, Maurice, Lamas, Claire, Pham-Scottez, Alexandra, and Doyen, Catherine, *L'anorexie mentale: déni et réalités* (Rueil-Malmaison: Doin, 2008)

Couser, Thomas, *Recovering Bodies: Illness, Disability and Life Writing* (Madison, WI: University of Wisconsin Press, 1997)

Crow, S.J., Peterson, C.B., Swanson, S.A., Raymond, N.C., Specker, S., Eckert, E.D., and Mitchell, J.E., 'Increased mortality in bulimia nervosa and other eating disorders', *American Journal of Psychiatry*, 166, 12 (2009), 1342–46

Dahlgren, Camilla Lindvall, 'Transitioning from DSM-IV to DSM-5: A systematic review of eating disorder prevalence assessment', *International Journal of Eating Disorders*, 49 (2016), 975–97

Dally, P. and Gomez, J., *Anorexia Nervosa* (London: William Heinemann Medical Books, 1979)

Damlé, Amaleena, 'The becoming of anorexia and text in Amélie Nothomb's *Robert des noms propres* and Delphine de Vigan's *Jours sans faim*', in Amaleena Damlé and Gill Rye (eds), *Women's Writing in Twenty-First-Century France: Life as Literature* (Cardiff: University of Wales Press, 2013), pp. 113–26

Dare, Christopher and Crowther, Catherine, 'Psychodynamic models of eating disorders', in Szmukler et al. 1995, pp. 125–39

Darmon, Muriel, *Devenir anorexique. Une approche sociologique* (Paris: La Découverte, 2003)

de Santé, Haute Autorité, 'Anorexie mentale: prise en charge. Recommendations', https://www.has-sante.fr/portail/jcms/c_985715/fr/anorexie-mentale-prise-en-charge

Deleuze, Gilles and Parnet, Claire, *Dialogues* (Paris: Flammarion, 1977)

Duker, Marilyn and Slade, Roger, *Anorexia Nervosa and Bulimia: How to Help* (Milton Keynes/Philadelphia, PA: Open University Press, 1988)

Eisler, Ivan, 'Family models of eating disorders', in Szmukler et al. 1995, pp. 155–76

Eisler, Ivan, Simic, Mima, Blessitt, Esther, Dodge, Liz et al., 'Maudsley Service Manual for Child and Adolescent Eating Disorders', https://www.national.slam.nhs.uk/wp-content/uploads/2011/11/Maudsley-Service-Manual-for-Child-and-Adolescent-Eating-Disorders-July-2016.pdf (2016)

Faludi, Susan, *Backlash: The Undeclared War Against American Women* (New York: Crown Publishing Group, 1991)

Ferreday, Debra, 'Anorexia and abjection: A review article', *Body & Society*, 18, 2 (2012), 139–55

Freeman, Christopher, *Overcoming Anorexia Nervosa: A Self-Help Guide Using Cognitive Behavioral Techniques* (London: Robinson, 2009 [first published 2002])

French, Marilyn, *The War Against Women* (New York: Summit Books, 1992)

Garfinkel, P.E. and Garner, D.M., *Anorexia Nervosa: A Multidimensional Perspective* (New York: Brunner/Mazel, 1982)

Geary, James, *I Is an Other: The Secret Life of Metaphor and How it Shapes the Way We See the World* (New York: HarperCollins, 2011)

Gilmore, Leigh, *The Limits of Autobiography: Trauma and Testimony* (London: Cornell University Press, 2001)

Githire, Njeri, 'The semiotics of (not)-eating: Fasting, anorexia, and hunger strike in Ananda Devi's *Le Voile de Draupadi*', *Nottingham French Studies*, 48, 1 (2009), 82–93

Goodheart, Kristin, Clopton, James R. and Robert-McComb, Jacalyn J. (eds), *Eating Disorders in Women and Children: Prevention, Stress Management* (Boca Raton, FL: CRC Press/Taylor & Francis, 2000)

Gordon, Richard A., *Anorexia and Bulimia: Anatomy of a Social Epidemic* (Oxford: Blackwell, 1990 [second edition published 2000])

Gowers, S.G. et al., 'Treatment aims and philosophy in the treatment of adolescent anorexia nervosa in Europe', *European Eating Disorders Review*, 10 (2002), 271–80

Grilo, Carlos M., *Eating and Weight Disorders* (Hove/New York: Psychology Press, 2006)

Habermas, T., 'Further evidence on early case descriptions of anorexia nervosa and bulimia nervosa', *International Journal of Eating Disorders*, 11 (1992), 351–59

Habermas, T., 'The psychiatric history of anorexia nervosa and bulimia nervosa: Weight concerns and bulimic symptoms in early case reports', *International Journal of Eating Disorders*, 8 (1989), 259–73

Halmi, A.K., Eckert, E., Marchi, P., Sampugnaro, V., Apple, R. and Cohen, J., 'Comborbidity of psychiatric diagnoses in anorexia nervosa', *Archives of General Psychiatry*, 48 (1991), 712–18

Halmi, Katherine, 'Current concepts and definitions', in Szmukler et al. 1995, pp. 29–42

Havercroft, Barbara, 'Paper thin: Agency and anorexia in Geneviève Brisac's *Petite*', in Valerie Raoul et al. (eds), *Unfitting Stories: Narrative Approaches to Disease, Disability, and Trauma* (Waterloo, ON: Wilfred Laurier University Press, 2007), pp. 61–69

Hawkins, Hunsacker, *Reconstructing Illness: Studies in Pathography* (West Lafayette, IN: Purdue University Press, 1999)

Hébert, Philip C. and Weingarten, Michael A., 'The ethics of forced feeding in anorexia nervosa', *Canadian Medical Association Journal*, 144, 2 (15 January 1991), 141–44

Henke, Suzette A., *Shattered Subjects: Trauma and Testimony in Women's Life-Writing* (London: Macmillan, 1998)

Hepworth, Julie, *The Social Construction of Anorexia Nervosa* (London: Sage, 1999)

Herzog, D.B., Greenword, D.N., Dorer, D.J., Flores, A.T., Ekeblad, E.R., Richards, A., Blais, M.A., and Keller, M.B., 'Mortality in eating disorders: A descriptive study', *International Journal of Eating Disorders*, 28, 1 (2000), 20–26

Hoek, H.W., 'Review of the worldwide epidemiology of eating disorders', *Current Opinion in Psychiatry*, 29, 6 (November 2016), 336–39

Institut national de la santé et de la recherche médicale (Inserm), 'Anorexie mentale', http://www.inserm.fr/thematiques/neurosciences-sciences-cognitives-neurologie-psychiatrie/dossiers-d-information/anorexie-mentale (accessed 27 April 2015)

Jackson, C., Tabin, J., Russell, J., and Touyz, S.W., 'Themes of death: Helmut Thomas' anorexia nervosa (1987). A research note', *International Journal of Eating Disorders*, 14, 4 (1993), 433–37

Jackson, Laura, 'Purging the self: Transcribing the divided, anorexic subject in Geneviève Brisac's *Petite* and Camille de Peretti's *Thornytorinx*', in Adrienne Angelo and Erika Fülöp (eds), *Protean Selves: First-Person Voices in Twenty-First-Century French and Francophone Narratives* (Newcastle: Cambridge Scholars Publishing, 2014), pp. 166–79

Jansen, Anita, 'Eating disorders need more experimental psychopathology', *Behaviour Research and Therapy*, 86 (2016), 2–10

Jeammet, Philippe, *Anorexie Boulimie. Les paradoxes de l'adolescence* (Paris: Hachette Littératures, 2004)

Johnson, C. and Connors, M.E., *The Etiology and Treatment of Bulimia Nervosa: A Biopsychosocial Perspective* (New York: Basic Books, 1987)

Katzman, M.A., 'Feminist approaches to eating disorders: Placing the issues in context', in P. Bria, A. Ciocca, and S. De Risio (eds), *Psychotherapeutic Issues on Eating Disorders: Models, Methods and Results* (Rome: Società Editrice Universo, 1998), pp. 19–26

Katzman, M.A. and Lee, S., 'Beyond body image: The integration of feminist and transcultural theories in the understanding of self-starvation', *International Journal of Eating Disorders*, 22, 4 (1997), 385–94

Katzman, Melanie A. 'Eating disorders: Global marker of change', in Latzer et al. 2011, pp. 77–87

Kemp, Anna, '"Le passeport de la douleur ou rien": Fawzia Zouari's *Ce Pays dont je meurs* and the politics of pain', *Contemporary French Civilization*, 41 (2016), 49–67

Kemp, Anna, 'The child as artist in Amélie Nothomb's *Robert des noms propres*', *French Studies*, 66 (2012), 54–67

Kestemberg, E., Kestemberg, J., and Decobert, S., *La Faim et le Corps. Une étude psychanalytique de l'anorexie mentale* (Paris: Presses Universitaires de France, 1972)

Kristeva, Julia, *Pouvoirs de l'horreur: essai sur l'abjection* (Paris: Éditions du Seuil, 1980)

Lacan, Jacques, *Le Séminaire, Livre IV: la Relation d'objet* (Paris: Seuil, 1994)

Lacan, Jacques, *Les quatre concepts fondamentaux de la psychanalyse, Livre XI* (Paris: Seuil, 1973)

Lakoff, George and Johnson, Mark, *Metaphors We Live By* (Chicago, IL/London: University of Chicago Press, 1980)

Lasègue, E.C., 'On hysterical anorexia', *Med, Tms, Gaz.*, 2, 265 (1873), 265–66

Latzer, Yael, Merrick, Joav, and Stein, Daniel (eds), *Understanding Eating Disorders: Integrating Culture, Psychology and Biology* (New York: Nova Science Publishers, 2011)

Le Heuzey, Marie-France, *L'Enfant anorexique: Comprendre et agir* (Paris: Odile Jacob, 2003)

Lewis., B. and Nicholls, D., 'Behavioural eating disorders', *Paediatrics and Child Health*, 26, 12 (December 2016), 519–26

MacSween, Morag, *A Feminist and Sociological Perspective on Anorexia Nervosa* (London: Routledge, 1995)

Malson, Helen, *The Thin Woman: Feminism, Post-Structuralism and the Social Psychology of Anorexia Nervosa* (London/New York: Routledge, 1998)

Malson, Helen M. and Ussher, Jane M., 'Beyond this mortal coil: Femininity, death and discursive constructions of the anorexic body', *Mortality*, 2, 1 (1997), 43–61

McCarthy, Angela and Thomson, Margie, *Hungry Heart: Anorexia and Bulimia* (Auckland: Hodder Moa Beckett, 1996)

McEachern, Patricia, *Deprivation and Power: The Emergence of Anorexia Nervosa in Nineteenth-Century France* (Westport, CT/London: Greenwood Press, 1998)

McIlvanney, Siobhán, '"Il était une fois…": Trauma and the fairytale in Amélie Nothomb's *Robert des noms propres*', *Dalhousie French Studies*, 81 (2007), 19–28

Meares, R. and Hobson, R., 'The persecutory therapist', *British Journal of Medical Psychology*, 50 (1977), 349–59

Meuret, Isabelle, 'Entre secret et sacré: l'écriture "feminine" de Geneviève Brisac et Liliane Atlan', *Revue des Lettres et de Traduction*, 9 (2003), 307–18

Meuret, Isabelle, *L'anorexie créatrice* (Paris: Klincksieck, 2006)

Meuret, Isabelle, 'L'Anorexie: entre aliénation "mentale" et revendication d'altérité: le cas des écrivaines algériennes', *International Journal of Francophone Studies*, 12, 1 (2009), 19–35

Meuret, Isabelle, *Writing Size Zero: Figuring Anorexia in Contemporary World Literatures* (Brussels, Belgium/New York: Peter Lang, 2007)

Minuchin, S., Rosman, B. L., Baker, L., and Minuchin, S. *Psychosomatic Families: Anorexia Nervosa in Context* (Cambridge, MA: Harvard University Press, 2009)

Morello, Nathalie, 'Anorexia, anger, agency: Investigating quests for self in three contemporary narratives in French', in Francesca Calamita, Petra Bagley, and Kathryn Robson (eds), *Starvation, Food Obsession and Identity: Eating Disorders in Post-1968 Women's Writing* (Oxford: Peter Lang, 2017), pp. 121–41

Morgan, H.G., 'Fasting girls and our attitudes to them', *British Medical Journal*, 2, 6103 (1977), 1652–55

Mormont, Christian and Ansseau, Marc, 'Anorexie', in Marcel Crahay and Christine Goffinet (eds), *Regards croisés sur l'anorexie* (Liège: Les Editions de l'Université de Liège, 2001), pp. 11–13

Muschg, A., *Literatur als Therapie? Ein Exkurs über das Heilsame und das Unheilbare* [Literature as therapy? About the healable and unhealable] (Frankfurt: Suhrkamp, 1982)

Naish, J. M., 'Problems of deception in medical practice', *Lancet*, ii (1979), 139–42

Naudeau, J., 'Observations sur une maladie nerveuse accompagnée d'un dégoût extraordinaire pour les aliments', *J. méd. Chir. et pharmacol.*, 79 (1789) 197–200

Nicholson, J. and Nicholls, D., 'Clinical and diagnostic characteristics of eating disorders in children and adolescents', in Latzer et al. 2011, pp. 39–55

Orbach, Susie, *Fat is a Feminist Issue... How to Lose Weight Permanently – Without Dieting* (London: Arrow, 1988 [first published London: Paddington Press, 1978])

Orbach, Susie, *Hunger Strike: The Anorectic's Struggle as a Metaphor for our Age* (London: Penguin, 1993 [first published by Faber and Faber, 1986])

Palazzoli, Mara Selvini, *Self-Starvation: From Individual to Family Therapy in the Treatment of Anorexia Nervosa* (New York/London: Jason Aronson, 1978)

Paul, Thomas, Schroeter, Kirsten, Dahme, Bernhard, and Nutzinger, Detlev O., 'Self-injurious behaviour in women with eating disorders', *American Journal of Psychiatry*, 159, 3 (March 2002), 408–11

Peyser, Caroline, *Body and Soul: A Guide for Addressing Eating Disorders in a Jewish Education Setting* (Jerusalem: Academy for Torah Initiatives and Directions, 2005)

Probyn, Elspeth, *Carnal Appetites: FoodSexIdentities* (London/New York: Routledge, 2000)

Raimbault, Ginette and Eliacheff, Caroline, *Les indomptables. Figures de l'anorexie* (Paris: Odile Jacob, 2001 [first published 1989])

Ranzenhofer, L., Engel, S.G., Crosby, R.D., Haigney, M., and Tanofsky-Kraff, M., 'A pilot study of attachment style and emotional experience in adolescent girls with loss of control eating', *Advances in Eating Disorders: Theory, Research and Practice*, 4, 3 (2016), 250–63

Rastam, M. and Gilberg, G., 'The family background in anorexia nervosa: A population-based study', *Journal of American Academy Child Adolescent Psychiatry*, 31 (1991), 283–89

Raveneau, G., Feinstein, R., Rosen, L.M., and Fisher, M., 'Attitudes and knowledge levels of nurses and residents caring for adolescents with an eating disorder', *International Journal of Adolescent Medicine and Health*, 26, 1 (2014), 131–36

Reas, Deborah L., 'Impulsivity-related traits distinguish women with co-occurring bulimia nervosa in a psychiatric sample', *International Journal of Eating Disorders*, 49, 12 (2016), 1093–96

Robertson, Matra, *Starving in the Silences: An Exploration of Anorexia* (Sydney: Allen and Unwin, 1992)

Robson, Kathryn, 'Voicing abjection: Narratives of anorexia in contemporary French women's (life-)writing', *L'Esprit Createur*, 56, 2 (Summer 2016), 108–20

Rodgers, Catherine, 'Nothomb's anorexic beauties', in Susan Bainbrigge and Jeanette den Toonder (eds), *Amélie Nothomb: Authorship, Identity, and Narrative Practice* (New York: Peter Lang, 2003), pp. 50–63

Rodgers, Julie, 'Body politics in *Truismes*: "The tyranny of slenderness"', *Dalhousie French Studies*, 98 (Spring 2012), 29–39

Rodgers, Julie, 'Double voices and splintered selves: The dialectic of anorexia in Ying Chen's *Querelle d'un squelette avec son double*', in Francesca Calamita, Petra Bagley, and Kathryn Robson (eds), *Starvation, Food Obsession and Identity: Eating Disorders in Post-1968 Women's Writing* (Oxford: Peter Lang, forthcoming 2017), pp. 213–34

Russell, G.F.M. and Beardwood, C.J., 'Amenorrhoea in the feeding disorders: Anorexia nervosa and obesity', *Psychotherapy and Psychosomatics*, 18 (1970), 359–64

Sagi-Schwartz, Abraham, et al., 'Attachment and traumatic stress in female Holocaust child survivors and their daughters', *American Journal of Psychiatry*, 160, 6 (2003), 1086–92

Scheen, André J., 'L'anorexie mentale: aspects medicaux', in Marcel Crahay and Christine Goffinet (eds), *Regards croisés sur l'anorexie* (Liège: Les Editions de l'Université de Liège , 2001), pp. 89–96

Schmidt, Ulrike, Tiller, Jane, and Morgan, H. Gethin, 'The social consequences of eating disorders', in Szmukler et al. 1995, pp. 259–70

Seah, X.Y., Tham, X.C., Kamaruzaman, N.R., and Yobas, P., 'Knowledge, attitudes and challenges of healthcare professionals managing people with eating disorders: A literature review', *Archives of Psychiatric Nursing*, 31 (2017), 125–36

Senkbeil, Karsten and Hoppe, Nicola, '"The sickness stands at your shoulder...": Embodiment and cognitive metaphor in Hornbacher's *Wasted: A Memoir of Anorexia and Bulimia*', *Language and Literature*, 25, 1 (2016), 3–17

Senninger, Franck, *L'Anorexie: le miroir intérieur brisé* (Paris: Jouvence, 2004)

Siever, M.D., 'Sexual orientation and gender as factors in socioculturally acquired vulnerability to body dissatisfaction and eating disorders', *Journal of Consulting and Clinical Psychology*, 62, 2 (1994), 252–60

Silber, Thomas J., 'Anorexia nervosa in blacks and Hispanics', *International Journal of Eating Disorders*, 5, 1 (1986), 121–28

Slade, P.D., 'Body image in anorexia nervosa', *British Journal of Psychiatry*, 153 (suppl. 2) (1988), 20–22

Smolak, Linda, Levine, Michael P., and Striegel-Moore, Ruth, *The Developmental Psychopathology of Eating Disorders* (Mahwah, NJ: Lawrence Erlbaum Associate, Publishers, 1996)

Smyth, J.M., Stone, A.A., Hurewitz, A., and Kaell, A., 'Effects of writing about stressful experiences on symptom reduction in patients with asthma or rheumatoid arthritis', *Journal of the American Medical Association*, 281, 14 (1999), 1304–9

Smyth, Joshua M. and Pennebaker, James W., 'Translating emotional experiences into words as a coping tool', in C.R. Snyder (ed.), *Coping: The Psychology of What Works* (New York/Oxford: Oxford University Press, 1999), pp. 70–89

Sours, John A., *Starving to Death in a Sea of Objects: The Anorexia Nervosa Syndrome* (New York/London: Jason Aronson, 1980)

Spignesi, Angelyn, *Starving Women: A Psychology of Anorexia* (Dallas, TX: Spring Publications, 1983)

Stirn, A., Overbeck, G., and Pokorny, D., 'The core conflictual relationship theme (CCRT) applied to literary works: An analysis of two novels written by authors suffering from anorexia nervosa', *The International Journal of Eating Disorders*, 38, 2 (2005), 147–56

Striegel-Moore, R. H., Tucker, N., and Hsu, J. 'Body image dissatisfaction and disordered eating in lesbian college students', *International Journal of Eating Disorders*, 9 (1990), 493–500

Strober, M., 'Managing the chronic, treatment-resistant patient with anorexia nervosa', *International Journal of Eating Disorders*, 36 (2004), 245–55

Swift, W.J. and Letven, R., 'Bulimia and the basic fault: A psychoanalytic interpretation of the binging-vomiting syndrome', *Journal of the American Academy of Child Psychiatry*, 23 (1984), 489–97

Szmukler, G., Dare, C., and Treasure, J., *Handbook of Eating Disorders: Theory, Treatment and Research* (Chichester: J. Wiley & Sons 1995)

Szmukler, G.I. and Tantam, D., 'Anorexia nervosa: Starvation dependence', *British Journal of Medical Psychology*, 57 (1984), 303–10

Thoma, H., *Anorexia Nervosa* (New York: International Universities Press, 1967)

Touyz, S.T., Garner, D.M., and Beumont, P.J.V., 'The inpatient management of the adolescent patient with anorexia nervosa', in H.C. Steinhausen (ed.), *Eating Disorders in Adolescence: Anorexia Nervosa and Bulimia Nervosa* (Berlin: Walter de Gruyter & Co., 1995), pp. 247–70

Treasure, Janet and Holland, Anthony, 'Genetic factors in eating disorders', in Szmukler et al 1995, pp. 65–81

Treasure, Janet, Schmidt, Ulrike, and Macdonald, Pam (eds), *The Clinician's Guide to Collaborative Caring in Eating Disorders: The New Maudsley Method* (London/New York: Routledge, 2009)

Treasure, Janet, Todd, Gill and Szmukler, George, 'The inpatient treatment of anorexia nervosa', in Szmukler et al. 1995, pp. 275–91

Ushakov, G.K., 'Anorexia nervosa', in J. G. Howells (ed.), *Modern Perspectives in Adolescent Psychiatry* (Edinburgh: Oliver & Boyd, 1971), pp. 274–89

Vandereycken, W., 'Food for thought: Gerald Russell's writings on eating disorders', in Szmukler et al. 1995, pp. 401–6

Vandereycken, W., 'Naughty girls and angry doctors: Eating disorder patients and their therapists', *International Review of Psychiatry*, 5 (1993), 13–18

Vitiello, Joëlle, 'Le double meurtrier chez Sabrina Kherbiche', in Frédérique Chevillot and Colette Trout (eds), *Rebelles et criminelles chez les écrivaines d'expression française* (Amsterdam: Rodopi, 2013), pp. 129–45

Warin, Megan, *Abject Relations: Everyday Worlds of Anorexia* (Piscataway, NJ: Rutgers University Press, 2010)

Weinberger-Litman, S.L., Latzer, Y., and Stein, D., 'A historical, cultural and empirical look at eating disorders and religiosity among Jewish women', in Latzer et al. 2011, pp. 109–22

Wiley Emmett, Steven (ed.), *Theory and Treatment of Anorexia Nervosa and Bulimia: Biomedical Sociocultural & Psychological Perspectives: Biomedical, Sociocultural and Psychological Perspectives* (New York: Routledge, 1985)

Wilfley, D.E., 'Interpersonal analyses of bulimia: Normal weight and obese' (unpublished doctoral dissertation, University of Missouri, Columbia, 1989)

Wolf, Naomi, *The Beauty Myth: How Images of Beauty Are Used Against Women* (New York: William Morrow, 1991)

Woolf, Emma, *An Apple a Day: A Memoir of Love and Recovery from Anorexia* (London: Summersdale, 2012)

Yager, Joel et al., 'Practice guideline for the treatment of patients with eating disorders, Third edition', *The American Journal of Psychiatry*, 163, 7 (July 2006), 4–54

Zohar, Ada H., Giladi, Lotem, and Givati, Timor, 'Holocaust exposure and disordered eating: A study of multi-generational transmission', *European Eating Disorders Review*, 15 (2007), 50–57

Index

www.ingramcontent.com/pod-product-compliance
Lightning Source LLC
Chambersburg PA
CBHW071746250425
25721CB00004B/223
9781802077957